Neuroaesthetics

Edited by

Martin Skov

Danish Research Centre for Magnetic Resonance

Oshin Vartanian

DRDC Toronto

Foundations and Frontiers in Aesthetics

Series Editors: Colin Martindale and Arnold Berleant

Routledge
Taylor & Francis Group
LONDON AND NEW YORK

First published 2009 Baywood Publishing Company, Inc.

2 Park Square, Milton Park, Abingdon, Oxon OX14 4RN
711 Third Avenue, New York, NY 10017, USA

First issued in paperback 2017

Routledge is an imprint of the Taylor & Francis Group, an informa business

Library of Congress Catalog Number: 2008047653

Library of Congress Cataloging-in-Publication Data

Neuroaesthetics / edited by Martin Skov, Oshin Vartanian.
p. cm.
Includes bibliographical references and index.
ISBN 978-0-89503-336-9 (cloth : alk. paper) 1. Aesthetics--Physiological aspects. 2. Neuropsychology. I. Skov, Martin. II. Vartanian, Oshin, 1970–

BH301.P45N48 2009
153--dc22 2008047653

Back cover photographs

Martin Skov
Photograph by Susanne Østergaard, Hvidovre Hospital

Oshin Vartanian
Photograph by Steve Stober, www.stevestober.com

ISBN 13: 978-0-89503-336-9 (hbk)
ISBN 13: 978-0-41578-371-2 (pbk)

Table of Contents

This book is dedicated to the memory of Colin Martindale, a great patron of the arts

CHAPTER 1

Introduction: What is Neuroaesthetics?

Martin Skov and Oshin Vartanian

Neuroaesthetics is a young field of study, and it becomes youth to be imbued with a sense of curiosity and adventure. Considering that this book appears in an early stage in the history of this field, it is our hope that it captures the excitement that currently surrounds this topic. Against this backdrop, this book was conceived with two specific aims in mind. First, we wanted to highlight the diversity of approaches that are currently in use under the banner of neuroaesthetics. A single glance through the table of contents of this volume will reveal that this topic is being studied in many domains and from various methodological perspectives. The fact that researchers with experimental, evolutionary, neuropsychological, and neuroimaging perspectives are studying neuroaesthetics as it relates to visual art, literature, music, and film underscores the point that we are a differentiated bunch. We believe that in the long run, this diversity will serve the field well. Not only will the quintessentially interdisciplinary nature of this field be a breeding ground for generating hypotheses (see Zaidel, this volume), but it will also enable us to test foundational hypotheses across different domains.

Our second goal was more integrative in nature and involved distilling some of the key features that define what is common to these diverse strands of work. We will have a crack at this second goal in this introduction. Our aim here is to present a possible framework for neuroaesthetics by highlighting what we believe to be its defining features (see also Skov, this volume). Some (see Brown & Dissanayake, this volume) have argued that as a field, neuroaesthetics is too narrow in focus and that ideally, we should seek to understand the arts rather than only those aspects of it that have aesthetic functions. We take a somewhat different approach to this problem. We contend that neuroaesthetics should in fact encompass *more* than the study of the arts. We believe aesthetic functions to be phenomena that characterize our interactions with a very wide array of objects, far wider than what falls under the banner of the arts alone. Below we offer a working definition of neuroaesthetics that we hope captures these features.

NEUROAESTHETICS BEFORE AND NOW

At its base, neuroaesthetics is a certain way of doing aesthetics, using neuroscience as a method of enquiry where other approaches to aesthetics have used philosophical analysis or strictly psychological models. As such, neuroaesthetics studies how aesthetic behavior is underpinned by brain processes. Although real experimental work on this question has only started to appear in the last 20 years or so, the conceptual inclination to investigate the neural mechanisms underlying aesthetic behavior can be traced back to the eighteenth and nineteenth centuries. This era saw a general upheaval in the scientific understanding of the relation between mind and brain (Reed, 1997), giving rise to the idea in some researchers, such as Erasmus Darwin (1792), that mental states can be explained as physiological mechanisms. This idea, in turn, inspired a number of aestheticians, including Daniel Webb (*Observations on the Correspondence between Poetry and Music,* 1769) and Uvedale Price (*Essays on the Picturesque*, 1810), to suggest that aspects of the aesthetic experience have a physiological basis. For example, the American psychologist Henry Rutgers Marshall argued that the experience of beauty is rooted in the basic hedonic feelings of pain and pleasure (Marshall, 1892, 1893), and published a book called *Pain, Pleasure and Aesthetics* (1894) to address this issue.

Initially, this notion of a physiology of aesthetics prompted more speculation than experimentation, resulting in books with titles such as *Physiological Aesthetics* (Grant Allen, 1877), *Aufgaben der Kunstphysiologie* (Georg Hirth, 1897), and *Geschlecht und Kunst—Prolegomena zu einer Physiologischen Aesthetik* (Gustav Naumann, 1899). These, however, involved little or no data. This changed in the 1870s when the German physiologist Gustav Fechner came up with a way of studying the physiology of mental events by correlating changes in experience with measurable changes in the stimulus input; he quickly applied this experimental technique to dimensions of the aesthetic experience (Fechner, 1876). As Thomas Jacobsen shows in his chapter in this volume, Fechner's methodological invention became the inspiration for a rich experimental tradition, which up through the twentieth century has attempted to measure the behavioral response to the perception of art using various psychometric techniques (see also Martindale, 2007).

Still, for a true physiology of aesthetics, neuroaesthetics had to wait for basic neuroscience to advance. It is no accident that the influential effort to explain the behavioral data collected by the tradition of experimental aesthetics with recourse to cortical mechanisms—Daniel Berlyne's hypothesis that aesthetic preferences are determined by physiological arousal (1971)—appeared at a time when a revolution in the neurosciences was unfolding. Throughout the 1970s and 1980s numerous papers and books took advantage of basic neuroscience's increasing understanding of the neural underpinnings of perception, memory, emotion, and such to put forward theories of how the brain computes art behavior, especially visual art (Critchley & Henson, 1977; Gregory, Harris, Heard, & Rose, 1995; Livingstone, 1988; Miall, 1976; Rentschler, Herzberger, & Epstein, 1988). With the advent of noninvasive neuroimaging techniques such as PET and fMRI, allowing brain scientists to monitor brain activity as subjects experience art and other aesthetic objects, these theories finally became amenable to experimental scrutiny.

As this short historical sketch makes clear, the evolution of neuroaesthetics has followed a well-known trajectory within the neurosciences. First, the possibility of equating an aspect of mind to brain processes is introduced and hotly debated; next, models and hypotheses are advanced based on available, but not necessarily aesthetic-specific knowledge; and third; experimental work ensues. And just as the rise of the experimental study of consciousness and moral psychology has increased neuroscience's relevance to these fields of enquiry, we foresee a similar trend for aesthetics.

BASIC TENETS OF NEUROAESTHETICS

Neuroaesthetics is the study of the neural processes that underlie aesthetic behavior. But what, more precisely, does this mean? We suggest that there are forms of interaction with objects that can be called "aesthetic." The job of neuroaesthetics is to identify these aesthetic functions and to investigate their neurobiological causes.

By aesthetic function we mean the psychological processes that are evoked in the creator or the viewer of the object in the course of interacting with it. These psychological processes may involve perceptual, sensory, cognitive, emotional, evaluative, and social aspects among others, all of which are presumed to have a biological—neural—basis. We use the term "objects" rather than the "arts" because aesthetic processes typify our interactions with a much wider array of objects than artworks alone.

Currently, each of the components of this definition of neuroaesthetics is in need of further study. To begin with, a number of biological frameworks have been proposed for studying the aesthetic functions of objects (e.g., Berlyne, 1971). Biological framework is not a function of the specific technique used to study aesthetics. Rather, it relates to any biological theory that drives the investigation. For example, a behavioral experiment in aesthetics that measures reaction time would fall under a biological framework if the predictions under study were motivated by or derived from a biologically-based theory. We need to study the extent to which the predictions of these different biological frameworks apply across various domains (music, dance, etc.), or whether they serve a more specific purpose such as visual aesthetics (see Chatterjee, 2003). In addition, it is imperative that the biological frameworks that are proposed for understanding aesthetic functions make bridges with broader themes in biology, such as evolutionary theory (see Miller, 2000). In other words, biological frameworks within aesthetics must be compatible with larger themes in the biological sciences for the sake of coherence as well as exchange of ideas.

We also need a better understanding of the psychological processes evoked in the creator or the viewer of aesthetic objects in the course of interacting with them (Zaidel, 2005). Historically, it has proved easier to study aesthetic processes in the viewer rather than in the creator of objects, which has guided researchers in their focus, although everyone realizes that ultimately both sides of the coin need to be understood (see Fitch, von Graevenitz, & Nicolas, this volume). This bias is also reflected in much of the content of this book (but see the chapters by Brown & Dissanayake; Chatterjee; Zaidel). It is clear that understanding processes in the creator that give rise to aesthetic responses in viewers must be considered a core component of neuroaesthetics.

Finally, the criteria that demarcate art objects from other objects is not well understood (Skov, this volume). A reasonable approach is to study objects that are approached *as works of art* by the observer or the creator. For example, in Leder, Belke, Oeberst, and Augustin's (2004) model of aesthetic experience, the departing point is a consideration of the object of interest as an artwork. While this is a useful approach for our aesthetic experiences involving artworks, it does not capture the aesthetic experiences we have with objects that are not considered artworks. According to our definition of neuroaesthetics, aesthetic phenomena are common rather than unique, and are obviously evoked when we create paintings and watch movies, but also when we embrace a loved one. The probable reason for this is that the component neural processes involved in producing or appreciating art themselves are common, not unique. For instance, some neural mechanism may compute narrative structure in movies, novels, and operas, but also in our recounting of incidents at work or historical events. Even the function of experiencing some work of art as beautiful, which is seen as quintessentially aesthetic by most people (Jacobsen, Buchta, Köhler, & Schröger, 2004), is not unique to our interactions with art objects. We also find objects like faces, cars, and landscapes beautiful. In this way, there can be an aesthetic aspect to a range of other behavioral acts. Ultimately, we will need models that can account for our aesthetic experiences with all objects rather than just artworks, although the field's current focus on the latter is a justifiable starting point.

THE KEY QUESTIONS OF NEUROSAESTHETICS

Having thus defined the term neuroaesthetics, the next obvious question to ask is what the key issues are that require inquiry (see also Skov; Chatterjee; Jacobsen, this volume). Obviously, the main task is to pin down the behavioral features characteristic of aesthetic processes that can be investigated at the appropriate level of analysis. But there are other important issues, one of which is the evolutionary significance of aesthetic experience (see Brown & Dissanayake; Nadal et al.; Zaidel, this volume). Not only will this issue address the *why* of aesthetic experience, but also inform us about the *how* of the process, as the two are intricately linked. For example, whether aesthetic experience is found to be grounded in mate selection or enhancing group cohesion will inform the choice of processes that are investigated as mediators of its occurrence.

Many chapters in this book are devoted to the role of representation in art and, by extension, in aesthetics. Our understanding of factors that affect the aesthetic qualities of our mental representations depends on our understanding of representation in general. In this volume, Wade covers the fascinating history of visual representation and its eventual passage into visual neuroscience in colorful detail.

In their chapters, Grodal, Tervaniemi, and Miall tackle film, music, and literature respectively—perhaps the archetypal channels through which most humans currently enjoy aesthetic experiences. As editors, we find it gratifying that despite the obvious differences in domains of inquiry, similar themes are discussed by the authors as integral for understanding representation in their respective domains, such as the intricate links that exist between perception and action and their respective neural representations in the human brain.

Finally, the role of emotion in the aesthetic experience needs further exploration. Several chapters in the current volume address this issue. Chenier and Winkielman introduce the notion of processing fluency to account for the role of affect in aesthetic preference. Brown and Dissanayake and Vartanian take a different approach by introducing recent theories of emotion to the domain of aesthetics. The aim is to ground theories of emotion in aesthetics on advanced models of emotion processing in humans. Miall's discussion of the role of mirror neurons in empathy adds to this issue by accounting for the powerful experience of absorption in artworks (see also Grodal, this volume). It is fair to say that neurobiological theories of emotion in the aesthetic experience must be linked to neurobiological theories of emotion in other domains of human activity such as language processing.

We find it important to stress that work on these individual questions can influence one another with great benefits. For instance, the idea that the neural systems underlying aesthetic preference formation first evolved to facilitate mate selection can stimulate interesting questions as to how these systems may work. Do they react similarly to facial stimuli as to paintings? On the other hand, knowledge about the functional behavior of key structures such as the orbitofrontal cortex can, in turn, inform evolutionary hypotheses, as very elegantly demonstrated in the chapter by Nadal and colleagues.

THE OBJECTIVE OF THIS BOOK

With this book, we first and foremost hope to stimulate new research on these key questions. Although neuroaesthetics, as noted, can boast of a long intellectual history, and with experimental data starting to appear has generated a lot of interest recently, it is clearly in need of a coherent framework. In our selection of issues to include in the book, we have endeavored to outline such a framework, setting out a list of the most important questions to be investigated by future neuroaesthetecians and explaining how they relate to one another.

In suggesting this framework, we have especially been concerned with two themes. First, neuroaesthetics should encompass all forms of art, be it dance, music, literature, sculpture, or paintings. This also means that neuroaesthetic theory should not be dominated by idiosyncratic hypotheses motivated by examples from just one art form. Second, we hope to engage the broader scientific community about neuroaesthetics by demonstrating that aesthetic experience and artistic creativity do not rest upon obscure and esoteric psychological processes, but are rooted in basic neural processes such as perception, memory, emotion, and so on. As such, neuroaesthetics should be seen as a basic part of the larger neuroscience program.

LOOKING AHEAD

The beginning of psychological aesthetics is normally traced back to the publication of Gustav Theodor Fechner's seminal book *Vorschule der Aesthetik* in 1876. Following in the footsteps of this rich tradition, we view neuroaesthetics as a natural extension of Fechner's empirical spirit in understanding the link between the objective and subjective worlds inherent in aesthetic experience. We believe that the future for neuroaesthetics is bright, and that discoveries in this area will serve to more firmly place research in aesthetics within psychology and other related disciplines. Not only do we hope that puzzles in aesthetics can be solved through insights from biology, but that the contribution can be truly bidirectional (see Miller, 2001).

REFERENCES

Allen, G. (1877). *Physiological aesthetics.* New York: D. Appleton & Company.

Berlyne, D. E. (1971). *Aesthetics and psychobiology.* East Norwalk, CT: Appleton-Century-Crofts.

Chatterjee, A. (2003). Prospects for a cognitive neuroscience of visual aesthetics. *Bulletin of Psychology and the Arts, 4*, 55-60.

Critchley, M., & Henson, R. (1977). *Music and the brain. Studies in the neurology of music.* London: Heinemann.

Darwin, E. (1792). *Zoonomia; or, The laws of organic life* (Part I). London: J. Johnson.

Fechner, G. T. (1876). *Vorschule der Aesthetik [Experimental Aesthetics]*. Leipzig: Breitkopf & Härtel.

Gregory, R., Harris, J., Heard, P., & Rose, D. (1995). *The artful eye.* Oxford, New York, & Tokyo: Oxford University Press.

Hirth, G. (1897). *Aufgaben der kunstphysiologie.* München & Leipzig: Hirth's Kunstverlag.

Jacobsen, T., Buchta, K., Köhler, M., & Schröger, E. (2004). The primacy of beauty in judging the aesthetics of objects. *Psychological Reports, 94*(3), 1253-1260.

Leder, H., Belke, B., Oeberst, A., & Augustin, D. (2004). A model of aesthetic appreciation and aesthetic judgments. *British Journal of Psychology, 95,* 489-508.

Livingstone, M. (1988). Art, illusion and the visual system. *Scientific American, 258*, 68-75.

Marshall, H. R. (1892). The field of aesthetics psychologically considered. II: The differentiation of aesthetics from hedonics. *Mind, 1*(4), 453-469.

Marshall, H. R. (1893). Hedonic aesthetics. *Mind, 2*(5), 15-41.

Marshall, H. R. (1894). *Pain, pleasure and aesthetics.* New York: Macmillan.

Martindale, C. (2007). Recent trends in the psychological study of aesthetics, creativity, and the arts. *Empirical Studies of the Arts, 25,* 121-141.

Miall, D. S. (1976). Aesthetic unity and the role of the brain. *Journal of Aesthetics and Art Criticism, 35*, 57-67.

Miller, G. (2000). *The mating mind: How sexual choice shaped the evolution of human nature.* New York: Doubleday.

Miller, G. F. (2001). Aesthetic fitness: How sexual selection shaped artistic virtuosity as a fitness indicator and aesthetic preferences as mate choice criteria. *Bulletin of Psychology and the Arts, 2,* 20-25.

Naumann, G. (1899). *Geschlecht und Kunst—Prolegomena zu einer Physiologischen Aesthetik.* Leipzig: H. Haeffel.

Price, U. (1810). *Essays on the picturesque.* London: J. Mawman.

Reed, E. S. (1997). *From soul to mind. The emergence of psychology from Erasmus Darwin to William James*. New Haven & London: Yale University Press.

Rentschler, I., Herzberger, B., & Epstein, D. (1988). *Beauty and the brain. Biological aspects of aesthetics*. Basel: Birkhauser Verlag.

Webb, D. (1769). *Observations on the correspondence between poetry and music*. London: printed for J. Dodsky.

Zaidel, D. W. (2005). *Neuropsychology of art: Neurological, cognitive, and evolutionary perspectives*. Hove, UK: Psychology Press.

CHAPTER 2

Neuroaesthetic Problems: A Framework for Neuroaesthetic Research

Martin Skov

THE TASK OF NEUROAESTHETICS

As Dahlia Zaidel observes in her book *The Neuropsychology of Art*,

> The association between art and brain (. . .) has proven difficult because its components are elusive. What abilities of Michelangelo's mind went into painting the Sistine Chapel or sculpting *Moses* or the *Pietà?* What in Monet's mind controlled his water lily paintings, or in Gauguin's his *Ancestors of Tehamana* painting, or, in ancient artists, the cave walls at Lascaux and Altamira? Similarly, what were the components of Verdi's mind when he composed *Aida?* (2005, p. 1)

To these questions we would also have to add the following: What neural processes make us experience and appreciate art? How do we distinguish "a Monet" from "a Gauguin"? Why does Mona Lisa's smile seem enigmatic, and how does the brain resolve such puzzles evoked by works of art? Similarly, what is the reason that not only do some artworks please while others do not, but that some people like Monet and hate Gauguin, while it is the other way around for other people? Although we know more about the brain processes that underlie the perception and cognition of art than those that underlie the creation of art, we are still a far way from understanding either.

As a first approximation, neuroaesthetics can be defined simply as the scientific discipline that attempts to answer these and related questions. On the face of it, this seems like a straightforward enough endeavor. However, whereas, the neuroscientific research into language is built on an elaborate model of the structure of language, for instance, no similar model of the structure of art exists. This lack of a model describing the parts of the behavior to be studied means that it is difficult for the aspiring neuroaesthecian to start looking for the neural correlates of art appreciation or production. The neural components involved in the experience and creation of art are, as Zaidel states, elusive, because we lack both a "grammar" of art and a psychological model of how art behavior is computed by the brain.

Why haven't such models emerged? The main reason, I think, is that it has proven exceedingly difficult to define what art is in the first place. Even though thousands of authors throughout the ages have tried to pinpoint the properties that set art objects apart from other objects, in general, all such efforts have failed or proven controversial. Frustratingly, any property that has been advanced as unique to artworks has quickly been shown to be found also in non-art objects. The same goes for attempts to define what constitutes the "aesthetic experience" (Beardsley, 1969), the specific kind of experience afforded by art. Is "unity of experience," "disinterestedness," "beauty," or whatever experiential property that has been proposed as quintessential, really only evoked by works of art? Again, we can contrast this elusiveness with the case of language. It is difficult to build a model of the grammar of art if you cannot even agree on the equivalent of word classes, phonemes, or clauses.

Neuroaesthetics, therefore, at this time of its existence, is in a position where a prerequisite for any experimental work is the working out of good models of both what characterizes the art object and what characterizes the aesthetic experience. At least, researchers are in need of good motivated working lines of inquiry such as: style is a crucial part of art objects, and memory must play an important role in computing the experience of style (since you have to match the present perceptual input with a template to recognize the object you are looking at as a representative of a certain style); therefore, let's scan subjects as they look at "stylish" and "style-less" objects and look for differences in activity in the medial temporal lobe (MTL). The investigation of such provisional questions may in turn lead to a greater understanding of what style more precisely is: it may turn out, for example, that there is an important difference in how the MTL treats new and old styles, the first eliciting encoding processes and the latter recollection processes that may depend on activity in separate brain structures (see Miyashita, 2004). Recent evidence has indicated that structures such as the perirhinal cortex and the hippocampus may play differential roles in spatial and object recognition memory (Aggleton & Brown, 2005), suggesting that style in architecture and painting could rely on different neural systems. Furthermore, with a more detailed knowledge of how early perceptual and memory systems interact to produce the effect of style, it will also become possible to design studies investigating how style information influences other parts of the brain, including structures underlying emotion.

There are two important lessons to be extracted from this hypothetical example. First of all, the burgeoning field of neuroaesthetics, while primarily concerned with the question of *how* the brain computes art behavior, must advance with an eye to discussions of *what* art behavior is. In all likelihood, the memory processes underlying the computation of style, such as encoding of new percepts, recognition, or retrieval, are not unique to the experience of art objects. However, it is possible they perform a specific function in relation to the kind of objects we call artworks; for instance, the process of categorizing invented often fictive representations ("This mask represents the rain god Chac"), or even natural objects as expressed in unusual ways ("The brushstrokes used by Monet on his water lilies are *so* impressionistic!"). Yet, the claim of such specific functions rests on the assumption that style is a structural characteristic of most works of art. It doesn't have to be unique to art objects, but it must be a feature of most art. As a consequence, neuroaesthetics must work in tandem with other aesthetic subdisciplines that try to characterize in different ways the traits that typify art objects, including various disciplines—from archaeology over anthropology to art history—that work at cataloging and describing the many forms of art humankind has manufactured, and disciplines seeking to analyze the formal structures of these works of art (philosophy, semiotics, experimental psychology, etc.). It is worth emphasizing this point since some researchers working in these fields have expressed a fear that neuroaesthetics is seeking to usurp traditional aesthetics (e.g., Hyman, 2006). That is certainly not the case. In contrast, to a high degree, experimental neuroaesthetics cannot get started without using the insights from traditional aesthetics as a starting point.

On the other hand, as indicated by my imaginary example concerning style, the results from neuroaesthetic studies can prove helpful in revising and improving our understanding of what constitutes art objects and the aesthetic experience. This is my second point. Style may turn out to be an umbrella concept for a number of subforms, depending on variance in the percept (location, object) and other possible factors; it may also very well be the case that style is not exactly the same thing in music (or other modalities) as in painting. Experimental neuroaesthetics can unveil such potential differences which, then, when fed back into the descriptions and theories of traditional aesthetics can help us enrich and modify existing concepts and models. In other words, just as a model of *what* constitutes art is a prerequisite to investigations of *how* the brain computes art, studying the neurocognitive mechanisms that cause art behavior is of vital importance to the mission of traditional aesthetics: figuring out what art is. Indeed, it is beneficial to think of these two questions (*what* and *how*) as mutually intertwined.

To sum up these opening remarks, neuroaesthetics is a new scientific discipline whose object it is to identify and understand the neural processes involved in human art behavior—those processes that underlie both the construction and experience of art. However, to get off the ground, neuroaesthetics must have an idea what it is looking for, that is, the neuroaesthetics researcher should entertain some notion of what counts as an aesthetic property. This is in fact not easily done. Indeed, at this stage, a key challenge for neuroaesthetics lies in the very establishment of a model of the functional elements making up the neural system subserving art production and consumption. Such a model is best attained through the continuous posing of hypothetical models based on research into what art objects in actual fact look like and experimental testing of these hypotheses. Seen in this way, neuroaesthetics is but one subdiscipline of a number of biological approaches to art, with other disciplines investigating, *inter alia*, when art first appeared in the hominid line, what manifestations art behavior has taken historically (rock art, jewelry, dance, sculpture, architecture, music, etc.), or what the social and psychological function of art is. (I haven't mentioned the equally important evolutionary question of *why* specific forms of art behavior evolved. But, as I will briefly illustrate below, neuroaesthetics should also be seen as interrelated with this aspect of the wider domain of bioaesthetics: evolutionary hypotheses can inspire good neuroaesthetics experiments; and neuroaesthetics results, on the other hand, may inform evolutionary reasoning. For an example of this see Nadal et al., this volume.)

In the rest of this chapter, I put forward a number of problems I think should be viewed as central to neuroaesthetic research. Clearly, they are not in any way meant to be exhaustive. As already noted, neuroaesthetics is still in its infancy, and we are very far from having an exhaustive idea of what possible neural mechanisms could be involved in either the experience or the creation of art. But I think that, at least, all the problems I propose can be demonstrated to play a crucial role in art behavior, and as such, I hope they will inspire future neuroaesthetic research.

WHAT IS ART?

My overall aim is to identify a number of traits characterizing the phenomenon of art and to suggest some of the neurocognitive mechanisms that may be engaged by these traits. How do we go about this exercise? I believe the proper way to go is as follows: We already know that when experiencing a painting, the brain will activate basic neural systems such as visual perception, visual recognition, memory, emotion, and other mechanisms generally involved in seeing objects. Similarly, we also know that in order to create a work of art, the artist must activate neural systems underlying visual imagery (what to portray), motor control and visual perception (moving the brush in the right direction, etc.), and so on, in the same way processes general to other forms of visual depiction are activated. So, we can begin by asking what kinds of *functions* these systems may specifically be engaged in when it comes to experiencing and manufacturing art. To return to my example of style, we can for example ask if the general mechanisms of categorizing and attaching conceptual meaning to perceptual inputs perform any special task in connection with the process of seeing a painting as a Monet, or impressionistic. A speculative answer could be that, yes they do, because works of art are *created* intentionally—the artist has decided that colors, lines, and such should be arranged precisely as they are, in a unique way—the mechanisms of categorization and activation of conceptual meaning here take an extraordinary form, having, for instance, to erect novel and fictive clusters of conceptual elements ("A water lily by Monet is *purple* and *white*, painted with *open brushstrokes*, etc."). In this way, we move from something we know something about—visual perception, motor control—to evermore refined notions of how these basic mechanisms are used more specifically in seeing art, or in painting paintings. As far as I can see, this approach avoids postulating that art behavior is constituted by, or caused by, a set of wholly unique features; features that can, usually, be demonstrated to also be employed in nonart behavior. For instance, it is not necessary for the mechanisms of categorization or conceptual meaning involved in style to be unique to art. It is also perfectly OK if style can be said to be a property of nonart objects, such as when we experience a soccer team as having a certain style of play without equating, for whatever reasons, a game of soccer with art. The only important thing is that we have managed to identify a function that is actually an essential part of the behavioral domain we call art.

How would a list of such essential elements of art behavior look like then? In line with what I have already stipulated, I don't think it is possible at this point of time to produce a comprehensive list, but it is certainly possible to single out a number of the most significant features. Some of these features are very fundamental; they are general to all forms of art behavior. Others are more specific to the various modalities of art (mechanisms of motor activity in dance, mechanisms of audition in music, mechanisms of language in literature, etc.), although in some instances, they also play a role in the other modalities as well. Finally, some features figure prominently in artworks, but not necessarily in art behavior as such. I will call this type of features "devices," after the Russian formalists (Erlich, 1981). A device is a deliberate material construction crafted by the artist with the intention of producing a more or less specific effect in the observer—think rhyme, metrical structure, perspective, crescendo, pirouette, and so on. The presence of devices is integral to art, but no individual device is in itself essential to the art object; it is possible to create poems both with and without metaphors, for instance. We can think of devices as features that individuate each particular work of art—and consequently the experience of the individual art object—and as such devices are of great importance to neuroaesthetics. Not surprisingly a wide range has already been investigated in the lab, including metaphor (Rapp, Leube, Erb, Grodd, & Kircher, 2004), western tonal structure (Janata, Birk, Van Horn, Leman, Tillmann, & Bharucha, 2002), rhythm (Patel, 2003), narrative (Zalla, Phipps, & Grafman, 2002), and abnormally colored objects (Zeki & Marini, 1998), to name just a representative few. But in the end, devices are to be understood in the larger context of the role they play for art behavior: while we are inherently interested in uncovering the neurocognitive mechanisms driving metaphor, our primary objective remains understanding how metaphors contribute to the overall aesthetic experience.

I am convinced the following four features will turn out to be constitutive of art behavior in general. Once more, though, I stress that, as we garner more and more experimental data, they may very well be either revised or overturned, just as additional features may be added to them. I describe the four features briefly, and then, in the next two sections, proceed to suggest a number of neurocognitive mechanisms that are likely to subserve them, and that should therefore be targets of future neuroaesthetic enquiry.

1. At its core, all art is the result of an act of creation. This creative aspect is probably the most fundamental dimension in need of elucidation. Works of art result from the manipulation of some physical material by a human being with the intention of producing some specific form. I mean this in a very basic sense. Art does not necessarily have to take the form of "work," in this word's most traditional sense. It can also be more like an event, as in traditional dance or situational art (van Damme, 1996), and works of art can be construed as "open," that is, affected by the interpretation of the performer or the observer (Eco, 1989). However, even if

the work of art is an event, not an object, or is transitory or changing with time or context, it is always the case that there is some bounded material representation that only exists because the artist has brought it about, and which the observer uses as the starting point for erecting an aesthetic experience. It may also be objected that, even if it is true that the artist "brings about" the artwork, it is not always the case that physical materials are deliberately manipulated in a familiar way, such as musicians stringing together pitch, rhythm, and melody to form a song, or poets arranging words, syntax, and phonemes to craft a poem. Some modernist art attempts to minimize this aspect of making, using *objets trouvé* or emphasizing conceptual ideas over material form. Yet, although there is little ordinary craftsmanship in Duchamp's moving a readymade urinal into the museum, the intentional change of situational context is in itself an artful manipulation, and, in fact, Duchamp further modified the urinal by signing it and giving it a title, "Fontaine." The visitor is *meant* to experience an ordinary urinal as an oddball presence at a museum; the urinal is *placed* in the museum with the *express purpose of* making the observer debate what counts as a work of art, thereby making it a work of art itself.

2. Clearly, humans create other novel forms or objects that are not (necessarily) viewed as art, tools for instance, or linguistic utterances. Philosophers have tried to identify the difference between these forms of making and the act of creating art, most notoriously Kant's idea in *Kritik der Urteilskraft* that, while tools and other artifacts are made to serve a purpose, works of art are created to afford us with a disinterested, or nonpractical, experience (Kant, 1974). In my view, there are two big differences between works of art and other manmade objects. The first is the fact that the principal purpose of creating a work of art is to elicit an *experience* in some observer. We invent chairs to sit on, cars to transport us from one place to another, or iPods to make our music collection portable. We manufacture artifacts as instruments to help us facilitate some function. In contrast, works of art are created not to be used for some function, but to be experienced. As I said, Duchamp displayed his signed urinal in order for the persons who encounter it to *look* at it, to *realize* the dissonance between a urinal and the other objects traditionally exhibited in museums—indeed, to *experience this dissonance* as both a cognitive and an emotional effect and to *reflect* on the nature of art. To induce or provoke experience is the purpose of the art object. At the artist's end, this means that colors and words are chosen; motifs, themes, and subjects are aimed at; and new devices invented with the express purpose of instigating an effect in the observer. Very clearly, these effects vary immensely. Thrillers seek to evoke an intense sense of suspense in the observer; comedies try to make you laugh. In his *Poetics,* Aristotle suggested that tragic drama "is the mimesis of a serious and complete action of some magnitude; in language embellished in various ways in its different parts; in dramatic, not narrative form; achieving, through pity and fear, the catharsis of such passions" (Aristotle, 1941, §6). At the observer's end, the properties of the artwork are used as ingredients for cooking up a mental experience.

3. Why this proclivity for manipulating physical material in order to elicit experiential effects in the observer of the work of art (both other conspecifics and the artist herself)? Obviously in some instances the reason is just to make the observer

feel good, laugh, or pity the hero; in other instances the reason is to evoke novel, previously unconsidered ideas (urinals as art). As Ellen Dissanayake has argued forcefully in a series of papers and books, often the purpose of artistic creativity is also to make the work of art stand out, to "make it special" (Dissanayake, 1979, 1982, 2000; see also Brown & Dissanayake, this volume). The effect of experiencing a work of art as special sets it apart from other, everyday objects; for instance, an embellished tool can signal ownership or social status, or a huge palace built in rare materials can signify that this is the living quarters of the head of state. Dissanayake suggests that this inclination to shape or modify objects, places, behavior, and other parts of our surrounding world, reflects a human need to mark these modified things as out-of-context, a behavioral trait also found in animal play and ritual. Through exaggerations, stereotypification, rules, decoration, elaboration, and other forms of manufacturing, ordinary behavior and nonspecial objects, thus, "acquire a specialized communicative function" (Dissanayake, 1979, p. 27), such as the ability to communicate mood, thoughts, and feelings (for example, hostility or sexual arousal), or express important values or ideas, just as illustrated in the examples above. I think Dissanayake's hypothesis is highly attractive because it offers a plausible explanation for how the complex cultural products of modern "fine" art have evolved from earlier forms of behavior, at the same time as it clarifies why music, poetry, dance, and other types of art continue to feature prominently in almost every important situation of our lives, including baptism and burial, mating (parties!), social functions (coronations, inaugurations, etc.), and religious ceremony. Indeed, art devices, as defined above, are in many ways a subspecies of a general penchant for "making special."

4. As stated, works of art exist to be experienced. There is a long tradition in aesthetic theory for assuming that the mental process of forging an experience based on the perceptual properties of the artwork deviate in some significant respect from the mental process of experiencing nonart objects. A core assumption is that works of art, in contrast to ordinary objects, must be *interpreted*, that as percepts they are not readily "translated" into a meaningful mental representation, being constituted by novel, strange, or enigmatic parts. Hence, the Russian formalists argued that the stylistic devices employed by poets and authors deautomatize the reading process through "making strange" the habitual by presenting it in a novel light, giving rise to a heightened awareness of things and restoring sharpness to our perception (Shklovsky, 1965). David Miall and Don Kuiken have recently reexamined this hypothesis in a series of empirical reader-response studies, and have found that compared with nonpoetic segments, poetic segments of a story elicit increased reading times and greater affect ratings (Miall & Kuiken, 1994). In his chapter in this volume, Miall suggests that literature evokes a defamiliarization-reconceptualization cycle where the feelings evoked by passages containing stylistic devices "provide an alternative perspective directing the reader's search for a new understanding. The resulting reconceptualization occurs downstream from the initial encounter. . . ." This suggestion is reminiscent of Fitch and colleagues' proposal, in their chapter, that we go through a special "cognitive trajectory," composed of three stages, when experiencing art: "an initial stage of familiarity,

recognition or stability; a second stage of surprise, ambiguity, or tension; and a third stage of integration, resolution or synthesis." To this date there has been some, albeit not much, interest among psychologists in fleshing out what goes on during this integration of surprise elements and resolution of ambiguity (see, for instance, Solso, 1996, 2003). But as the chapters by Miall as well as Fitch et al. demonstrate, new ideas are starting to appear; crucially, ideas that can be tested empirically.

Together, I think these four features capture two essential characteristics of human art behavior—two characteristic traits that traditional aesthetics have tended to believe are distinctive of art, and that I believe most neuroaesthetecians will agree need elucidation. The first concerns the desire and ability to create works of art, that is, aggregations of physical materials that have been manipulated, embellished, or shaped with the intention of producing an experience in those who perceive them. The second concerns the nature of created materials: they tend to be "special" in some sense, that is, to deviate from ordinary objects or materials in a specific way and therefore to provoke a cognitive cycle of defamiliarization-reconceptualization processing on part of the beholder. The job of neuroaesthetics, now, is to identify the neural mechanisms that are the cause of these behavioral traits. Naturally, there will not be distinct anatomical regions dedicated to artistic creativity, material manipulation, making special, defamiliarization, or reconceptualization; these putative cognitive functions will turn out to be amalgams of more basic neural processes. Consider, as an example, poetic creativity. To compose a poem or a novel, the poet will engage in many of the same mental operations that she avails herself of when speaking in a nonpoetic way. A message must be intuited; this message must then be formulated lexically and syntactically, and expressed through the means of motor activity (Levelt, 1999). Diffuse neural networks in the temporal and parietal lobes, the prefrontal cortex, and in motor cortex underlie this complex process of producing a linguistic utterance (for reviews, see Bookheimer, 2002; Démonet, Thierry, & Cardebat, 2005; Gernsbacher & Kaschak, 2003). The question is how creating poetic utterances may differ from creating any other form of linguistic utterance, if at all. Together with Frederik Stjernfelt and Olaf Paulson, I have suggested that it could differ in a number of possible ways (Skov, Stjernfelt, & Paulson, 2007): (a) For one thing, the artist may be more prone to mental imagery, that is, the ability to dream up mental images invested with an intriguing meaning. Such bursts of "fantasy" could spring from the unusual coactivation of perceptual or conceptual features, such as horses with wings or men that drink blood and can assume the guise of a bat; possibly poets are born with a neural machinery facilitating such blending of conceptual information. (b) Another possibility is that poets might be especially good at putting their mental imagery into words. Research has shown that interactions between neurons in the inferior frontal gyrus (IFG) and the temporal lobe are important for the selection and integration of semantic features into larger phrasal and discursive entities (see Hagoort, 2005; Kan & Thompson-Schill, 2004; Thompson-Schill et al., 2005). Superior language skills in the poet could be rooted in some unknown structural or functional capacity—expanded grey matter, axonal connections, and such—strengthening IFG's control over the conceptual system in the temporal lobe. (c) Finally, no doubt the poet also taps into general brain mechanisms for creative problem solving, including hypothesis generation, evaluation, set shifting, and conflict resolution (Martindale, 1994), mechanisms that are currently the topic of intense investigation (for a recent review, see Vartanian & Goel, 2007). Whatever turns out to be the true source of poetic creativity, it stands to reason that creative excellence does not derive from just one neural process. In all probability, the process of creating poetic language calls upon several different neural mechanisms that may even interact in alternative ways from one poet to the next (one poet could be very imaginative, another could be highly proficient in coming up with *le mot juste* for a novel mental idea). And poetic creativity, it should be borne in mind, might furthermore engage neural mechanisms distinct from musical creativity or visual creativity.

The aspect of art behavior we presently know by far the most about is the reception of art. To start with, we can single out two core neural domains involved in art reception: representation and emotional response. Both representation and emotion will contribute neuronal mechanisms important to the creation of the essential features of art behavior.

REPRESENTATION

One of the principal purposes of a work of art, as I have written, is to elicit an experience in an observer. Since the work of art is composed of devices that make it appear special, this aspect of art behavior puts a premium on the process of building a mental representation. When observing a work of art, we will often encounter original and unique forms, invented by the artist, or at least novel organizations of familiar forms. A crucial part of the experience of art is the brain's ability to extract the perceptual features of these novel forms, or novel arrangements, and integrate them so that they make sense.

Modern neuroscience has come a long way in understanding how the visual system is organized in functional modules (Felleman & Van Essen, 1991; Zeki, 2005) and processing streams (Goodale & Milner, 1992), and how the brain recognizes objects (Kanwisher, 2003). Similarly, through neuroimaging and other new techniques, we are gradually beginning to also understand how the brain parses musical input into tonality, pitch, melody, rhythm, and so on (Koelsch & Siebel, 2005; Peretz & Zatorre, 2005) or language input into phonemes, lexical entities, syntactical structure, and such (Bookheimer, 2002; Démonet et al., 2005). A general structural organization for all three modalities appears to be that, as the perceptual input travels from the sensory periphery, through the posterior parts of the cortex, upstream toward the prefrontal cortex, the early parts of the brain are in the business of extracting perceptual features (contrasts, light, color, symmetry, auditory complexity, etc.); structures in the temporal and parietal lobes classify and integrate these features according to various principles, and relate the resulting object categorization to other nodes of knowledge in the brain's conceptual system; while structures located in the prefrontal cortex incorporate the ensuing information into the behavioral program of the organism.

Neuroaesthecians have utilized this emerging understanding of how the brain handles perceptual input to suggest various models of how representations of art emanate from more basic processes (Chatterjee, 2003; Leder, Belke, Oeberst, & Augustin, 2004; Livingstone, 1988; Solso, 1996; Zeki, 1999). A good example is Helmut Leder and colleagues' model, depicted in Figure 1. It assigns a number of putative art-specific processes to the general mechanisms of perceptual analysis, memory, and object categorization, including identification of context, organization, familiarity, prototypicality, classification of style and content, and "cognitive mastering" of the work of art, to name the most important.

The Leder model can be viewed as an information-processing model, stipulating a flow of information from one component process to the next (perceptual analysis → implicit memory integration → explicit classification → cognitive mastering → evaluation). It is probably true that all these stages will be engaged by any work or art, but it should be recognized, I think, that works of art can differ in the respect that they tap different parts of the system. As the insightful Semir Zeki (1999) has remarked, artists tend to focus on a limited number of perceptual and cognitive features, targeting select brain mechanisms. For instance, the portrait painter concentrates on face processing, the abstract painter on geometrical figures or color, and so on. In the same way, some works of art are more stimulus driven, while others appeal predominantly to our mental world of ideas (e.g., conceptual art). A monochrome painting by Yves Klein relies comparably little on the beholder's ability to relate perceptual information to past experiences, whereas highly intertextual works of art, such as David Lynch's *Twin Peaks,* can only be comprehended through the active, and possibly effortful, participation of memory. Thus, depending on the nature of the work of art, the computational impact of Leder's putative five stages on the individual art experience will vary. Also, it is unlikely that the flow of information only moves upstream, from posterior to anterior parts of the brain. Not only has it been known for a long time that top-down information modulates even the processing of neurons in early visual cortex (Churchland, Ramachandran, & Sejnowski, 1994), but several psychophysical studies have demonstrated that modulating the context of the artwork, by simply attaching a title to it, will influence the observer's appreciation and understanding of the artwork (Cupchick, Shereck, & Spiegel, 1994; Leder, Carbon, & Ripsas, 2006; Russell, 2003). A more likely assumption is that information flows back and forth, as it were, between the various mechanisms suggested by Leder et al.'s model. It remains to be seen exactly how perceptual analysis, memory, object recognition, and prefrontal processes interact, functionally and temporally, during the construction of mental representations of art.

Models such as the one proposed by Leder et al. will be vital to developing concrete hypotheses as to how the artist manages to make the work of art appear to be special. A work of art made special is in essence one that provokes a strange, or nonnormal, representation in the brain of the observer. In terms of Leder et al.'s model, it is possible to perturb the system at every stage, i.e. to tweak whatever representative mechanism employed by the individual art object. For instance, since the relative size of a percept is an indication of how far from the observer it is located (the closer the percept is to the observer, the more space it will occupy

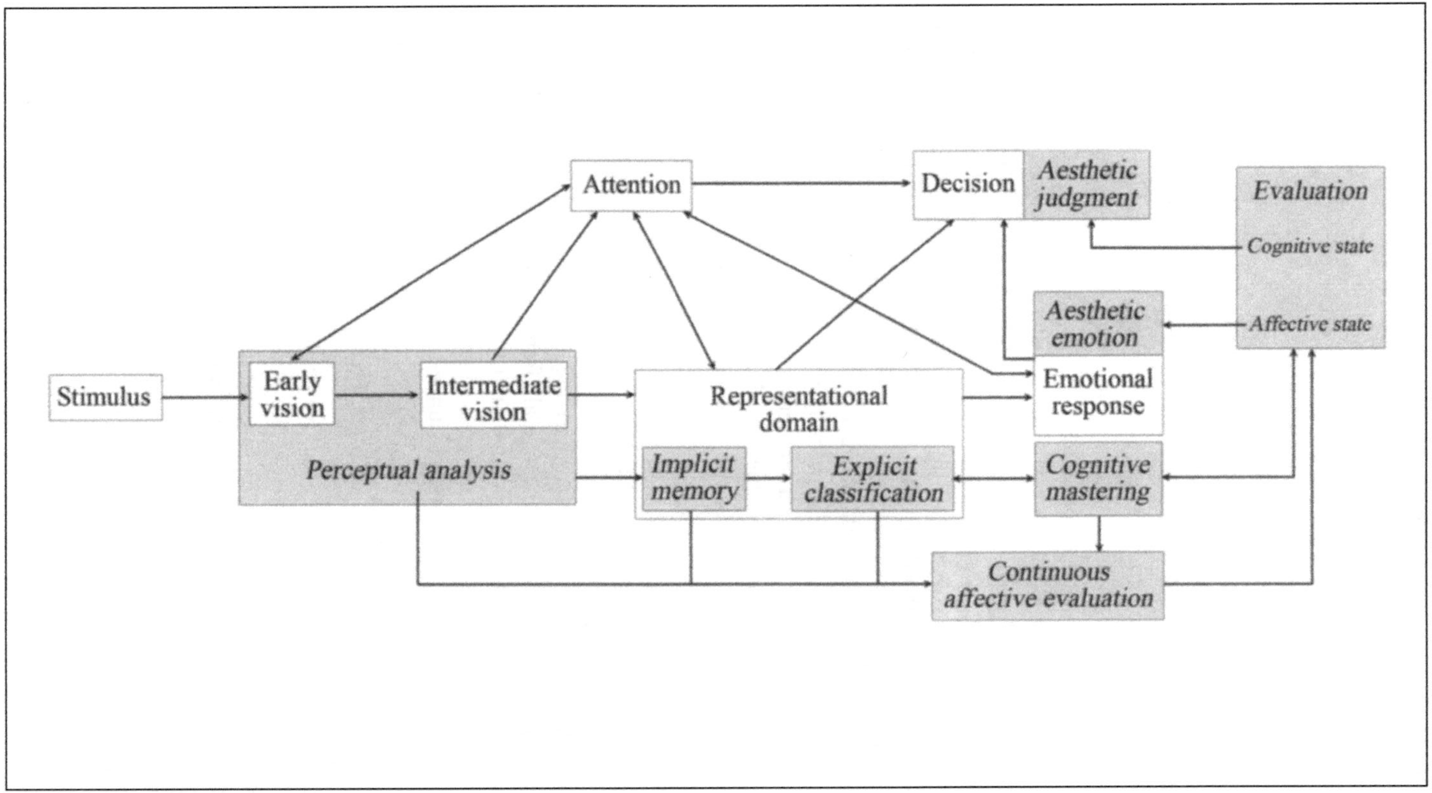

Figure 1. A model of possible neurocognitive mechanisms involved in the brain's forming a mental representation of the work of art, based on the perceptual properties exhibited by the art object. After Leder et al. (2004). (© Illustration by Marcos Nadal.) Reproduced by permission from Marcos Nadal.

on the retina of the eye), by varying the two-dimensional size of a painting's elements, an artist can co-opt the perceptual system of the brain into inducing illusions of depth (Solso, 2003). That's one way of achieving specialness. Another way to achieve the effect is to break the observer's expectation by, for example, disturbing the proportion of well-known objects, changing the normal color of a thing, juxtapose unrelated concepts, or frame the parts of the representation in an unusual way. Indeed, often the artist will employ more than one strategy in one and the same work of art. Consider Balthus' painting *La Rue* (http://artchive.com/artchive/B/balthus/balthus_street.jpg.html). This painting very effectively transforms an everyday street into an alternative, highly strange street. For instance, the colors used are not normal for everyday streets, and the people occupying it seem odd in one way or another. All in all there is a rather unsettling quality to the painting, as if this is a slightly sinister or *Unheimlich* street. This effect, at least in me, stems from the manipulation of a range of factors. Several of people promenading, for example, have been given a sickly yellow skin color. The perspective of the scene seems tilted because of the horizontal line in the back of the picture that slopes downward to the right. Both the "girl" playing with a red ball in the front of the picture and the "boy" sitting on a woman's arm in the back look more adult than childlike, and, of course, the man putting his arm around the girl in the left field of the painting gives off an obscure impression of attacking her (sexually, playfully?); a strange act to unfold in broad daylight, in the middle of a street, surrounded by other people. Together, these and other factors conspire to both build in the mind of the beholder the representation of "a street" as an extremely estranged location, perceptually as well as conceptually, and to evoke a somewhat disturbing feeling of disquiet. What is the man doing to the girl? Why do two of the persons have the body of a child and the head of an adult? What kind of place is this anyway?

It is probably critical that the defamiliarizing devices employed by the artist serve a meaningful purpose within the overall frame of representation. *Together* the odd face colors, the slanted perspective, and the adult faces on the bodies of children, and so on, give rise to an experience of seeing a strange street, populated with bizarre people, involved in mysterious undertakings. It is possible to imagine removing some of the elements used by Balthus. Taking away the buildings and the lines designating the road and pavements, for instance, we would have just the free-floating persons, eliminating the sense of looking at curious people, engaged in queer acts, *in a specific setting*. Likewise, we could also imagine Balthus having painted only the man in yellow, located at the middle of the painting. This would leave us with a Munch-like expressionist painting, where the yellow color, the position of the arm, and the enigmatic smile would suddenly stand as signs of this man's inner, psychological world instead of as signs of the nature of the strange street. In other words, artistic devices function as parts of a whole. This is a very important point: The objects we call art do not spring from just the shaping of a material form in any old unusual way, but from doing so with a communicative purpose. This gives the mental representations they evoke a characteristic uniqueness; in *La Rue,* the combination of colors, lines, body positions, body-head incommensurability, unsettling feeling, and so on, make for a street that looks like no other street, or like no other depiction of a street for that matter.

In order to fuse the artistic devices of a work of art into a meaningful whole, the brain must employ some mechanism for integrating information coming from separate neural processes, or more likely, several different mechanisms for integrating information. These integrative mechanisms should be added as a part to Leder's model. Experimental data show that, for instance, music can influence semantic processing (Koelsch, Kasper, Sammler, Schulze, Gunter, & Friederici, 2004), affect the emotional reaction to pictures (Baumgartner, Lutz, Schmidt, & Jäncke, 2006), or activate the motor system (Zatorre, Chen, & Penhune, 2007). Another type of integration is exemplified by the metaphor that integrates conceptual information from two separate semantic domains (Fauconnier & Turner, 2000). A third is exemplified by conflict resolution: conceptual, perceptual, or otherwise. Presumably these mechanisms rely on axonal connections, synchronization of neuronal firings, reactivation of perceptual and conceptual information, selection of information, shift of attention and working memory maintenance, as well as different forms of top-down modulation. Happily, experiments are starting to elucidate the various neuronal processes involved in these mechanisms. For instance, in an early fMRI study, Zeki and Marini (1998) compared viewing red strawberries with blue strawberries and found that the latter condition elicited extraordinary activity in prefrontal structures. Other studies of metaphor processing indicate that temporal structures in the right hemisphere maintain weak, diffuse semantic activation of a broader semantic field, initiated by a given linguistic utterance, including distant and contextually irrelevant features, whereas structures in the left temporal lobe underlie semantic activation of features related to the dominant, literal, or contextually relevant meaning of the utterance (Jung-Beeman, 2005; see also Miall, this volume). This coarse semantic activation appears to facilitate indirect semantic relations, unusual interpretations, jokes, and indeed metaphors (Schmidt, DeBure, & Seger, in press; St. George et al., 1999), presumably by bypassing the dominant semantic meaning and giving access to more distant features. More studies along these lines can be expected to further illuminate how information is integrated in the experience of art.

EMOTION

Naturally, the representational aspect of our experience of art objects is the one artists influence most directly, through the manipulations of the perceptual properties of the work of art. The experiential character of engaging with a work of art, as opposed to an ordinary object, stems primarily from the manipulation of the perceptual, memory, and cognitive processes involved in generating a mental representation. We need to be able to pick up on the specialness of a visual or auditory form in order to react to it. However, it is at the same time clear that a crucial part of experiencing something as special is some form of emotional reaction accompanying such a mental representation. I recognize the skin color employed in Balthus' painting as abnormal because I have a visual system that informs me that such a type of color is unusual on human skin; but I react to this abnormality with the feeling of sickness—the persons look sickly. Likewise, I feel that the combination of children's bodies with adult heads is odd and unsettling. And for some reason that I may at first be unable to explain, the whole scenery comes off as somewhat sinister. No doubt, the brain's emotional response to the work of art is a very important component of the aesthetic experience.

Unfortunately, in contrast to models of the mechanisms underlying representation such as Leder's, there are at present no attempts to tally up the emotional mechanisms employed by experiences of art. Of course, our neurobiological understanding of the processes involved in emotion is very much inferior to our understanding of visual perception or memory. But we are beginning to know enough (Barrett, Mesquita, Ochsner, & Gross, 2007; Dalgleish, 2004; Panksepp, 2005) to start speculating what function emotion might play in the experience of art. Whereas the neurocognitive mechanisms underlying representation compute the nature of the object we experience, our emotions in different ways gauge its *value*. Emotional values are related to the physiological state of the experiencing organism, as wells as to its behavioral goal. For instance, thirst may signal a physiological deficiency that acts as a motivational feeling. Pleasure and displeasure, on the other hand, can help the organism choose between different behavioral choices and also function as reinforcement signals in a process of learning ("If the yellow fluid I tried to drink in order to quell my thirst tasted bad, I should avoid it in the future"). It is an important question how such functions—valence; imputing saliency to an object; allocating attention due to the value of an object (for instance, a threatening face); predicting reward; and so on—is employed by works of art, and for what reason. From time to time, philosophers have suggested that emotional reactions could play a pivotal part in the experience of art, but there is still no consensus if this is true. (I am thinking of such oft-quoted reactions to art as beauty, catharsis, the sublime, shock of the new, and so on.) I will, very provisionally, suggest a few functions that emotional responses could enjoy in the experience of art.

First, it is rather obvious that very many works of art provoke what is sometimes called basic emotions (Barrett & Wager, 2006). We feel sad when the hero dies and happy when the heroine finally, at the end of the romantic comedy, gets her kiss. Often the evocation of such feelings appears to be the primary objective of the work of art. This is not the case only in genre work, where one emotional reaction is sought above all else; the comedy, the thriller, the horror movie, the romance. Often works of art are characterized by their ability to evoke emotional transformations, as when a character in a novel is first seen as evil, but is later learned to be a nice guy. Indeed, it is often seen as a hallmark of "good" art that there are no easy solutions, that we cannot easily make up our minds as to whether or not a person, or some action, is good or bad. Similarly, our emotional reaction to a symphony might be muddled or unclear, composed of positive and negative emotions in rapid alternations. Remarkably, art is probably one of the few areas of life where we voluntarily expose ourselves to unpleasant objects: mutilated bodies, violence, dissonance, boring serial repetitions of the same notes, evil acts of behavior, disproportional bodies, unsettling streets with strange and sinister persons, and such. Hence, art is not only employed in the service of inducing positive emotions, as when we dance together, enhance the mood through music, or by reading an entertaining book; we also willfully use art to induce sadness, fear, nausea, or displeasure.

The second function of the emotional system in the experience of art is to assert what could be called the aesthetic value of the work of art. In contrast to the various emotional reactions discussed above, the aesthetic value concerns how much the observer likes the art objects. Aesthetic values are often referred to as distinct feelings—beautiful, delightful, interesting, superb, etc.—but it is still unknown if they really differ in a physiological sense or if we are just giving different names to the same basic form of pleasure. We do know, though, from countless psychological experiments, that the aesthetic value of an object is influenced by numerous factors, including the physical properties of the stimulus, learning, personality traits, mood, and a range of top-down factors (context, titles, frames change, and other things). Several neuroimaging studies indicate strongly that aesthetic values are predominantly computed by reward processes associated with such brain structures as the striatum, amygdala, orbitofrontal cortex, and the anterior cingulate. (I am not going to review this literature as this is done in Oshin Vartanian's chapter in this volume.) It is possible for artists to seek a high aesthetic value of their work of art by selectively highlighting some properties but not others. For instance, the poet may be concerned to balance the meter of the poem with the right number of syllables and semantic content of each sentence, but disregard phonetic features such as alliteration. For the artist, the work of art might be seen as "brilliant" because he has accomplished this formal objective. On the other hand, some readers may not react to these properties, and could thus find it boring even if the artist likes it. Why exactly people respond differently to the same set of perceptual properties is one of the key questions facing neuroaesthetics. Different strokes for different folks.

Together, these two ways of engaging the brain's emotional system through the use of art suggest different ways of making a manmade object special. The appeal to basic emotions through empathy with representations of human characters or actions, or otherwise through emulation of emotionally salient situations, is perhaps more concerned with the *content* side of the representation where the striving for aesthetic value seems more directed at the *form* elements making up the representation. Maybe this hypothetical difference reflects different needs of making special.

CONCLUSION

In this chapter, I have attempted to lay out a general framework for future neuroaesthetic research. I propose that neuroaesthetic researchers should make it clear why they think a research question belongs to the field of aesthetics or not. For experimental research to start, we need to specify what neurocognitive mechanisms underlie art behavior; a prerequisite to such models is a reflection of what constitutes art behavior. I believe my brief discussion of putative mechanisms involved in the representational and emotional aspects of the experience of art objects furnish the reader with a meaningful structure within which to understand the more detailed discussions to come in the rest of the book's chapters.

REFERENCES

Aggleton, J. P., & Brown, M. W. (2005). Contrasting hippocampal and perirhinal cortex function using immediate early gene imaging. *Quarterly Journal of Experimental Psychology B, 58,* 218-233.

Aristotle. (1941). Poetics. In R. McKeon (Ed.), *The basic works of Aristotle.* New York: Random House.

Barrett, L. F., & Wager, T. D. (2006). The structure of emotion. Evidence from neuroimaging studies. *Current Directions in Psychological Science, 15,* 79-83.

Barrett, L. F., Mesquita, B., Ochsner, K. N., & Gross, J. J. (2007). The experience of emotion. *Annual Review of Psychology, 58,* 373-403.

Beardsley, M. C. (1969). Aesthetic experience regained. *Journal of Aesthetics and Art Criticism, 28*(1), 3-11.

Baumgartner, T., Lutz, K., Schmidt, C. F., & Jäncke, L. (2006). The emotional power of music: How music enhances the feeling of affective pictures. *Brain Research, 1075,* 151-164.

Bookheimer, S. (2002). Functional MRI of language. *Annual Review of Neuroscience, 25,* 151-188.

Chatterjee, A. (2003). Prospects for a cognitive neuroscience of visual aesthetics. *Bulletin of Psychology and the Arts, 4,* 55-60.

Churchland, P. S., Ramachandran, V. S., & Sejnowski, T. J. (1994). A critique of pure vision. In C. Koch & J. L. Davis (Eds.), *Large-scale neuronal theories of the brain* (pp. 23-60). Cambridge, MA & London: The MIT Press.

Cupchik, G., Shereck, L, & Spiegel, S. (1994). The effects of textual information on artistic communication, *Visual Arts Research, 20,* 62-78.

Dalgleish, T. (2004). The emotional brain. *Nature Review Neuroscience, 5,* 582-589.

Démonet, J.-F, Thierry, G., & Cardebat, D. (2005). Renewal of the neurophysiology of language: Functional neuroimaging. *Physiology Review, 85,* 49-95.

Dissanayake, E. (1979). An ethological view of ritual and art in human evolutionary history. *Leonardo, 12,* 27-31.

Dissanayake, E. (1982). Aesthetic experience and human evolution. *Journal of Aesthetics and Art Criticism, 41*(2), 145-155.

Dissanayake, E. (2000). *Art and intimacy.* Seattle & London: University of Washington Press.

Eco, U. (1989). *The open work.* London: Hutchison Radius.

Erlich, V. (1981). *Russian formalism. History—Doctrine* (3rd ed.). New Haven & London: Yale University Press.

Fauconnier, G., & Turner, M. (2000). Conceptual integration networks. *Cognitive Science, 22,* 133-187.

Felleman, D., & van Essen, D. (1991). Distributed hierarchical processing in the primate cerebral cortex. *Cerebral Cortex, 1,* 1-47.

Gernsbacher, M., & Kaschak, M. (2003). Neuroimaging studies of language production and comprehension. *Annual Review of Psychology, 54,* 91-114.

Goodale, M., & Milner, D. (1992). Separate visual pathways for perception and action. *Trends in Neuroscience, 15,* 20-25.

Hagoort, P. (2005). On Broca, brain, and binding: A new framework. *Trends in Cognitive Sciences, 9,* 416-423.

Hyman, J. (2006). Art and neuroscience. Downloaded from www.interdisciplines.org/artcognition/papers/15 (accessed January, 23, 2006).

Janata, P., Birk, J. L., Van Horn, J. D., Leman, M., Tillmann, B., & Bharucha, J. J. (2002). The cortical topography of tonal structures underlying western music. *Science, 298*, 2167-2170.

Jung-Beeman, M. (2005). Bilateral brain processes for comprehending natural language. *Trends in Cognitive Sciences, 11*, 512-518.

Kan, I., & Thompson-Schill, S. (2004). Selection from perceptual and conceptual representations. *Cognitive, Affective, & Behavioral Neuroscience, 4,* 466-482.

Kant, I. (1974). *Kritik der Urteilskraft.* Frankfurt am Main: Suhrkamp. (Original work published 1778.)

Kanwisher, N. (2003). The ventral visual object pathway in humans: Evidence from fMRI. In L. Chapula & J. Werner (Eds.), *The visual neurosciences* (pp. 1179-1189). Cambridge, MA: The MIT Press.

Koelsch, S., & Siebel, W. A. (2005). Towards a neural basis of music perception. *Trends in Cognitve Sciences, 9*, 578-584.

Koelsch, S., Kasper, E., Sammler, D., Schulze, K., Gunter, T., & Friederici, A. D. (2004). Music, language and meaning: Brain signatures of semantic processing. *Nature Neuroscience, 7*, 302-307.

Leder, H., Belke, B., Oeberst, A., & Augustin, D. (2004). A model of aesthetic appreciation and aesthetic judgments. *British Journal of Psychology, 95*, 489-508.

Leder, H., Carbon, C.-C., & Ripas, A.-L. (2006). Entitling art: Influence of title information on understanding and appreciation of paintings. *Acta Psychologia, 121,* 176-198.

Levelt, W. (1999). Producing spoken language: A blueprint of the speaker. In C. Brown & P. Hagoort (Eds.), *The neurocognition of language* (pp. 83-122). Oxford: Oxford University Press.

Livingstone, M. (1988). Art, illusion and the visual system. *Scientific American, 258,* 68-75.

Martindale, C. (1994). Biological bases of creativity. In R. J. Sternberg (Ed.), *Handbook of creativity* (pp. 137-152). Cambridge, MA: Cambridge University Press.

Miall, D. S., & Kuiken, D. (1994). Foregrounding, defamiliarization, and affect: Response to literary stories. *Poetics, 22*, 389-407.

Miyashita, Y. (2004). Cognitive memory: Cellular and network machineries and their top-down control. *Science, 306*, 435-440.

Panksepp, J. (2004). Affective consciousness: Core emotional feelings in animals and humans. *Consciousness and Cognition, 14,* 30-80.

Patel, A. D. (2003). Language, music, syntax and the brain. *Nature Neuroscience, 6*, 674-681.

Peretz, I., & Zatorre, R. J. (2005). Brain organization for music processing. *Annual Review of Psychology, 56,* 89-114.

Rapp, A. M., Leube, D. T., Erb, M., Grodd, W., & Kircher, T. T. J. (2004). Neural correlates of metaphor processing. *Cognitive Brain Research, 20,* 395-402.

Russell, P. A. (2003). Effort after meaning and the hedonic value of paintings. *British Journal of Psychology, 94*, 99-110.

Schmidt, G., DeBure, C., & Seger, C. (in press). Right hemisphere metaphor processing? *Brain and Language.*

Shklosky, V. (1965). Art as technique. In L. T. Lemon & M. J. Reis (Eds.), *Russian formalist criticism: Four essays* (pp. 3-24). Lincoln, NE: University of Nebraska Press. (Original work published 1917.)

Skov, M., Stjernfelt, F., & Paulson, O. B. (2007). Language and the brain's 'mental cinema.' In B. Grundtvig, M. McLaughlin, & L. W. Petersen (Eds.), *Image, eye, and art in Calvino. Writing visibility* (pp. 185-194). Leeds, UK: Maney Publishing.

Solso, R. L. (1994). *Cognition and the visual arts.* Cambridge, MA & London: The MIT Press.

Solso, R. L. (2003). *The psychology of art and the evolution of the conscious brain.* Cambridge, MA & London: The MIT Press.

St. George, M., Kutas, M., Martinez, A., & Sereno, M. I. (1999). Semantic integration in reading: Engagement of the right hemisphere during discourse processing. *Brain, 122,* 1317-1325.

Thompson-Schill, S. (2005). Dissecting the language organ: A new look at the role of Broca's area in language processing. In A. Cutler (Ed.), *Twenty-first century psycholinguistics: Four cornerstones* (pp. 173-189). Mahway, NJ & London: Lawrence Erlbaum.

Thompson-Schill, S., Bedny, M., & Goldberg, R. F. (2005). The frontal lobes and the regulation of mental activity. *Current Opinion in Neurobiology 15,* 1-6.

Van Damme, W. (1996). *Beauty in context. Towards an anthropological approach to aesthetics.* Leiden, New York, & Köln: E. J. Brill.

Vartanian, O., & Goel, V. (2007). Neural correlates of creative cognition. In C. Martindale, P. Locher, & V. Petrov (Eds.), *Evolutionary and neurocognitive approaches to aesthetics, creativity and the arts* (pp. 195-207). Amityville, NY: Baywood.

Zaidel, D. W. (2005). *Neuropsychology of art: Neurological, cognitive, and evolutionary perspectives.* Hove, UK: Psychology Press.

Zalla, T., Phipps, M., & Grafman, J. (2002). Story processing in patients with damage to the prefrontal cortex. *Cortex, 38,* 215-231.

Zatorre, R. J., Chen, J. L., & Penhune, V. B. (2007). When the brain plays music: Auditory-motor interactions in music perception and production. *Nature Review Neuroscience, 8,* 547-558.

Zeki, S. (1999). *Inner vision.* Oxford: Oxford University Press.

Zeki, S. (2005). The Ferrier lecture 1995. Behind the seen: The functional specialization of the brain in space and time. *Philosophical Transactions of the Royal Society of London B, 360,* 1145-1183.

Zeki, S., & Marini, L. (1998). Three cortical stages of colour processing in the human brain. *Brain, 121,* 1669-1685.

CHAPTER 3

Neuroaesthetics and the Psychology of Aesthetics

Thomas Jacobsen

As the term neuroaesthetics already denotes, cognitive neuroscientists have rediscovered the traditional discipline of empirical aesthetics. Over the past years, more and more researchers have begun to employ neuroscientific tools in the psychological study of aesthetic processing, or started to direct research in functional (cognitive) neuroscience toward the study of aesthetic processing. This chapter will trace how their endeavors are largely rooted in the classical, pragmatically dualistic approach of psychophysics. Here, objective measures of neural activity are correlated with reports of individual, subjective experience.

Mental aesthetic processing, aesthetic appreciation or production, is a very interesting topic, its complex realm of issues seemingly resisting a unified approach. This chapter will briefly review work showing that aesthetic processing, the evaluation or production of beauty, ugliness, prettiness, harmony, elegance, shapeliness, or charm (see Jacobsen, Buchta, Köhler, & Schröger, 2004), is governed by a host of factors such as stimulus symmetry, complexity, novelty, familiarity, artistic style, appeal to social status, and individual preferences. Humans appreciate a wide range of entities aesthetically: paintings, sculpture, music, opera, theater, literature, design, buildings, faces, flowers, landscapes, food, machinery, habitats, and various other objects of everyday life. Cultures differ in what is considered beautiful and within cultures, people differ. Moreover, the degree of agreement between individuals differs between content domains. Therefore, aesthetic processing can be usefully considered from an evolutionary, historical, cultural, educational, cognitive, (neuro)biological, individual, personality, emotional, and situational perspective, and probably many more. Hence, it has been argued that human aesthetics, as a whole, is best approached from a number of different perspectives at several different levels of analysis. This chapter also reviews a framework of seven such vantage points for today's Psychology of Aesthetics (Jacobsen, 2006).

Neuroaesthetics, as a strongly interdisciplinary field, focuses on the mind and body perspectives, emphasizing both. But other vantage points will be taken into account as well in order to create a general and unified approach to account for the mental processing of aesthetics.

HISTORY

Gustav Theodor Fechner summarized his major work on psychological aesthetics in the book *Vorschule der Aesthetik*, which was published in Leipzig in 1876 (Fechner, 1876). If one takes this year of publication to mark the beginning of a strongly empirical Psychology of Aesthetics, this discipline is more than 130 years old, and can be considered the second oldest branch of Experimental Psychology, following Fechner's Psychophysics. In contrast to most of the very popular philosophical aesthetics of his days, Fechner argued for an empirical "aesthetics from below," which assembles pieces of objective knowledge. This empirical aesthetics was called "Experimental Aesthetics" by Fechner, but other expressions such as "Empirical Aesthetics," "Psychological Aesthetics," or "Psychoaesthetics" are common as well. Today's Psychology of Aesthetics still follows Fechner's tradition. It often establishes transformational relations between objective observations from a third-person perspective, on the one hand, and participants' reports based on individual, inherently subjective experience, on the other hand. In neuroaesthetics, the former comprises measures like electroencephalograms (EEG), event-related potentials (ERP), magnetoencephalograms (MEG), functional magnetic resonance (fMRI), or positron emission tomography (PET). The latter are irreducible. In this way, this part of neuroaesthetics is one particular version of inner psychophysics.

To this day, Fechner's works represent an excellent source of inspiration for experimental psychological aesthetics, and neuroaesthetics as well. Many of his concepts have not yet been adopted to today's inventory of psychological terminology, some aspects of his work have fallen into oblivion. His concept of the aesthetic threshold, for example, implies that a stimulus has to cause the crossing of a specific individual threshold to trigger experiences that are aesthetically pleasant or unpleasant. This concept was subjected to empirical and experimental testing, and the results were published in a very renowned psychological journal, the *Psychological Review*, in 1906 (Martin, 1906). In years since, however, Fechner's concept of the aesthetic threshold, or the *aesthetische Schwelle,* has rarely been used by international experts.

When considering the history of experimental aesthetics, a few major trends can be identified. Following Fechner's seminal writings, there are a number of contributions that stand out in particular. Gestalt psychology had a strong influence on the psychology of art and aesthetics. In this context, Rudolf Arnheim's work represents an important application of the famous Gestalt laws of perception of art and aesthetics (Arnheim, 1974). Particular importance should be attached to Daniel Berlyne's work (1971, 1974). He advocated a psychobiological approach, mainly during the 1960s and 1970s, and managed to revive experimental aesthetics on a large scale after it had attracted much less attention in the decades before. He emphasized the importance of physiological arousal and suggested inverted-U-shaped relations between so-called collative variables (complexity, novelty, etc.) and aesthetic appreciation. Berlyne's impetus can still be felt today. Also, Hans Eysenck (1983), an eminent theorist in personality-structure research, contributed a great number of mostly comparative and psychometric publications to experimental aesthetics. Another milestone is Colin Martindale's (1988) cognitive theory. He put particular emphasis on the determining role of a person's structure of knowledge to aesthetic processes. According to their main orientations, these trends all contributed specific findings to the psychology of aesthetics.

TERMINOLOGY

The meaning of the word aesthetics is multifold and changing over time. Two main clusters of meaning can be identified. One is related to processes of sensation, as illustrated by its derivatives like anaesthetic, the absence of sensation, and synaesthetic, involuntary cosensation. The second cluster is related to the meaning of aesthetics as it is discussed in the arts, philosophy, or art history. In a recent study of German college students, a bipolar beautiful-ugly dimension clearly appeared to be the primary and prototypical descriptive dimension to address the aesthetics of objects (Jacobsen et al., 2004). This result, of course, converges with the main conceptualization of aesthetics in Philosophical and Psychological Aesthetics: beauty. At a secondary level, there is a conceptual system entailing a larger number of concepts (elegant, harmonious, shapely, small, big, round, colored, etc.). The descriptive approach of such a study yields information about a given state, without negating potential change due to historical, educational, cultural, and other influences. The study showed that in contemporary Western culture, the latter range of the meanings of the word aesthetics dominates. The former meaning, related to sensation, however, is entailed in that a sensory component is mandatory for aesthetic processing. For instance, an aesthetic judgment of beauty requires sensory processes, whereas a memory-based judgment of beauty does not. Consequently, aesthetic processing is sensation-based evaluation of an entity with respect to the above conceptual system, primarily the beauty dimension. The sensory subcomponents of aesthetic processing can be mentally simulated using imagination. Throughout this text, the word aesthetics will be understood as referring to beauty, the arts, shapeliness, elegance, harmony, and the like, rather than to the study of perception per se.

Psychology is the science of experience and behavior. The Psychology of Aesthetics is the subdiscipline of psychology that is concerned with the mental processing of aesthetics. Here, the term "entity" refers to an object of aesthetic processing. At this, an entity may be a thing, a living being, an event, a scenery, or an environment.

Neuroaesthetics can be construed as both a neuro (cognitive) psychology of aesthetics or part of functional (cognitive) neurology. The term itself mirrors the newly established connection between cognitive neuroscience and the second-oldest branch of experimental psychology. Three basic research strategies are conceivable for this new field. One is the correlational, psychophysical approach described above, which is adopted in most neuroimaging studies. The two other strategies comprise approaches that establish unidirectional causal relationships between mind and matter, like in neuropsychological studies, on the one hand, or long-term training studies using *in vivo* morphometry, on the other hand. Either way, previous behavioral findings, along with other empirical or historical observations, are highly relevant for the development of this emerging field.

STATUS

A host of factors influencing aesthetic experience and behavior has been identified in the course of research (Arnheim, 1974; Berlyne, 1971, 1974; Fechner, 1876). It is known that symmetry or asymmetry of an object (e.g., Berlyne, 1971; Fechner, 1876; Jacobsen & Höfel, 2002), complexity or simplicity (Berlyne, 1970, 1971), novelty or familiarity of an object (Berlyne, 1970, 1971), proportion or composition (Höge, 1995; Locher, 2003), semantic content as opposed to formal qualities of design (Martindale, 1988), the protypicality of an object (Hekkert & van Wieringen, 1990), and the significance or mere exposure of a stimulus (e.g., Leder et al., 2004) affect aesthetic experience and judgments. In addition, aspects of a person's emotional state (e.g., Konecni, 1979), the interestingness of a stimulus (Berlyne, 1971), appeal to social status or financial interest (Konecni, 1979; Ritterfeld, 2002), education, and historical, cultural or economical background in general (Jacobsen, 2002; Konecni, 1979; Ritterfeld, 2002) are known to influence aesthetic judgments. Various situational aspects play a role, as we might appreciate an object differently in a museum than in a supermarket, for example. In addition, aesthetic judgment is also determined by interindividual differences (Berlyne, 1971; Fechner, 1876; Jacobsen, 2002, 2004; Jacobsen & Höfel, 2002; Martindale, 1988; Whitfield, 1984). Naturally, there are numerous other findings. However, this short list already shows that aesthetic experiences and behavior are subject to a complex network of stimulus-, person-, and situation-related influences.

Present-day Psychology of Aesthetics is characterized by a mosaic of empirical discoveries. Often, however, the problems that have to be faced today are the same as in the past; for instance, the conflict between the degree of experimental control and the range of generalizability of the findings. The logic of the experiment calls for clearly defined conditions that are preferably varied only in regard to one or a few well-defined aspects while the other factors remain constant. This methodological background applied to the study of aesthetics often implies a sacrifice of stimulus complexity for the sake of maximum experimental control. In the scope of these experiments, participants are asked to judge the beauty of geometrical shapes or just simple lines. But, can individuals come up with genuine aesthetic judgments for these kinds of objects? Usually, individuals are more inclined to make an aesthetic judgment about paintings, sculptures, buildings, or melodies that are much more complex. These objects, however, mostly combine variations of a multitude of stimulus dimensions hampering adequate experimental control or rendering it to even impossible. If, for this reason, researchers often restrict themselves to simple, easy-to-control stimuli, they will be very much restricted in their statements about combinatory effects and interactions between the factors investigated. In the worst case, it is impossible to come to any conclusions about the objects of interest. This is a challenge, a challenge of successfully bridging art and science that still stands today.

Since the days of Fechner, psychology has developed significantly and become a fully established scientific discipline. Today, the main stream of psychological aesthetics works with experimental or empirical methods. Thus, it has accepted and continued Fechner's original conceptual and methodological intention of "bottom-up aesthetics" in contrast to a theoretical and introspective kind of psychological aesthetics, and thus clearly follows this tradition.

The Psychology of Aesthetics is not, however, a strong academic discipline today. How can the status of a discipline be measured? Perhaps by the number of its full-time scientists, the number of publications, the status of specialist journals in which the articles are published, the number of specialist journals in the field, professional societies, and the like. When measured by these parameters, the discipline shows a great potential for development in comparison with others. There is no general textbook for the Psychology of Aesthetics, neither in German nor in English. Essentially, the discipline has only one specialist journal, the *Empirical Studies of the Arts* (Höge, 1995), the organ of the International Association of Empirical Aesthetics, although the American Psychological Association's Division 10—Society for the Psychology of Aesthetics, Creativity and the Arts—has recently launched a new journal entitled *Psychology of Aesthetics, Creativity, and the Arts*. Furthermore, there are only a few scientists who completely devote their work to psychological aesthetics, and for those who do attend to it, it is their second or third area of research activity. This leads to a situation that is very much in contrast to other subdisciplines in psychology, where scientists are almost forced to focus completely on a single field of research. Moreover, the Psychology of Aesthetics frequently is not an integral part of standard psychological curricula. It often depends on the individual teachers' interest in the field whether or not students of psychology become familiar with it. Thus, it is not unusual to encounter qualified psychologists who consider experimental aesthetics to be a trend in modern art rather than the second oldest branch of experimental psychology.

The Psychology of Aesthetics consists of fragmented subdisciplines. It is not a homogenous discipline. Experimental aesthetics as outlined above mainly deals with research on art, with artifacts in the widest sense. In order to cover the full range of aesthetic behavior and experience, however, the Psychology of Aesthetics would have to include a wide range of subject areas. Research on human attractiveness in social psychology, for instance, deals with aspects of human beauty (see Langlois & Roggmann, 1990). Market research covers numerous aspects of the identification of aesthetic preferences. Although the focus here is on the application, aesthetic experience and behavior are of immediate relevance for the marketing of products. There are numerous overlapping areas in the psychology of art and in psychological aesthetics. Aesthetic processing, however, is not limited to art, therefore the two fields should not be equated. Also, there are many similarities with the psychology of music (see Tervaniemi, this volume). Anthropology and evolutionary biology deal with the origins and bases of aesthetic behavior (see Nadal et al., this volume). In architecture, researching and integrating aesthetic aspects of buildings are natural components of the work. The (other) applied arts adopt similar approaches. To a far lesser extent, this is also true for media and literary studies. Art history can provide a cornucopia of insights. In addition, oral and facial surgery, and dentistry (see Höfel, Lange, & Jacobsen, 2007) contribute to the empirical research of aesthetics in their fields. As a consequence, the Psychology of Aesthetics, being rather fragmented at present, could develop into an interdisciplinary and integrating approach, bridging and uniting a large number of disciplines and applications. The latter also holds true for neuroaesthetics.

FRAMEWORK

The framework reviewed here adopts seven vantage points on the topic of aesthetic processing (Jacobsen, 2006). Each vantage point can have different levels of analysis. These are not mutually exclusive. Rather, they are concerned with the processing of aesthetics, while approaching it in a multifold way from different angles, covering a broad range of partly interrelated topics. These seven perspective pillars have been called Mind, Body (which are at the heart of neuroaesthetics), Content, Person, Situation, Diachronia, and Ipsichronia. They are reviewed below (see Figure 1).

Mind

The vantage point on aesthetic processing from the perspective of modern academic psychology. The Psychology of Aesthetics is an integral part of psychological science. A number of investigators have adopted a cognitive terminology in accounting for aesthetic processing (e.g., Martindale, 1988). The preference-for-prototype model, for example, holds that prototypical exemplars of a given category will be preferred over less typical ones (Hekkert & van Wieringen, 1990). This demonstrates the applicability of a very influential cognitive model (Rosch, 1975) to the psychological study of aesthetic processing. The systematic transfer of contemporary psychological concepts, however, has yet to be carried out.

There are many possibilities to establish connections with modern psychological theories. Judgments of taste may serve as an example. A determining judgment requires the mental representation of the object to be judged as well as the assessment by the judge. In the case of a determining judgment, both are "retrieved." Cognitive social psychology disposes of very elaborate research and a conceptual framework for these mental processes, the so-called concept of "attitudes" (see Petty, Wegener, & Fabrigar, 1997 for a review). A theoretical link of rather broad scope is quite possible here. However, this link has only been elaborated for limited

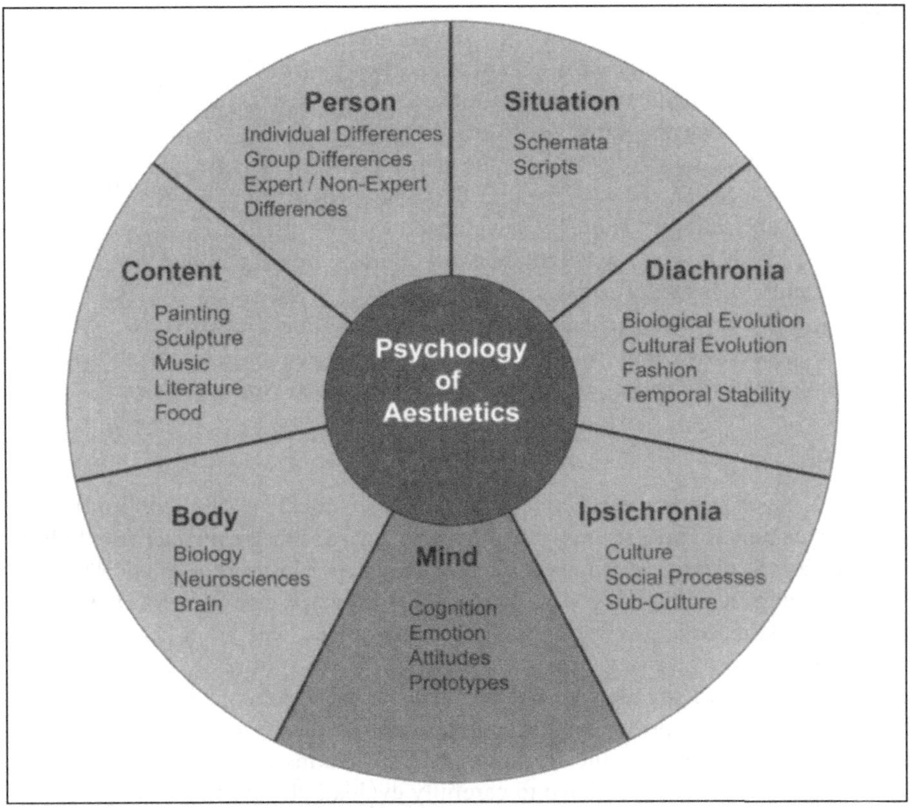

Figure 1. An illustration of a framework for the Psychology of Aesthetics (from Jacobsen, 2006). The topic is viewed from seven different vantage points which are not mutually exclusive. These are called Diachronia, Ipsichronia, Mind, Body, Content, Person, and Situation. Eventually, this work can converge on a unified theory of processing aesthetics. (© Illustration by Thomas Jacobsen.)

content domains, such as furniture, for instance (Ritterfeld, 2002). In addition, cognitive social psychology has developed a theoretical inventory that could be used more intensely for research into the Psychology of Aesthetics.

This also applies to the psychology of emotions (e.g., Konecni, 1979). How does mood influence the aesthetic judgment? What is the effect of emotional styles? Certainly, there are a number of other perspectives from which one could view emotions in psychological aesthetics (see Chenier & Winkielman, this volume). Especially philosophical aesthetics could be an almost inexhaustible source. Psychological penetration of many concepts is yet to be undertaken. Famous philosophical concepts, such as the distinction between reflecting and determining aesthetic judgments or between artificial and natural beauty remain to be studied in psychology and neuroaesthetics.

Body

The perspective of the body embraces the heart of neuroaesthetics. Aesthetic processing is examined by taking somatic aspects into consideration. Together, mind and body also cover the entire realm of aesthetic processing. Biology contributes to our understanding of aesthetics. The neurosciences, in particular, have made dramatic advances in the last decade. Our knowledge about brain function has increased substantially. These achievements will be used also in research on aesthetics. Furthermore, the integration of findings from cognitive neuroscience also becomes increasingly feasible. As several contributors to this book make clear, not only have researchers begun to investigate brain activity directly during aesthetic processing, but insights about how acquired lesions affect aesthetic processing (see Chatterjee, Zaidel, this volume) have also begun to appear.

Content

Human aesthetic processing relates to a large number of different entities (as introduced above). These realms differ vastly in regard to their characteristics, which in turn leads to differences in aesthetic processing. For instance, evolution has left humans being more tuned to certain stimulus characteristics than to others. The sensory modalities are governed by different principles. The brain has specialized areas for processing certain stimulus categories. Some entities are highly socially relevant, others less so. We are educated and trained to become experts in certain domains, like music, poetry, or dance, whereas we remain novices in others. All these factors contribute to the impact of content realms on aesthetic processing. Therefore, investigators will have to carefully evaluate the generalizability of their findings. For instance, does the gestalt law that accounts for a given preference in the visual modality (Arnheim, 1974) extend to music or culinary preferences? Most likely not. Color preferences, for example, appear to be highly context dependent (Whitfield, 1984).

Person

This perspective focuses on individual processing characteristics and preferences. From the ancient Roman saying *De gustibus non est disputandum,* it is commonly known that there is no accounting for taste. There is, however, discussion about matters of taste, sometimes quite violent arguments. A systematic examination of interindividual differences in aesthetic processing remains to be carried out. To date, relatively little is known about such interindividual differences of aesthetic processing within homogenous groups.

In a recent study, aesthetic judgments of beauty of 49 novel, formal graphic patterns were collected from nonartist participants (Jacobsen et al., 2004). The data were subjected to individual analyses resulting in models reflecting the individual's strategy of aesthetic judgment. Individual case modeling provides the means to capture these interindividual differences. The study also derived a group model based on averaged data. This model, however, could sufficiently account for only one half of the participants' strategies, whereas the individual models gave much more precise account thereof. Thus, it appears reasonable to assume that some nomothetic studies may have camouflaged marked individual differences by using data averaging. Hence, one may debate the justification of mere nomothetic approaches given such a data pattern. So it is argued that the idiographic approach should be additionally adopted, if such an equivocal empirical situation is encountered. In that sense, there is (no) accounting for taste, indeed.

Some differences between individuals are, however, reasonably well accounted for at the level of group differences. Experts and nonexperts, laymen or novices differ with regard to their abilities and skills. Experts are equipped with specific, structured knowledge of their area of expertise. Knowledge systems show different degrees of complexity. These different cognitive systems in turn can lead to different aesthetic processing. The typical study contrasted the performance of groups of experienced judges with the performance of groups of naïve or inexperienced judges (e.g., Nodine, Locher, & Krupinski, 1993). There is also a considerable literature based on personality structure research (see Eysenck, 1983). Besides the consideration of individuals versus groups, the comparison of cultures is another important perspective.

Situation

The combination of a given time and a given place—the situation—affects aesthetic processing. The perspectives of content, person and situation, taken together, also provide full coverage of the topic of aesthetic processing.

Encountering a can of tomato soup in a supermarket, for instance, will most likely entail different mental processing than when it is encountered in a museum. Such situational conditions elicit the use of a mentally stored script or schema (Baldwin, 1992). Schemata or scripts are organized memory representations that store domain-specific knowledge that is used to guide behavior in a given situation. Hence, schemata can drastically reduce processing load. They are predominantly socially determined, thus culturally limited, and individually acquired. Being in a museum, a theater, an opera house, or a gallery usually facilitates aesthetic processing, because a respective cognitive schema is put to use. A gas station or supermarket script, on the other hand, does not. Consequently, one and the same entity will be processed differently due to a different mindset induced by the currently active schema. The right schema will help to activate a mental mode of aesthetic contemplation, or aesthetic productivity. Given the laboratory nature of most of neuroaesthetics research, this will be a hard-to-implement, albeit important, perspective.

Diachronia

This is the perspective that takes change over time into account. It can be pursued at different levels of analysis; for instance, from the perspective of evolutionary biology or evolutionary anthropology. The *biological evolution* afforded substantial changes, from nonhuman to human primates. The question about the origins of and reasons for aesthetic behavior are at the center of attention here. Why do individuals produce splendid and elaborate tools and weapons if they are not intended for use? Why do faces have to show a certain degree of symmetry to be perceived as beautiful? What is the share of evolution in the development of our aesthetic faculties and skills (Wundt, 1900/1920)? These questions lead to a classical complex of questions in psychology: the nature-nurture debate. This question, probing into the relation between heredity and biological setup, on the one hand, and the impact of a cultural superstructure, on the other hand, was, for example, the subject of a heated debate in intelligence research and is very popular in current linguistic research (see Gazzaniga, 2004).

The above leads to the other side of the nature-nurture question, to one aspect of historical change, cultural development, or as it is sometimes termed, *cultural evolution,* which explains the main variance of aesthetic processing today. Another perspective of psychological aesthetics is the historic one, especially connected with the history of civilization. Aesthetic judgments and preferences change over time (Höfel & Jacobsen, 2003; Jacobsen, 2002). Aesthetic usage is changed by the availability of tools, the development and availability of materials, and production techniques, while conversely, there are temporal changes, unaffected by what is feasible.

Here, *fashion* comes into play. Fashion, another aspect of historical change, can be due to mere trends that are either based on or independent from current technical development. Trends can lead to extreme instantiations of an ideal of beauty, including unpractical clothes, plastic surgery, and (self-)mutilations. Considering these two aspects, the historical vantage point can open up an important perspective on aesthetic behavior and experience, which can also contribute to finding answers for questions that are essentially psychological in nature.

In addition to these levels of analysis of diachronia at a group level, there are individual levels. During ontogenesis, individuals can acquire different degrees of developmental refinement (Parsons, 1987) through aesthetic education and other developmental achievement. Furthermore, aesthetic processing is subjected to differing degrees of *individual temporal stability*, also governed by novelty or mere exposure of stimuli (Berlyne, 1971, Höfel & Jacobsen, 2003; Leder, Belke, Oeberst, & Augustin, 2004).

Ipsichronia

This vantage point focuses on comparisons within a given time slice. Together with diachronia, it also covers the entire realm of aesthetic processing. A wide range of entities of aesthetic processing is subjected to cultural and social processes. Hence, effects of culture, influences of social roles, social status, or cultural differences are taken into consideration (Baldwin, 1992; Ritterfeld, 2002).

Comparisons of cultures can be a very informative method (Wundt, 1900/1920). Contrasting the main tendencies of a culture and its predominant ideals of beauty with those adopted by subcultures is becoming an increasingly more important research endeavor. When looking at the picture of a man in his shirt sleeves in the 1950s, for example, the answer to the question what is missing would have been "the tie." This was the correct answer in the most widely used intelligence test. Today, people in Western metropolitan areas would perhaps rather miss a tattoo or facial piercing. This is certainly true for some subcultural groups. A systematic survey of cultural shaping of maybe universal aesthetic tendencies would be an interesting facet in an interdisciplinary approach. There are numerous examples of aesthetic preferences that are contingent on a given culture or subculture. Research in the Psychology of Aesthetics can benefit from research in other disciplines on cultural specificities in order to avoid the proposition of psychological models that are culture dependent, and therefore not general. When using the present framework, one of the researchers' tasks is to extract the information that is relevant for the Psychology of Aesthetics from the cornucopia of material provided by the seven perspectives.

PROSPECT

As mentioned above, the Psychology of Aesthetics today is quite heterogeneous. In a strongly interdisciplinary approach, all above-mentioned disciplines of the Arts and the Sciences would make their contributions. The ultimate goal would be a unified theory of mental processing of aesthetics, which describes and explains the whole network of stimulus-, personality-, and situation-related factors. This is a huge challenge. To face it, it could be helpful to approach the subject matter from the different perspectives introduced above, identify and extract psychologically relevant aspects, and gradually integrate these step-by-step. Nonetheless, an inherently complex and finely textured theoretic structure will eventually emerge.

Such a strongly interdisciplinary approach is not impossible. Cognitive neuroscience, in general, has impressively demonstrated the success of this basic approach (see Gazzaniga, 2004 for a review). For the Psychology of Aesthetics, in general, and neuroaesthetics, in particular, this approach remains to be undertaken. In our lab, we decided to pursue a cognitive neuroscience approach to the study of aesthetic judgment. To this end, we constructed new stimulus material that allowed controlling for the factors influencing aesthetic judgment introduced above. Symmetry and complexity were varied in the material (see Figure 2). Other factors were adequately controlled.

First ERP data were presented in 2000 (Jacobsen & Höfel, 2000, 2003). Results showed a double dissociation in temporal course as well as neural sources between an evaluative aesthetic-judgment task and a descriptive symmetry-judgment task, both using identical stimuli and task structure. A frontal negativity was elicited under the aesthetic judgment and a posterior sustained negativity was elicited under the symmetry-judgment task. Data of not aesthetic minus aesthetic in the time window between 300 and 400 milliseconds for the frontal negativity and symmetrical minus nonsymmetrical in the time window between 600 and 1100 milliseconds after stimulus onset are shown in Figure 3. In the meantime, these findings have been replicated (Höfel & Jacobsen, 2007a, 2007b; Roye, Höfel, & Jacobsen, 2008).

Figure 2. Stimulus examples from Jacobsen and Höfel (2000, 2003) and Jacobsen, Schubotz, Höfel, and Cramon (2006). The graphic patterns in rows 1 and 2 are not symmetric, ranging from not beautiful to beautiful (line by line). Patterns in rows 3 and 4 are symmetric, also ranging from not beautiful to beautiful. (© Illustrations by Thomas Jacobsen.)

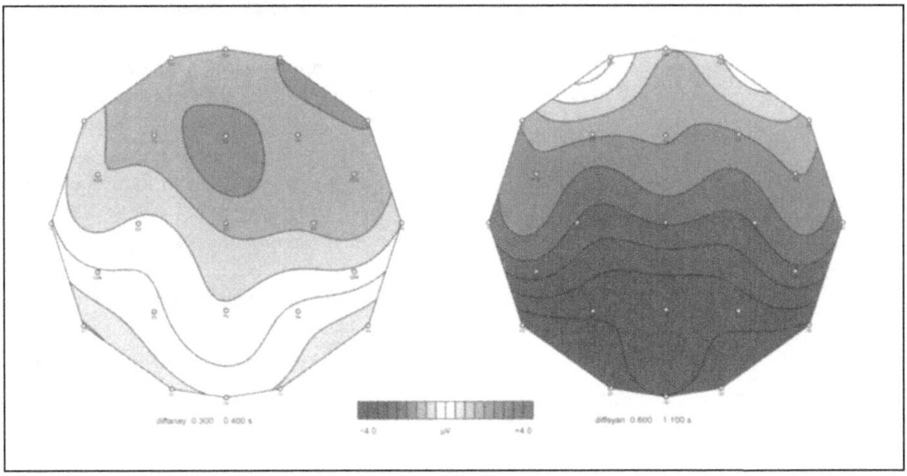

Figure 3. See p. 145 for full color.

In a subsequent study, functional MRI was used to investigate the neural correlates of aesthetic judgments of beauty of geometrical shapes. Participants performed evaluative aesthetic judgments (beautiful or not?) and descriptive symmetry judgments (symmetric or not?) on the same stimulus material. Symmetry was employed because aesthetic judgments are known to be often guided by criteria of symmetry. Novel abstract graphic patterns were presented to minimize influences of attitudes or memory-related processes and to test effects of stimulus symmetry and complexity.

Behavioral results confirmed the influence of stimulus symmetry and complexity on aesthetic judgments. Direct fMRI contrasts showed specific activations for aesthetic judgments in the frontomedian cortex (BA 9/10), bilateral prefrontal (BA 45/47), posterior cingulate, left temporal pole, and the temporoparietal junction (Figure 4). In contrast, symmetry judgments elicited specific activations in parietal and premotor areas subserving spatial processing. Interestingly, beautiful judgments enhanced BOLD signals not only in the frontomedian cortex, but also in the left intraparietal sulcus of the symmetry network. Moreover, stimulus complexity caused differential effects for each of the two judgment types.

These findings indicate aesthetic judgments of beauty to rely on a network partially overlapping with structures underlying evaluative judgments of social and moral cues and substantiate the significance of symmetry and complexity for our judgment of beauty.

Neuroaesthetics integrally deals with the body/brain and the mind vantage points introduced above. The other five perspectives also add to making predictions about mental processing, behavioral performance, and the dynamic configurations of underlying brain networks. Neuroaesthetics, in its correlational approach, constructs

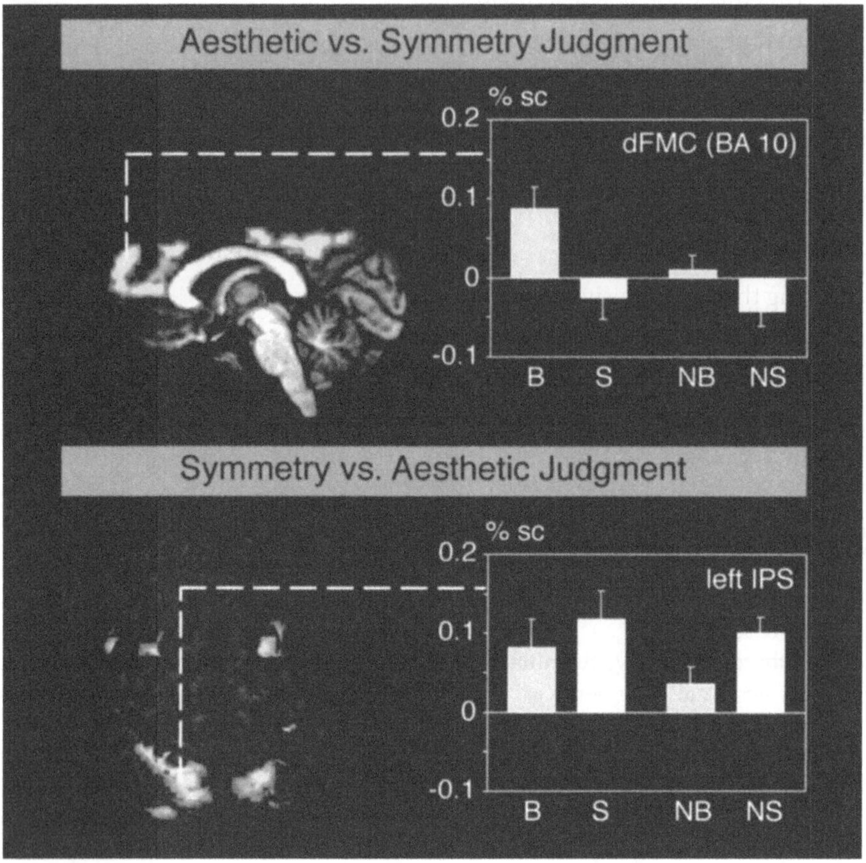

Figure 4. See p. 146 for full color.

transformational relations between irreducibly and individually subjective mental processes and states, and their objectively, externally observed neural underpinnings. Therefore, neuroaesthetics is following Fechner's tradition, not only because of his Experimental Aesthetics, but also, and more centrally so, because it is a brilliant example of modern psychophysics. Today, inner psychophysics has come a long way due to the availability of modern neuroscientific methods. The basic methodological approach, however, is the same. In a pragmatically dualistic approach, subjective experience and external observation (EEG, ERP, MEG, fMRI, PET, and the like) are correlated or, when possible and ethically feasible, causal relationships are established (neuropsychology, TMS).

All the factors introduced above, known to affect aesthetic processes, are very likely to exert an effect also on neuroscientific measures. Therefore, neuroaesthetics has to set out to take on an exciting and vastly complex challenge.

REFERENCES

Arnheim, R. (1974). *Art and visual perception: The new version*. Berkeley, CA: University of California Press.

Baldwin, M. W. (1992). Relational schemas and the processing of social information. *Psychological Bulletin, 112*(3), 461-484.

Berlyne, D. E. (1970). Novelty, complexity, and hedonic value. *Perception & Psychophysics, 8*(5-A), 279-286.

Berlyne, D. E. (1971). *Aesthetics and psychobiology*. East Norwalk, CT: Appleton-Century-Crofts.

Berlyne, D. E. (1974). *Studies in the new experimental aesthetics: Steps toward an objective psychology of aesthetic appreciation*. Oxford: Hemisphere.

Eysenck, H. J. (1983). A new measure of good taste in visual art: The Visual Aesthetic Sensitivity Test. *Leonardo, 16*(3), 229-231.

Fechner, G. T. (1876). *Vorschule der Aesthetik* [Experimental Aesthetics; "Pre-school" of aesthetics]. Leipzig: Breitkopf & Härtel.

Gazzaniga, M. S. (2004). *The cognitive neurosciences III*. Cambridge, MA: The MIT Press.

Hekkert, P., & van Wieringen, P. C. W. (1990). Complexity and prototypicality as determinants of the appraisal of cubist paintings. *British Journal of Psychology, 81*(4), 483-495.

Höfel, L., & Jacobsen, T. (2003). Temporal stability and consistency of aesthetic judgments of beauty of formal graphic patterns. *Perceptual and Motor Skills, 96*(1), 30-32.

Höfel, L., & Jacobsen, T. (2007a). Electrophysiological indices of processing aesthetics: Spontaneous or intentional processes? *International Journal of Psychophysiology, 65*(1), 20-31.

Höfel, L., & Jacobsen, T. (2007b). Electrophysiological indices of processing symmetry and aesthetics: A result of judgment categorization or judgment report? *Journal of Psychophysiology, 21*(1), 9-21.

Höfel, L., Lange, M., & Jacobsen, T. (2007). Beauty and the teeth: Perception of tooth color and its influence on the overall judgment of facial attractiveness. *International Journal of Periodontics & Restorative Dentistry, 27*(4), 349-357.

Höge, H. (1995). Fechner's experimental aesthetics and the golden section hypothesis today. *Empirical Studies of the Arts, 13*(2), 131-148.

Jacobsen, T. (2002). Kandinsky's questionnaire revisited: Fundamental correspondence of basic colors and forms? *Perceptual and Motor Skills, 95*(3), 903-913.

Jacobsen, T. (2004). Individual and group modeling of aesthetic judgment strategies. *British Journal of Psychology, 95*(1), 41-56.

Jacobsen, T. (2004). Kandinsky's color-form correspondence and the Bauhaus colors: An empirical view. *Leonardo, 37*(2), 135-136.

Jacobsen, T. (2006). Bridging the arts and sciences: A framework for the psychology of aesthetics. *Leonardo, 39*(2), 155-162.

Jacobsen, T., Buchta, K., Köhler, M., & Schröger, E. (2004). The primacy of beauty in judging the aesthetics of objects. *Psychological Reports, 94*(3), 1253-1260.

Jacobsen, T., & Höfel, L. (2000). Descriptive and evaluative judgment processes: An event-related potential analysis of processing symmetry and aesthetics. *Journal of Cognitive Neuroscience, 12*(Supplement), 110.

Jacobsen, T., & Höfel, L. (2002). Aesthetic judgments of novel graphic patterns: Analyses of individual judgments. *Perceptual and Motor Skills, 95*(3), 755-766.

Jacobsen, T., & Höfel, L. (2003). Descriptive and evaluative judgment processes: Behavioral and electrophysiological indices of processing symmetry and aesthetics. *Cognitive, Affective & Behavioral Neuroscience, 3*(4), 289-299.

Jacobsen, T., Schubotz, R. I., Höfel, L., & v. Cramon, D. Y. (2006). Brain correlates of aesthetic judgment of beauty. *NeuroImage, 29*(1), 276-285.

Konecni, V. J. (1979). Determinants of aesthetic preference and effects of exposure to aesthetic stimuli: Social, emotional and cognitive factors. *Progress in Experimental Personality Research, 9,* 149-197.

Langlois, J. H., & Roggman, L. A. (1990). Attractive faces are only average. *Psychological Science, 1*(2), 115-121.

Leder, H., Belke, B., Oeberst, A., & Augustin, D. (2004). A model of aesthetic appreciation and aesthetic judgments. *British Journal of Psychology, 95*(4), 489-508.

Locher, P. J. (2003). An empirical investigation of the visual rightness theory of picture perception. *Acta Psychologica, 114*, 147-164.

Martin, L. J. (1906). An experimental study of Fechner's principles of aesthetics. *Psychological Review, 13*, 142-219.

Martindale, C. (1988). Aesthetics, psychobiology, and cognition. In F. H. Farley & R. W. Neperud (Eds.), *The foundation of aesthetics, art and art education*. New York: Praeger.

Nodine, C. F., Locher, P. J., & Krupinski, E. A. (1993). The role of formal art training on perception and aesthetic judgment of art compositions. *Leonardo, 26*(3), 219-227.

Parsons, M. (1987). *How we understand art: A cognitive developmental account of aesthetic experience*. Cambridge, MA: Cambridge University Press.

Petty, R. E., Wegener, D. T., & Fabrigar, L. R. (1997). Attitudes and attitude change. *Annual Review of Psychology, 48*, 609-647.

Ritterfeld, U. (2002). Social heuristics in interior design preferences. *Journal of Environmental Psychology, 22*(4), 369-386.

Rosch, E. (1975). Cognitive representations of semantic categories. *Journal of Experimental Psychology: General, 104*(3), 192-233.

Roye, A., Höfel, L., & Jacobsen, T. (2008). Aesthetics of faces: Behavioural and electrophysiological indices of evaluative and descriptive judgment processes. *Journal of Psychophysiology, 22*(1), 41-57.

Whitfield, A. (1984). Individual differences in evaluation of architectural colour: Categorization effects. *Perceptual and Motor Skills, 59*(1), 183-186.

Wundt, W. (1900/1920). *Völkerpsychologie (10 Bde.), Bd. III: Die Kunst*. Leipzig: Kröner-Engelmann.

CHAPTER 4

The Arts are More than Aesthetics: Neuroaesthetics as Narrow Aesthetics

Steven Brown and Ellen Dissanayake

Neuroaesthetics is a young enough field that there seems to be no established view of its proper subject matter. Morphologically, the term implies the scientific study of neural aspects of the perception of artworks such as paintings, or elements of artworks such as musical intervals. We are concerned, however, that practitioners of this new field may not be aware of the tremendous ambiguities inherent in the terms "aesthetics" and "art," ones that limit a proper understanding of human art behavior. Connotations of these terms are particularly inappropriate and misleading when considering the experiences, practices, and functions of the arts in preindustrial, folk, aboriginal, or Pleistocene societies, and even in contemporary popular culture.

It is only during the last two centuries that the terms "Art" (with an implied capital A, connoting an independent realm of prestigious and revelatory works) and "aesthetics" (as a unique, and even reverential, mode of attention toward such works) have taken on their present elitist meanings and become unavoidably intertwined (Davies, 2006; Shiner, 2001). The word "aesthetic" (from the Greek *aiesthesis*, having to do with the senses) was first used in 1735 by a German philosopher in a book on poetry (Baumgarten, 1735/1954), and since that time has been employed in two different, but not always distinct, ways. Enlightenment philosophers and their followers gradually developed the now elitist notion of "*the* aesthetic"—a special form of disinterested knowledge and appreciation—to describe the emotional response elicited by the perception of great works of art (Shiner, 2001).

While this meaning of aesthetic has strong historical connections with the arts and with artworks, a second usage has come to refer to any value system having to do with the appreciation of beauty, such as the beauty of nature. In recent decades, for example, some ethologists and evolutionary psychologists have adopted this second, broader notion of aesthetics in a new field, originally called "landscape aesthetics" (Appleton, 1990; Orians, 2001; Ruso, Renninger, & Atzwanger, 2003) or "Darwinian aesthetics" (Thornhill, 1998), but generally called "evolutionary aesthetics" (Voland & Grammer, 2003) today. Evolutionary aesthetics investigates sensory preferences in animals and humans that promote selective attention and positive emotional responses toward objects in the environment that lead to adaptive decision making and problem solving (Orians, 2001). Objects perceived in this manner are considered to be beautiful (Thornhill, 1998). Following Darwin (1871), who noted that animals (especially birds) seemed to appreciate beauty and who attributed the spectacular colors and patterns of male birds to female choice, some workers in evolutionary aesthetics have proposed that human art arose by sexual selection in a similar manner to the courtship displays performed by male birds to attract females for mating (e.g., Miller, 2000, 2001).

Although workers in evolutionary aesthetics do not overtly adhere to the elitist philosophical connotations of aesthetics, some nevertheless write as though their findings are applicable to an understanding of human responses to art and beauty (e.g., Thornhill, 1998). Judging by the work published thus far under the banner of neuroaesthetics, this field seems to be expressly concerned with art, not least the masterpieces of European visual art and even abstract paintings (e.g., Kawabata & Zeki, 2004; Solso, 1994; Vartanian & Goel, 2004; Zeki, 1999). We suspect that this interest in elite visual art arises from the implicit association of both art and aesthetics with the eighteenth century Eurocentric notions of these concepts.

In this chapter, we suggest that present-day neuroaesthetics is limited in three important respects by a narrow, culture-bound sense of aesthetics/art. First, its aesthetic data—based on sensory percepts and preferences—apply to a much wider range of objects than art objects. Neuroaesthetics, like evolutionary aesthetics and other scientific notions of aesthetics, is predicated on a class of emotions whose biological function is to generate an appraisal of the *properties of objects*. However, aesthetic emotions, seen here as general appraisals of like or dislike, are superordinate: they are critical in all living creatures for assessing a wide variety of objects important for biological survival, as in evolutionary aesthetics, where they include landscapes, food quality, the appearance and behaviors of conspecifics, and so forth. Strictly speaking, it is this broad area—not works of art alone—that defines the domain of neuroaesthetics; a better goal for the field would be to develop a general, superordinate theory of aesthetic responses that applies to all appraised objects rather than one linked to artworks (or landscapes or mates, for that matter). As presently conceived, neuroaesthetics has no way of distinguishing art from nonart. Characterizing the neural responses elicited by viewing a modern abstract painting begs the question that what is being assessed is a response to art. In the next section, we present a view of art as a behavior of "artification," a neologism that allows us to think of art as an activity, in other words as something that people do (to "artify").

Second, the arts themselves deal with a much broader realm of human experience than aesthetic responses or preferences for features. A focus on such responses and preferences, even in individual artworks, reduces the arts to the level of receiver psychology and social functionlessness, as presupposed in many philosophical approaches to the fine arts based on Enlightenment principles. Although complex behaviors such as creating art (like choosing a mate or finding a suitable habitat) include an aesthetic dimension, they are in no way reducible to it, nor is it the most important thing about them. Introducing another neologism, we propose a new field, "neuroartsology," as a comprehensive neuroscientific approach to the arts, which is conceived in the broader framework of art as an evolved behavior.

Third, because aesthetic experience, broadly speaking, concerns the emotional appraisals of objects (be they art objects or otherwise), we find it necessary to ground neuroscientific studies of aesthetic responses where they belong, in a larger theory of emotion. Until recently, biological theories of emotion have been strongly dominated by the "basic emotion" theory (BET), dating back to Darwin (1872). We believe that the BET provides an inadequate basis for the understanding of not only aesthetic responses but of many other emotions that accompany the production and perception of the arts. To take the starkest example (and the one most central to this volume), while there is indeed a basic emotion for the negative-valenced appraisal of disgust, there is no basic emotion corresponding with its positive-valenced counterparts of liking, attraction, ecstasy, and so on. Hence, neuroaesthetics, no less than evolutionary aesthetics, is in need of a richer theory of emotion than the one provided by the BET. In a later section, we discuss the Clore/Ortony theory as one promising alternative, and attempt to relate it to neuroimaging work in the field of emotion.

In summary, neuroaesthetics should not be limited to the arts but should instead focus on all types of aesthetically appraised objects and phenomena; and a proper understanding of the arts does not benefit from a narrow neuroaesthetics of perceptual preferences, but instead requires a neuroartsology that seeks to explain the full array of cognitive, neural, and cultural phenomena involved in the universal behaviors of artification.

WHAT IS ART AND WHAT IS IT FOR?

Although aesthetics is a confused term, the concept of art is, if anything, even more conflicted and contested. And as with the term aesthetics, the modern use of art is derived from the eighteenth century philosophy of fine art and its focus on artworks that were largely created for a wealthy elite, mainly the church and the court. It is therefore burdened with Eurocentric conceptions regarding the practices and meanings of classical/fine art. However, a comprehensive scientific understanding of art must include its manifestations in all human cultures. A foray into the arts of non-Western cultures not only compels us to confront art practices that are removed from the "disinterested" aesthetic practices of Western fine art, but also forces us to consider the arts as behaviors that may have no necessary connection with beauty (Dissanayake, 2007).

When we look at the contexts for the production of the arts in premodern (traditional, aboriginal) societies around the world and throughout time, we find that they are notably practiced in ritual ceremonies (Alcorta & Sosis, 2005; Dissanayake, 1988, 2006). Indeed, ceremonies, whatever else they may be, are collections of arts (conceived of as artified behaviors). Despite wide cultural variability, ritual ceremonies, as behavioral manifestations of cognitive belief systems about the way the world works (Alcorta & Sosis, 2005), have some common characteristics. They are *performed at times of perceived uncertainty*, when individuals and groups wish to influence the outcomes of circumstances that they perceive as vital to their livelihood and survival (Dissanayake 1992, 2008; Rappaport, 1999; Turner, 1969). They are typically *multimodal*, combining singing, instrument playing, dancing, literary language, dramatic spectacle, and the decoration of bodies, surroundings, and paraphernalia. In addition, they are typically *participative*: even when an audience observes specialists performing, they join in by clapping, moving, shouting, singing, and so forth. As John Chernoff, a scholar of West African drumming, has observed: "the most fundamental aesthetic in Africa is that without participation, there is no meaning" (Chernoff, 1979, p. 23).

The arts in ceremonial contexts provide a multitude of critical social functions for cultures small and large, including historiographic functions related to a society's ancestry and identity; discursive functions related to the justification and feasibility of planned endeavors; functions related to the marking of time (e.g., calendrical rituals [harvests], life-cycle rituals [weddings, funerals, births]); communication with deities; relief of anxiety and stress; social coordination, to name but a few. A major purpose of arts activities is to foster cooperation in support of collective endeavors, such as hunting, foraging, resisting enemies, building infrastructure, and the like. The arts are also the major means of maintaining social harmony and ameliorating conflicts within groups. The group benefits of the arts across cultures are strong and widespread. Reducing the arts' adaptive function to individual sexual display, as sexual selectionists have proposed (Miller, 2000), makes the arts into a completely competitive enterprise, when there is an abundance of evidence to suggest that the arts do precisely the opposite, foster cooperation and obviate individual competitiveness. Hence, while we acknowledge the existence of sexual display in the context of arts-suffused rituals, we reject a reduction of the arts to sexual display. In fact, if a connection is indeed to be found here, it is more likely that sexual display is a secondary offshoot of the group-assembly aspect of ceremonial rituals rather than the reverse (Brown, 2000). Once the group comes together for the business of collective survival, there can be opportunities for sexual display within such a context.

We suggest that it is profitable to consider the arts not as objects (paintings, songs), qualities of objects (beauty, consonance), cues to sensory-cognitive preferences, or passive registrations of sensory/cognitive stimuli, but as behaviors of artification—things that people do. Over several decades, one of us [ED] has gradually refined such a concept (Dissanayake, 1988, 1992, 2000, 2008). Artification (originally called "making special") refers to the universally observed penchant of human individuals (and groups) to "make ordinary reality extraordinary" (Dissanayake, 1992, p. 49).

An understanding of artification and its manifestations in human ritual practices is made clearer by an application of the ethological concept of "ritualization," as developed in the study of other animals (Tinbergen, 1952). Briefly, ritualized behaviors are communicative displays that take ordinary, unremarkable behaviors drawn from everyday life (e.g., preening, nest building, pecking for food) and use them in an altered manner and novel context in order to communicate something entirely different from their original source. Ethologists have described the alterations that occur during ritualization in both animals and humans (Eibl-Eibesfeldt, 1989, pp. 439-440), and have shown that, compared with the precursor behavior, the ritualized version becomes (a) *simplified*: it is formalized, stereotyped, or patterned; (b) *repeated*, often with a "typical intensity" or regularity of pace that departs from desultory performance of ordinary actions; (c) *exaggerated*; and (d) *elaborated*, sometimes with (e) *manipulation of expectation*. These alterations or operations serve to attract attention to and sustain interest in the new message, which is often concerned with aggression or courtship.

The human behavior of artification, like ritualization, uses operations such as formalization, repetition, exaggeration, and elaboration performed on components of ordinary behaviors to make them notable and extraordinary. In the most elementary sense, ordinary body movements, when artified (or stylized) through formalization, repetition, elaboration, and exaggeration, become "dance," ordinary language is made poetic or literary, and ordinary materials (bodies, artifacts, surroundings) are rendered extraordinary with paint, carving, and accoutrements of countless kinds. More broadly, a dance in a traditional culture becomes further enhanced as a narrative reenactment of historical (mythical) events. Artified behaviors, like ritualized behaviors, attract attention, sustain interest, and shape emotion. Indeed, while not themselves art, the preferences investigated by evolutionary aesthetics and neuroaesthetics are often themselves artified or used in artifications, as when appealing colors or shapes emphasize or enhance an important object, event, or message.

Lest artification be seen exclusively in terms of its ability to stimulate aesthetic responses, we point out that the result of such an activity has an important *cognitive* consequence, mainly to generate a new signification for something compared with its ordinary meaning or use. For example, ornamentation of objects like weapons or vessels is a way of giving them special power; the placement of a crucifix in a new church is a way of sanctifying and protecting it; and the utterance of special texts like prayers or incantations is a way of making contact with remote deities. Hence, the emphases that underlie the "alterations" of artification involve not only changes in context or performance properties such as repetition and exaggeration but include cognitive changes in the signification and function of an object or event. Arts behaviors are among the most important mechanisms that link ritual practices with cognitive belief systems (Alcorta & Sosis, 2005).

Interestingly, human infants are born with predispositions to respond to the operations of ritualization (or artification) on the vocalizations, facial expressions, and head/body movements of adult caretakers. In the universal dyadic behavior of "baby talk," adults spontaneously (that is, without being taught) simplify, repeat, elaborate, and exaggerate their utterances, expressions, and kinetic movements, thereby attracting infant attention and sustaining their interest. Adults temporally coordinate these signals with infant responses, as evidenced by studies that show that, by eight weeks, infants expect contingent responses from their adult partners

(Murray & Trevarthen, 1985; Nadel, Carchon, Kervella, Marcelli, & Réserbet-Plantey, 1999).

Such coordinated, dyadic behavior is hypothesized by Dissanayake (2000, 2008) to have originated as a behavioral adaptation that addressed the "obstetric dilemma" of two million years ago when the anatomical trend toward a narrowed pelvis in fully bipedal *Homo erectus* conflicted at childbirth with a concomitant anatomical trend toward enlarged brains and skulls. Among other adaptations (e.g., separable pubic symphysis in females at parturition, compressible infant skull, extensive postnatal brain growth), the gestation period was significantly reduced (Falk, 1998; Gould, 1977; Portmann, 1941), resulting in helpless infants dependent on their caretakers for years, rather than weeks or months as in other primates. A mother's simplification, repetition, elaboration, and exaggeration of affinitive communicative behaviors (e.g., smiling, open eyes, eyebrow flash, head bob, head nod, soft undulant vocalization, touching, patting, kissing) served to reinforce affinitive neural networks in her own brain and, when performed on a shared temporal basis, also set up a means of neural coordination of behavior and of matching of affective change between the pair (Beebe, Lachmann, & Jaffe, 1997; Trevarthen, 1979). Mother-infant interaction would seem to operate like a ritualized behavior, where signals from one context (affinitive, prosocial behaviors, observable in human adults and other primates) are altered and come to mean something different or, in this case, foster an adaptive mutual emotional bond. Dissanayake (2000, 2008) suggests that human sensitivity to and competence for the operations of artification originated phylogenetically in evolved interactions between ancestral mothers and their immature infants.

A THEORY OF EMOTION

We have argued that the concept of aesthetics, unencumbered by its Eurocentric conflation with art, applies to a wide array of objects (as in evolutionary aesthetics), and that a neural theory of the arts requires much more than a neuroaesthetic analysis of sensory preferences for art objects. An understanding of the proper connection between neuroaesthetics and the arts requires not only a functional analysis of the behaviors comprised in the arts but, equally importantly, a grounding of aesthetic responses in a theory of human emotion.

We understand emotions as being responses to events or objects in the environment, driven by appraisals of goodness or badness. They are strongly tied to goal-driven motivational states important for survival, as related to feeding, self-defense, mating, migration, and so forth. The concept of emotion requires three critical facets: valence, intensity, and focus. Valence refers to the fact that the vast majority of emotions fall binarily into the categories of positive and negative (Ortony & Turner, 1990). In other words, most emotional appraisals are experienced as either "good for me" or "bad for me." In contrast to this discrete division, emotions vary in intensity along a graded scale from weak to strong. Frustration and gladness are low-intensity emotions compared with highly intense counterparts like rage and ecstasy. Synthetic schemas that unite valence and intensity include the "circumplex" or "pleasure-arousal" model, in which valence (pleasure) and intensity (arousal) are seen as orthogonal dimensions on a two-dimensional plot (Reisenzein, 1994).

While significant, such schemes still lack a third critical ingredient in the psychology of emotion, namely focus. The most universally accepted scheme for focus is the Basic Emotion Theory (BET), first suggested by Darwin (1872) but elaborated in the twentieth century by Ekman and colleagues (Ekman, 1992, 1999). The BET scheme comprises some 5 to 8 discrete emotion types that are shown to have strong biological underpinnings, both by the unique facial expressions that accompany them and by their universal expression across cultures. The BET has been a major driving force for neuroimaging work on emotion and, not surprisingly, the major emotions analyzed in neuroimaging studies (mostly fear) are components of the BET scheme (Hennelotter & Schroeder, 2006). Of these basic emotions, only disgust can be categorized as an aesthetic emotion although there are clearly nonaesthetic meanings of disgust in addition to aesthetic ones.

To our way of thinking, the BET greatly underrepresents the number of human emotions as well as the richness of human emotional life. Psychologists who have cataloged human emotions find there to be literally hundreds of emotions, not merely a handful (see Clore, 1994). We are sympathetic to the criticisms of the BET put forth by Clore, Ortony, and others (e.g., Ortony & Turner, 1990), and find that their perspective on emotional focus provides a more promising way of understanding the complexities of human emotion than the BET.

In the Clore/Ortony scheme (Clore, 1994; Clore & Ortony, 2000), emotions are categorized with regard to three foci: outcomes, objects, or agency. To these, we add a fourth category, what we call the "social interaction" focus.

1) *Outcomes*. The first category deals with valenced reactions to the *consequences of outcomes*. These are the *motivational* emotions, spanning the range from happiness (being pleased with an outcome) to sadness (being displeased with an outcome). Joy is a positive outcome-emotion, one that has a higher intensity than happiness, while grief and sadness are analogous negative-valence emotions.

2) *Objects*. The second category deals with valenced reactions to the *aspects of objects and events*. Importantly for this volume, *it is this category that comprises the aesthetic emotions*, spanning the range from liking/attraction to disliking/disgust. This is also the category that is invoked when people discuss preferences and taste. Hence, feelings of aesthetic attraction, whether for a face, a food item, a melody, or a building, fall into this category, as do negative-valenced counterparts such as hate and disgust. Regarding neuroaesthetics, it is telling that BET does not contain a positive-valenced aesthetic term (e.g., attraction, liking, love), only the negative-valenced emotion of disgust.

3) *Agency*. The third category of emotion involves valenced reactions to the *actions of agents,* and includes the spectrum from approval to disapproval. This category comprises a large part of what people think of as *moral* emotions (judgments of the appropriateness of behavior), including assessments of praiseworthiness or shamefulness. Interestingly, the negative-valenced basic emotion of disgust sits in two focus categories. On the one hand, disgust can be an aesthetic assessment of the properties of an object (e.g., of feces, spoiled food), but on the other, it can be a

moral assessment of the actions of an agent (e.g., of a politician, boss, or store clerk). Hence, a scheme such as that proposed by Clore and Ortony permits an appreciation of the "multifocus" nature of emotion terms in a way that the BET simply cannot.

4) *Social interaction*. The fourth category of focus, which we offer here as a refinement of the Clore/Ortony scheme, involves valenced reactions to social interactions with other people. While similar to the moral emotions discussed under agency, these emotions go beyond simple appraisals of agency, and can probably be best encapsulated by the comfort/discomfort emotional spectrum. Do we feel that people are on our side or against us? Are they supporting our goals or thwarting them? When our ego feels threatened by someone whom we perceive as being better or more competent than ourselves, it is this fourth category that is experienced. On the positive side, this involves emotions like love, trust, and affiliation that are so central to the experience of the arts. These are rewarding emotions that are not aesthetic in nature but that definitely reinforce aesthetic assessments. We will talk more below about the interplay between attraction (an aesthetic emotion) and affiliation (a social-interaction emotion). On the negative side is a basic emotion which, like disgust, has complex multifocus connotations, namely fear. Fear is an "outcome" emotion related to predictions of negative consequences for future events (e.g., stage fright related to a class presentation), but fear is also a strong social-interaction emotion related to a perception of people's intent to thwart our goals or hurt us (i.e., being afraid of someone).

Beyond these four general foci of emotion, there is an important interplay among emotions of a similar valence that tend to act in a mutually reinforcing manner. We propose that there is a union of emotions that vary in focus but are similar in valence. For example, people tend to evaluate as morally good those things that they think of as aesthetically beautiful, and as bad those things they assess as ugly. Hence, in mythology, the wicked witch is ugly and the good prince is handsome. In numerous premodern societies (e.g., Basongye, Dinka, Igbo, Javanese, Lega, Senufo, Temne, Wahgi, among many others), the good (refined, wholesome) and the beautiful are conceptually inseparable (Dissanayake, 1992; van Damme, 1996). Socially, we assess as morally good those people who support our goals and around whom we feel comfortable. We tend to find them attractive (if not immediately, at least over time). So, aesthetic and moral evaluations of a given object tend to be parallel (Brown & Volgsten, 2006). Situations where they fail to be so tend to cause feelings of cognitive dissonance; we are confused if the ugly witch is benevolent or the handsome prince is evil. In sum, we tend to make parallel appraisals of multiple aspects of objects or situations, and these appraisals tend to be mutually reinforcing along the lines of valence.

To summarize, an understanding of aesthetics must be rooted in a theory of human emotion, which includes the dimensions of valence, intensity, and focus. BET lacks sufficient theoretical sophistication for an accurate understanding of focus. We believe that the Clore/Ortony theory is a richer view of emotion. Of the four foci of emotion that we discussed, "aspects of objects" is the one most directly related to aesthetic emotions. However, our plea is to look beyond aesthetic emotions and recognize the complex network of emotions involved in the arts, not least the interactions between aesthetic emotions and other socially important emotions.

ORBITOFRONTAL CORTEX AND THE APPRAISAL OF VALENCE

As just discussed, emotions are based on a valenced appraisal of an object or event, that is, an assessment of the goodness or badness of something in terms of individual goal attainment. The appraisal process is in many ways a comparison between "exteroceptive" perception—the perception of things occurring in the external world around us—and "interoceptive" perception—a reporting of the status of our internal environment as related to the functional state of our organs vis-à-vis physical and emotional needs. There are "visceral afferent" systems that report on the state of our homeostatic mechanisms, such as the need for food, warmth, or sleep. When we perform a goal-directed behavior, a comparison is made between our intended goal and the current visceral state. We make judgments of the outcomes based on whether they promote our goals (positive valence, rewarding) or oppose them (negative valence, aversive). Hence, when we perceive things around us in the context of goal-directed behavior, parallel sensory signals arrive from exteroceptors and interoceptors, and they must be compared. An "appraisal of valence" system makes an assessment of the compatibility between exteroceptive inputs and interoceptive inputs. Based on this comparison, an emotion of positive or negative valence, and of a given intensity, is registered.

In thinking about brain centers for the four foci of emotion previously mentioned, it is interesting to consider the paralimbic cortex of the orbitofrontal cortex (OFC, mainly human Brodmann area 11, but also including anteroventral portions of the cingulate cortex) as a promising candidate for a multifocus and multimodal brain area dealing with the appraisal of valence (Rolls, 2004). This is one of the few brain areas that shows consistent responsiveness to objects of both positive and negative valence. Interestingly, the orbitofrontal cortex is perhaps primarily a higher-level sensory cortex for smell and taste, serving as a secondary olfactory and gustatory cortex (Rolls, 2005). This, in and of itself, may indicate something significant about the origins of aesthetics in the appraisal of food sources (and perhaps conspecifics as well via odor and taste mechanisms).

Neuroimaging studies of aesthetic emotions, especially those of positive valence, have demonstrated activations in the orbitofrontal cortex in response to a wide diversity of rewarding stimuli, including music (Blood & Zatorre, 2001; Blood, Zatorre, Bermudez, & Evans, 1999; Brown, Martinez, & Parsons, 2004), paintings (Kawabata & Zeki, 2004), faces (Aharon, Etcoff, Ariely, Chabris, O'Connor, & Breiter, 2001; Nakamura et al., 1998; O'Doherty, Winston, Critchley, Perrett, Burt, & Dolan, 2003), odors (Anderson et al., 2003), tastes (Small, Gregory, Mak, Gitelman, Mesulam, & Parrish, 2003), and touches (Francis et al., 1999). Hence, there is ample evidence of multisensory processing within the context of a given emotional focus (namely, aesthetic appraisals of objects and events). Beyond such multisensory processing is crossmodal processing. For example, the conjunction of olfaction and gustation within neurons of the OFC is thought to mediate the higher-order sensation of flavor (Rolls, 2005). Cross-modal associations occur in OFC even in very young infants and include visual, kinesic, and vocal modalities (Schore, 1994).

Other brain areas that have been implicated in emotional processing show more valence specificity than the OFC. For example, positive emotions are associated with areas like the ventral striatum (nucleus accumbens), ventral tegmental area, periaqueductal gray, and their associated dopaminergic and opiate neurotransmitter systems (Burgdorf & Panksepp, 2006). Negative emotions are associated with areas like the amygdala and anterior/ventral insula. So, the orbitofrontal cortex is perhaps the best candidate for a superordinate emotion area that spans both valence and focus. It is also one of the cortical receiving areas for visceral afferents, which thus provides clues regarding the mechanism by which it can make an appraisal of valence. By mediating a comparison between exteroceptive information from all the sensory pathways (via their "what" or object-recognition pathways) and interoceptive information from the organ systems, the orbitofrontal cortex is in a good position to generate an assessment of "good for me" vs. "bad for me" and hence assign valence to the emotional appraisal of a stimulus. In addition, the OFC is a paralimbic area that is closely connected with mnemonic areas like the parahippocampal gyrus and hippocampus, thus modulating the memorability of stimuli. It also projects extensively to subcortical motivation-emotion integration centers, especially in the right hemisphere (Tucker, 1992). The importance of the OFC for the appreciation of art objects like symphonies and sculptures may derive evolutionarily from the function of this part of the cortex in making appraisals of the olfactory and gustatory properties of food sources and perhaps conspecifics as well. The OFC is also important for affiliative interactions, which is the topic of the next section.

AFFILIATION vs. ATTRACTION

Both anthropologists of music and popular music theorists agree that Western thinking about the arts is based on an *objectification* of artworks (see also cultural theorist Shiner, 2001). Art genres are seen to be composed of collections of discrete "artworks" (e.g., books, symphonies, ballets) having individual authorship (Stockfelt, 2006). Because aesthetic emotions are those that relate to the properties of objects, it is perhaps natural to reduce the arts to the appraisal of objects, namely, aesthetic responses. However, as described above, we believe that a theory of the arts based exclusively on the properties of objects is inadequate. Having described the four foci of emotions in our modification of the Clore/Ortony theory, we feel it important to emphasize that the efficacy of the arts in terms of human behavior is dependent upon the production and perception of *all types* of emotions and not just object-based aesthetic emotions. We suggest that one of the most significant (and understudied) emotions that drives the arts is social affiliation, an emotion of strong reward value. This is tied in with our view that one of the most important functions of the arts is to create and reinforce a sense of social unity so as to promote cooperation and cohesion within social groups. In fact, affiliative interactions are the very basis for group formation, including family units and friendships. There is a strong developmental basis for this, as ritualized affinitive signals exchanged between mothers and infants in baby talk attune infants' cognitive and affective capacities in ways that provide a foundation for the skills at work in later production and perception of the arts (Miall & Dissanayake, 2003). While affiliation sits in our category of social-interaction emotions, it is highly tied in with moral emotions about the appropriateness of social actions and with motivational emotions about their goals and consequences. And as per our discussion of emotion above, all of these different emotion types should be mutually reinforcing. Hence, object-based aesthetic emotions are part of a suite of responses that includes the rewarding emotions of affiliation, anticipation, and moral righteousness.

There is a small amount of neuroimaging literature devoted to affiliation, including maternal love and romantic love. It is telling that the experience of affiliative emotions activates the orbitofrontal cortex as well as other reward centers of the brain such as the periaqueductal gray (Bartels & Zeki, 2004; Carter et al., 1999; Miller & Rodgers, 2001; Nitschke, Nelson, Rusch, Fox, Oakes, & Davidson, 2004). This latter area contains a high concentration of receptors for vasopressin and oxytocin—both of which are implicated in the experience of affiliation in animals (Nelson & Panksepp, 1998; Young & Wang, 2004; see also papers in Pedersen, Caldwell, Jirikowski, & Insel, 1992)—and projects to the orbitofrontal cortex. This finding is consistent with our claim above that the orbitofrontal cortex transcends the focus of emotion, and that interactions between emotions of more than one focus may come together in this brain area, thus providing a biological explanation for why the wicked witch should be ugly or the good prince should be handsome. We can speculate that the functional properties of the orbitofrontal cortex provide important insight into the human affinity toward multimodal processing so central to ritualized behaviors, extending from mother-infant interaction all the way to the artifications of groupwide ceremonies. Additionally, the contribution of oxytocin to stress reduction supports an argument that some social participation in the arts, in addition to other functions, may relieve individual anxiety (Dissanayake, 2007; Üvnas-Moberg, 1999).

The bottom line for us is that the arts provide a marriage of the four emotional foci of outcome, object, agency, and social interaction. It is misleading and reductionist to relegate the arts to a narrow domain of aesthetics only. It does not do justice to either the arts or the richness of the emotions that accompany them. Activities like music making and dance in small-scale cultures are consummate ways of eliciting the organismic properties of a group and ultimately solidifying the sense of common cause that is so important for group actions, not least costly ones like hunting or warfare. Aesthetic approaches to the arts focus on objects rather than behaviors and therefore neglect most of the functional consequences of the arts.

NEUROARTSOLOGY, NOT NEUROAESTHETICS

Although we appreciate the pitfalls in proposing neologisms, we believe that a deep understanding of the evolution and neuroscience of the arts will only come about from a "neuroartsology" and not a neuroaesthetics. To the extent that aesthetic responses are a critical facet of the experience of the arts, neuroaesthetics will no doubt provide important enlightenment for the neural study of the arts. And yet, neuroartsology will cover much more ground than that offered by neuroaesthetics. As mentioned, the arts take advantage of all aspects of cognitive life and capitalize on all four categories of human emotions described in this chapter, not only aesthetic emotions. In addition, neuroartsology places a strong emphasis on the behavioral functions of producing and perceiving art. It does not reduce the products of artification to the aesthetic responses of perceivers, responses that are little different from responses to any other salient stimulus. Perhaps most importantly, neuroartsology encompasses a host of cognitive and behavioral mechanisms of the arts that have no direct aesthetic functions or consequences. Features of the arts such as pitch-combination rules in music, rhythmic entrainment in dance or music, role-playing in drama or dance, or image creation through drawing or painting need not have any direct aesthetic function and may instead be serving social roles related to motivating people to take up arms, communicating with deities, educating people about their ancestral lineages, or assuaging anxiety and generating catharsis after a misfortune. Aesthetic emotions are unquestionably an integral part of the arts, but they are neither necessary nor sufficient to characterize them. Thus, a narrow focus on aesthetic responses is ultimately a distraction from the larger picture of what the arts are about. Finally, to the extent that the arts are perceived as rewarding, this is not so only because artworks are appealing objects. There is a wide variety of rewarding emotions that occur when people create and experience art apart from simply object-based emotions, including the pleasure of social communion and the moral zeal of common cause.

REFERENCES

Aharon, I., Etcoff, N., Ariely, D., Chabris, C. F., O'Connor, E., & Breiter, H. C. (2001). Beautiful faces have variable reward value: fMRI and behavioral evidence. *Neuron, 32,* 537-551.

Alcorta, C. S., & Sosis, R. (2005). Ritual, emotion, and sacred symbols: The evolution of religion as an adaptive complex. *Human Nature, 16,* 323-359.

Anderson, A. K., Christoff, K., Stappen, I., Panitz, D., Ghahremani, D. G., Glover, G., et al. (2003). Dissociated neural representation of intensity and valence in human olfaction. *Nature Neuroscience, 6,* 196-202.

Appleton, J. (1990). *The symbolism of habitat.* Seattle: University of Washington Press.

Bartels, A., & Zeki, S. (2004). The neural correlates of maternal and romantic love. *Neuroimage, 21,* 1155-1166.

Baumgarten, A. (1735/1954). *Reflections on poetry.* Berkeley: University of California Press.

Beebe, B., Lachmann, F. L., & Jaffe, J. (1997). Mother-infant interaction structures and presymbolic self and object representations. *Psychoanalytic Dialogues, 7,* 133-182.

Blood, A. J., & Zatorre, R. J. (2001). Intensely pleasurable responses to music correlate with activity in brain regions implicated in reward and emotion. *Proceedings of the National Academy of Sciences, 98*, 11818-11823.

Blood, A. J., Zatorre, R. J., Bermudez, P., & Evans, A. C. (1999). Emotional responses to pleasant and unpleasant music correlate with activity in paralimbic brain regions. *Nature Neuroscience, 2*, 382-387.

Brown, S. (2000). Evolutionary models of music: From sexual selection to group selection. In F. Tonneau & N. S. Thompson (Eds.), *Perspectives in ethology. 13: Behavior, evolution and culture* (pp. 231-281). New York: Plenum.

Brown, S., Martinez, M. J., & Parsons, L. M. (2004). Passive music listening spontaneously engages limbic and paralimbic systems. *NeuroReport, 15*, 2033-2037.

Brown, S., & Volgsten, U. (2006). Is Mozart's music *good*? In S. Brown & U. Volgsten (Eds.), *Music and manipulation: On the social uses and social control of music* (pp. 365-369). New York: Berghahn.

Burgdorf, J., & Panksepp, J. (2006). The neurobiology of positive emotions. *Neuroscience and Biobehavioral Reviews, 30*, 173-187.

Carter, C. S., Lederhandler, I. I., & Kirkpatrick, B. (Eds.). (1999). *The integrative neurobiology of affiliation*. Cambridge, MA: MIT Press.

Chernoff, J. M. (1979). *African rhythm and African sensibility*. Chicago: University of Chicago Press.

Clore, G. L. (1994). Why emotions require cognition. In P. Ekman & R. J. Davidson (Eds.), *The nature of emotion: Fundamental questions* (pp. 181-191). New York: Oxford University Press.

Clore, G. L., & Ortony, A. (2000). Cognition in emotion: Always, sometimes, or never? In L. Nadel, R. Lane, & G. L. Ahern (Eds.), *The cognitive neuroscience of emotion* (pp. 24-61). New York: Oxford University Press.

Darwin, C. (1871). *The descent of man and selection in relation to sex*. London: J. Murray.

Darwin, C. (1872). *The expression of emotion in man and animals*. London: J. Murray.

Davies, S. (2006). *The philosophy of art*. Malden, MA: Blackwell.

Dissanayake, E. (1988). *What is art for?* Seattle: University of Washington Press.

Dissanayake, E. (1992). *Homo aestheticus: Where art comes from and why*. Seattle: University of Washington Press.

Dissanayake, E. (2000). *Art and intimacy: How the arts began*. Seattle: University of Washington Press.

Dissanayake, E. (2006). Ritual and ritualization: Musical means of conveying and shaping emotion in humans and other animals. In S. Brown & U. Volgsten (Eds.), *Music and manipulation: On the social uses and social control of music* (pp. 31-57). Oxford: Berghahn.

Dissanayake, E. (2007). What art is and what art does: An overview of contemporary evolutionary hypotheses. In C. Martindale, P. Locher, & V. Petrov (Eds.), *Evolutionary and neurocognitive approaches to aesthetics, creativity, and the arts* (pp. 1-14). Amityville, NY: Baywood.

Dissanayake, E. (2008). If music is the food of love, what about survival and reproductive success? *Musicae Scientiae*, 169-195.

Eibl-Eibesfeldt, I. (1989). *Human ethology*. Hawthorne, NY: Aldine de Gruyter.

Ekman, P. (1992). Are there basic emotions? *Psychological Review, 99*, 550-553.

Ekman, P. (1999). Basic emotions. In T. Dalgleish & M. Power (Eds.), *Handbook of cognition and emotion* (pp. 45-60). Sussex, UK: John Wiley and Sons.

Falk, D. (1998). Hominin brain evolution: Looks can be deceiving. *Science, 280*, 1714.

Francis, S., Rolls, E. T., Bowtell, R., McGlone, F., O'Doherty, J., Browning, A., et al. (1999). The representation of pleasant touch in the brain and its relationship with taste and olfactory areas. *NeuroReport, 10*, 453-459.

Gould, S. J. (1977). *Ontogeny and phylogeny*. Cambridge, MA: Harvard University Press.

Hennelotter, A., & Schroeder, U. (2006). Partially dissociable neural substrates for recognizing basic emotions: A critical review. *Progress in Brain Research, 156*, 443-456.

Kawabata, H., & Zeki, S. (2004). Neural correlates of beauty. *Journal of Neurophysiology, 91*, 1699-1705.

Miall, D. S., & Dissanayake, E. (2003). The poetics of babytalk. *Human Nature, 14*, 337-364.

Miller, G. (2000). *The mating mind: How sexual choice shaped the evolution of human nature.* New York: Doubleday.

Miller, G. (2001). Aesthetic fitness: How sexual selection shaped artistic virtuosity as a fitness indicator and aesthetic preferences as mate choice criteria. *Bulletin of Psychology and the Arts, 2*, 20-25.

Miller, W. B., & Rodgers, J. L. (2001). *The ontogeny of human bonding systems: Evolutionary origins, neural bases, and psychological mechanisms.* Dordrecht: Kluwer.

Murray, L., & Trevarthen, C. (1985). Emotional regulation of interaction between two month-olds and their mothers. In T. Field & N. Fox (Eds.), *Social perception in infants* (pp. 177-197). Norwood, NJ: Ablex.

Nadel, J., Carchon, I., Kervella, C., Marcelli, D., & Réserbet-Plantey, D. (1999). Expectancies for social contingency in 2-month-olds. *Developmental Science, 2*, 164-173.

Nakamura, K., Nagumo, S., Ito, K., Sugiura, M., Kato, T., Nakamura, A., et al. (1998). Neuroanatomical correlates of the assessment of facial attractiveness. *NeuroReport, 9*, 753-757.

Nelson, E., & Panksepp, J. (1998). Brain substrates of infant-mother attachment: Contributions of opioids, oxytocin, and norepinepherine, *Neuroscience and Biobehavioral Reviews, 22*, 437-452.

Nitschke, J. B., Nelson, E. E., Rusch, B. D., Fox, A. S., Oakes, T. R. & Davidson, R. J. (2004). Orbitofrontal cortex tracks positive mood in mothers viewing pictures of their newborn infant. *NeuroImage, 21*, 583-592.

O'Doherty, J., Winston, J., Critchley, H., Perrett, D., Burt, D. M. & Dolan, R. J. (2003). Beauty in a smile: The role of medial orbitofrontal cortex in facial attractiveness. *Neuropsychologia, 41*, 147-155.

Orians, G. H. (2001). An evolutionary perspective on aesthetics. *Bulletin of Psychology and the Arts, 2*(1), 25-29.

Ortony, A., & Turner, T. (1990). What's basic about basic emotions? *Psychological Review, 97*, 315-331.

Pedersen, C. A., Caldwell, J. D., Jirikowski, G. F., & Insel, T. R. (Eds.). (1992). Oxytocin in maternal, sexual and social behaviors. *Annals of the New York Academy of Sciences, 652.*

Portmann, A. (1941). Die Tragzeit der Primaten und die Dauer der Schwangerschaft beim Menschen: Ein Problem der vergleichende Biologie. *Revue Suisse de Zoologie, 48*, 511-518.

Rappaport, R. A. (1999). *Ritual and religion in the making of humanity.* London: Cambridge University Press.

Reisenzein, R. (1994). Pleasure-arousal theory and the intensity of emotions. *Journal of Personality and Social Psychology, 67*, 525-539.

Rolls, E. T. (2004). Convergence of sensory systems in the orbitofrontal cortex in primates and brain design for emotion. *The Anatomical Record, 281A*, 1212-1225.

Rolls, E. T. (2005). Taste, olfactory, and food texture processing in the brain, and the control of food intake. *Physiology and Behavior, 85*, 45-56.

Ruso, B., Renninger, L., & Atzwanger, K. (2003). Human habitat preferences: A generative territory for evolutionary aesthetics research. In E. Voland & K. Grammer (Eds.), *Evolutionary aesthetics* (pp. 279-294). Berlin: Springer-Verlag.

Schore, A. N. (1994). *Affect regulation and the origin of the self: The neurobiology of emotional development.* Hillsdale, NJ: Erlbaum.

Shiner, L. (2001). *The invention of art: A cultural history*. Chicago: University of Chicago Press.

Small, D. M., Gregory, M. D., Mak, E. Y., Gitelman, D., Mesulam, M. M., & Parrish, T. (2003). Dissociation of neural representation of intensity and affective valuation in human gustation. *Neuron, 39,* 701-711.

Solso, R. L. (1994). *Cognition and the visual arts*. Cambridge, MA: MIT Press.

Stockfelt, O. (2006). Music and reuse: Theoretical and historical considerations. In S. Brown & U. Volgsten (Eds.), *Music and manipulation: On the social uses and social control of music* (pp. 315-335). New York: Berghahn.

Thornhill, R. (1998). Darwinian aesthetics. In C. Crawford & D. L. Krebs (Eds.), *Handbook of evolutionary psychology: Ideas, issues, applications* (pp. 543-572). Mahwah, NJ: Erlbaum.

Tinbergen, N. (1952). Derived activities: Their causation, biological significance, origin, and emancipation during evolution. *Quarterly Review of Biology, 27,* 1-32.

Trevarthen, C. (1979). Communication and cooperation in early infancy: A description of primary intersubjectivity. In M. Bullowa (Ed.), *Before speech: The beginning of human communication* (pp. 321-347). Cambridge, MA: Cambridge University Press.

Tucker, D. M. (1992). Developing emotions and cortical networks. In M. R. Gunnar & C. A. Nelson (Eds.), *Development, behavior, neuroscience* (pp. 75-128). Hillsdale, NJ: Erlbaum.

Turner, V. (1969). *The ritual process: Structure and anti-structure.* London: Routledge and Kegan Paul.

Üvnas-Moberg, K. (1999). Physiological and endocrine effects of social contact. In C. S. Carter, I. I. Lederhendler, & B. Kirkpatrick (Eds.), *The integrative neurobiology of affiliation* (pp. 245-261). Cambridge, MA: MIT Press.

van Damme, W. (1996). *Beauty in context: Towards an anthropological approach to aesthetics*. Leiden: E. J. Brill.

Vartanian, O., & Goel, V. (2004). Neuroanatomical correlates of aesthetic preference for paintings. *NeuroReport, 15,* 893-897.

Voland, E., & Grammer, K. (Eds.). (2003). *Evolutionary aesthetics.* Berlin: Springer-Verlag.

Young, L. J., & Wang, Z. (2004). The neurobiology of pair bonding. *Nature Neuroscience, 7,* 1048-1054.

Zeki, S. (1999). *Inner vision: An exploration of art and the brain.* Oxford: Oxford University Press.

CHAPTER 5

Bio-Aesthetics and the Aesthetic Trajectory: A Dynamic Cognitive and Cultural Perspective

W. Tecumseh Fitch, Antje von Graevenitz, and Eric Nicolas

Figure 1. Looking at Fontana. (© Illustration by W. Tecumseh Fitch.)

INTRODUCTION: BEYOND "GREAT ART": EXPLORING THE AESTHETIC EXPERIENCE ON ITS OWN TERMS

There is a long tradition in aesthetics that takes as its goal the making of judgments about the "value" of particular pieces of art, often by a well-educated aesthetic elite. This approach often focuses on the understanding and interpretation of some canon: a group of work agreed to constitute "great art." One can find this attitude unashamedly expressed in introductory textbooks on art appreciation and art history, which may explicitly state an aim to "develop a technique of general critical analysis by which the student can arrive at his own evaluation and judgment of works of art" (Wold & Cykler, 1976, p. 1), and thus to give the reader access to the shared judgments of the aesthetic elite. Referring to popular music, illustration, or cartoon, the same authors tell us that art "which aims merely to amuse and to provide a pleasant diversion . . . has little or no lasting quality." In particular, "art which caters to the masses . . . is of little aesthetic value and will not be considered." We feel that, despite its long tradition, such a conception of aesthetics—the study of what makes art beautiful, criteria for judging greatness in art—makes a poor foundation for a biologically based approach to aesthetics. Instead, a future discipline of bioaesthetics should focus on the broadly shared capacity of any normal human to have *any* aesthetic experience.

The starting point for the current chapter is thus to reject the traditional prescriptivist perspective in favor of a more neutral and descriptive study of the aesthetic experience itself, whatever its object, and whatever the cultural background of the viewer or listener. Specifically, the goal for any future bioaesthetics should be to link the subjective phenomena that constitute varieties of aesthetic experience with the cognitive and neural mechanisms that make such experiences possible. In attempting to build bridges between the "bio," the "neuro," and the "aesthetic," we need a more basic and inclusive conception of aesthetics, which includes the broadly (and probably universally) shared capacity for perceiving and enjoying everyday music and artwork possessed by untrained nonelite perceivers, one that is already present in a basic form in a four- or five-year-old child. Rather than focus exclusively on canonical works, then, we suggest a realignment of focus on the normal perceiver's cognitive experience of any art. In this chapter, then, we take some initial steps toward a basic and descriptive understanding of what is happening when an ordinary person perceives some event or object "aesthetically," whether the effect is pleasing or provocative, soothing or irritating. We will discuss artworks that we happen to like, but we avoid any prescriptive evaluations about "good" or "bad" art. This theoretical move parallels the refocusing that typifies modern linguistics, which rejects the prescriptive role of the language maven (i.e., "'ain't' is not proper English") in favor of a more neutral, descriptive approach to the linguistic capabilities of the person in the street (or, equally interesting, those of young children). For linguistics, this change of focus led to the discovery of a vast complexity, mostly unconscious, and thus overlooked by language mavens, underlying the linguistic capacity of any normal human. We believe that similar complexity awaits future bio- and neuroaestheticians who take seriously *any* artwork that elicits an aesthetic response from some group of perceivers. Indeed, an important component of such study must certainly be popular art, which successfully "caters to the masses," and this will thus be a primary focus in the discussion below.

Ultimately, a comprehensive descriptive approach to aesthetics should include both the psychological experience of a *perceiver* of a piece of art and the less replicable psychological experience of the *creator* of that artwork. Both are obviously important, but in this chapter we will focus on the perceiver for simple reasons of logical priority and empirical tractability. The empirical study of the creative side of the aesthetic process, while not impossible, is far more challenging, and we prefer to start with the low-hanging fruit, which alone presents plenty of challenges.

Taste in art is famously variable among individuals. However, in this chapter we suggest that there is a very basic cognitive trajectory that typically characterizes the mental and emotional experience of the perceiver of successful art, regardless of the medium utilized. Broadly speaking, this "aesthetic trajectory" includes at least three temporal stages: an initial stage of familiarity, recognition, or stability; a second stage of surprise, ambiguity, or tension; and a third stage of integration, resolution, or synthesis. Often, especially in visual art, a sort of tension or ambiguity remains, and this keeps the viewer "coming back for more," inviting repeated viewings to resolve or better understand the piece. Equally often, particularly in music, the resolution is quite complete and satisfying, but the experience of tension and resolution is itself pleasing and invites repeated listenings. This sort of trajectory is perhaps most familiar in music, film, and the other temporal arts, because the temporal form of the piece is more or less synchronized with the temporal unfolding of the perceiver's cognitive and emotional experience. However, it seems likely that a similar trajectory also characterizes our perception of static visual art such as painting, sculpture, or architecture. In fact, a near analog of the three-stage cognitive trajectory we propose here has been considered a principle of dramatic narrative since Aristotle identified it in his *Poetics*: the basic structure of exposition, introduction of conflict leading to climax, and denouement (later elaborated by Gustav Freytag as the "pyramidal" structure of a plot), which characterizes a near-universal range of storytelling. In the narrative arts, such an aesthetic "arc" is intuitively recognizable to such an extent that we will leave the reader to assess its relevance to the underlying cognitive dynamic we propose here.

Thus, we suggest, a basic dynamic progression of cognitive states is characteristic of aesthetic experience, even for art in forms that do not themselves change. *The aesthetic response is a kind of mental movement, even if the object of contemplation remains still.* To the extent that this characterization is correct, it provides a unifying theme for characterizing our experience of the arts in general, and one which allows various nontrivial points of contact with psychology and the cognitive neurosciences (see Empirical Approaches to Bioaesthetics, page 93).

Background Assumptions

Before embarking on our discussion of the aesthetic trajectory, we should briefly state a few background assumptions of the approach we adopt. First, we take the perspective of modern cognitive science, which attempts to characterize the underlying principles of all of cognition using such shorthand terminology as "hypothesis formation" or "rules and representation." It is understood that most of the cognitive processes thus described are unconscious and are often resistant to conscious introspection (to varying degrees "encapsulated"). Classic examples of this approach are provided in vision, where it is now clear that gazing upon even a simple image sparks a complex series of neural events in multiple brain regions that unfold extremely rapidly (in less than one second) and are mostly completely unconscious (Marr, 1982). Many of the mechanisms involved, such as those subserving color or depth perception, are highly resistant to any conscious introspection. It is typically only when the system is "broken" in some way, as by various visual illusions, or by brain damage, that the complexity of the underlying system is laid bare. Our discussion thus makes no assumptions about the degree to which the perceiver is consciously aware of the various stages we posit. Indeed, our background assumption is that most of the perceptual work occurs without conscious awareness, and that the most prominent conscious component of aesthetic experience is the emotional effect of these unconscious perceptual processes.

Second, in our attempt to build bridges between the biological sciences and aesthetics, we are seeking a very basic, lowest-common-denominator set of cognitive processes. The particular process we have identified is, we hope, rather obvious to both professional aestheticians (see Langer, 1942) and to the average art appreciator who has a certain degree of insight into his experience. We thus make no claim to deep novel insights here, and do not attempt to deal with many issues about beauty, interpretation, creativity, and the like that are the more traditional focus of aesthetic debate. We will be quite satisfied if the psychologist, the aesthetician, and the average art appreciator find our suggestions about the aesthetic trajectory rather obvious.

The third preliminary is a justification of our focus in this chapter on the aesthetic experience of the perceiver of a work of art, rather than on that of the creator. The creator is the traditional focus of aesthetics, which seems logical because without a creator there would be nothing for the perceiver to perceive. However, this ignores the fact that *the creator is herself a perceiver*: the process of creation itself generally entails an interplay between the artist's creative action and perceptual evaluation. This is even true when a composer "hears" the music in her head during an internal composition process: the underlying cognitive processes on which we focus here are also in this case called into play, and a better understanding of them may therefore also shed light on the creator's side of the process. Logically, then, the production of art presupposes an ability to perceive it aesthetically (if only on the part of the creator him- or herself), and a crucial component of the creative process is the perception of the developing piece as it is being created. Thus, our focus here should not be taken to indicate a lack of interest in, or failure to appreciate the importance of the creator's role in aesthetics. Indeed, we agree wholeheartedly with Zeki's argument that successful artistic creators are themselves practicing neuroaestheticians, and that the artist has much to teach the scientist interested in understanding the human aesthetic capacity (Zeki, 1999). We will provide a number of examples below where artists either have had, or promise to have, important roles to play in neuro- and bioaesthetics.

Another justification for our focus here on the perceiver's experience is specifically tailored to this volume on neuroaesthetics: empirical accessibility. Aesthetic experience in ordinary perceivers can easily be studied experimentally (e.g., with psychological rating tasks or brain imaging studies). Put simply, the perceiver's aesthetic experience is far more reliably elicited and controllable than that of the creator. We can easily and repeatedly expose naïve viewers to novel artworks and gauge their responses in various ways, while even the most confident and prolific creator has incomplete control over the creative process, and must to some extent "await the muse" (though we will turn at the end briefly to the musical performer, particularly the jazz improviser, as an important intermediate case). Furthermore, a perceiver's experience is replicable to at least some extent within and among individuals. We can listen to the same piece of music, or view the same painting, again and again, and while the experience each time is by no means identical, certain basic aspects of our aesthetic response will typically remain consistent. Even those aspects that change with repetition, as when one tires of hearing a song, may clarify key facets of the stages of the "trajectory." This reproducibility also allows perceivers some introspective insight into the perceptual experience, a form of insight that both artists and appreciators have long valued. In contrast, the creation of a piece of art is a singular and unique, and, we suspect, a largely empirically inaccessible experience.

Finally, and probably most controversially, we suspect that in general there is a nonrandom correspondence between the cognitive processes experienced by the perceiver and those intended by the creator. Depending on the situation, this may be relatively direct (e.g., a close temporal "sympathy" between creator and listener during an improvised solo) or quite indirect and vague, but it is in part the belief that such a connection exists that makes the perceiver's experience relevant to future exploration of the creative experience (to which we return in the conclusion).

Overview of the Chapter

Having stated our goal of exploring the aesthetic trajectory in various arts, and having justified our focus on the perceiver's aesthetic experience, we will begin the chapter with a more detailed description of the aesthetic trajectory using examples from painting and music, mostly from the twentieth century. Although our conception of the aesthetic trajectory certainly encompasses representational art, the idiom of nonrepresentational visual art provides a clearer illustration of the fundamental points, unobscured by more complex issues of representation, illusion, and symbolism (Gombrich, 1959). Nonrepresentational art also seems more directly comparable to music, which provides our paradigm case of the aesthetic trajectory because its temporal development and dynamics can accurately be notated. Our discussion begins by focusing on the "synchronic" experience of individual perceivers during a brief span of time; and only later turns to the "diachronic" social and cultural phenomena, the development of traditions and art "forms."

In the section entitled "The Aesthetic Trajectory and Cultural Change" (see p. 76), we discuss a broader, longer-scale cultural evolution. We argue that there is no incompatibility between biological and cultural perspectives with regard to art, and that indeed both viewpoints are necessary for any rich understanding of human aesthetic capabilities. We suggest that the dynamics of the aesthetic trajectory enforce a continual search for novelty over a longer cultural timescale, and thus constitute a force for cultural change. Last year's pleasing novelty becomes part of this year's new style, and of next year's old hat. Thus, the model we consider here highlights a firm link between individual aesthetic experience and the diachronic cultural change so typical of the arts.

In the section entitled "A Useful Framework for Aesthetic Analysis," we explore an important difference between the visual and temporal arts by considering the question of notation. In the visual arts, the work itself is a kind of notation of the artist's actions, and thus a separate notation system appears unnecessary. By contrast, in music the development of notation systems provided a permanence to the otherwise fleeting artistic object (the transitory performance), though at the price of failing to capture many of the expressive details that go into such a performance. Music notation is an abstraction of the temporal structure of a piece and, as such, provides an unparalleled opportunity to identify precisely where specific aesthetic stages are likely to occur. This makes musical notation a useful medium for representing and discussing, and an empirical tool for neural investigations of the aesthetic trajectory.

Music notation also has relevance to cultural and historical considerations, which in turn provide opportunities for further study toward evaluating suggestions about biological universals underlying the aesthetic faculty. By allowing communication of artistic ideas across time and space, the existence of a parallel system of representation had a profound effect on the development of Western music, and despite the present-day ubiquity of audio recordings, notation remains a crucial component of many musical subcultures. As an illustrative example, we explore the evolution of the notational system used in jazz, which although based on traditional Western notation, involved some significant additions that have evolved over the last half century (and are still evolving), reflecting the needs of a more improvisational medium. The parallels between the more abstract and improvisatory art of the twentieth century, including abstract art, jazz, and experimental art music (e.g., Cage and Glass), appear to warrant further exploration from the dynamic perspective advocated here.

We end in the final section by illustrating the sorts of experiments that could test and extend the ideas proposed here, by considering some ways in which these hypotheses about perception could be extended to understand the creative process, and by highlighting a number of unresolved issues and questions for future research.

THE AESTHETIC TRAJECTORY

"Art is the lie that reveals the truth." Picasso

Representational Art

Consider Figure 2, an image of a row of poplars along a waterfront, painted by French Impressionist Claude Monet (1891, Coll. Metropolitan Museum of Art, New York). At first sight, this is a very simple piece, and it may well recall an image the viewer has seen in reality before. This initiates the first stage of the aesthetic trajectory: a feeling of recognition and familiarity that invites and binds the viewer's attention to the piece. However, as the eye plays over it, the painting begins to seem more adventurous. The color choices invite us to consider individual brushstrokes, and the fact that the "image" is a flat canvas rectangle covered with paint becomes hard to ignore. One notices further that the mirrored space between

Figure 2. See p. 147 for full color.

the trees on the painted surface of the water could be seen as (a) spaces or "holes" of air, (b) a reflection of these on the surface of the water, or (c) a row of white rectangles of paint on the canvas. In general, we don't "see" all of these interpretations at one time: we toggle among them, and we can to some extent guide our perception toward one or another. This kind of mental movement, a destabilization of our ordinary comfortable perceptual certainty, is the second stage of the aesthetic trajectory. The initial familiarity has evolved into novelty, uncertainty, and ambiguity. This creates a palpable tension between the reality of the object itself (strokes of paint on canvas) and the image it represents (a row of poplars by the water).

An important aesthetic "trick" here is one that was central to the Impressionist movement and advanced theoretically by Cézanne: by allowing the brushstrokes to retain their obvious "brushstroke" quality and allowing the texture of the canvas material to remain prominent (often showing through between the brushstrokes), many Impressionist paintings force the viewer to acknowledge the painting-as-object almost immediately. This contrasts with the highly finished, polished techniques of the Salon painters that constituted the Western European norm of that time. By confronting the reality of the art object itself, a movement away from one's initial sense of familiarity is generated, and with this comes uncertainty and ambiguity, with a heightened emotional tension. But, finally, one can resolve this tension by stepping back, as it were, and relaxing one's orientation back into the original percept of the image as trees. This is the third stage of the aesthetic trajectory: a (partial) resolution of the tension caused by the second stage of novelty. So, crucially, the last stage of this cycle represents an integration or synthesis of the earlier two, and not simply a return to the initial familiarity. It is this partial resolution that gives us pleasure, and its incompleteness (in many artworks) is what keeps us coming back for more. One can repeat the process as often as desired, and indeed many paintings invite us to do so. Thus, an aesthetic experience will often consist of multiple passes through the simplified three-stage process we have just illustrated, which we intend as a distillation of the aesthetic dynamic rather than as a complete characterization.

There is a fundamental similarity between the mental movement just described and the cognitive movement one experiences viewing the Necker cube in Figure 3. Such figures are termed "bistable" because the visual system perceives them in one of two ways and tends to flip, given time, between these two interpretations. Bistable figures of this sort provide the canonical evidence that vision is not simply a veridical "absorption" of a real visual stimulus onto the retina and into the brain, but in fact a process of interpretation by the viewer (Wundt, 1908). This notion of vision as an active (if unconscious) type of hypothesis testing was already clear to early physiologist/psychologists like Helmholtz (1911), and has been accepted by most subsequent psychophysicists and neuroscientists (for discussion see Gombrich, 1959; Zschocke, 2006). However, the aesthetic trajectory goes beyond simple bistability, because the third integrative stage, the "resolution," leaves one with a feeling of satisfaction quite beyond the curious shifting that one feels

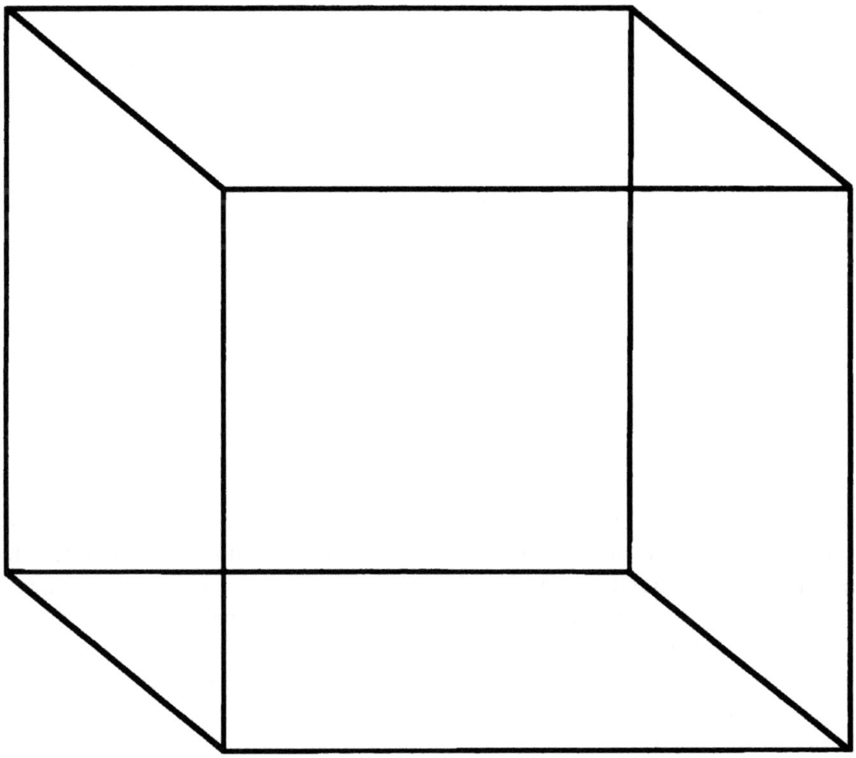

Figure 3. Necker Cube. (© Illustration by W. Tecumseh Fitch.)

watching the Necker cube flip states. Thus, while bistability provides a nice illustration of the active cognitive side of perception, we do not consider such bistable figures to be art, because they lack the crucial resolution/synthesis component of the aesthetic trajectory.

The Monet painting typifies an ambiguity one can experience with most representational art (Gombrich, 1959): the main source of "mental movement" is an oscillation between the percept of the image (which is what usually strikes one first) and of the art object itself (as paint on canvas, marks on a page, or a carved block of marble). The bistability of image and object creates the precondition for aesthetic experience that is consummated by the viewer's attempt to integrate these two percepts into a unified whole. Ultimately, one may attain a satisfactory overall feeling about both aspects, thinking both "what a pleasing image" and "what a skilled painting." By allowing and indeed encouraging us to see the painting as an object, the Impressionists heightened this bistable tension and paved the way for the more abstract art that followed.

Abstract Art

> Many things in engineering went out of use on the strength of man's discovery of new possibilities in nature. The same should be true of artistic-aesthetic questions. (Kazimir Malevich, 1976, p. 11)

The move to nonrepresentational or nonfigurative—abstract—art came close on the heels of Impressionism, Expressionism, and Cubism, and abstract art is in many ways a logical extension of the ideas developed by the Impressionists, especially Cézanne. But with the abandonment of representational imagery, and thereby of the traditional bistability between image and object that figurative paintings ensured, abstract artists were forced to develop other sources of familiarity, and of tension and ambiguity.

In a painting widely viewed as initiating the twentieth-century paradigm shift toward abstract art (e.g., Gooding, 2001), the Russian painter Kazimir Malevich came up with a very simple and elegant solution to this problem with his "Black Suprematist Square" of 1915 (Collection of Tretjakov Gallery, Moscow) (Figure 4). The painting, a simple black square on a simple white canvas, can be seen as a black surface superimposed on a white surface, a black cube floating in empty white space, or quite differently, as a black hole within a white surface, opening into an empty black void. Even viewed as purely two-dimensional, the piece has two conflicting interpretations, each of which contains its opposite. The viewer cannot be certain which is "correct," for whichever way one chooses to interpret the image, the other interpretation seems equally possible. But, unlike the Necker cube, the experience of which stalls at the second perceptual stage (is it protruding? is it receding? and so on), "Black Suprematist Square" compels viewers toward the resolution of this tension upon which art depends. One partial resolution comes from Malevich's choice of the square: a symmetrical geometrical form seen by the neoclassicists as the epitome of order and stability, and viewed by scholastics as the symbol of Earth. Malevich equated the equality of its sides with the equality of all humans. So the shape of the square itself provides one route to resolution of tension and ambiguity: the viewer creates a resolution in a richer, more fully interpreted square. Another source of resolution was made possible via the painting's spatial context in the original exhibition: it was hung in a quite unconventional place, in the upper corner of the room (as if freed from the architecture), in a manner strongly reminiscent of Russian Orthodox icon paintings. By this path, the tension could be relieved by seeing the painting as, after all, a continuation of a deep stream of Russian religious art.

The nearly unconstrained possibilities of abstract art for generating familiarity and tension led to a profusion of aesthetic approaches in the last century. These can be challenging for the viewer to perceive, understand, and integrate, and from the beginning abstract artists often accompanied their works with written interpretive guidelines or manifestos to help this process along (a practice ridiculed by Wolfe, 1975). Such documents, despite their occasional pretentiousness, offer a valuable tool for the art historian and aesthetician interested in abstract art, as we rarely have such detailed interpretive guidelines from the artist for representational pieces.

Figure 4. Malevich Square. (© Illustration by W. Tecumseh Fitch.)

Malevich's writings discuss his highly ambitious aesthetic goals for his black square in some detail. The painting, like the "Suprematist" movement that took it as its symbol, explicitly handed over the lion's share of creativity in art to the viewers, who, in seeing and imagining the various possible interpretations of the piece, *themselves* created the image. The artist, in presenting such a simple image, intentionally bows out of the creative process as much as possible. This granting of almost limitless freedom to the creative viewer was seen as politically meaningful, as a harbinger for the freedom of the citizen that Malevich foresaw on the dawn of the Russian Revolution. Malevich's artistic goals with this piece thus included the political goal of mental and aesthetic liberation of the people, through his self-proclaimed "universal" art form. Thus, at least at its inception in Russia, abstract art was seen as the very opposite of the elitist institution of representational art represented by the European Salons. Malevich felt, with this new approach, that he had "dragged [him]self out of the rubbish-filled pool of academic art" (Malevich, 1915). The aesthetic goals of this simple square were nothing if not ambitious.

Although Malevich made no explicit mention of the influence on his work of contemporary psychological theories about visual perception, he was probably well aware of the perceptual theories of the Gestalt psychologists, especially of Wilhelm Wundt (see Zhadova, 1982, p. 45). Malevich's wife, the daughter of a psychologist, may have drawn her husband's attention to the widely discussed publication of Wundt's internationally successful *Outline of Physiological Psychology* (Wundt, 1908). The three volumes had many editions in the original German, a language that Malevich could probably read, and was translated into Russian in 1912. In volumes 2 and 3 of this work, Wundt discussed optical illusions and aesthetic perception, arguing that the viewer has the freedom to make up his own mind about even the simplest geometrical forms, especially drawn cubes (see Figure 5). Wundt describes his perception of a black square on a white surface as a suspended form, or, reversed, as a hole in a plain surface, as an endless plurality of sensations. Malevich's aesthetic claims in the manifesto accompanying his piece directly echo

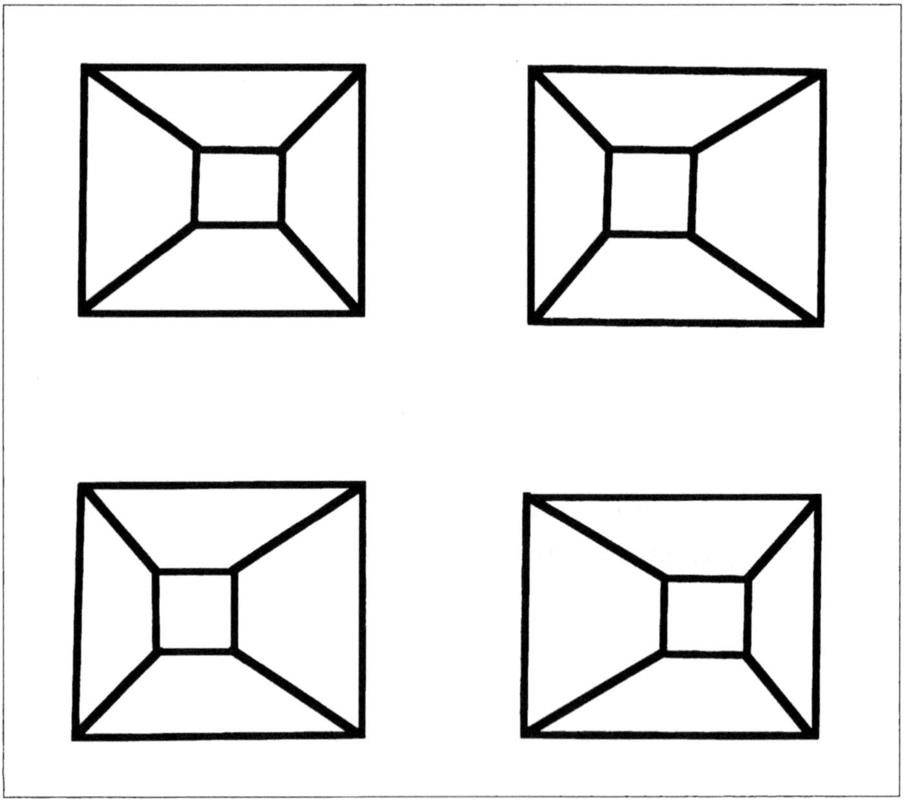

Figure 5. Wundt cubes. (© Illustration by W. Tecumseh Fitch.)

Wundt's arguments about visual perception itself. Thus, two of our central themes in this chapter—the focus on the creative process in the viewer, and of the importance of the viewer's mental movement—echo the explicit goals of this early abstract artist, as well as the leading Gestalt psychologists of his time. It is safe to say that these preoccupations have continued through the present day in abstract art, and that they also resonated in later representational and figurative art (e.g., that of Surrealists like Magritte). We shall return to these broader cultural issues below, but first must consider how the aesthetic trajectory is realized in the nonstatic artistic idioms.

Music and the Temporal Arts

The distinction between abstract and representational art parallels a similar distinction concerning abstraction and meaning in music and language (Langer, 1942). In an important sense, we can see representational painting as akin to (meaningful) poetry: poetry simultaneously explores sound structure (via rhyme, alliteration, cadence, etc.) and semantic structure (built up from word meanings) in the same way that painting can simultaneously explore physical structure (brushstrokes, color choices) and imagistic structure (the representational visual image brought to mind). The semantic, representational element is not present in the same way in abstract art, nor in music. It is not surprising that precisely when Malevich was advancing his new, fully abstract art, poets in his creative circle in Moscow, as elsewhere (the Italian Futurists, and later Dadaists) were experimenting with meaningless poetry—poetry "freed" from the shackles of grammar and meaning (Zhadova, 1982). But of course, human experimentation with abstraction, with sound for sound's sake, began long before this, with the advent of music. Although no one knows precisely when humans began making music, beautifully formed bone flutes from the Paleolithic period clearly indicate that humans made music by 35,000 years ago (Hahn & Münzel, 1995), during the same period that our ancestors were producing Lascaux and similar cave paintings. So music is at least as old as representational art. But beginning with Darwin, many theorists have suggested that music goes far further back and indeed preceded the evolution of language in protohumans (for reviews see Fitch, 2006b; Mithen, 2005). Unlike visual art, music was, in an important sense, abstract from the very beginning. How does an art form that unfolds through time and lacks explicit propositional meaning elicit the three basic stages of the aesthetic trajectory? How does an ever-changing stimulus elicit a feeling of familiarity? How is familiarity transformed, leading to a feeling of surprise or tension?

Consider the Beatles' 1968 hit song "Revolution," composed by John Lennon and Paul McCartney (Figure 6). The song starts off with the "feel" of a rock and roll song in the key of A, a feel that was very familiar at that time to the English-speaking popular music community. The first bars of this song, with lyrics "You say you want a revolution" continue this, and already the listener has a strong feeling of familiarity and comfort. However, the loud and intentionally distorted electric guitar sound was quite novel at the time and gives a hint of the novelty soon to unfold (indeed, this aspect of the recording is sometimes cited as a

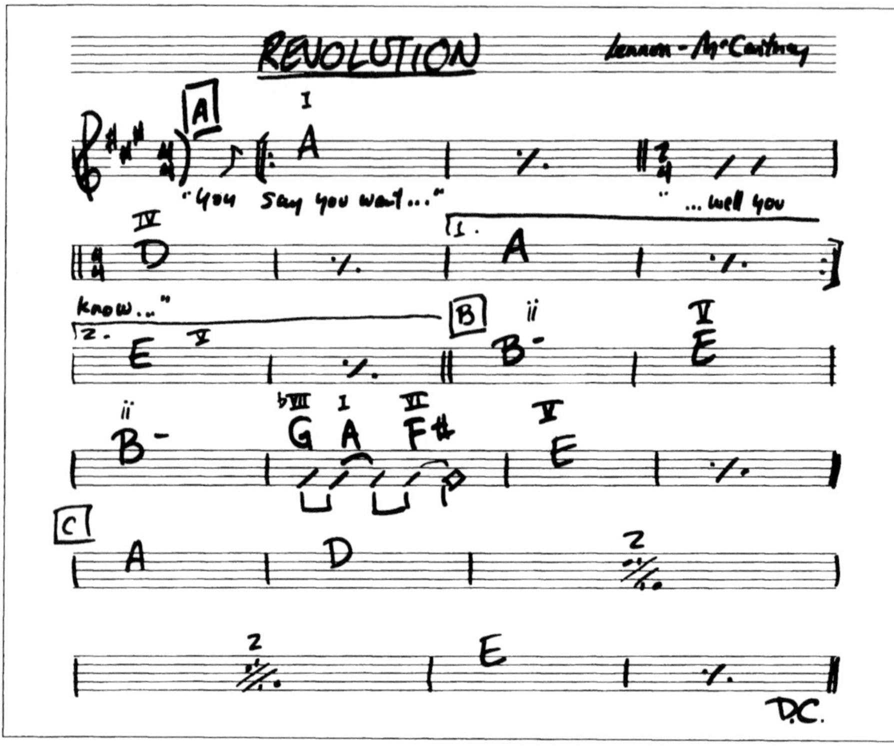

Figure 6. Score for "Revolution." (© Illustration by E. Nicolas and W. Tecumseh Fitch.)

precursor of "heavy metal"). Almost immediately following the establishment of the familiar-sounding harmonic rhythm and Chuck Berry-derived guitar riff, the composers throw a small wrench into our comfortable familiarity by violating the metrical structure of a standard rock or blues song. Standard rock form is 4/4 or "common time" all the way through, meaning that each measure contains exactly four beats. But the "well, you know" phrase of the lyric cuts its measure two beats short, and the chord change at "know" occurs two beats "too soon" for the established meter. This violates our metrical expectations and creates a bit of uncertainty in the listener, who is then, however, promptly reassured by a return to the standard meter. Then this entire form is repeated again. This time we unconsciously expect the 2/4 bar, and this unconscious expectation is rewarded. This change from the standard metrical form is quite subtle (despite the authors' thorough familiarity with the song, we had never noticed it before we sat down to notate it), but already has instantiated the desired three-part dynamic of the aesthetic trajectory: we have experienced familiarity, surprise ("expectancy violation" being the more standard musicological phrase), and resolution. But there is much more to come.

In part B of the song, initiated with the lyric "but if you talk about," we move to a B minor chord not yet heard in the song and the choice of which itself transgresses the stylistic expectations already established of a "rootsy" blues-based (typically I-IV-V or "three-chord") rock and roll tune. However, by standard rules of Western harmony, this chord, the diatonic ii minor, fits perfectly in the song's key of A; it then moves to the dominant chord, E, so this change is unsurprising harmonically and at the same time unexpected stylistically. Returning next to the B minor chord, we are lulled into a false sense of security, and this is where the bomb explodes: over the lyric "count me out," for one short measure we are presented rapidly with the chord series G, A, F#, and in a startling syncopated rhythmic phrase to boot. The G major and F# major chords violate standard rules of Western harmony and are essentially totally unpredictable and unexpected. Resting on the F#, we suddenly have a feeling that the song could go anywhere. We are harmonically disoriented and confused. But quickly, the song relaxes into the (familiar) dominant chord and proceeds into an absolutely straightforward rock chorus that could not be more predictable and familiar. The chords accompanying the chorus ("and you know its gonna be alright") are, true to the lyrics, the utterly unchallenging I-IV-V that provide the skeleton for thousands of folk, blues, and rock songs, and, almost as if to further emphasize this effect of restored familiarity, a background vocal line of 1950's-style "shoobie-doos" are added to near-comic, or ironical, effect.

Repetition and Familiarity in the Temporal Arts

This song, indisputably popular, provides in a microcosm a nicely compressed instance of how the aesthetic trajectory is achieved in music. There are two primary sources of familiarity, both based on repetition. At the local level, within a song, repetition creates a basic, perceptual expectation of continuation. In the same way in which we rapidly habituate to a continued noise or tone, we unconsciously extract the structure of a repeated musical phrase, and when a subsequent phrase matches that structure exactly or approximately, we gain an immediate feeling of familiarity. The same can happen over longer time spans but still within a piece, as when a theme or motif is repeated in a longer (e.g., symphonic) piece. We can call such within-piece repetition "local repetition." At a broader cultural level, an entire musical community possesses standard song forms and styles, harmonic and metrical structures, and instrumental combinations that a member of that community will recognize when listening to a particular new piece for the first time. Using such culturally contingent knowledge, a piece can be categorized as instantiating a previously familiar form or style. We can call such between-piece repetition, which depends on the listener's previous experience and knowledge, social or cultural repetition.

Thus, in the nonrepresentational sphere of music, the primary tool for creating familiarity is repetition of different sorts. Although we have used a popular Western song to illustrate this idea, these principles apply to a very considerable portion of existing human music of all cultures and times. Local repetition, following some shared metrical or harmonic system, is found in the choice of either 3/4 or 4/4 meters (and their most common variants, 6/8 and 2/4), and the use of a diatonic scale, for almost all Western art music until the twentieth century. A "scale" is a restricted set of pitches (usually between five and ten) from which all of the notes of a piece are constructed; as such, scales appear to be a near-universal feature of human music (Nettl, 2000). Stringed instruments equipped with "drone strings," used in much of the Eastern hemisphere, provide examples of the widespread use of tonal repetition in many non-Western musical cultures. In addition, individual notes or clusters of notes, repeated regularly to give a microlevel repetition, are a common feature of virtually all known music.

An example of repetition taken to an extreme is the piece "Vexations" written but kept secret by the French composer Eric Satie, and first performed in 1963 by John Cage and his colleagues. The piece demands that a short chordal motif be performed 840 times *trés lent*; the first public performance of the piece in 1963 stretched from 6 p.m. until after noon of the following day, with several pianists taking turns playing (the only person to attend the entire performance was reputedly Andy Warhol). Satie considered the piece to represent a kind of "musical furniture," where the repetition was to lead to a dissolution of one's sense of time and change, to be perceived paradoxically as a kind of rest: movement at a standstill. This piece, although chordally complex and unfamiliar, would achieve the necessary familiarity by brute force, and thus takes one of the tools available to the musician to its logical extreme.

Social repetition is also universal in human music (Cross, 2003; Nettl, 2000). Throughout the world, lullabies and other children's songs are sung repeatedly, and this simplest form of social repetition is sought avidly by young listeners (Trehub & Trainor, 1998). In Western classical music, stylistic forms are ubiquitous, from the "Kyrie Eleison" form of the Catholic mass to the four-part form of the classical sonata. The ragas of Indian classical music, though akin in some ways to scales, go beyond local repetition in that they have both an associated "mood" and particular orders of notes that are stylistically normal, as well as a huge wealth of accumulated cultural tradition about the sorts of ornament that are appropriate. Similarly, West African percussion and its many derivatives (Afro-Caribbean forms like rumba, mambo, and salsa, or Afro-Brazilian forms such as afoxé and samba) are built upon complex rhythmic ostinatos (termed "claves" in the Caribbean tradition) that generate a metrically ambiguous rhythmic structure (Amira & Cornelius, 1992; Locke, 1983; Titon, Koetting, McAllester, Reck, & Slobin, 1984; Temperley, 2000). But in addition, certain ostinatos and different specific patterns built upon them take on a specific social significance, either religious, as in the different drum patterns corresponding to different deities in the Santeria music of Cuba or Candomble in Brazil. Thus repetition, at many different levels, seems to provide the basis for familiarity in human music, either universally or nearly so.

It will be immediately clear that these dual types of repetition, though highlighted in music, are by no means unique to it. The repetition of the poplars in the Monet painting also create a local familiarity, and the match of the image both to reality ("I've seen trees like this before") and to an existing style of landscape painting create a social familiarity. Although the latter form is predominant in representational painting, local repetition plays a more dominant role in abstract art, as well as in other visual arts (especially architecture). In dance, repetition again plays a central role in building expectations, while in film the self-referential quoting of earlier films, in terms of photography, set design, costume, dialogue, and such is one of the core creative building blocks of the director and screenwriter.

Returning to Malevich and abstract art, the immediate follow-ups to Malevich's black square involved both types of repetition, and consisted for example of two black squares, or two squares, one red and one black, in a single artwork. The local repetition within the canvas, and the social repetition between these pieces and the Black Suprematist Square that they quote, create familiarity. But how are we to interpret this repetition? Is it a matter of just more of the same, or does this new dual shape contrast the earlier one? We cannot judge, for whichever choice we make, the other remains potentially valid. Again, there is a bistability, with the added resonance of the social repetition within the young style of Russian Suprematism. Again, Wundt may have been a source of inspiration for Malevich, as Wundt's tome presented an analogous figure of two adjacent squares (to be interpreted as two cubes, side by side).

We have focused here on the first stage of the aesthetic trajectory, the establishment of familiarity, because we wish to argue that this is an essential precondition for aesthetic appreciation of any art form. While the routes to familiarity are various, *some* type of familiarity is a requirement of aesthetic engagement. But once familiarity is achieved, there seems to be little hope of cataloging the many ways in which we can be surprised or confused, or in which that surprise and ambiguity can successfully be resolved. Indeed, much of the creative work of the artist lies in the second and third components, and many of the differences between artistic movements lie in the degree to which they remain comfortably familiar versus surprising (or even shocking) to the perceiver. At the avant-garde end of the spectrum, our sense of familiarity may be stretched to the breaking point, while at the more conservative end (typically the more popular, it must be said), our expectations may be only slightly violated and our ability to synthesize and resolve may be only mildly exercised. But whatever the artistic style, a familiarity must exist—even if only, as in cases of self-consciously avant-garde art, in a formal declaration that the object, installation, performance, or event to be viewed is *to be considered* art—before the perceiver can be surprised, and before the crucial integration and resolution of the aesthetic trajectory can be completed.

Summarizing, a broadening of scope is required to understand the dynamic aspects of the aesthetics of music and the temporal arts. This dynamic perspective leads to observations that are also relevant to the static visual arts. Although the spatial repetition of trees in Monet's poplars occurs in a different dimension and sensory modality than the repetition of notes and motifs in music, they both play the same role of stabilizing our percept, fulfilling a low-level cognitive expectation, and creating a feeling of familiarity and comfort. Similarly, the social repetition of forms and styles, which occurs in many different ways and over different time scales, provides a second crucial route to familiarity, albeit one that makes greater demands on the cultural, historical, and other kinds of understanding on the part of the viewer/listener. Just as Malevich's two squares will have less significance to the viewer unfamiliar with abstract art in general and Suprematism in particular, the listener unfamiliar with rock and roll or Ghanaian *agbekor* drumming will find less to grab on to, less that is familiar, in these forms. In the extreme case, he may be wholly unable to grasp the music as familiar in any way, and thus unable even to embark on the aesthetic trajectory.

Thus, although a biological approach to aesthetics should start by considering perceptual and neural processing shared by all humans, we cannot afford to focus solely on these aspects if we hope to understand human aesthetic experience in its full complexity. Bioaesthetics needs further to incorporate some understanding of the social and cultural factors that shape, and in some cases wholly determine, the use of these capacities in the skilled viewer/listener. As a step in this direction, we now turn to a brief exploration of the cultural evolution of art forms and styles, which we suggest can also be more richly understood from the viewpoint we adopt in this chapter.

THE AESTHETIC TRAJECTORY AND CULTURAL CHANGE

Although biology and culture are sometimes positioned as mutually exclusive explanatory factors (the infamous Nature versus Nurture debate), this is an illusory dichotomy that retards or blocks any genuine insight into the complexity of biological explanation. Indeed, it has become increasingly clear to students of animal behavior that the capacity for social learning itself has a strong biological basis, and that there are simple forms of cultural transmission among many different vertebrate species (Avital & Jablonka, 2000; Bonner, 1983; Boyd & Richerson, 1985; Galef, 1992). Further, it has recently become clear that our nearest living cousins, the chimpanzees, have certain foraging and social behaviors that are passed down the generations (McGrew, 2004; Whiten et al., 1999), now known as "chimpanzee cultures." However, most scholars agree that the human capacity for culture goes far beyond these relatively simple examples of social learning, and that this capacity is a uniquely powerful aspect of human biology (Tomasello, 1999). While language is typically and correctly highlighted as an extremely powerful tool for cultural transmission, music and art also have important trans-generational or cultural components. In general, language, music, and other art forms contain both a shared, socially learned component and a creative, individually distinctive component. In attempts to understand any specific utterance or artwork, both of these will play a crucial role. Any attempt to focus exclusively on one or the other (e.g., denying the creative: "language is a rehearsal of prelearned utterances"—or denying the social: "great art is a purely creative act of the individual") does violence to the more complex reality. Similarly, any attempt to apportion the role of each factor with some simple formula ("language/art/music is 40% culture and 60% individuality") is equally misguided. Because of the continuous interaction and feedback between these two factors, both are 100% involved and necessary in culturally transmitted behaviors. Better metaphors are needed.

An Instinct to Learn

An elegant and powerful model of a biologically based cultural capacity has been developed by Peter Marler, one of the most seminal living ethologists and a lifelong student of animal communication. Marler's early work helped to demonstrate the fact that most songbirds (which make up about half of all bird species) *learn* their song: a young bird must hear examples of the song of its species in order to itself produce a normal song (Catchpole, 1973; Marler & Slabbekoorn, 2004). Birds raised in an aviary with other species, but without access to conspecific song, will sing either a completely abnormal song, or (in some cases) will learn the song of another species. Crucially, most birds do not simply mimic the song of adults exactly: in many species, individuals create new, novel songs that are built upon but not identical to the songs they hear as nestlings. There is a creative aspect to birdsong, which ensures that each generation hears slightly different songs from those of the previous generation. Because of this process of song transmission across generations, with slight novelties introduced by creativity or erroneous copying, "dialects" of birdsong develop, such that conspecific birds in different regions sing quite different songs. But just as a human child of Chinese descent can learn perfect English, a young bird exposed to a different dialect than that of its parents will learn the new dialect. Equally crucially, young birds exposed to the song of many different species will unerringly home in on the song of their own species. In a manner that is not yet understood, a bird of a particular species appears to be born with a proclivity for the song "style" of its own species, to which it will attend preferentially. So a bird's propensity to learn is constrained in certain ways: it is not a simple "general purpose system" that will learn anything it hears.

These facts have forced students of birdsong to go beyond simple-minded nature/nurture dichotomies. Marler's model of birdsong acquisition instead gives equal weight to both biological and cultural factors, which are inextricably intertwined in an "instinct to learn" (Marler, 1991). Birds, like human children, are born with a *readiness* to master their species-specific communication system, but they are not born *knowing* this system. Part of this biologically given readiness is a proclivity to attend to certain types of auditory stimuli (conspecific voices) and not others (dog barking, machine noises, etc.). Another component is a set of constraints on what can and cannot be learned: there are limits to the sorts of artificial birdsongs (or artificial languages) that a youngster can absorb. These facts show an obvious parallel with the facts of human language acquisition, and it seems clear that a model of the human cultural capacity as an "instinct to learn" is an important improvement over previous metaphors. This instinct to learn model has recently been put forth explicitly to model the acquisition of human music (Fitch, 2006a; Marler, 2000).

The Cultural "Ratchet" and Stylistic Change

When the aesthetic trajectory is combined with our human cultural instinct to learn from previous generations, a powerful engine for cultural change results. The need for novelty (the middle component of the aesthetic trajectory) ensures that each generation will creatively experiment and discover novel forms of ambiguity and surprise. The dual needs for familiarity and synthesis will keep creativity within bounds sufficient to ensure a certain continuity with the works of the past. Each generation can build upon the aesthetic successes of its forebears, "ratcheting" onward in whatever direction it desires, typically conditioned by the mood and tastes of the day. In all art forms, the "cultural ratchet" operates across generations, with youngsters mastering, and then moving beyond, the forms practiced by their elders. The permanence of many works of visual art (painting, sculpture, architecture, etc.), which may far outlast their creators, makes this process all the more complex, since a learner need not be present at the creation of a piece to see it and learn from it. However, such permanence did not occur for language until the advent of writing, some 5000 years ago, or for music until much later. Western musical notation developed far enough to play this role by about the fifteenth century (Read, 1969). For dance, it is only with the advent of film and video that a similarly permanent and accurate recording system has developed.

A propensity for cultural change and development thus seems to result inevitably from the combination of the aesthetic trajectory with our human tendency to absorb the culture of our youth. In particular, the desire for novelty would seem to ensure gradual change in all but the most stringently policed art forms. At the most conservative extreme, we might place music or art created for use in religious rituals. The continuous performance over many centuries of Gregorian chants provides an example in Western art music. A striking example in non-Western music is provided by various religious music derived from West African (especially Yoruba) cultures and carried to the New World by slaves centuries ago (e.g., Santería in Cuba, Candomblé in Brazil, or voudoun in Haiti; see Amira & Cornelius, 1992). Both comparisons among these long-separated forms, and with present-day Yoruba forms, reveal a remarkable preservation of both style and content over centuries, in hundreds of extremely complex rhythms and songs, without the benefit of any notational or writing system. Because of the essentially conservative social uses to which it is put, religious music or art can form a long-lived source of cultural heritage, passed down with considerable fidelity over many generations, even without the benefit of any external record. Thus, it can influence successive versions of more rapidly changing styles, such as popular music intended only for enjoyment and dancing.

The thirst for newness reaches an extreme in works produced by the avant-garde, but even here, an essential cultural continuity in art forms should be acknowledged. Even the most radical rejection of previous forms and styles is never free of the influence of previous generations. For all its innovations, Cubism still treated traditional subjects (portraits, nudes, still lifes) in a semirepresentational manner. Malevich's "Black Suprematist Square," though proclaimed (and decried) as "the end of art," was still an object made of paint on canvas, hung in a gallery, by an artist who had copied the Impressionists and Cubists (Zhadova, 1982), and thus from a broader viewpoint remained very much in line with tradition. The same is true of musical forms explicitly rejecting contemporary practice. The "grunge" revolution in popular music, peaking in the mid-1990s with the music of Nirvana, was characterized by an explicit rejection of the highly polished studio music then commercially dominant, but was still built unmistakably upon previous tried-and-true musical styles (particularly the rock music of the 1950s and 1960s); grunge used standard musical instruments, was played in music clubs where people danced, and was distributed through traditional music-industry channels. Even the avant-garde is firmly tied to the past (without which, after all, its rebellion is meaningless), and the most novel and creative work reacts to and builds upon earlier works. Finally, last year's newest thing becomes this year's standard and next year's old hat, so some form of cultural change is virtually guaranteed.

Does such cultural change constitute progress? In at least some cases, one can discern directionality in cultural change: a style seems to be heading in some specific direction over multiple generations. From a bioaesthetic perspective, considering such a possibility need not entail accepting any outmoded Hegelian notion of a trend toward perfection (any more than the acceptance that each biological species grows ever-better suited to its environment entails that any species is "more perfect" than another). Progressive change, in a particular aesthetic direction, is not merely a matter of retroactively imposing schematic coherence upon disorderly historical reality, but a testable observation with multiple historical corollaries. A classic example is the increasing verisimilitude that characterized Western painting from the early Renaissance to the late nineteenth century (explored in penetrating detail by Gombrich, 1959). There can be little doubt that a desire for the illusion of reality was a major force for change during this long period, or that successive generations, through the accumulation of technical insight and proficiency, came ever closer to this goal. During this period, it is entirely valid, as Zeki has argued at length, to characterize artists as practicing neuroaestheticians who were exploring the properties of the human perceptual system long before brain scanning was possible (Zeki, 1999). Indeed, contemporary visual neuroscience has made abundant and profitable use of the many visual illusions and technical tricks developed by artists over the centuries. This provides an important reminder that the interchange between art and science is a two-way street. The development of representational painting in post-Renaissance Europe is justly regarded as an apogee of human artistic achievement, and resulted precisely from the accumulation, over time, of innumerable small perceptual and technical insights achieved by many different artists widely separated in space and time. Similar comments could be made about an apparent trend toward understated simplicity in Chinese and Japanese brush painting over multiple generations. When an overarching goal such as realistic representation, or simplicity, drives successive generations, the accumulation of small novelties can clearly result in progress.

Of course, in popular art forms, novelty often becomes an end in itself. It is a truism that each generation, as it ages, tends to see the style of the younger generation as a step downwards, while the younger generation holds its new styles up as a fresh new alternative to previous styles and practices. Who is right? As we emphasized at the beginning of this chapter, we think it is important for the field of bioaesthetics to avoid debating such loaded issues, whether by glorifying or decrying the changes that occur. We can simply accept that change appears to be embedded in the cultural dynamics of art, and try to understand how and why such change occurs. We can also use those things that *do not* change as important clues to the nature of our basic cognitive proclivities and constraints. Thus, the student of art history has an important role to play in bioaesthetics.

Summary

We have now reached the end of the more theoretical portion of this chapter. We argued that the aesthetic experience of a perceiver of any successful piece of art can be characterized as an "aesthetic trajectory," consisting at a minimum of three phases of familiarity, novelty, and synthesis. Although the unfolding of such a trajectory is most obvious in the temporal art forms such as music, we have argued that it applies equally well to the cognitive experience of the viewer of static art forms such as painting. Repetition, in several forms, plays a crucial role in the establishment of a feeling of familiarity. At one, local, extreme, repetition may be purely perceptual (the immediate repetition of a visual form, or a repeated sonic motif). In addition, there is typically a repetition of styles and forms within an artistic community, which we have termed social repetition. Other, intermediate levels of repetition are also possible (e.g., the theme and variations of a symphonic piece, or an artist revisiting a theme throughout his or her oeuvre), and in general a single piece may instantiate all of these different forms of repetition. The thirst for novelty, combined with our human proclivity to absorb the culture of our youth (our instinct to learn), leads to a continual change in artistic styles, sometimes in particular directions that can be considered progressive, and sometimes simply in the direction of novelty. But one generation's novelty is the next generation's standard to be surpassed, so cultural change is assured unless countered by a powerful opposing force.

In the next part of this chapter, we will provide an illustration of how these issues can be explored empirically by considering a detailed example: the development of jazz improvisation. Our empirical data will come from the study of music notation, which we argue provides a critical resource for understanding both the aesthetic trajectory in general, and cultural development in particular. Thus, we start with a general consideration of music notation as a tool for research in bioaesthetics.

NOTATION: A USEFUL FRAMEWORK FOR AESTHETIC ANALYSIS

Notational systems, designed to be an *aide-mémoire*, are probably very old: some of the oldest "symbolic" objects have been interpreted as notational. Perhaps the oldest human artifact with some potential abstract or symbolic value is a piece of carved ochre discovered in Blombos Cave, in South Africa (Henshilwood et al.,

2002) dated to about 70,000 years ago. Although earlier marks on bone have been discovered (e.g., at Kozarnika Cave, in Bulgaria, dated to at least 1.2 million years ago), the Blombos ochre is the first to have a clear pattern that could not be a product of butchery, sharpening, or other utilitarian purposes. Abundant evidence for such nonrepresentational but nonutilitarian markings does not appear until far later in the archaeological record, mostly in Europe, by about 30,000 years ago (Marshack, 1976). Of course, interpretation of such markings is something of a Rorschach test for archaeologists, and many uses for these early engraved objects have been envisioned, from calendars or kill counters to early abstract art: "marks for marks' sake." What these finds indicate clearly is that humans have been purposely creating marks for at least 30 millennia, and probably much longer. By the time for which we can unambiguously determine the usage of such marking systems (with the advent of interpretable cuneiform writing in Mesopotamia), marks were used for counting and arithmetic, as records of language, and for music notation (Kilmer & Tinney, 1996; West, 1994). Musical notational systems have subsequently and independently developed in many cultures (e.g., the sargam system of Indian classical music). The current Western system, developed in Europe in the Middle Ages, is now in worldwide use and serves as a lingua franca for the representation of an immense variety of different music, from simple folk tunes to the most complex modern symphonic works.

It is an interesting fact that notation systems of this sort have not (successfully) developed for the visual arts or dance. In the case of drawing and painting, the work itself can be seen as a kind of notation: the marks are a direct record of the actions of the artist. Although brushstrokes or pencil marks are not ordered in time, they remain as indelible representations of the artist's movements in space, and we can get some clues to the relative order in which they were applied by examining overlap and other clues (especially with modern techniques such as x-ray, mass spectrometry, and the like). A skilled artist, familiar with the techniques of the period in question, can thus reconstruct a fairly accurate mental model of what the artist did, and when, simply by examining the finished work. Some abstract art, such as the paintings of Jackson Pollock, fairly cry out to be interpreted in terms of the movements of the artist, and thus might be interpreted as "scores" in a more literal sense.

In the case of dance, the situation is more complex, for there have been several attempts to create accurate dance notation systems, none of which have been particularly successful. The most widespread of these is Labanotation (Hutchinson, 1961), which has achieved some currency and is mastered by many dance students (similar notation systems apparently exist for Indian classical dance). Nonetheless, a tradition analogous to that in music has not developed. Choreographers seldom create pieces notated in Labanotation that are then performed, from these scores, by dancers; beginning dancers do not learn their steps from dance notation. Today, film and video provide lasting records of dance pieces, but these are direct representations of the performance, rather than codified abstractions of it. Given the ease of film and video recording and manipulation, it seems unlikely that such a dance-notation culture will develop. Nonetheless, dance-notation systems exist, and a set of potential experimental subjects can read and interpret them. Thus, although we will not discuss dance further here, most of our comments concerning music notation and its value for empirical investigations of aesthetics are probably applicable *mutatis mutandis* to Labanotation or similar systems as well.

Music Notation and the Aesthetic Trajectory

At an abstract level, the notated score for a musical piece represents a mapping between marks laid out spatially on a page and musical events (notes, phrases, metric structures, etc.) unfolding in time. For a performer, these musical structures have a corresponding motor component, so a score also can be transformed into a series of actions. In either case, a spatial dimension in the visual domain is mapped onto the flow of time in the other dimension. Like the relation between speech and writing, the relation between music and a score is a bidirectional mapping between space and time. Thus, a notated score allows us to specify moments or durations of time quite precisely. This makes notation a potentially important tool in studying the dynamics of the aesthetic trajectory.

An essential point is that music notation is an abstraction. A score represents not only individual notes, but their *relationships* to one another within some initial harmonic and metrical context, as well as to an ongoing gestalt conception of a changing location in harmonic and rhythmic space. Drastic or subtle changes in this gestalt can be notated explicitly on a local level (e.g., with accidentals, notes from outside the key that are to be played within a given measure) or at the level of the piece (e.g., with changes in key or time signature). The composer can be very specific (e.g., denoting each specific note to be played, and even which fingers to use in playing it), or she can provide a much broader and more flexible sense of what is expected of the performer (e.g., with the chord spelling used in jazz; see below). But because music notation provides an abstract representation of a piece, it provides explicit information of various types that are absent or only implicit in an audio recording of a piece, or in a computer-based notational system like MIDI (which represents each note as an isolated event; see Dannenberg, 1993). Thus, we suggest that music notation provides an abstract "inside view" of a composer's intentions and a performer's actions, and can provide a useful framework for empirical inquiry.

Western musical notation, though far from perfect, provides a widely accessible and well-codified symbolic means of representing the pitch and timing of each note of a musical piece, along with additional information about harmony, rhythmic "feel," and interpretive clues to more subtle aspects of performance including dynamics, tempo, and timbre. The system is accurate and perceptually efficient enough to allow a skilled musician who has never heard a piece to re-create it "on the fly," "sight reading" it in real time. Many trained Western musicians are so skilled at interpreting music notation that this process is automatic and seems almost effortless. Nonetheless, many difficulties dogged the cultural evolution of this system over several centuries, and music notation poses serious difficulties for the reader not trained in the system. Because we do not assume that our readers all are familiar with music notation, we will start with a discussion of another Beatles piece that will be familiar to many readers, "Here, There and Everywhere" (Figure 7),

Figure 7. Score for beginning of "Here There and Everywhere."
(© Illustration by E. Nicolas.)

giving a brief introduction to the structure of a musically notated piece and focusing on harmonic aspects of notation. We will then illustrate the value of this system for representing the stages in the development of the aesthetic trajectory.

Basic Concepts in Western Music Notation

A musical score is essentially a text that is read horizontally, like Latin script, from the upper left to lower right of the page. A set of five parallel horizontal lines, called a *staff*, spans the width of each page, and is divided by thick vertical bars into *measures* (also termed "bars"). The *clef*, the symbol found at the very beginning of each staff, specifies that a particular location on the staff is to be interpreted as a given note, and all other notes are relative to this one. The clef in this piece, shaped somewhat like an upright cello, is called the G or treble clef, because the spirals circle the line for the note G. At the beginning of a piece, we generally find several important indications about its overall structure. In addition to the name of the piece and its composer, we find a *key signature* that specifies the *harmonic* structure of the piece and a *time signature* that indicates its *rhythmic* structure. The key signature is found just to the right of the clef symbol (e.g., the three # marks, *sharp signs*, at the beginning of "Revolution," denoting the key of A, or the single #, meaning G major, at the beginning of "Here . . ."). These marks specify which notes, if any, are to be raised or lowered from their "standard" pitches. The standard pitches correspond to the white keys of the piano keyboard, and each of the black keys corresponds to a *sharp* or a *flat* note: a raising or lowering by a half-step of one of the standard pitches. A key contains seven notes, which are considered, in traditional Western terms, to be normal or standard members of the key. These seven notes are the *diatonic* notes of the key (and an exclusive use of these notes leads, as discussed below, to "pure" diatonic harmony). Because each key contains a different set of sharps or flats, the composer specifies the "black-key" notes, the sharps or flats present in a given key, all at once, at the beginning of the piece, using the key signature. This says to the reader: "Always, for this piece, interpret a note written at this location on the staff as sharp, or flat (as the case may be), unless otherwise instructed." In a piece that uses entirely the standard, white-key pitches, and is thus in the key of C, there are no sharps or flats, and the key signature is null (blank).

Because the key signature and time signature indicate the "default settings" for a piece, they constitute a set of default rules for interpretation of the rest of the score. These can be thought of as a form of musical "grammar" (Bernstein, 1981; Sloboda, 1985; Sundberg & Lindblom, 1976). Any deviations from these defaults are specified using additional symbols. Thus, any note preceded by an accidental mark is *de facto* a "deviant" in a Western harmonic sense (though as we shall see below, what counts as "deviant" varies considerably from style to style). Such explicit indications of deviance can provide a clear indication of expectancy violation or harmonic tension in a piece. This is one very simple and direct example of the value of musical notation in explicitly locating crucial aesthetic moments in a score and the corresponding musical performance.

Accidentals and Modulation: Harmonic Tension and Resolution

"Here, There and Everywhere" provides a clear example of the generation of considerable harmonic tension. The first section of this piece, (here called the "A section" and indicated by the boxed letter A), is entirely diatonic in the home key of G. Thus, the sequence of chords (indicated by the letter symbols) conform to pure diatonic harmony, building a cadence which is, moreover, the sequence of diatonic chords in their most familiar scale order—I, ii, iii, IV. However, the entry into the B section is presaged by the appearance of an accidental note (the B♭ on the word "want") and a chord (F7) which is non-diatonic, and quite surprising as a result. Suddenly, with little preparation, we have entered a new and rather distant key: the key of B♭. Such a change of key is termed *modulation*, and is one of the primary sources of harmonic surprise and tension in Western music. The very appearance of an accidental symbol here is a clear indication of an increase in tension. And this is where the song gets interesting and challenges the listener.

The piece momentarily sits comfortably in this new key, going through another very ordinary set of chord changes for just long enough to assure us that this *is* the new key, before heading back to the old key of G (via a "pivot chord," D7) and repeating the harmony and melody from the beginning of the piece (indicated by the Italian phrase "da capo," "from the head," abbreviated DC as in "DC al Coda" here). Thus, we see in this fragment of notation the symbolic outline of the aesthetic trajectory. A key signature, and the initial measures, creates the necessary feeling of familiarity. A modulation, indicated by the appearance of any accidental and surprising chord, creates a tension, which is then resolved by a return to the original key.

Even more rarefied examples of this "chord oscillation" form of harmonic tension and release can be found in many Nirvana songs (and in the chord progressions of many songs in the pop genres they have influenced). In the simplest form, an entire song section may contain just two chords: the first sets the expectation of a key signature, and the second breaks this expectation (examples include the A sections of "Something in the Way" and "About a Girl" and many others). In a way then, grunge harmony is a logical extension and purification of a harmonic "trick" for creating and resolving tension that was not uncommon in prior popular music (including many Beatles songs, or in Cole Porter songs from a previous period). What is striking about this grunge approach, to an ear trained in traditional harmony, is that it makes no concession to one's ordinary expectation that a modulation will entail a number of chords in both keys. The opening chord of Porter's "Night and Day" and the surprising modulation that introduces its second section are separated by 32 mellifluous bars, whereas many Nirvana songs make the same surprising intervallic move from one chord to the next. In the grunge harmonic strategy, and in an increasingly familiar style of rock songwriting that makes use of it, two keys are simply juxtaposed, harmonic tension and relaxation are distilled to their most basic essence, and the rest is left as an exercise to the listener.

We have given these examples of modulation from the popular music of the late twentieth century for two reasons. The first is that these pieces are undeniably popular (in the literal sense), selling millions of copies, and their appeal has spread far beyond the confines of the West, winning many listeners without the inducements of advertising. For some reason, these pieces have had a long-lasting and worldwide appeal to humans, and thus seem good candidates for aesthetic study of the sort we urge in this chapter. The second and perhaps more interesting reason to focus on pop music is that neither Lennon and McCartney (the composers of most Beatles songs), nor Kurt Cobain (who composed most Nirvana songs) were schooled in Western harmony, nor could they read or write music. These songs were created, like most human music, "by ear" and passed on via a folk tradition of direct performance and hearing (often involving electronic reproduction but no less "folk," in our intended sense, for that), without the benefit of any notational system. Nonetheless, the pieces can be readily notated, and the notation does reflect crucial aspects of the familiarity/tension/resolution trajectory under discussion. It seems clear then that Western notation can extend far beyond its original domain of European religious and art music and serve as a practical symbolic framework for analyzing and discussing this trajectory.

We hope that these examples illustrate the basic point of this section: music notation provides a view into the abstract cognitive structure of a piece, a view corresponding to at least some of the aesthetic properties of the piece. A more detailed consideration of the many other musical complexities that can be represented and studied in this fashion is beyond the scope of this chapter, to say nothing of the many inadequacies of standard musical notation, particularly in the rhythmic domain. Happily, such inadequacies have led many composers to devise notational innovations, ensuring that notation is always changing to fit the demands of new music, which is itself evolving in the cultural sense (Gaare, 1997). The reader interested in learning more about contemporary music notation will find an excellent brief introduction in Cooper (1982) and an encyclopedic, authoritative explication in Read (1969). For our purposes, the previous examples are enough to illustrate how the abstract representation of a musical piece provided by its notation can be used to specify quite precisely the times at which various sorts of tension and resolution occur. This in turn opens doors to various experimental approaches to exploration of the aesthetic trajectory at a cognitive and neural level (considered in the section entitled "Conclusion"). We now discuss the utility of notation in exploring our second question, that of the cultural evolution of musical styles, by considering a particular evolving aspect of musical notation in detail: the harmonic notation used in jazz.

The Cultural Evolution of Jazz Notation: An Illustrative Example

We will now illustrate the value of notational systems in exploring cultural issues in aesthetics by considering the historical development of jazz notation. From its earliest beginnings in the streets of New Orleans, jazz music was steeped in the Western musical tradition, and particularly the complex harmonies and melodic lines that are distinctive of this tradition. However, the deeper roots of jazz in the earlier music of African Americans bears unmistakable traces of its West African musical origins, particularly in its use of rhythm and its focus on improvisation. Jazz thus represents a kind of fusion of two independent cultural streams, African and European, and integrates the complex rhythmic and improvisational elements of the former with the complex harmonic and melodic structures of the latter (Cooke, 1998; Dale, 2004; King, 1997). From the very beginning, jazz was an improvisational form, and this remains one of its most distinctive differences from Western "classical" music as performed today. Although Bach or Mozart themselves were consummate improvisers, and Baroque/Classical musical traditions sometimes had a "cadenza" section for the soloist to improvise in, this tradition has been all but lost in contemporary practice, where written notes are "the law" and any deviation simply a mistake. In contrast, the jazz soloist is expected to "play around" with an established melody in a way that is simply forbidden in contemporary performance of a Bach or Beethoven piece. An accomplished jazz performer is expected to do so creatively, generating a new and different solo every time he or she plays a piece. Nor is improvisation limited to the soloist: in general, the other members of the jazz ensemble are also improvising more or less continuously on a more subtle rhythmic and harmonic level. For a beginner in this aspect of jazz, a nice introduction is provided by King (1997).

In this section, we will explore the development of jazz notation to illustrate how this distinctive improvisational aspect of a well-known musical tradition is reflected in (and documented by) changes in its notation. The composer of a jazz piece does not, and cannot, write out every note of the piece for each instrument, because music written and played exactly this way would cease to be jazz—it would lose one of the most distinctive and appreciated characteristic of the jazz style. This is not due to any intrinsic shortcoming of Western notation, nor even to the level of difficulty of jazz (indeed some high-school jazz bands play from complete classical-music-style scores, exactly as written). Instead, it is due to a pressure from within the style of performance: the value placed on performers' impromptu creativity. Thus, the jazz score has developed to be less like a precise protocol for performance and more like a recipe for concocting an infinite number of variants of a piece. Each piece has a musical "grammar," a set of harmonic and rhythmic ideas that specifies a range of possible expressions and excludes many others. A jazz score embodies the inimitable creative role of the performer. Of course, a classical score also leaves plenty of room for the performer's creativity and emotional nuance, and in general, no two performances of a piece will be exactly the same in any musical idiom. But while this room for creativity is in classical music left implicit, an extranotational matter for conductors' and players' discretion, in jazz notation it is made explicit, and substantive creativity is expected of the performer. Thus, an important virtue of jazz (and of other improvisatory music) is that it elides the traditional creator/performer dichotomy, and thus provides one empirical route for the exploration of the neural bases of creativity in performers who, in improvising, compose spontaneously for a living.

Jazz music developed in the southern United States in the 1900s (Cooke, 1998). Building on earlier styles like ragtime and particularly the blues, it used mostly standard European instruments in a distinctively African American way, and thus could be written in rough form relatively easily using standard Western notation (Russo, 1961). (We leave aside here rhythmic issues such as "swing," which still defy exact notation.) The jazz ensemble will typically include a rhythm section, which also expresses the harmony (typically a keyboard or stringed instrument such as guitar or banjo, a bass, and often some drums or percussion) along with one or more horns, which act as solo instruments. In larger jazz "orchestras," horns compose sections that may trade roles with instruments from the rhythm section, which also play solos. A vocalist may or may not be present. The unpredictable nature of the instruments available had a strong effect on jazz notation early on: a system was needed that was adaptable to whatever instruments happened to be present. This led to the development of chord notation that remains at the core of jazz notation (and indeed has spread to most popular music today). The system of interpretation underlying jazz-chord symbols constitutes a relatively simple grammar—a set of explicit rules for moving from chord notation to sets of notes and back.

Chord notation is, in essence, a simple idea (although some of the rarer examples can be complex and difficult). A chord is a set of three or more notes, typically sounded simultaneously, that plays a harmonic role in a musical composition. Jazz-chord notation allows the composer or arranger to denote virtually any imaginable chord with a sequence of letters, numbers, and a few additional symbols. The most important component of a chord's name is termed its "root" (a letter between A and G, which may include sharps or flats). The most basic unadorned chord is considered to be a major triad based on this root (the three-note complex made up of root, third, and fifth). Thus, a C chord is the set of three notes {C, E, G}. A large set of more complex chords is built upon this basic armature by either modifying one or more of these notes, or adding additional "coloring" notes. For example, a minor chord (written with "m," "min," or "-" after the chord's letter name) is an instruction to flat, or lower by half a step, the third. Thus "Cm" indicates the triad C, E♭ and G. A diminished chord flats both the third and fifth, and thus "Cdim" indicates {C, E♭, G♭}. This basic level of jazz-chord notation simply borrows the terms for chords, and the basic use of the diatonic scale, from classical music, with no significant change. Additional coloring notes are denoted in ascending order from the root. The most common example is the "7," which always refers to the flatted or "dominant" seventh in jazz (rather than the "major" 7, which is standard in the diatonic scale, in jazz written "maj7"). (This already reflects an important difference between jazz and classical practice, since a classically trained musician would see the diatonic "major" seventh as the "default" 7.) The dominant 7 of C is B♭, so the chord written C7 would be {C, E, G, B♭}. The symbol "Cm7" combines the minor third with the dominant seventh to yield the notes {C, E♭, G, B♭}. These simple examples illustrate the basic principles underlying jazz-chord notation. However, there are far more complex notational devices (e.g. writing "9" indicates that *both* the dominant seventh and the ninth, or second degree from the root, should be added). The protocol for writing and interpreting these more complex aspects of jazz-chord notation is sketched in Table 1.

Of particular interest are various notational devices that specify a choice to be made by the performer. For example, when a chord is called a "13" (e.g., A13), the spelling of the chord for the use of the rhythm section (i.e., the harmonic component of the accompaniment) specifies the presence not only of the "13" note, the sixth scale degree from the root, but also of the dominant seventh and the major third; if however the seventh is to be avoided, or the *natural* seventh used as an improvising option, the chord will be called a "6" instead. But a convention has evolved that further enriches the meaning for the jazz soloist of the symbol 13: it encourages the use, in constructing improvised melodic ideas for the duration of the chord, of the "tension notes" that lie *between* the mandatory flat 7 and the 13. Furthermore, a "flat 13" denotation conveys an implicit instruction to the modern soloist to make use of a more complex tonal palette than would be intended by a "sharp 5" denotation, although the specified chord spelling notes are identical. To take another example, sophisticated jazz charts make use of the term "altered chord," rendered "alt," to indicate for the soloist a kind of scale from which notes may be played for that chord's duration, including but not limited to both the raised and the lowered 9ths, encouraging a densely chromatic sound via the juxtaposition of both the natural and the flatted thirds in proximity with the natural and the flatted seconds. Not only might further instances be cited: the rate of cultural evolution is rapid enough in improvised music such that new instances are continually in the process of being coined, and new generations of music notators update chord symbols, with their implicit stylistic instructions, as they come into common use, as we will discuss further.

Table 1. "Chord Spelling": Principles of Jazz Harmonic Notation

Symbol	Alternates	Spoken	Signifies to:
min	m, -	minor	flat the third[a]
B♭5	-5	flat five	flat the fifth
7	B♭7	seven	add dominant (flat) seven[b]
maj7	Δ	major seventh	add diatonic seven
dim	°	diminished	flat third, flat five
dim7	°7	diminished seventh	", ", add doubly flatted seven
m7b5	ø	half-diminished	flat third, flat five, dom. seven
aug, +5	+, #5	augmented	sharp five
sus 4	sus	"sus 4," "suspended 4"	omit third, add fourth
6		sixth	add sixth[c]
9		nine	add dom 7 *and* nine (second)
11		eleven	", and eleven (fourth)
13		thirteen	", and thirteen (sixth)

[a]In jazz, "minor" always and only refers to the third. Intervals that are termed "minor" in classical terminology are typically called "flat" in jazz (e.g., the classical "minor sixth" is termed "flat sixth," enabling jazz musicians readily to specify minor *or* major chords containing dominant *or* natural sevenths, as in "C-/maj7," the second chord in "My Funny Valentine": root, flat 3rd, optional 5th, natural 7th).

[b]The default seventh interval in jazz is the non-diatonic flattened seven, termed the "dominant" seven.

[c]The term "flat six" is avoided: this would be called a "sharp five" or augmented.

There are two relevant points here. The first is that the practice of jazz (e.g., the habitual use of the flatted 7) has had an influence on the notation system, such that "typical" chords tend to have shorter symbolic representations than chords that are less frequently encountered. Thus, the notational system reflects actual practice, and the study of this notational system can provide insights into the conception of musical practice that lies behind it. Second, and crucially, these chord symbols leave a huge amount of flexibility to the ensemble about how the notes required will be played. All of the notes might be played by a single instrument (such as the guitar or piano), or several might be played by the bass and the remainder on the banjo. The specific register in which the notes are played is left up to the performers, which implies a considerable variety of possible realizations of any particular chord, and thus a vast number of possible versions of an entire song. Thus, the jazz composer specifies not a specific single instantiation of a piece, but a whole open-ended set of possible instantiations.

As a concrete example, let us consider two different versions of Cole Porter's "Just One of Those Things," one of many Porter tunes that has become a jazz standard (Figure 8). The figure shows the beginning of an old version presumably

Figure 8. "Just One of Those Things."
(© Illustration by W. Tecumseh Fitch and E. Nicolas.)

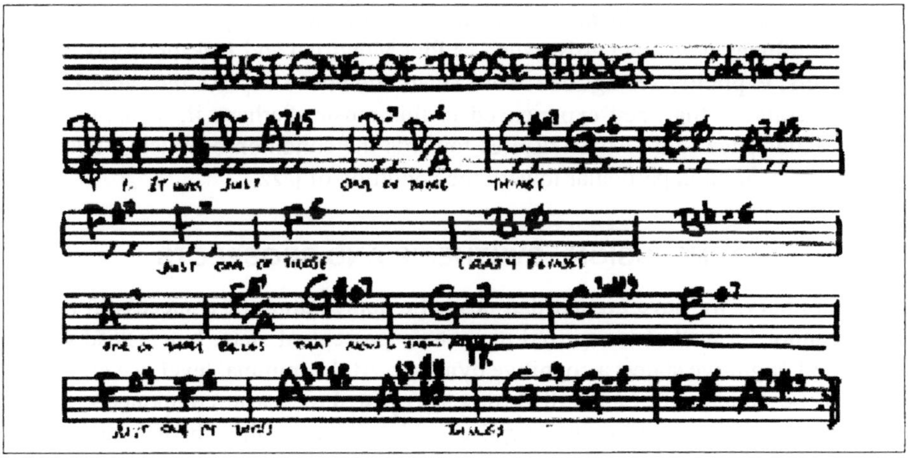

Figure 8. (Cont'd.)

quite close to that written by Porter himself, and a contemporary jazz "chart" that compresses the entire song onto a single page. There are numerous differences, the most conspicuous being the addition of many chords, and the substitution of some chords with their more "jazzy" counterparts. The actual Broadway-style introduction to the piece is omitted from the jazz chart (this is almost always the case, and indeed with few exceptions, one rarely hears such introductions performed in jazz standards). The lyrics are not provided, but the melody is written out as it would typically be played by one of the instruments of a jazz ensemble at the beginning of the piece. It is this melody, plus a broad harmonic structure, that thus binds these two versions together, so that we can call them "the same piece"—but virtually everything else has changed.

Part of the ongoing vitality of jazz resides in this generativity. Although jazz has its canon of standards, just like classical music, the jazz listener can expect a given standard to sound different every time they hear it performed (or, for recorded music, by every ensemble), and would be disappointed to hear an ensemble perform a note-for-note replica of another ensemble's performance. Such lack of improvisation would be quite out of keeping with the jazz aesthetic, which thus imposes quite daunting demands on the jazz performer, considerably beyond what is required of a classical performer on the same instrument. These differences in style have led to changes in notational practice, which are thus tangible, historical records of a cultural evolution that is still in progress today.

It would be remiss to end without mentioning the close links between jazz and "experimental" music with other artistic styles in the twentieth century. On one hand, the scores of composers like John Cage, and many of his followers in the Fluxus movement, are themselves thought of as works of visual art ("suitable for framing"). Some are in fact impossible to perform, and the standard notion of a score as instructions for performance is undermined. In the other direction, jazz has influenced many artists in other modalities, from the Beat poets to avant-garde cinema; influential abstract artists such as Piet Mondrian and Jackson Pollock were jazz lovers, explicitly seeing their work as an attempt to express the same kind of vital generativity that they experienced in this music. Perhaps if, as art historian Walter Pater once said "All art aspires towards the condition of music," twentieth century art aspired in particular toward the condition of jazz.

CONCLUSION: SYNTHESIS AND PROSPECTS

In summary, we have argued that aesthetic appreciation of a successful artistic work cannot be well characterized as a static perceptual state, but instead entails a series of cognitive states: a cognitive dynamic. At the minimal level, we argue that this can be condensed, or distilled, down to just three basic components, which we have glossed as familiarity, surprise, and resolution, though of course much more complex cognitive dynamics can be built on this basis. We have dubbed the form of mental movement consisting of combinations of these states "the aesthetic trajectory," and have suggested that it characterizes an important element of aesthetic appreciation of *any* artwork, regardless of modality, although we have only provided illustrative examples from painting and music. The long tradition in literary studies, derived from Aristotle's *Poetics*, suggesting a three-stage structure for successful narrative—exposition or "rising action," conflict and "climax," and denouement or "falling action"—that pleasingly corresponds to our model of the aesthetic trajectory, suggesting that a study of dramatic and literary art from a cognitive or bioaesthetic perspective may reveal links between universal properties of storytelling and underlying cognitive processes.

We emphasize that the capacity for aesthetic enjoyment is something any normal human is capable of (not just an educated 'aesthetic elite'), and that a characterization and understanding of this general capacity, both as it exists in any normal adult, and how it develops during infancy and childhood, should be a basic research topic for scholars interested in developing a biological approach to aesthetics.

Acknowledging the existence of a biologically based aesthetic capacity, common to all humans, by no means forces one to exclude or ignore the profound cultural component of human artistic endeavor—quite the contrary. As we see it, the combination of the basic human propensity for culture (our instinct to learn) *combines* with the aesthetic trajectory to mandate a process of continual cultural change. The desire for familiarity ensures a certain degree of cultural continuity, while the aesthetic need for novelty, surprise, and ambiguity acts as an engine for change. Indeed, just as we have characterized the basic appreciation of art as a dynamic process, it seems that a continually changing *cultural* notion of art is an almost unavoidable consequence of some basic facts about our species. Thus, we suggest that a richer biological understanding of the basic human aesthetic capacity could shed important light on the process of cultural change as studied by art historians. Just as historical change in languages (e.g., the development of Latin into Italian or French) can shed light on the human capacity for language, the study of change in artistic cultures (whether Pre-Columbian pottery or painting in Renaissance Europe) may shed light on more basic commonalities in human aesthetic appreciation. Thus, an interest in culture or the cultural development of artistic styles is in no sense opposed to or incompatible with a biological approach to aesthetics: both topics are equally important, indeed inextricably intertwined, and the study of culture should be seen as an essential component of a biological approach to aesthetics. This dynamic approach to aesthetic appreciation opens numerous doors for empirical investigation. In the next section, we will briefly sketch some of these.

Empirical Approaches to Bioaesthetics

At the most fundamental level, the cognitive dynamic of the aesthetic trajectory, like all cognitive activity, must have its basis in brain function. A first stab at understanding this basis could use standard brain-imaging techniques to attempt to extract the "neural signature" of the stages of the aesthetic trajectory by examining brain activity in human subjects contemplating artistic works. It is important to note that contemporary cognitive neuroscientists have moved beyond the over-simplified "neophrenology" that characterized some early brain-imaging studies, and we would be extremely surprised if future studies turned up an "aesthetic appreciation" area of the brain (or even a brain area corresponding to the "novelty" or "resolution" stages of the aesthetic trajectory). Far more likely is the possibility that certain types of coherence and incoherence among multiple brain regions, and within the neurons of a particular region, are the crucial aspects of neural activity underlying aesthetic appreciation. Given that most of the neurons underlying visual versus auditory processing are located in different brain regions, we should expect that a more abstract conceptual approach will be necessary to identify and isolate any aesthetic commonalities in the perception of music and painting. In particular, contemporary techniques such as MEG (magneto-encephalography), which combines good spatial accuracy with excellent temporal accuracy, seem promising in this regard.

Emotional Responses to Music: Empirical Techniques

To get a sense of the promise of the tools currently available, consider the recent explosion of research on the cognitive neuroscience of music (Peretz & Zatorre, 2003). This has become one of the fastest-growing areas in cognitive neuroscience and is already the topic of several book-length reviews. Although aesthetic experience of music as we have discussed it here is rarely mentioned explicitly, much of the work discussing emotion in music is closely related to our focus in this chapter (for reviews, see Juslin & Sloboda; 2001, Trainor & Schmidt, 2003). The most basic techniques for examining this are subject self-report (Sloboda, 1991) and physiological measures (heart rate, respiration, etc.), and by both of these measures music can induce powerful emotional responses (Krumhansl, 1997; Nyklicek, Thayer, & Van Doornen, 1997). Sloboda found, in particular, that expectancy violations (the second stage of our aesthetic trajectory) were the regions of a musical piece where "shivers" were most typically, and reliably, induced in music listeners. This ability of music to generate intensely pleasurable "thrills" or shivers has been further explored in brain-imaging studies (e.g., Blood & Zatorre, 2001). In this PET study of cerebral blood flow, the brain regions whose activation correlated with physiological and subjective measures of thrills were the same as those involved with emotion in other, nonmusical contexts. Using EEG measures of alpha-band power in babies listening to music, Trainor and Schmidt (2003) showed that this capacity to respond emotionally to music develops early in life, and while not present at three months, is already well developed by one year of age. Similar measures applied to emotionally arousing pictures and music reveal a synergistic interaction between the two domains (Baumgartner, Esslen, & Jäncke, 2006). These data, considered together, should remove any doubt that an individual's emotional reactions to a piece of music are powerful and measurable using a variety of techniques; the data are consistent with our proposal that the second stage of surprise (expectancy violation) is a crucial part of the emotional and aesthetic experience of a musical piece.

Well-tested techniques are also available to explore more basic perceptual aspects of expectancy violation, including unconscious (automatic or "preattentive") aspects of perceptual processing. A nice example is the MMN (mismatch negativity), typically studied using MEG techniques. This is a rapid and automatic neural response, centered in or near the auditory cortex, to "oddball" or deviant stimuli. When a series of stimuli of a particular type (e.g., notes of a particular frequency) are played repeatedly, an occasional deviant from this type (a note at a different frequency) will elicit an MMN. This effect is not dependent on the subject's attention, and MMNs will still appear if the subject is playing video games, reading, or even in a coma (Tervaniemi, 2003). Thus, the MMN is the neural signature of a low-level, automatic, and typically unconscious process. Although MMNs are classically used to study relatively basic aspects of audition, such as pitch or timbre (Tervaniemi, Winkler, & Näätänen, 1997), the same techniques have also been applied to musical processing at a far higher level by (Koelsch, Gunter, Friederici, & Schröger, 2000). These researchers played series' of chords, with sets of five chords arranged in a cadence that set up a harmonic expectancy, and then typically resolved to the expected tonic. Cadences that violated standard harmonic rules generated an EEG signal, strongest in the right hemisphere and thus labeled the ERAN (early right anterior negativity), similar to that elicited in the left hemisphere by linguistic violations of syntax. Again, these effects can be elicited preattentively. Furthermore, an ERAN is observed to harmonic violations even in listeners with no musical training, demonstrating that this is not an effect of education associated with music theory or learning an instrument, but instead a more basic and universal aspect of the human musical capacity.

These results, together with those from many similar studies (Peretz & Zatorre, 2003), clearly illustrate the power of the suite of noninvasive tools now available for investigating the neural basis of the aesthetic response to music, at multiple levels of analysis. In most cases, the data analysis depends on the fact that music unfolds temporally, and that specific points in a score can easily be isolated as the point at which tension increases or a resolution occurs. This makes for a reassuring convergence of experimental results and theory, since these temporal locations of moments of tension and relaxation play a prominent role in modern musicology (e.g., Lerdahl, 2001; Lerdahl & Jackendoff, 1983). The score has become an important empirical tool: we essentially are searching for correlations between the cycles of tension and resolution, as manifested in the score, with events in the neural data elicited by its performance.

However, the reliance in these musicological studies on the temporal specificity of the aesthetic response poses a serious problem for attempts to apply the same principles to the perception of static visual art like painting or sculpture. For how are we to know, as experimenters, precisely when the "aha" moments corresponding to surprise or recognition of ambiguity, or to a resolution or synthesis of that ambiguity, occurs in the visual arts? The very fact that the mental movement associated with a viewer's aesthetic experience is internally generated, a creative act on the part of the viewer, might seem to pose insurmountable problems for empirical study. Furthermore, the emotional reactions subjects show to visual stimuli (e.g., faces with various expressions) and music are not necessarily identical at any level, even in terms of raw physiological reaction, much less associated brain regions (Trainor & Schmidt, 2003). There is no assurance, then, that we can simply expect auditory reactions (such as the MMN or the ERAN) to serve as valid indicators of aesthetic reactions to visual art.

Empirical Investigations of the Aesthetic Trajectory in Visual Art

We see two potential ways, which are not mutually exclusive, around these problems. The first is to use some form of self-report, in which the viewer indicates (e.g., via a button press, or a verbal "aha") when they notice some surprising or confusing aspect of the piece they are viewing. The second approach is to use modern eye-tracking equipment, at least initially in combination with self-report, so that eye movements themselves become the index of surprise or ambiguity. Particularly with carefully chosen or generated artistic stimuli that have relatively well-defined "surprising" components (e.g., a work by René Magritte or M. C. Escher that has a particularly surprising region in the image that typically takes a viewer some time to fixate on visually and notice), such a combined approach could be used to identify eye movements to the region of interest, the electronic "signatures" of surprise (like the MMN previously discussed in the auditory domain), and the brain regions with which these are associated. Once measures of this sort were isolated and validated, they could become powerful tools for exploring the aesthetic appreciation of a more general set of artworks, where the elements of surprise and resolution are more subtle, multifaceted, or various. Exploration of the aesthetic experience in a viewer of a piece of visual art, using a combination of eye movements with brain imaging or EEG, thus may provide a promising route by which to explore the issues raised in the current chapter. There is no apparent barrier to applying to the visual arts techniques already successfully developed in neuromusicological research.

Another very promising route to bridging the gaps between different aesthetic modalities is to use video, which has both temporal *and* visual components. One could easily design videos in which a surprising or resolving element occurs at a particular moment in time, thus making it possible unambiguously to document neural or physiological reactions to those elements. Such elements seem far more likely to map onto the visual surprise that occurs during the viewing of static art than do those from the auditory domain. Finally, the combination of music with video raises further possibilities. Music added to video can have powerful effects on the perception and emotional reaction to the visual events, and the craft of film scoring provides many well-known examples that could easily be utilized in experimental investigations. This is another domain in which the insights of the "artist-as-practicing-neuroaesthetician" could profitably be explored in an experimental setting.

An empirical approach to aesthetics that sought to bridge the gaps between the different arts would lead rapidly to fascinating questions. Is there a neural signature of the recognition, novelty, or resolution stages we hypothesize to be typical of most aesthetic experience, and shared by static and temporal arts? Does this apply across visual artistic domains as diverse as painting, sculpture, and architecture? Are there shared brain regions activated by certain emotional or aesthetic reactions to *any* form of art, regardless of modality? This would be a fascinating and important discovery, if so.

A neural approach would also allow us to consider the evolutionary origins of our human aesthetic capacity, using a comparative approach to examine perception in other species. While the question of "animal aesthetics" remains largely unexplored, it does not seem to us preposterous to suggest that basic certain aspects of human aesthetic experience may be shared with nonhuman animals, and thus have a biological basis that can be better understood from a comparative perspective (see Figure 9). To what extent may phenomena similar to human aesthetic reactions be observed in the brains of nonhuman animals? Although clearly they cannot share their reactions to art with us using language, animals might nonetheless share some protoaesthetic reaction to stimuli that we consider art, and noninvasive neural techniques may be the best way to uncover such commonalities. Do animals share with humans certain proclivities for symmetry or bright colors, or even a pleasurable reaction to the resolution of ambiguity that we suggest is a core component of human aesthetic pleasure? All of these are empirical questions that seem, to us, well worth exploring.

Incorporating the Creator

In this chapter, we have focused nearly entirely on the aesthetic experience of the perceiver, arguing that without the exercise of an aesthetic capacity (at the very least, the artist's own), there would be no point in creating art. But it is of course equally true that without creators there would *be* no art. So it would be remiss if we said nothing at all about the cognitive processing that underlies artistic creation. The main point we wish to make is that many of the same processes that

Figure 9. Dog looks at abstract art. (© Illustration by W. Tecumseh Fitch.)

underlie perception are fully operative, and necessarily so, during the creation of a work of art. Thus, an important first step in understanding the psychology of a particular creator would be to understand her perceptual proclivities, using just the sorts of techniques outlined above. The fact that a creator also acts as a perceiver of her own developing artwork also raises the possibility that other perceivers might have analogous aesthetic experiences when they view the finished piece.

To evaluate this potential correspondence between creator and perceiver, consider the analogy to the telling and experiencing of jokes. Jokes can be seen as embodying highly compressed, linguistic versions of our aesthetic trajectory, in the sense that they demand a creative act of the listener. The punch line includes an element of surprise, often building on an unnoticed ambiguity occurring at an earlier point in the setup. To "get" a joke means to resolve this ambiguity by retrospectively modifying the previously established conception of the situation. While this process may not always lead to laughter, there is typically pleasure in this creative act of completion or resolution. If, for whatever reason, this creative act of completion on the part of the listener does not occur, the joke has been unsuccessful. Thus, we can see the basic outline of the aesthetic trajectory, though typically highly compressed in time (the moment of surprise is followed almost immediately by its resolution). Crucially, to get a joke means that the listener has both noticed and understood the surprising element and has experienced essentially the same resolution and synthesis as that intended by the teller. Someone might genuinely find the situation presented in the setup of a joke funny, and even laugh at its conclusion, without this precise correspondence to the teller's intention, but in normal parlance, they don't get the joke unless they experience a very specific particular surprise and resolution. There is in a successful joke exchange, thus, a fundamental symmetry between teller and listener. Of course, the teller of the joke is not actually surprised by the element that is surprising to the listener, since they knew the joke already, and were almost certain to have been pleasantly surprised the first time they heard it, since they then take the trouble to tell it themselves. Note that the same may be true of a listener: one may have heard a joke before and nonetheless opt not to "stop me if you've heard this one," happily expecting to find it funny again in the same way (just as one may experience the same artwork repeatedly and achieve a similar, if subtly altered, aesthetic reaction each time). It would seem that literal surprise is not a fundamental difference in the performance and experience of joke telling, and is not crucial to its effectiveness; a close correspondence between what the joke-narrative intentionally withholds and what the hearer's imagination supplies, however, is. Thus, the successful joke provides a powerful instance of aesthetic pleasure resulting directly from, and depending crucially upon, an identity between the creator's (or teller's) intention and the perceiver's (or listener's) interpretation.

We suggest that the same is true of the creation or performance of a piece of art: part of the pleasure comes precisely from the similarity of the aesthetic experience on the part of creator and perceiver. When we take pleasure in a work of representational art, a crucial aspect of the experience is the feeling that we are *sharing* the aesthetic experience of the creator. We at least imagine that we are seeing the poplars *as Monet saw them*. It is presumably true that there were many other things on Monet's mind while painting this work (most obviously, the meta-artistic awareness that he was in the process of making a painting, along presumably with a whole suite of other incidental concerns: cold, hunger, the price of pigments, Cézanne's health, and so on). Nonetheless, the notion that while Monet was painting, he was in a sense discovering, in himself, a way of seeing, which the painting then potentially shares with others, seems like a reasonable and valid way to conceptualize the relationship between creator and perceiver. We are well aware that in stating this potential, we risk being accused of the infamous "Intentional Fallacy" so much decried in postmodernist criticism (Wimsatt & Beardsley, 1946). However, while it is clearly true that no perceiver can hope to recover *all* of a creator's intentions, it does not follow that the perceiver can recover *none* of them. Indeed, this appears to us a wholly implausible claim.

Fundamentally, then, we can hope to understand an important component of the creator's cognitive experience in the same terms that we have outlined here for that of the perceiver. Furthermore, there is good reason to think that the creator's perceptual dynamic will have something basic in common with that of other perceivers, and that an important part of the pleasure of art is the sense, not wholly futile, that a *sharing* of aesthetic experience is occurring. In his insightful exploration of music cognition, John Sloboda has argued persuasively against the "pharmaceutical" model of art (that art's function is to generate emotional effects in perceivers), as well as against the "linguistic" model (that art exists to accurately communicate specific meanings and messages from creator to perceiver; see Sloboda, 2005). If we abandon these models, as we think that we must, perhaps a more apt model is based on an architectural metaphor: the artist creates a space, with particular dimensions and characteristics that invite certain types of experience on the part of the perceiver. An invitation is all this can be, because the onus is on any individual entering this space to follow through with an actual aesthetic experience, and it is always possible that the perceiver will decline the invitation entirely (either by necessity or choice), or even put this metaphoric space to an aesthetic use wholly unforeseen by its creator. Either way, this potential for creativity is a fundamental aspect of the aesthetic experience that is shared between artist and appreciator. We would thus hope that many of the ideas we have advanced here concerning aesthetic appreciation will have equal relevance to the understanding of artistic creation.

ACKNOWLEDGMENTS

We thank copyright lawyer Wallace Collins and saxophonist Michael Karn for their advice.

REFERENCES

Amira, J., & Cornelius, S. (1992). *The music of Santería,* New York: Talman.

Avital, E., & Jablonka, E. (2000). *Animal traditions: Behavioural inheritance in evolution.* Cambridge, MA: Cambridge University Press.

Baumgartner, T., Esslen, M., & Jäncke, L. (2006). From emotion perception to emotion experience: Emotions evoked by pictures and classical music. *International Journal of Psychophysiology, 60*, 34-43.

Bernstein, L. (1981). *The unanswered question: Six talks at Harvard (Charles Eliot Norton Lectures).* Cambridge, MA: Harvard University Press.

Blood, A. J., & Zatorre, R. J. (2001). Intensely pleasurable responses to music correlate with activity in brain regions implicated in reward and emotion. *Proceedings of the National Academy of Sciences, USA, 98*, 11818-11823.

Bonner, J. T. (1983). *The evolution of culture in animals.* Princeton: Princeton University Press.

Boyd, R., & Richerson, P. J. (1985). *Culture and the evolutionary process.* Chicago: University of Chicago Press.

Catchpole, C. K. (1973). The functions of advertising song in the sedge warbler (*Acrocephalus schoenobaenus*) and reed warbler (*A. scirpaceus*). *Behaviour, 46*, 300-320.

Cooke, M. (1998). *Jazz.* London: Thames & Hudso.

Cooper, H. (1982). *The basic guide to how to read music.* New York: Putnam: Perigee.

Cross, I. (2003). Music, cognition, culture and evolution. In I. Peretz & R. J. Zatorre (Eds.), *The cognitive neuroscience of music* (pp. 42-56). Oxford: Oxford University Press.

Dale, R. (2004). *Teach yourself Jazz.* London: Hodder Headline.

Dannenberg, R. B. (1993). Music representation issues, techniques, and systems. *Computer Music Journal, 17*, 20-30.

Fitch, W. T. (2006a). On the biology and evolution of music. *Music Perception, 24*, 85-88.

Fitch, W. T. (2006b). The biology and evolution of music: A comparative perspective. *Cognition, 100*, 173-215.

Gaare, M. (1997). Alternatives to traditional notation. *Music Educators Journal, 83*, 17-23.

Galef, B. G., Jr. (1992). The question of animal culture. *Human Nature, 3*, 157-178.

Gombrich, E. H. (1959). *Art and illusion: A study in the psychology of pictorial representations.* London: Phaidon.

Gooding, M. (2001). *Abstract art.* London: Tate Publishing.

Hahn, J., & Münzel, S. (1995). Knochenflöten aus dem Aurignacien des Geissenklösterle bei Blaubeuren, Alb-Donau-Kreis. *Fundberichte aus Baden-Württemberg, 20*, 1-12.

Helmholtz, H. v. (1911). *Handbuch der Physiologischen Optik*. Hamburg: Voss.

Henshilwood, C., D'Errico, F., Yates, R., Jacobs, Z., Tribolo, C., Duller, G., et al. (2002). Emergence of modern human behavior: Middle Stone Age engravings from South Africa. *Science, 295*, 1278-1280.

Hutchinson, A. (1961). *Labanotation*. Norfolk, CT: New Directions.

Juslin, P., & Sloboda, J. A. (Eds). (2001). *Music and emotion: Theory and research*. Oxford: Oxford University Press.

Kilmer, A. D., & Tinney, S. (1996). Old Babylonian music instruction texts. *Journal of Cuneiform Studies, 48*, 49-56.

King, J. (1997). *What jazz is: An insider's guide to understanding and listening to jazz*. New York: Walker and Co.

Koelsch, S., Gunter, T. C., Friederici, A. D., & Schröger, E. (2000). Brain indices of music processing: "Non-musicians" are musical. *Journal of Cognitive Neuroscience, 12*, 520-541.

Krumhansl, C. L. (1997). An exploratory study of musical emotions and psychophysiology. *Canadian Journal of Experimental Psychology, 51*, 336-353.

Langer, S. K. (1942). *Philosophy in a new key: A study in the symbolism of reason, rite and art*. Cambridge, MA: Harvard University Press.

Lerdahl, F. (2001). *Tonal pitch space*. New York: Oxford University Press.

Lerdahl, F., & Jackendoff, R. (1983). *A generative theory of tonal music*. Cambridge, MA: The MIT Press.

Locke, D. (1983). *Drum Gahu: The rhythms of West African drumming*. New York: Talman.

Malevich, K. S. (1915). From Cubism to futurism to suprematism: The new realism in painting. In T. Andersen (Ed.), *The artist, infinity, suprematism. Unpublished writings 1913-1933* (p. 51). Copenhagen: Borgen.

Malevich, K. S. (1976). *The world as non-objectivity. Unpublished writings 1913-1933*. Copenhagen: Borgen.

Marler, P. (1991). The instinct to learn. In S. Carey & R. Gelman (Eds.), *The epigenesis of mind: Essays on biology and cognition* (pp. 37-66). Hillsdale, NJ: Lawrence Erlbaum Associates.

Marler, P. (2000). Origins of music and speech: Insights from animals. In N. L. Wallin, B. Merker, & S. Brown (Eds.), *The origins of music* (pp. 31-48). Cambridge, MA: The MIT Press.

Marler, P., & Slabbekoorn, H. (2004). *Nature's music: The science of birdsong*. New York: Academic Press.

Marr, D. (1982). *Vision: A computational investigation into the human representation and processing of visual information*. San Francisco: W. H. Freeman & Co.

Marshack, A. (1976). Some implications of the paleolithic symbolic evidence for the origin of language. *Current Anthropology, 17*, 274-282.

McGrew, W. C. (2004). *The cultured chimpanzee*. Cambridge, MA: Cambridge University Press.

Mithen, S. (2005). *The singing Neanderthals: The origins of music, language, mind, and body*. London: Weidenfeld & Nicolson.

Nettl, B. (2000). An ethnomusicologist contemplates universals in musical sound and musical culture. In N. L. Wallin, B. Merker, & S. Brown (Eds.), *The origins of music* (pp. 463-472). Cambridge, MA: The MIT Press.

Nyklicek, I., Thayer, J. F., & Van Doornen, L. J. P. (1997). Cardiorespiratory differentiation of musically-induced emotions. *Journal of Psychophysiology, 11*, 304-321.

Peretz, I., & Zatorre, R. J. (Eds). (2003). *The cognitive neuroscience of music*. Oxford: Oxford University Press.

Read, G. (1969). *Music notation: A manual of modern practice*. New York: Crescendo: Taplinger Publishing.

Russo, W. (1961). *Composing for the jazz orchestra*. Chicago: University of Chicago Press.

Sloboda, J. A. (1985). *The musical mind: The cognitive psychology of music*. Oxford: Clarendon.

Sloboda, J. A. (1991). Music structure and emotional response: Some empirical findings. *Psychology of Music, 19*, 110-120.

Sloboda, J. A. (2005). *Exploring the musical mind: Cognition, emotion, ability, function*. Oxford: Oxford University Press.

Sundberg, J., & Lindblom, B. (1976). Generative theories in language and music descriptions. *Cognition, 4*, 99-122.

Temperley, D. (2000). Meter and grouping in African music: A view from music theory. *Ethnomusicology, 44*, 66-96.

Tervaniemi, M. (2003). Musical sound processing: EEG and MEG evidence. In I. Peretz & R. J. Zatorre (Eds.), *The cognitive neuroscience of music* (pp. 294-309). Oxford: Oxford University Press.

Tervaniemi, M., Winkler, I., & Näätänen, R. (1997). Pre-attentive categorization of sounds by timbre as revealed by event-related potentials. *NeuroReport, 8*, 2571-2574.

Titon, J. T., Koetting, J. T., McAllester, D. P., Reck, D. B., & Slobin, M. (Eds). (1984). *Worlds of music: An introduction to the music of the world's peoples*. New York: Schirmer Books.

Tomasello, M. (1999). *The cultural origins of human cognition*. Cambridge, MA: Harvard University Press.

Trainor, L. J., & Schmidt, L. A. (2003). Processing emotions induced by music. In I. Peretz & R. J. Zatorre (Eds.), *The cognitive neuroscience of music* (pp. 310-324). Oxford: Oxford University Press.

Trehub, S. E., & Trainor, L. J. (1998). Singing to infants: Lullabies and play songs. *Advances in Infant Research, 12*, 43-77.

West, M. L. (1994). The Babylonian musical notation and the Hurrian melodic texts. *Music & Letters, 75*, 161-179.

Whiten, A., Goodall, J., McGrew, W. C., Nishida, T., Reynolds, V., Sugiyama, Y., et al. (1999). Cultures in chimpanzees. *Nature, 399*, 682-685.

Wimsatt, W. K., & Beardsley, M. C. (1946). The intentional fallacy. *Sewanee Review, 54*, 468-488.

Wold, M., & Cykler, E. (1976). *An introduction to music and art in the Western world*. Dubuque, IA: Wm. C. Brown and Co.

Wolfe, T. (1975). *The painted word*. New York: Farrar, Straus and Giroux.

Wundt, W. M. (1908). *Grundzüge der physiologischen Psychologie*. Leipzig: Wilhelm Engelmann.

Zeki, S. (1999). *Inner vision: An exploration of art and the brain*. Oxford: Oxford University Press.

Zhadova, L. A. (1982). *Malevich: Suprematism and revolution in Russion art 1910-1930*. London: Thames and Hudson.

Zschocke, N. (2006). *Der irritierte Blick: Kunstrezeption und Aufmerksamkeit*. Munich: Wilhelm Fink Verlag.

CHAPTER 6

Constraining Hypotheses on the Evolution of Art and Aesthetic Appreciation*

Marcos Nadal, Miquel Capó, Enric Munar, Gisèle Marty, and Camilo José Cela-Conde

> If it were our purpose in this chapter to say what is actually known about the evolution of human cognition, we could stop at the end of this sentence. (R. C. Lewontin, 1990)

Researchers have attempted to explain the evolution of aesthetic appreciation and art for a long time. By the early twentiethth century, and even before the end of the nineteenth century, Darwinian-grounded reasoning had already led to some interesting conclusions. For instance, Clay (1908) argued that the pleasure we take in looking at or listening to beautiful things played an important adaptive role throughout the evolution of our species. According to him, this affective dimension of aesthetic appreciation grew out of the need to assess the suitability of environments. This viewpoint anticipated current models of the origins of aesthetic preference based on the emotional reactions to environments depending on their resources and potential dangers (Kaplan, 1992; Orians, 2001; Orians & Heerwagen, 1992; Smith, 2005). Other early work on "the primitive source of the appreciation of beauty" (Allen, 1880, p. 30), as well as its evolutionary history, was based on sexual selection, also a popular explanation in recent studies (Etcoff, 1999; Miller, 2001):

*This research was made possible by research grant PRIB-2004-10057 from the *Conselleria d'Economia, Hisenda i Innovació, Govern de les Illes Bolears* to the Clinica Rotger, Palma de Mallorca.

> Man in his earliest human condition, as he first evolved from the undifferentiated anthropoidal stage must have possessed certain vague elements of aesthetic feeling: but they can have been exerted or risen into conscious prominence only, it would seem, in the relation of primaeval courtship and wedlock. He must have been already endowed with a sense of beauty in form and symmetry (. . .). He must also have been sensible to the beauty of colour and lustre, rendered faintly conscious in the case of flowers, fruits, and feathers, but probably attaining its fullest measure only in the eyes, hair, teeth, lips, and glossy black complexion of his early mates (. . .). In short, the primitive human conception of beauty must, I believe, have been purely anthropinistic—must have gathered mainly around the personality of man or woman; and all its subsequent history must be that of an apanthropinisation (. . .), a gradual regression or concentric widening of aesthetic feeling around this fixed point which remains to the very last its natural centre. (Allen, 1880, pp. 450-451)

Richard Lewontin's (1990) skepticism regarding our knowledge about the evolutionary history of cognitive processes stems from its largely speculative nature. The views expressed by Allen (1880) and Clay (1908) on this topic, as well as the later accounts (Etcoff, 1999; Kaplan, 1992; Miller, 2001; Orians, 2001; Orians & Heerwagen, 1992; Smith, 2005), are susceptible to Lewontin's (1990) criticisms. In paraphrasing this author, we must admit, first, that most hypotheses about the evolution of art and aesthetic appreciation lack a solid grounding in facts, and, for the most part, we have no means to assess their validity. Second, it is extremely difficult to determine that aesthetic appreciation has actually been shaped by natural selection, given that this involves demonstrating that survival probabilities differed among individuals with different variants of this trait. Third, even if there actually were differences in reproductive rates, the driving force of natural selection requires individuals to differ genetically in relation to the particular trait, and there is no certain proof of such differences for aesthetic appreciation. These and other points led Lewontin to caution against taking plausible scenarios for demonstrated truth about the evolution of cognition, and we believe the same can be said about art and aesthetic appreciation.

Most of our knowledge about the evolution of our lineage relies on inferences from fossil remains, material culture, and ancient DNA. However, there is little in the fossil record—not to mention ancient DNA—that can be used to ground hypotheses about the evolution of cognitive traits. Even the suitability of using material remains, such as tools, signs of habitation, or burials, to infer mental capabilities is a matter of much controversy. We believe that explanations of the evolution of aesthetic appreciation should be firmly grounded on knowledge about the evolution of our species, the cognitive processes involved underlying this mental faculty, as well as the evolution of their neural correlates. In this chapter, we will review facts from paleoanthropology and comparative neuroscience, which should be accounted for by (and could serve as constraints on) hypotheses about the evolution of art and aesthetic appreciation. In this attempt, we will focus most of our attention on the possible evolution of the brain regions that have been implicated in aesthetic preference by recent neuroimaging studies.

HUMAN EVOLUTION AND ARCHAEOLOGICAL EVIDENCE OF AESTHETIC PRODUCTION

The basis for our classification of living beings was set by Linnaeus (1735). The highest place in this scheme was occupied by the order *Primata* (the first): humans and their closest relatives. The idea of evolution as an ascending scale is common among popular thinking, and it has permeated research in human evolution since its scientific beginnings. Until fairly recently, human paleontology favored a similar linear model. Human evolution was regarded as a straight line leading from our ancestors shared with apes to modern humans. Several stages were identified along this line, including the Australopithecine, Paranthropine, and Neanderthal phases (Brace, 1965). This sequential view found support in a seemingly ordered fossil record, with older specimens resembling current apes and recent ones exhibiting many more similarities to ourselves.

However, by the end of the 1970s new fossil evidence had made such a simple conception of human evolution untenable. The Kenyan Koobi Fora site yielded hominid remains that belonged to the same time interval but showed striking morphological differences. Some specimens were characterized by a robust appearance and a small cranium, while others were gracile and had slightly larger crania. The variation among these exemplars is such that they are currently included in three different species: *Paranthropus boisei*, *Homo habilis*, and *Homo ergaster*. This was the first sign of a previously unrecognized complexity and variety of human ancestry, but certainly not the last. In fact, recent findings in Central and Eastern Africa, as well as Southeast Asia, suggest that more than one hominid form has existed at each point in time almost since the very beginning of our family, and probably until only 20,000 or 30,000 years ago.

Most researchers would agree that fossil remains and molecular data indicate that hominids first appeared about 6 or 7 million years ago, somewhere in the African continent. The earliest specimens, from sites dated to between 5 and 7 million years ago have been attributed to three different species: *Sahelanthropus tchadensis*, *Orrorin tugenensis*, and *Ardipithecus ramidus*. Given the fragmentary state of these remains, and the difficulties inherent in their comparison, there is much discussion as to the validity of their hominid status. The earliest undisputed evidence of completely bipedal hominids is close to 4 million years old. This is the estimated age of some of the *Australopithecus anamensis* and *Australopithecus afarensis* specimens found in East Africa. Their most notable features include the presence of primitive traits, such as a small braincase, large canines, large molars, and certain remnants of arboreal specializations.

One of the most important events in human evolution was the splitting of the robust and gracile lineages between 3.5 and 2.5 million years ago. This divergence led to two distinct hominid adaptive strategies. One of the lineages became specialized in a diet consisting of hard vegetable materials and developed massive jaws, molars, and sagittal crests. The other lineage, the gracile one, turned to extrasomatic adaptations to survive. Undisputed evidence indicates *Homo habilis* was the first hominid to develop a stone-tool industry, known as Oldowan, the earliest evidence of which dates to about 2.5 million years ago. When climate changes led to the disappearance of the robust lineage, close to 1 million years ago, it had spread across Africa and diverged into at least 3 distinct species (*Paranthropus boisei*, *Paranthropus aethiopicus*, *Paranthropus robustus*). Conversely, by 1.7 million years ago, the gracile lineage had arrived at Asia and developed a new, more sophisticated and varied lithic industry: Acheulean. Pleistocene hominids diverged into different species, including *Homo georgicus* in the Caucasus, *Homo erectus* in Asia, and *Homo ergaster* in Africa.

By 300,000 years ago, Neanderthals had settled in subglacial Europe and the Middle East. Meanwhile, in warmer East Africa, a new species was about to appear. The earliest exemplars of our species, *Homo sapiens*, are between 150,000 and 200,000 years old. This new species began sweeping across the old continents when temperatures rose, about 70,000 years ago. They arrived at Australia probably about 50,000 years ago, and moved into Europe before 30,000 years ago, displacing the Neanderthals, and crossed the Bering Strait into America between 30,000 and 15,000 years ago.

Each of these hominid species is characterized by a set of distinctive features, and they represent different adaptive alternatives. Although they share common ancestors, they cannot be placed along a single morphological or cognitive line leading from apes to humans. The branching of lineages within the hominid family probably led to different ways of solving adaptive problems, and for a long period of time hominids survived without manufacturing stone tools, let alone works of art.

There are different views on the origin of human behavioral modernity, which includes the capacity to create objects and depictions for aesthetic appreciation, as well as those endowed with a symbolic function. These approaches can be placed on a continuum between two contrary hypotheses. One of these, which we will refer to as the "revolution hypothesis," sees the archaeological record as pointing to a recent and rapid emergence of modern human behavior between 50,000 and 40,000 years ago. Some of the proponents of this perspective have argued that this sharp shift to the kinds of archaeological remains found in European Upper Paleolithic sites, such as intentional burials; ornamentation of tools, bodies and cave walls; elaboration of bone and ivory objects; novel blade technologies; as well as evidences of complex exchange relations, among others, are evidence of a substantial change in human cognition (Mellars, 1991) and its neural substrates (Klein, 1995). This rich archaeological record is seen to contrast with Middle Paleolithic remains, which are viewed as evidence of a simpler and less varied lithic technology, lower effectiveness of resource exploitation, and absence of symbolic behavior (Hensilwood & Marean, 2003).

Conversely, at the other end of the continuum, a number of reinterpretations of the archaeological record have recently questioned the place and time of the appearance of modern human cognition. They have shown that the revolution hypothesis ignores problems with the application of European-based prehistoric periodization systems to other regions; differences in the abundance and richness between European, African, and Asian archaeological sites; and population movements (Hensilwood & Marean, 2003). The alternative explanation, which we will refer to as the "gradualist hypothesis," argues that, contrary to the predictions made by the revolution hypothesis, the set of behaviors taken to indicate human cognitive modernity did not appear at the same time and place. McBrearty and Brooks (2000) have presented abundant evidence supporting the notion that the Upper Paleolithic remains found in Europe are the result of a gradual and continuous accumulation of novel behaviors during a long period of time. In fact, as work progresses in African archaeological sites, it is becoming increasingly clear that such activities as the use of ochre, engraving, bone working, as well as complex subsistence strategies, appeared much earlier than posited by the revolution hypothesis (d'Errico et al., 2003; Hensilwood, d'Errico, Marean, Milo, & Yates, 2001). For instance, ornamental sea shells, eggshells, and perforated bones have been found in some African sites dated to 100,000 years. Decorative stones have appeared in 130,000-year-old Nigerian sites. The use of ochre has been documented in a number of sites spanning the last 300,000 years (McBrearty & Brooks, 2000). However, early evidence of aesthetic appreciation is not restricted to the African continent. A gradual, though later, transition to fully modern behaviors is also apparent in the South Asian archaeological record (James & Petraglia, 2005). The recent accumulation of new data, together with the reinterpretation of earlier evidence, seems to confirm Martin's (1998) observation that the mosaic nature of evolution makes the origin of human uniqueness at a particular point in time a very unlikely scenario.

Hence, recent revisions of the archaeological record from a global, not just European, perspective suggest that the origin of art, symbols, and aesthetic appreciation is diffuse, extended in space, and continuous in time, with deep roots in our Middle Paleolithic ancestors' cognitive and neural structures. The evidence for this origin appears throughout a long period of time, initially scarcely, but later growing in abundance and variety. Only by neglecting the African and Asian archaeological record is it possible to be surprised at the "sudden" artistic explosion of the European Aurignacian. This set of cultural manifestations had been gradually growing since the appearance of our own species and left some early samples, not in Europe, but in Africa. The murals found in caves in Southern France and Northern Spain are sophisticated and beautiful manifestations of cognitive processes that were probably present at the dawn of our own species, some of which might have been inherited from earlier ancestors. Rather than signs of a cognitive modification (or neural or genetic, for that matter), they seem to be the result of a long process of cultural evolution that gradually led to increasingly sophisticated and varied expressions of an underlying modern creative capability and aesthetic preference, which are, possibly, as old as our species.

EVOLUTION OF THE NEURAL BASES OF AESTHETIC PREFERENCE

To consider language, moral reasoning, or aesthetic appreciation as single and unitary cognitive processes may suggest that each of these cognitive faculties owes to a single, separate piece of computing machinery. However, viewing cognitive mechanisms as the result of the modification and novel combination of previously existing subcomponents has proved very fruitful in beginning to understand their structure and evolution (Marcus, 2004). Evolutionary approaches to human behavior and cognition must not lose sight of the fact that such human behaviors as admiring the beauty of a sculpture or creating an artwork are the result of the interplay of different cognitive processes, probably none of which are exclusive to the task. This has been highlighted by recent models of aesthetic experience (Chatterjee, 2003; Leder, Belke, Oeberst, & Augustin, 2004). Most contributions to the study of the evolution of aesthetic appreciation implicitly or explicitly assume that this cognitive trait appeared at some stage in human evolution, most commonly during the Pleistocene (Orians & Heerwagen, 1992). However, this assumption needs to be justified, given that it is not inconceivable that humans share some of the cognitive and neural underpinnings of aesthetic appreciation with other primates, and thus, may predate humans themselves. This, which might intuitively seem far-fetched, has recently been demonstrated for language. Some of the cognitive processes involved in language comprehension and acquisition, and hence, presumed to be specifically human traits, have been identified in monkeys (for reviews of this research, see Tincoff & Hauser, 2005; Weiss & Newport, 2006). Similarly, Flack and de Waal's (2000) division of human morality into four building blocks allowed them to identify its possible evolutionary roots in our primate relatives. This suggests that not all the constituent cognitive operations subservient to human morality and language appeared after the human and chimpanzee lineages diverged. In fact, it suggests that they appeared long before humans, and that human language and morality evolved, in part at least, by using preexisting building blocks. In this section, we will explore the question of whether brain regions involved in aesthetic preference show any kind of special feature in humans, or whether they seem to have changed little since our lineage separated from our closest living relatives. It is very possible that not all the neural structures involved in aesthetic preference (and the functions they perform), have undergone the same degree of transformation since the appearance of the human lineage. We believe that differences and similarities between human and nonhuman primates in the brain regions shown to be involved in aesthetic preference by neuroimaging studies, can offer clues to researchers approaching these cognitive processes from an evolutionary perspective.

A caveat before we proceed: As Sejnowski and Churchland (1989) pointed out, the brain can be organized in several hierarchical levels. These include systems, maps, networks, individual neurons, synapses, and molecules. As with any other cognitive operation, there is no way of determining which level of analysis is the most relevant to the study of the neural correlates of aesthetic preference. Additionally, the evolutionary emergence of such a capacity may owe to alterations in any set of these levels. In this case, though, information about the neural underpinnings of this cognitive operation is limited to one of these levels (systems), and the little knowledge we have about how the human brain evolved prevents reasonable hypotheses about modifications at most of the other levels. Hence, our analysis will be restricted to the higher levels in the organizational hierarchy of the brain.

Cognitive Operations Involved in Aesthetic Preference

In order to address the question previously outlined, we first need to determine the building blocks of aesthetic appreciation. The models elaborated by Chatterjee (2003) and Leder and colleagues (2004) provide reasonable guidelines to carve aesthetic appreciation into basic components. Although Chatterjee's (2003) proposal is a model of aesthetic preference for a broad range of visual objects grounded on visual neuroscience, and Leder and colleagues' (2004) an information-processing model of aesthetic judgment of artworks, they represent complementary views of cognitive and affective operations involved in aesthetic appreciation (Vartanian & Nadal, 2007). Given that our main concern here is the relation between brain and aesthetic appreciation, Chatterjee's (2003) framework is better suited to our purposes. Chatterjee suggested that aesthetic preference involves three processing stages, common to the perception of any visual stimulus. During early visual processes, simple components are extracted and analyzed in different brain areas. Operations in the intermediate stage segregate some elements and group others, forming coherent representations. In late stages, certain regions of the object are selected for further scrutiny, memories are activated, objects are recognized and associated with meanings. In the case of visual stimuli found to be aesthetically pleasing or displeasing, these operations elicit emotional processes, which feed back into the system of via attentional mechanisms. There is a second output, resulting from decision-making processes. Chatterjee (2003) suggested that the involvement of visual brain regions in processing aesthetic stimuli is the same as in the processing of any other kind of visual stimuli. What sets aesthetic preference apart from other cognitive processes involving visual stimuli is precisely the engagement of additional nonperceptual processes, such as emotions and decision making.

Recent neuroimaging studies have revealed a basic picture of the neural correlates of these cognitive and affective processes. Affective processes involved in aesthetic appreciation seem to be mediated by the orbitofrontal cortex (Kawabata & Zeki, 2004), caudate nucleus, anterior cingulate cortex, as well as the strengthening of early visual processes in the occipital cortex (Vartanian & Goel, 2004). Recognition and meaning attribution in aesthetic appreciation seem to be related with activity in the temporal pole (Jacobsen, Schubotz, Höfel, & von Cramon, 2005), and decisions seem to be mediated by the lateral prefrontal cortex and the frontal pole (Cela-Conde et al., 2004; Jacobsen et al., 2005). If indeed these are the main brain regions that support aesthetic preference, it follows that knowledge about their evolution is basic to understand the evolution of aesthetic preference itself.

A comprehensive understanding of the evolution of the human brain, as well as of certain specific regions, requires taking into account general principles of brain evolution that operate across a broad range of animals, accounting for current brain features that seem to be specifically human, and tracing these features in the fossil record. Space limitations will allow us only to briefly outline some of the main ideas and to require us to restrict ourselves to our regions identified by neuroimaging studies of aesthetic preference, which were noted above. Readers who wish to delve deeper in research on human brain evolution will find Rilling (2006) and

Schoenemann (2006) good critical reviews of current knowledge both clarifying and interesting.

Evolution of the Human Brain

After the human lineage split from the lineage leading to chimpanzees, there was no appreciable increase in brain size. The cranial capacity of early australopithecines, such as *Australopithecus afarensis*, is close to 400 cc, almost identical to that of current chimpanzees. In relation to body size, cranial capacity did not vary much within the robust lineage. However, an extra-allometric increase in brain size accompanied the appearance of the first specimens of our own genus, *Homo habilis*. This means that although there is no evidence of increased body weight in comparison with other species, the cranial capacity of *Homo habilis* is estimated at 700 to 750 cc. There is a general agreement that this represents a notable increase and is somehow related with the appearance of lithic cultures. The cranium of *Homo erectus*, reaching 900 to 1,000 cc, was larger than that of *Homo habilis*, though so was its body. Hence, this increase in brain size seems to owe to a general increase in body size (Hublin, 2005). Conversely, brain growth in later hominids, such as Neanderthals or modern humans, seems to have been extra-allometric, given that the sizes of their bodies did not vary much; but the average cranial capacity in our species is about 1,350 cc.

Comparative studies suggest that the subcortical components of the brain have not undergone a dramatic change in size or organization during human evolution. This means that the primary source of increase in cranial capacity observed in the human fossil record is related to increases in the cerebral cortex. Moreover, there is evidence suggesting that in fact most of the cortical expansion that occurred after the human lineage split from that of chimpanzees is due to the enlargement of the neocortex (Changeux, 2005; Zilles, 2005). However, it appears that not all functional regions of the neocortex have undergone the same increase in size. Whereas primary sensory and motor regions seem to have grown little, or even occupy a smaller relative area than in other primates, there seems to have been an extraordinary increase of the multimodal association cortex during human evolution (Changeux, 2005; Zilles, 2005). This conservation is also apparent at finer levels of analysis. The study of cytoarchitectonic and neurochemical properties of motor and somatosensory cortices of macaques and humans carried out by Zilles and colleagues (1995) revealed great similarities between both species, suggesting that brain regions involved in the processing of somatosensory and motor information are largely conserved in these species. Thus, our review of the findings on the evolution of human brain areas involved in aesthetic preference will focus on multimodal association cortical regions.

The Visual System

Vartanian and Goel's (2004) neuroimaging study of aesthetic preference for paintings revealed that activity in occipital visual regions was greater when participants gave a higher preference rating to the stimulus they were seeing than when they gave a lower score. Previous studies suggest that preferred stimuli engage attentional mechanisms (Kaestner & Ungerleider, 2000; Poghosyan, Shibata, & Ioannides, 2005) or affective processes (Lang et al., 1998) that enhance their processing at early visual stages.

Although the region occupied by the primary visual cortex in humans is 1.5 times larger than it is in chimpanzees, in relative terms it is almost half the size expected for a primate brain of 1,350 cc. It seems, thus, that throughout the course of human evolution, occipital regions that carry out the initial processing of visual information have expanded less than the overall brain. But whereas size variations are relatively easy to measure, the comparative study of the organization of the visual cortical system in monkeys and humans is hampered by the lack of broad consensus regarding their partition into discrete areas. Several reviews on homologies between monkeys and humans in the cytoarchitecture and function of the visual cortex note that the only undisputed homologies refer to areas V1, V2, V3, and MT/V5 (Orban, Van Essen, & Vanduffel, 2004; Sereno & Tootell, 2005; Van Essen, 2005). As Orban and colleagues (2004) note, the retinotopic organization and functions of brain areas involved in early visual processing—V1 and V2—are largely conserved in humans. However, there are indications of certain derived aspects in area V1 of the human brain. Specifically, Preuss and Coleman (2002) reported evidence showing that humans differ from other primates in certain features related to the cortical representation of the magnocellular visual pathway. The data suggest some of these modifications appeared in the common ancestors of African apes and humans, whereas others appeared along the human lineage. Given that the magnocellular system is related to the processing of luminance contrasts, and that the perception of motion is impaired in isoluminant conditions, this system appears to be essential in analyzing motion. Other features that are associated with processing along the magnocellular stream include perspective, relative size of objects, and depth perception.

Whereas early visual areas tend to be homologous in humans and monkeys, as we move up the visual system hierarchy, homologies become less clear. For instance, area V3 supports virtually identical representations of the visual field in humans and macaques. However, Orban and colleagues (2004) noted that human area V3A is sensitive to motion cues and uses them to extract three-dimensional information, whereas the monkey area V3A does not share this function. Similarly, it seems that even though the posterior region of MT/V5 is conserved in humans, the homologues of the anterior part still remain unclear. It is not easy to determine the monkey homologue of human area V4 because its ventral and dorsal regions have evolved in different ways among primate species. Further downstream, additional differences have been identified. Studies reported by Orban and colleagues (2004) using comparative functional magnetic resonance imaging (fMRI) data and computerized brain warping suggest that the ventral and dorsal visual streams have not evolved in the same fashion along the human lineage. Specifically, the areas included in the ventral stream, related to object representation and categorization, have undergone a smaller expansion than those parts of the dorsal stream involved in the representation of space and the analysis of visual information to organize action (Orban et al.,

2004). Barton (2006) noted that the fact that the parietal areas of the dorsal stream receive only information from the magnocellular system adds to the aforementioned idea of an enhancement of the magnocellular cortical representations during human evolution. The relative conservation of the ventral stream in humans is further evidenced by studies showing activity in human and monkey homologue brain areas during the perception of symmetry (Sasaki, Vanduffel, Knutsen, Tyler, & Tootell, 2005), representation (Munakata, Santos, Spelke, Hauser, & O'Reilly, 2001), and categorization of visual objects (Sigala, Gabbiani, & Logothetis, 2002).

Temporal Poles

The neuroimaging study of aesthetic judgment carried out by Jacobsen et al., (2005) revealed that rating the beauty of visual geometric stimuli was associated with a greater activity in the left temporal pole, compared with when participants rated the symmetry of the stimuli. Backed by the results from previous work, the authors suggested that this region could be involved in the creation of a broad affective and semantic context based on past experiences in which to frame decisions about beauty of visual stimuli.

Rilling and Seligman (2002) compared several aspects of the temporal lobe across a broad sample of primates, including humans. Their results revealed that during human evolution, the temporal lobe grew in surface and volume, as well as in white matter, resulting in a larger-than-expected proportion of the brain. However, there is evidence suggesting that the temporal lobe of humans is not merely an allometricaly enlarged ape temporal lobe. The amount of white matter in the human temporal lobe is greater than predicted by primate allometric trends, suggesting that temporal-lobe connectivity patterns have undergone a certain amount of reorganization since the appearance of the human lineage, which is consistent with Schenker, Desgouttes, and Semendeferi's (2005) results. Rilling (2006; Rilling & Seligman, 2002) suggested that this reorganization might be related to the appearance and expansion of language-related areas in the temporal lobe of humans, especially in the left hemisphere. They based this hypothesis on studies that have shown that language areas occupy a large portion of the human lateral temporal lobe, including the temporal pole. In monkeys, this region appears to be mostly involved in object recognition. Thus, it seems that in humans, the visual-object processing stream has shifted ventrally to allow for the expansion of language and speech-related areas on the lateral surface.

Despite this difference in the functional involvement of lateral and ventral regions of the human and nonhuman primate temporal lobes, it seems that most of the functions of the temporal pole are homologous. Recent studies carried out with monkeys suggest that regions in the left temporal lobe of humans, including the temporal pole, which have been involved in the processing of speech, might have a long evolutionary history of processing information relative to vocal communication. Poremba, Malloy, Saunders, Carson, Herscovitch, and Mishkin (2004) found that the right and left temporal poles of macaques are specialized in the processing of acoustic stimuli. But whereas activity in the right hemisphere was associated with a broad spectrum of sounds, including nonvocal sounds, ambient background noise, and human speech, activity in the left dorsal temporal pole was greater than in the right hemisphere for species-specific monkey vocalizations. The authors believe this could represent a precursor of auditory language processing in the human brain. Belin's (2006) review of the comparative processing of vocal information also emphasizes this coincidence of lateralized function in human and nonhuman primates.

But there seems to be additional functional homologies. The human temporal pole has been related to the use of past experiences to generate a broad semantic and emotional context in which to interpret the information being processed. Kondo, Saleem, and Price (2003) showed that the temporal pole of monkeys is strongly connected with orbital and medial prefrontal networks, suggesting its involvement in the integration of emotional, mnemonic, and sensory processes. This functional homology converges with the results reported by Croxson and colleagues (2005), showing that the connectivity patterns of the temporal and prefrontal cortex of humans and macaques are very similar.

Finally, the temporal pole seems to play a central role in object recognition in humans. Lesions to this region impair the ability to recognize and recall specific entities, especially familiar objects and faces (Nakamura & Kubota, 1996). This function also finds a homologue in the monkey. It has been shown that neurons in the anterior temporal cortex are involved in the higher-order processing of object-related visual information and can become sensitive to the presentation of exemplars of a trained category (Vogels, 1999). Likewise, other studies, reviewed by Nakamura and Kubota (1996), suggest lesions to the monkey temporal pole produce deficits in the recognition of the experimenters' gloves, food, or live snakes, but not in the discrimination of unfamiliar objects or patterns.

Frontal Lobes: General Features

Terrence Deacon (1997) argued that the human prefrontal cortex is about twice the expected size for a hominoid brain the size of ours. This increase has often been associated with humans' unique cognitive traits, such as language or symbolic representation; but Ralph Holloway's (1996) results indicated that the volume of this region lay within predicted values, casting doubts on the relation between the size of the prefrontal cortex and human cognitive faculties. In order to reach an empirical clarification of this matter, Semendeferi and Damasio (2000) used structural magnetic resonance to measure the sizes of different brain regions of modern humans, chimpanzees, gorillas, orangutans, and gibbons. Images were reconstructed to produce three-dimensional renderings of the cerebral hemispheres, which allowed the authors to calculate total hemispheric volumes, as well as the volumes of the frontal, occipital, and the combination of temporal and parietal lobes. Their results revealed a great homogeneity in the relative volumes of those sectors. Thus, their results provided no evidence of an increase in size in any part of the prefrontal cortex during human evolution (Semendeferi & Damasio, 2000).

It might be the case that variation in sheer size is not the key to understanding the evolution of neural correlates of cognitive processes. It is known that increases in primate brain size involve an expansion of cortical area rather than thickness. And given that this surface expansion does not involve an equal increase in cranial size, the cortex must increase the degree of folding. Zilles, Armstrong, Schleicher, and Kretschmann (1988) compared the pattern of rostro-caudal gyrification indices—the extent to which the cortex is folded, forming sulci and convolutions—of human and nonhuman primate brains. They found that the human pattern, which revealed maximum gyrification indices for the prefrontal, posterior temporal, and anterior parietal cortex, was strikingly different from that of prosimians and monkeys. When compared with brains of chimpanzees, gorillas, and orangutans, the human brain does not appear that special, except for one fact: the unusually high gyrification index of the prefrontal cortex.

With techniques that afforded greater precision, Rilling and Insel (1999) continued the research on the gyrification of primate brains. They used structural magnetic resonance to measure the brains of 44 specimens belonging to 11 different primate species. Their results confirmed that, overall, larger brains have greater gyrification indices. However, there are two regions in the human brain that exceed the expected value: the prefrontal cortex and the posterior temporal-parietal cortex. The authors suggested that the increase in gyrification of these regions during human evolution could constitute part of the neural bases that led to the appearance of some of our unique cognitive faculties.

Increases in the surface of prefrontal and parietal cortices necessarily lead to an increase in intracortical connectivity if function is to be maintained. This, in turn, would require increasing the proportion of white matter in these areas. Schoenemann, Sheehan, and Glotzer (2005) searched for evidence of this increase in white matter in the human prefrontal cortex. They measured grey matter, white matter, and volumes of the prefrontal cortex, as well as the total cortex, of male and female individuals belonging to 11 different primate species. Results revealed that the correlation between the percentage of prefrontal white and grey matter was very weak. This suggests that connectivity might vary throughout evolution with relative independence from variations in neural numbers. Furthermore, there were significant differences in the proportion of white matter in the prefrontal area between human and nonhuman primates, whereas there were no such differences with regard to grey matter (Schoenemann et al., 2005). Taken together, these results suggest that white matter in the prefrontal cortex—either through increase in number of glial cells, reorganization of connectivity patterns, or both—might have played a crucial role in the development of sophisticated cognitive processes supporting a variety of characteristically human traits. However, Sherwood, Holloway, Semendeferi, and Hof (2005) criticized the proxy for prefrontal cortex used in this study, as well as the composition of the sample included, and suggested that the increase in prefrontal white matter is much smaller than suggested by Schoenemann and colleagues' (2005) results. In fact, it is difficult to ascertain whether this overabundance of prefrontal white matter represents an extra-allometric increase, or whether, as argued by Sherwood et al. (2006), it is associated with elevated energetic costs derived from maintaining longer axonal projections and larger dendritic arbors in such a large brain as ours. In any case, given the evidence presented by Bush and Allman (2004), which showed that primates have a greater amount of grey matter in the frontal cortex relative to the rest of the cortex than carnivore mammals, it seems that the increase in prefrontal white matter throughout human evolution represents the extension of a general primate trend.

Orbitofrontal Cortex

Activity in the orbitofrontal cortex was identified by Kawabata and Zeki (2004) while participants decided about the beauty of diverse artistic visual stimuli. The fact that many studies have observed activity in this region in association with primary (Francis et al., 1999; O'Doherty, Deichmann, Critchley, & Dolan, 2002) and abstract (O'Doherty, Kringelbach, Rolls, Harnak, & Andrews, 2001) rewarding stimuli, suggests that its role in aesthetic preference might be to represent the reward value of each visual stimulus.

The comparison of the orbitofrontal cortex of a large number of macaques and humans revealed that their sulcal patterns were very much alike (Chiavaras & Petrides, 2000), though the human pattern was more variable and showed a greater degree of intricacy. In both species, there are four main sulci in each hemisphere. These form five main gyri: a medially positioned gyrus rectus, parallel to which runs the medial orbital gyrus. Between the latter and the lateral orbital gyrus lay the anterior orbital gyrus and the posterior orbital gyrus. Thus, there seems to be a high degree of conservation regarding the sulcal pattern of the human orbitofrontal cortex.

Semendeferi and colleagues' (1998) comparative analysis of Brodmann's area 13, located in the posterior orbitofrontal cortex included a quantitative study of the microstructural organization of this area and estimated its volume for humans, chimpanzees, bonobos, gorillas, orangutans, and gibbons, as well as rhesus monkeys. Although they included relatively small samples, some of their results might turn out to be relevant to the study of the evolution of aesthetic appreciation. Despite overall similarities, which led Semendeferi, Armstrong, Schleicher, Zilles, and Van Hoesen (1998) to consider the state of area 13 in humans as primitive, meaning conservative, there are several features that distinguish humans from other sampled apes. For instance, area 13 in humans and bonobos is relatively smaller than in other apes, which, together with other features, suggests an increased number of orbitofrontal cortex cytoarchitectonic regions. The cell density of this area in humans was the lowest of all hominoids, and together with gibbons, they showed the lowest grey-level indices, meaning that there is greater space filled by axons and dendrites.

This picture of a mosaic of primitive and derived aspects of the organization of the human orbitofrontal cortex was also the result of Van Essen's (2005) comparison with macaques. The overall layout of the cortical areas is much the same in both species, as is their neighboring relations. As for relative sizes, lateral orbitofrontal areas seem to be the most conserved. Although there are some differences between the medial and posterior areas of both species, it is the anterior region, occupied by area 10, which shows the largest amount of differences. Whereas in humans this area occupies 4.5% of the cortex and is constituted by five subdivisions, in macaques it represents 1.4% of the cortex and shows two subdivisions (Van Essen, 2005), confirming Semendeferi and colleagues' (1998) aforementioned prediction.

Rolls' (2004) review of the functions of the primate orbitofrontal cortex suggests that this region is functionally conserved in humans in that, as in monkeys, it includes representations of smell, taste, food texture, ventral-stream visual information, as well as facial information. These representations are used to identify the stimuli being processed and to establish their reward value. Moreover, the orbitofrontal cortex of monkeys and humans seems to be a crucial element in learning stimulus-reward associations and correcting them when contingencies are altered.

Anterior Frontal Cortex

As previously mentioned, Jacobsen and colleagues (2005) recorded activity in the frontal pole while participants performed aesthetic judgments of geometric visual stimuli. In light of previous studies (e.g., Zysset, Huber, Ferstl, & von Cramon, 2002), it seems that this brain region plays a fundamental role in a broad spectrum of evaluative judgments. Petrides and Pandya (1999) compared the neural organization of Brodmann's area 10, the designation of the cytoarchitectonic region occupying the frontal pole, in macaques and humans. Their results revealed that the architectural features that distinguish this area from the neighboring ones are largely the same in both species. This suggests that there has been little change in the types and distribution of neurons across cortical layers in this brain area throughout human evolution.

Semendeferi, Armstrong, Schleicher, Zilles, and Van Hoesen (2001) carried out a quantitative and qualitative analysis of Brodmann's area 10. They compared data from macaque, gibbon, orangutan, gorilla, chimpanzee, bonobo, and human brains. Although their results are preliminary, due to relatively small sample sizes, they reveal some interesting commonalities and differences among hominoids. For instance, the study showed that area 10 is found in the frontal pole in humans as well as Asian and African apes, except for gorillas, which exhibit a rather particular organization of this area. On the other hand, there are certain features that set humans apart from other hominoids with regard to this specific brain region. First, it is larger, both in relative and absolute terms, than that of other apes. However, when the data are transformed into logarithmic scales and regressed for all hominoids, the observed value for the size of area 10 in humans is just above the expected value. Holloway (2002) calculated this increase to represent approximately 6%. Second, although in humans the absolute number of neurons is larger, the neural density is the lowest among hominoids, allowing greater space for connections within the same and other areas. Specifically, Semendeferi and colleagues (2001) noted that "Humans seem to have more space available for connections in layers II and III, which may indicate increased communication between area 10 and other higher-order association areas in our species" (Semendeferi et al., 2001, p. 238).

Lateral Prefrontal Cortex

The studies carried out by Cela-Conde and colleagues (2004) and Jacobsen and colleagues (2005) revealed that rating the beauty of visual artworks and geometric designs engages the lateral prefrontal cortex. The hypothesis that this activity might be related to decision-making processes involving beauty of the visual stimuli presented in the studies is supported by previous studies (Heekeren, Marrett, Bandettini, & Ungerleider, 2004; Krawczyk, 2002).

Van Essen's (2005) review of the compared cortical organization of monkeys and humans revealed that the expansion of the prefrontal cortex was uneven during hominid evolution, suggesting that the lateral areas are the ones that have expanded the most. Despite this difference in the relative expansion of cortical areas, there seems to be a great similarity between humans and other primates regarding the neural architecture and functions of the lateral prefrontal cortex. Petrides and Pandya (1999) carried out a comparison of the cytoarchitecture and connection patterns of the human and macaque dorsolateral prefrontal cortex, which encompasses Brodmann's areas 8, 9, and 46. Results showed that there are no novel cytoarchitectonic areas in the human brain. In fact, they all exhibited similar characteristics in humans and macaques, such that the same architectonic features can be used to identify these areas in both species. This architecture is homologous to the extent that even the same subdivisions of the areas, namely 8Av, 8Ad, 8B, 9/46d, and 9/46v, were to be found in both species. A similar picture emerged after the comparative analysis of the ventrolateral prefrontal cortex of humans and macaques (Petrides & Pandya, 2001), which includes Brodmann areas 47/12 and 45. The cytoarchitectural criteria used to distinguish these two areas in monkeys and humans were largely the same as those used to differentiate both of them from the areas in the dorsolateral cortex. Again, even the finer-grained subdivisions of area 45 (45A and 45B) were distinguishable in both species.

At a functional level, similarities between monkeys and humans regarding the lateral prefrontal cortex have also been documented. Petrides (2005) noted that the lateral cortex of both monkeys and humans is functionally organized along a caudal-rostral axis. Lesion studies have shown that the caudal region of the prefrontal cortex (area 8) in monkeys contributes to the flexible switching of attention between stimuli and the selection of competing responses according to learned conditional rules. At the rostral end of the axis, the mid-lateral prefrontal cortex is involved in more abstract processes of cognitive control. Here, there is a further functional organization along a dorsal-ventral axis. Lesions to the mid-dorsolateral (areas 46 and 9/46) region result in impaired performance of working memory tasks that require monitoring the selection of stimuli or the occurrence of expected events. Lesions to the mid-ventrolateral prefrontal cortex (areas 47/12 and 45) affect the performance of executive functions, including the selection and comparison of stimuli stored in short- and long-term memory, as well as the performance of judgments based on them. Petrides (2005) reviewed several neuroimaging studies carried out with human participants to clarify the organization of lateral prefrontal areas, the results of which converge with the lesion studies carried out on monkeys.

Thus, the functions performed by the lateral cortex in humans—selection, monitoring and judgment—are also structured along both a caudal-rostral and a dorsal-ventral axis. Taking into account the aforementioned results obtained from monkey-lesion studies, it would seem that the functional organization of the human lateral cortex is a primitive trait. There are, however, certain differences. For instance, it is obvious that the recruitment of these functions for particular human cognitive abilities, such as language or even aesthetic appreciation, is absent in other primate species. Second, the kinds of information upon which these functions are carried out also seem to differ. Denys and colleagues (2004) used fMRI with human and nonhuman primate participants to show that the activation of the prefrontal cortex was much stronger in monkeys than humans when presented with visual objects. The authors interpreted this finding as the result of the multisensory nature of information reaching the human cortex, in contrast with the primarily visual information received by the monkey prefrontal cortex. Alternatively, it could also be due to the selective gating of visual information reaching the human prefrontal cortex (Denys et al., 2004).

Anterior Cingulate Cortex

The studies carried out by Vartanian and Goel (2004) and Jacobsen and colleagues (2005) recorded activity in this region while participants performed aesthetic preference tasks. Evidence from prior studies (Hornak et al., 2003; Lane, Reiman, Axelrod, Yun, Holmes, & Schwartz, 1998) suggests that its involvement in aesthetic preference might be related to the conscious awareness of emotions elicited by aesthetically pleasing visual stimuli. Although the anterior cingulate cortex is cytologically distinguishable from the posterior cingulate cortex in both monkeys and humans, there are also significant differences between both species. The most obvious one is the presence of two new areas in humans: 33 and 32. Moreover, the results obtained by Nimchinsky, Gilissen, Allman, Perl, Erwin, and Hof (1999) suggest that the anterior cingulate cortex of great apes and humans is characterized by a unique kind of neurons. These neurons, called spindle cells, and found in layer Vb, have not been found in other mammals, including other primate species. In humans, these cells represent 5.6% of pyramidal cells in traverse sections of this layer, and are found in clusters of 3 to 6 neurons. Among other hominoids, bonobos revealed the closest trend to humans, with spindle neurons, which in their case represent 4.8% of pyramidal cells, also clustering in packs of between 3 and 6. Conversely, no clusters were observed in common chimpanzees, gorillas, or orangutans, and relative abundance was 3.8%, 2.3%, and 0.6%, respectively. None were observed in gibbon samples. These results suggest that new kinds of neurons restricted to the anterior cingulate cortex appeared during the evolution of hominoids. These neurons became relatively more numerous along the lineage leading to humans and began to cluster together. Allman, Hakeem, and Watson (2002) noted that the greatest concentration of spindle cells in the human anterior cingulate cortex is found in its ventral region, the activity of which has often been recorded during the performance of emotional tasks (see Bush, Luu, & Posner, 2000 for a review). Nimchinsky and colleagues (1999) hypothesized that the main function of these neurons is to integrate affective information and transmit it to motor regions related to vocalization, facial expression, or autonomic functions. Allman and colleagues (2002) suggested that increased proportion of spindle cells could be related to the enhancement of emotional stability and self-control, and that, together with an enlarged anterior frontal cortex, it was a key factor in coping with the economic needs of human extended families.

Summary

Studies such as those highlighted in this section can constitute a starting point for hypotheses about the evolution of aesthetic preference, because they provide an initial sketch of the modifications that the neural underpinnings of this cognitive faculty have undergone during human evolution. Our review has revealed that some areas shown by neuroimaging studies to be involved in aesthetic preference are relatively conserved in humans, while others exhibit a number of derived features.

The orbitofrontal cortex presumably supports the representation of reward value of visual stimuli during aesthetic-judgment tasks. It seems that to a large extent, its sulcal pattern, cytoarchitecture, and functions are conserved in the human brain. The only derived features appear to be an enlargement of area 10 and a reduction in neural density. A similar picture emerges after reviewing the comparative literature on the frontal pole, involved in the decision-making stage of aesthetic preference: relative enlargement and reduction of the density of neurons. There is also a great cytoarchitectonic similarity between humans and monkeys in the other regions shown to be involved in decisions about the beauty of visual stimuli, the mid-dorsolateral and mid-ventrolateral cortex. In addition to a considerable enlargement during the evolution of our species, the main difference between both species is that in humans, these lateral regions seem to receive multisensory information, rather than mainly visual. Overall, the complexity of prefrontal-cortex connectivity patterns seems to have increased after our lineage split from chimpanzees some seven million years ago.

Activity within the temporal pole has been related to the creation of a mnemonic and emotional context for aesthetic preference. Our review has revealed that this region performs very similar functions in monkeys and humans, essential for the categorization and recognition of familiar objects, and the integration of emotion, memory, and sensory information. Even if temporal regions involved in language have expanded in humans, pushing areas of the object-centered visual stream further ventrally, they seem to bear a close phylogenetic relation to those underlying the processing of species-specific calls in monkeys.

Occipital visual areas, whose activity during aesthetic preference has been interpreted as the correlate of emotional or attentional engagement, show a mosaic of novel and primitive features. Whereas areas supporting early visual processing seem to be largely conserved, those involved in later stages seem to have changed somewhat. Specifically, the processing of spatial information and the organization of visual information to guide movement seems to have been emphasized during human evolution, rather than object-centered visual analyses.

Finally, our review of comparative work on the anterior cingulate cortex, which probably plays a role in the conscious awareness of the affective state during aesthetic preference, has revealed two major modifications in cytoarchitecture: the appearance of two novel cytoarchitectonic brain areas, and the clustering of a kind of neuron unique to great apes and humans.

THE PRODUCT OF GENES AND CULTURE

The fact that structural and cytoarchitectonic modifications of the brain that occurred throughout the human lineage owe, ultimately, to changes in the developmental course of neural tissue has sometimes been overlooked by studies of brain evolution (Martin, 1998). Although these developmental processes are guided by genes, the relation between brain features and genes is, at present, far from straightforward. It is now known, for instance, that the expression of a certain gene may depend on the tissue, the developmental stage, as well as the context provided by other active genes. Furthermore, it seems that genes are largely pleiotropic, meaning that they are related to several aspects of brain development and function. Changeux (2005) hypothesized that the expansion of human frontal brain regions, as well as others, might be the outcome of an extended influence of (probably few) developmental genes. This hypothesis is backed by results showing striking differences in the regulation of gene expression in the cerebral cortex of humans when compared with other primates (Cáceres et al., 2003). Results by Oldham, Horvath, and Geschwind (2006) revealed that these differences are not common to all brain regions, and suggest that expression patterns might be especially derived in the association cortex, while relatively conserved in the primary visual cortex. Uddin and colleagues (2004) cautioned, however, that changes in gene-expression regulation in the brain are not restricted to the human lineage, but that they have also occurred in chimpanzees, as well as other ape and primate species.

Enard and colleagues (2002) studied the expression levels of mRNA and the expression patterns of proteins in samples from human, orangutan, chimpanzee, and macaque tissues. Their results showed that there are more gene-expression differences between humans and other species in the brain than in other organs. This finding suggests that changes to gene-expression levels in the brain have been especially marked during human evolution. Similar results were reached by Dorus and colleagues (2004), who analyzed the evolution rate of proteins related to genes underlying biological functions of the nervous system in several species of primates and rodents. They found that primates showed a higher evolution rate than rodents, especially for genes involved in the development of the nervous system. This trend was not as prominent for genes related to routine physiological processes. Moreover, their results also revealed that, within the primate order, these genes had undergone an especially rapid evolution along the human lineage, a finding they related to the increased size and complexity of the human brain. Pollard and colleagues (2006) identified a series of chromosomal regions that are typically conserved in mammals but seem to have suffered a highly accelerated evolution throughout the human lineage. Their results reveal that many of these chromosomal regions house genes that carry out regulatory and neurodevelopmental functions. Rates of change in amino-acid sequences that are faster than expected under a neutral model are usually taken as a sign of positive selection and of increased evolutionary success (Amadio & Walsh, 2006). Hence, modifications to developmental processes in the brain seem to have been guided by strong positive selective pressures. However, a caveat was introduced by Shi, Bakewell, and Zhang (2006), who argued that accelerated evolution might not be a feature of many genes expressed in brain tissue, and that results obtained in this kind of study might be biased by the criterion used to include specific genes in the study, as well as the composition of the outgroups used for comparison.

Thus, the origins and evolution of aesthetic appreciation, as well as other characteristically human cognitive mechanisms, might not owe solely to increases in the relative sizes of certain neocortical regions per se, but also to the timing of their development. The normal maturation of neural circuits requires a precise developmental timing and the organism's interaction with its environment. This has been shown by Majdan and Shatz' (2006) study of the effects of visual deprivation on gene expression during the development of the visual cortex in mice, among many others. The authors reported that the regulation of some genes involved in the maturation of neural circuitry is dependent on the history of sensory experience, suggesting an intricate relation between environmental stimulation and gene expression in the development of the neural substrates of visual processing.

Changeux (2005) reviewed some of the evidence showing that the developmental phases in which the maximum number of synapses is achieved and then trimmed are unusually long in humans. This is a crucial point, given the importance of connectivity in understanding human brain evolution. Changeux (2005) noted that the increase of cerebral-cortex surface affords the possibility of creating a larger amount of connections among neurons. And an increase in connectivity would lead to a greater arborization of dendrites and axons, which is precisely what is observed in the prefrontal cortex when compared with other brain regions, such as the primary visual cortex. Whereas earlier phases are relatively insensitive to environmental influence, these extended periods, which last throughout human infancy, are especially sensitive to external information. Hence, the brain of human beings is influenced by external factors at a crucial stage in development—when neural connections are being forged, strengthened, or eliminated.

Brain epigenetic capacities to store stable representations of the outside world give human beings the opportunity to create an artificial world of cultural objects at the social level. In other words, the origin of culture and of its transmission from generation to generation lies in the considerable increase of synapse numbers and multiple nested processes of activity-dependent synapse selection that take place postnatally in the human brain. This epigenetic evolution also has another consequence: it permits the diversification of cultures that human beings have developed throughout their recent history. In other words, the postnatal epigenetic evolution of brain connectivity opens the way to cultural evolution (Changeux, 2005, p. 89).

Hence, the malleability of neural connectivity at early stages of development makes the human brain especially susceptible to environmental influences. In the case of humans, though, an important part of this environment is constituted by cultural elements. Laland, Odling-Smee, and Feldman (2001) summarized a large body of work showing the important role of the creation of a cultural environment throughout human evolution. Just as humans grow up surrounded by biological elements, such as certain plants, animals, climate, and so on, they also develop in a rich cultural surrounding, which includes language, social interactions, and the use of colors, shapes, objects, movements, and sounds, among other features, for aesthetic purposes. Obviously, the cultural milieu in which we grew up did not appear suddenly in human evolution. It is the result of a slow and gradual accumulation of cultural practices and traditions. Tomasello (1999), who described this process as "the ratchet effect" has argued that social learning skills and innovation are the base of cumulative cultural evolution. Children's imitative learning from adults assures that the cultural practices will not be lost from one generation to the next. On the other hand, innovation allows more effective novel cultural variants to be transmitted to future generations. Thus, each generation does not need to create cultural elements from scratch, they modify those they learned from their parents and will transmit those modifications to their own children. In the case of aesthetic appreciation, generation after generation, humans increased the sophistication and broadened the variation of aesthetic expression, creating many new forms of providing aesthetic pleasure. These, in turn, became the cultural environment in which a new generation would be immersed, and, according to the literature reviewed above, may have influenced certain aspects of the organization of neural development and connectivity. Lewontin (1990) emphasized the need to study cognitive traits both as the consequence and cause of evolution, just as any other kind of traits. Hence, paraphrasing Lewontin (1990), evolutionary approaches need to study the evolution of such phenomena as aesthetic preference and creativity, as well as their consequences on human evolution. The way in which this reciprocal influence between biological and cultural evolution has affected aesthetic appreciation has yet to be systematically explored.

CONCLUSIONS: TOWARD A FRAMEWORK FOR THE EVOLUTION OF AESTHETIC PREFERENCE

We have assembled a collection of diverse bits and pieces in this chapter. We will now briefly sketch some of the implications of these pieces for hypotheses concerning the evolution of aesthetic preference, as if we were laying down some of the side pieces of a jigsaw puzzle without knowing many of details of the final image. But before we do so, we wish to acknowledge two of the most important limitations of the present work. First, in our review of comparative neurology, we have focused on the higher levels of brain organization. This is because comparative data at the lower levels are scarce, and not because we believe they are less important for the question at hand. Second, although in some instances we have assumed a correspondence between anatomical and cognitive change, there is a daunting lack of knowledge about the cognitive impact of neuro-anatomical changes during evolution. In spite of these two shortcomings, we believe the following conclusions represent valuable constraints for evolutionary approaches to aesthetic preference, and even possibly to other related phenomena, such as creativity.

Aesthetic preference is the result of the interaction of several component cognitive processes. This fact has been reflected in recent cognitive models based on a large corpus of psychological and neuropsychological studies (Chatterjee, 2003; Leder et al., 2004). Neuroimaging studies have confirmed that there is no single brain center for aesthetic preference, and that different component processes are associated with activity in different brain regions. The reward value of aesthetically pleasing visual stimuli seems to be represented in the orbitofrontal cortex (Kawabata & Zeki, 2004) and caudate nucleus (Vartanian & Goel, 2004). It has been argued that the anterior cingulate cortex, the activity of which was recorded by Vartanian and Goel (2004) and Jacobsen and colleagues (2005) during aesthetic preference tasks, is involved in the conscious awareness of emotional processes. Attentional or emotional mechanisms engaged by preferred stimuli enhance early visual processes in the occipital cortex (Vartanian & Goel, 2004). Activity in the temporal pole seems to provide an emotional and mnemonic context for decisions about beauty (Jacobsen et al., 2005). And, finally, making decisions about the beauty of visual stimuli has been associated with activity in frontopolar and lateral prefrontal regions (Cela-Conde et al., 2004; Jacobsen et al., 2005). It is a certain temporal and spatial distribution of neural activity that enables each human to enjoy viewing certain artworks and designs but not others. Hence, the question of the evolution of aesthetic preference becomes the question of the evolutionary history of those components, their neural bases, and their interaction.

A consequence of shifting our focus to the component processes is that their evolution might be relatively independent. The possibility that they may have different origins is opened. Also, comparative studies become a powerful tool to determine their putative precursors. In fact, our review has shown that, to a very large extent, the component cognitive processes, as well as their neural bases, are present in our close living relatives. Hence, we can assume that they were also present in the common ancestors of humans and monkeys. According to the parsimonious criterion underlying modern phylogenetic reasoning, this is a much likelier scenario than assuming they appeared independently in two closely related lineages. It would seem, therefore, that aesthetic preference has evolved through the recruitment of preexisting cognitive processes and neural structures, rather than by substantive changes in brain and cognition.

This does not mean that there has been no modification of cognitive processes and neural structure during human evolution. We mean to say that humans acquired aesthetic preference by virtue of gradual and quantitative changes in certain brain regions. Specifically, an increase in the complexity of prefrontal connectivity patterns, the elaboration of the dorsal visual stream, together with cytoarchitectonic novelties in the anterior cingulate cortex. Presumably, these modifications afforded a richer integration of multimodal information and the generation of abstract representations, an improved analysis of spatial relations, together with a heightened ability for cognitive control, respectively.

These changes in the brain bases of aesthetic preference may have occurred at different times throughout human evolution. Furthermore, they might have been driven by diverse selective pressures, which need not have been related to aesthetic preference originally. Hence, evolutionary approaches to this human experience can, and probably must, include more than one hypothesized selective advantage, and even evolutionary mechanism.

The development of connectivity patterns in the human brain is sensitive to environmental factors. It is possible that this increased plasticity has played a relevant role in the evolution of aesthetic preference. At least during the last 200,000 years the exposure of human infants to diverse cultural practices, including those designed to embellish the environment—body painting, ornamental objects, bone carving, and so on—has surely been a keynote aspect in the development of an aesthetically tuned mind. The cultural production of aesthetic elements has been slow and gradual, with many different local traditions and forms of expression. Evolutionary approaches to aesthetic preference need to account for the interplay between cultural and biological evolution.

REFERENCES

Allen, G. (1880). Aesthetic evolution in man. *Mind, 5*, 445-464.

Allman, J., Hakeem, A., & Watson, K. (2002). Two phylogenetic specializations in the human brain. *The Neuroscientist, 8*, 335-346.

Amadio, J. P., & Walsh, C. A. (2006). Brain evolution and uniqueness in the human genome. *Cell, 126*, 1033-1035.

Barton, R. A. (2006). Primate brain evolution: Integrating comparative, neurophysiological, and ethological data. *Evolutionary Anthropology, 15*, 224-236.

Belin, P. (2006). Voice processing in human and non-human primates. *Philosophical Transactions of the Royal Society B, 361*, 2091-2107.

Brace, C. L. (1965). *The stages of human evolution.* Englewood Cliffs, NJ: Prentice-Hall.

Bush, E. C., & Allman, J. M. (2004). The scaling of frontal cortex in primates and carnivores. *Proceedings of the National Academy of Sciences USA, 101*, 3962-3966.

Bush, G., Luu, P., & Posner, M. I. (2000). Cognitive and emotional influences in anterior cingulate cortex. *Trends in Cognitive Sciences, 4*, 215-222.

Cáceres, M., Lachuer, J., Zapala, M. A., Redmond, J. C., Kudo, L., Geschwind, D. H., et al. (2003). Elevated gene expression levels distinguish human from non-human primate brains. *Proceedings of the National Academy of Sciences USA, 100*, 13030-13035.

Cela-Conde, C. J., Marty, G., Maestú, F., Ortiz, T., Munar, E., Fernández, A., et al. (2004). Activation of the prefrontal cortex in the human visual aesthetic perception. *Proceedings of the National Academy of Sciences USA, 101*, 6321-6325.

Changeux, J.-P. (2005). Genes, brains, and culture: From monkey to human. In J.-R. D. S. Dehaene, M. D. Hauser, & G. Rizzolatti (Eds.), *From monkey brain to human brain* (pp. 73-94). Cambridge, MA: MIT Press.

Chatterjee, A. (2003). Prospects for a cognitive neuroscience of visual aesthetics. *Bulletin of Psychology of the Arts, 4*, 55-60.

Chiavaras, M. M., & Petrides, M. (2000). Orbitofrontal sulci of the human and macaque monkey brain. *The Journal of Comparative Neurology, 422*, 35-54.

Clay, F. (1908). The origin of the aesthetic emotion. *Sammelbände der Internationalen Musikgesellschaft, 9*, 282-290.

Croxson, P. L., Johansen-Berg, H., Behrens, T. E. J., Robson, M. D., Pinsk, M. A., Gross, C. G., et al. (2005). Quantitative investigation of connections of the prefrontal cortex in the human and macaque using probabilistic diffusion tractography. *The Journal of Neuroscience, 25*, 8854-8866.

d'Errico, F., Hensilwood, C., Lawson, G., Vanhaeren, M., Tillier, A.-M., Soressi, M., et al. (2003). Archaeological evidence for the emergence of language, symbolism, and music. An alternative multidisciplinary perspective. *Journal of World Prehistory, 17*, 1-70.

Deacon, T. W. (1997). *The symbolic species.* New York: W. W. Norton & Company.

Denys, K., Vanduffel, W., Fize, D., Nelissen, K., Sawamura, H., Georgieva, S., et al. (2004). Visual activation in prefrontal cortex is stronger in monkeys than in humans. *Journal of Cognitive Neuroscience, 16*, 1505-1516.

Dorus, S., Vallender, E. J., Evans, P., Anderson, J. R., Gilbert, S. L., Mahowald, M., et al. (2004). Accelerated evolution of nervous system genes in the origin of *Homo sapiens*. *Cell, 119*, 1027-1040.

Enard, W., Khaitovich, P., Klose, J., Zöllner, S., Heissig, F., Giavalisco, P., et al. (2002). Intra- and interspecific variation in primate gene expression patterns. *Science, 296*, 340-343.

Etcoff, N. (1999). *Survival of the prettiest.* New York: Doubleday.

Flack, J. C., & De Waal, F. B. M. (2000). 'Any animal whatever.' Darwinian building blocks of morality in monkeys and apes. *Journal of Consciousness Studies, 7*, 1-29.

Francis, S., Rolls, E. T., Bowtel, R., McGlone, F., O'Doherty, J., Browning, A., et al. (1999). The representation of pleasant touch in the brain and its relationship with taste and olfactory areas. *Neuroreport 10*, 453-459.

Heekeren, H. R., Marrett, S., Bandettini, P. A., & Ungerleider, L. G. (2004). A general mechanism for perceptual decision-making in the human brain. *Nature, 431*, 859-862.

Hensilwood, C. S., d'Errico, F., Marean, C. W., Milo, R. G., & Yates, R. (2001). An early bone tool industry from the Middle Stone Age at Blombos Cave, South Africa: Implications for the origins of modern human behaviour, symbolism and language. *Journal of Human Evolution, 41*, 631-678.

Hensilwood, C. S., & Marean, C. W. (2003). The origin of modern human behavior. *Current Anthropology, 44*, 627-651.

Holloway, R. L. (2002). How much larger is the relative volume of area 10 of the prefrontal cortex in humans? *American Journal of Physical Anthropology, 118*, 399-401.

Hornak, J., Bramham, J., Rolls, E. T., Morris, R. G., O'Doherty, J. O., Bullock, P. R., et al. (2003). Changes in emotion after circumscribed surgical lesions of the orbitofrontal and cingulate cortices. *Brain, 126*, 1691-1712.

Hublin, J.-J. (2005). Evolution of the human brain and comparative paleoanthropology. In J.-R. D. S. Dehaene, M. D. Hauser, & G. Rizzolatti (Eds.), *From monkey brain to human brain* (pp. 57-71). Cambridge, MA: MIT Press.

Jacobsen, T., Schubotz, R. I., Höfel, L., & von Cramon, D. Y. (2005). Brain correlates of aesthetic judgment of beauty. *Neuroimage, 29*, 276-285.

James, H. V. A., & Petraglia, M. D. (2005). Modern human origins and the evolution of behavior in the later Pleistocene record of South Asia. *Current Anthropology, 46*, S3-S16.

Kaestner, S., & Ungerleider, L. G. (2000). Mechanisms of visual attention in the human cortex. *Annual Review of Neuroscience, 23*, 315-341.

Kaplan, S. (1992). Environmental preference in a knowledge-seeking, knowledge-using organism. In J. H. Barkow, L. Cosmides, & J. Tooby (Eds.), *The adapted mind: Evolutionary psychology and the generation of culture* (pp. 581-598). New York: Oxford University Press.

Kawabata, H., & Zeki, S. (2004). Neural correlates of beauty. *Journal of Neurophysiology, 91*, 1699-1705.

Klein, R. G. (1995). Anatomy, behavior, and modern human origins. *Journal of World Prehistory, 9*, 167-198.

Kondo, H., Saleem, K. S., & Price, J. L. (2003). Differential connections of the temporal pole with the orbital and medial prefrontal networks in macaque monkeys. *The Journal of Comparative Neurology, 465*, 499-523.

Krawczyk, D. C. (2002). Contributions of the prefrontal cortex to the neural basis of human decision making. *Neuroscience and Biobehavioral Reviews* (26), 631-664.

Laland, K. N., Odling-Smee, J., & Feldman, M. W. (2001). Cultural niche construction and human evolution. *Journal of Evolutionary Biology, 14*, 22-33.

Lane, R. D., Reiman, E. M., Axelrod, B., Yun, L.-S., Holmes, A., & Schwartz, G. E. (1998). Neural correlates of levels of emotional awareness: Evidence of an interaction between emotion and attention in the anterior cingulate cortex. *Journal of Cognitive Neuroscience, 10*, 525-535.

Lang, P. J., Bradley, M. M., Fitzsimmons, J. R., Cuthbert, B. N., Scott, J. D., Moulder, B., et al. (1998). Emotional arousal and activation of the visual cortex, and fMRI analysis. *Psychophysiology 35*, 199-210.

Leder, H., Belke, B., Oeberst, A., & Augustin, D. (2004). A model of aesthetic appreciation and aesthetic judgments. *British Journal of Psychology, 95*, 489-508.

Lewontin, R. C. (1990). The evolution of cognition. In D. N. Smith (Ed.), *An invitation to cognitive science, Vol. 3: Thinking* (pp. 229-246). Cambridge, MA: MIT Press.

Linnaeus, C. (1735). *Systema Naturae per Naturae Regna Tria, Secundum Classes, Ordines, Genera, Species cum Characteribus, Synonymis, Locis.* Stockholm: Laurentii Sylvii.

Majdan, M., & Shatz, C. J. (2006). Effects of visual experience on activity-dependent gene regulation in cortex. *Nature Neuroscience, 9*, 650-659.

Marcus, G. (2004). *The birth of the mind: How a tiny number of genes creates the complexities of human thought.* New York: Basic Books.

Martin, R. D. (1998). Comparative aspects of human brain evolution: Sclaing, energy costs and confounding variables. In N. G. Jablonski & L. C. Aiello (Eds.), *The origin and diversification of language* (pp. 35-68). San Francisco: The California Academy of Sciences.

McBrearty, S., & Brooks, A. (2000). The revolution that wasn't: A new interpretation of the origins of modern human behavior. *Journal of Human Evolution, 39*, 453-563.

Mellars, P., A. (1991). Cognitive changes and the emergence of modern humans in Europe. *Cambridge Archaeological Journal, 1*, 63-76.

Miller, G. F. (2001). Aesthetic fitness: How sexual selection sharped artistic virtuosity as a fitness indicator and aesthetic preferences as mate choice criteria. *Bulletin of Psychology and the Arts, 2*, 20-25.

Munakata, Y., Santos, L. R., Spelke, E. S., Hauser, M. D., & O'Reilly, R. C. (2001). Visual representation in the wild: How rhesus monkeys parse objects. *Journal of Cognitive Neuroscience, 13*, 44-58.

Nakamura, K., & Kubota, K. (1996). The primate temporal pole: Its putative role in object recognition and memory. *Behavioural Brain Research, 77*, 53-77.

Nimchinsky, E. A., Gilissen, E., Allman, J. M., Perl, D. L., Erwin, J. M., & Hof, P. R. (1999). A neuronal morphologic type unique to humans and great apes. *Proceedings of the National Academy of Sciences USA, 96*, 526-5273.

O'Doherty, J. O., Deichmann, R., Critchley, H. D., & Dolan, R. J. (2002). Neural responses during anticipation of a primary taste reward. *Neuron, 33*, 815-826.

O'Doherty, J. O., Kringelbach, M. L., Rolls, E. T., Hornak, J., & Andrews, C. (2001). Abstract reward and punishment representations in the human orbitofrontal cortex. *Nature Neuroscience, 4*, 95-102.

Oldham, M. C., Horvath, S., & Geschwind, D. H. (2006). Conservation and evolution of gene coexpression networks in human and chimpanzee brains. *Proceedings of the National Academy of Sciences USA, 103*, 17973-17978.

Orban, G. A., Van Essen, D., & Vanduffel, W. (2004). Comparative mapping of higher visual areas in monkeys and humans. *Trends in Cognitive Sciences, 8*, 315-324.

Orians, G. H. (2001). An evolutionary perspective on aesthetics. *Bulletin of Psychology and the Arts, 2*, 25-29.

Orians, G. H., & Heerwagen, J. H. (1992). Evolved responses to landscapes. In J. H. Barkow, L. Cosmides, & J. Tooby (Eds.), *The adapted mind: Evolutionary psychology and the generation of culture* (pp. 556-579). New York: Oxford University Press.

Petrides, M. (2005). Lateral prefrontal cortex: Architectonic and functional organization. *Philosophical Transactions of the Royal Society B, 360*, 781-795.

Petrides, M., & Pandya, D. N. (1999). Dorsolateral prefrontal cortex: Comparative cyto-architectonic analysis in the human and macaque brain and corticocortical connection patterns. *European Journal of Neuroscience, 11*, 1011-1036.

Petrides, M., & Pandya, D. N. (2001). Comparative cytoarchitectonic analysis of the human and the macaque ventrolateral prefrontal cortex and corticocortical connection patterns in the monkey. *European Journal of Neuroscience, 16*, 291-310.

Poghosyan, V., Shibata, T., & Ioannides, A. A. (2005). Effects of attention and arousal on early responses in striate cortex. *European Journal of Neuroscience, 22*, 225-234.

Pollard, K. S., Salama, S. R., Lambert, N., Lambot, M.-A., Coppens, S., Pedersen, J. S., et al. (2006). An RNA gene expressed during cortical development evolved rapidly in humans. *Nature, 443*, 167-172.

Poremba, A., Malloy, M., Saunders, R. C., Carson, R. E., Herscovitch, P., & Mishkin, M. (2004). Species-specific calls evoke asymmetric activity in the monkey's temporal poles. *Nature, 427*, 448-451.

Preuss, T. M., & Coleman, G. Q. (2002). Human-specific organization of primary visual cortex: Alternating compartments of dense Cat-301 and Calbindin immunoreactivity in layer 4A. *Cerebral Cortex, 12*, 671-691.

Rilling, J. K. (2006). Human and nonhuman primate brains: Are they allometrically scaled versions of the same design? *Evolutionary Anthropology, 15*, 65-77.

Rilling, J. K., & Insel, T. R. (1999). The primate neocortex in comparative perspective using magnetic resonance imaging. *Journal of Human Evolution, 37*, 191-223.

Rilling, J. K., & Seligman, R. A. (2002). A quantitative morphometric comparative analysis of the primate temporal lobe. *Journal of Human Evolution, 42*, 505-533.

Rolls, E. T. (2004). Convergence of sensory systems in the orbitofrontal cortex in primates and brain design for emotion. *The Anatomical Record Part A, 281A*, 1212-1225.

Sasaki, Y., Vanduffel, W., Knutsen, T., Tyler, C., & Tootell, R. (2005). Symmetry activates extrastriate visual cortex in human and nonhuman primates. *Proceedings of the National Academy of Sciences USA, 102*, 3159-3163.

Schenker, N. M., Desgouttes, A.-M., & Semendeferi, K. (2005). Neural connectivity and cortical substrates of cognition in hominoids. *Journal of Human Evolution, 49*, 547-569.

Schoenemann, P. T. (2006). Evolution of the size and functional areas of the human brain. *Annual Review of Anthropology, 35*, 379-406.

Schoenemann, P. T., Sheehan, M. J., & Glotzer, L. D. (2005). Prefrontal white matter volume is disproportionately larger in humans than in other primates. *Native Neuroscience, 8,* 242-252.

Sejnowski, T. J., & Churchland, P. S. (1989). Brain and cognition. In M. I. Posner (Ed.), *Foundations of cognitive science* (pp. 301-356). Cambridge, MA: MIT Press.

Semendeferi, K., Armstrong, E., Schleicher, A., Zilles, K., & Van Hoesen, G. W. (1998). Limbic frontal cortex in hominoids: A comparative study of area 13. *American Journal of Physical Anthropology, 106*, 129-155.

Semendeferi, K., Armstrong, E., Schleicher, A., Zilles, K., & Van Hoesen, G. W. (2001). Prefrontal cortex in humans and apes: A comparative study of area 10. *American Journal of Physical Anthropology, 114*, 224-241.

Semendeferi, K., & Damasio, H. (2000). The brain and its main anatomical subdivisions in living hominoids using magnetic resonance imaging. *Journal of Human Evolution, 38,* 317-332.

Sereno, M. I., & Tootell, R. B. H. (2005). From monkeys to humans: what do we now know anout brain homologies? *Current Opinion in Neurobiology, 15*, 135-144.

Sherwood, C. C., Holloway, R. L., Semendeferi, K., & Hof, P. R. (2005). Is prefrontal white matter enlargement a human evolutionary specialization? *Nature Neuroscience, 8*, 537-538.

Sherwood, C. C., Stimpson, C. D., Raghanti, M. A., Wildman, D. E., Uddin, M., Grossman, L. I., et al. (2006). Evolution of increased glia-neuron ratios in the human frontal cortex. *Proceedings of the National Academy of Sciences USA, 103*, 13606-13611.

Shi, P., Bakewell, M. A., & Zhang, J. (2006). Did brian-specific genes evolve faster in humans than in chimpanzees? *Trends in Genetics, 22*, 608-613.

Sigala, N., Gabbiani, F., & Logothetis, N. K. (2002). Visual categorization and object representation in monkeys and humans. *Journal of Cognitive Neuroscience, 14*, 187-198.

Smith, C. U. M. (2005). Evolutionary neurobiology and aesthetics. *Perspectives in Biology and Medicine, 48*, 17-30.

Tincoff, R., & Hauser, M. D. (2005). Cognitive basis for language evolution in nonhuman primates. In K. Brown (Ed.), *Encyclopedia of language and linguistics* (pp. 533-538). New York: Elsevier.

Tomasello, M. (1999). *The cultural origins of human cognition.* Cambridge, MA: Harvard University Press.

Uddin, M., Wildman, D. E., Liu, G., Xu, W., Johnson, R. M., Hof, P. R., et al. (2004). Sister grouping of chimpanzees and humans as revealed by genome-wide phylogenetic analysis of brain gene expression profiles. *Proceedings of the National Academy of Sciences USA, 101*, 2957-2962.

Van Essen, D. (2005). Surface-based comparisons of macaque and human cortical organization. In J.-R. D. S. Dehaene, M. D. Hauser, & G. Rizzolatti (Eds.), *From monkey brain to human brain* (pp. 3-19). Cambridge, MA: MIT Press.

Vartanian, O., & Goel, V. (2004). Neuroanatomical correlates of aesthetic preference for paintings. *Neuroreport, 15*, 893-897.

Vartanian, O., & Nadal, M. (2007). A biological approach to a model of aesthetic experience. In L. Dorfman, C. Martindale, & V. Petrov (Eds.), *Aesthetics and innovation* (pp. 429-499). Cambridge, MA: Cambridge Scholars Publishing.

Vogels, R. (1999). Categorization of complex visual images by rhesus monkeys. Part 2: Single-cell study. *European Journal of Neuroscience, 11*, 1239-1255.

Weiss, D. J., & Newport, E. L. (2006). Mechanisms underlying language acquisition: Benefits from a comparative approach. *Infancy, 9*, 241-257.

Zilles, K. (2005). Evolution of the human brain and comparative cyto- and receptor architecture. In J.-R. D. S. Dehaene, M. D. Hauser, & G. Rizzolatti (Eds.), *From monkey brain to human brain* (pp. 41-56). Cambridge, MA: MIT Press.

Zilles, K., Armstrong, E., Schleicher, A., & Kretschmann, H.-J. (1988). The human pattern of gyrification in the cerebral cortex. *Anatomy and Embryology, 179*, 173-179.

Zilles, K., Schlaug, G., Matelli, M., Luppino, G., Schleicher, A., Qü, M., et al. (1995). Mapping of human and macaque sensoriomotor areas by integrating architectonic, transmitter receptor, MRI and PET data. *Journal of Anatomy, 187*, 515-537.

Zysset, S., Huber, O., Ferstl, E., & von Cramon, D. Y. (2002). The anterior frontomedian cortex and evaluative judgment: An fMRI study. *Neuroimage, 15*, 983-991.

CHAPTER 7

Prospects for a Neuropsychology of Visual Art

Anjan Chatterjee

Can we learn anything from the neuropsychology of art? Neuropsychology has been instrumental in advancing our knowledge of various cognitive systems, such as perception, memory, and language. But its impact on the study of aesthetics has thus far been minimal. Why is that? Certainly, an important factor is that as a domain of inquiry, the neuropsychology of art (and neuroaesthetics in general) is in its infancy. The data from which one might draw inferences are sparse. Rather than in peer-reviewed papers, these data are often found in book chapters, rendering them inaccessible to search engines. Beyond the constraints of limited data and impediments to its access, fundamental questions within the field about proper methods remain unanswered. Furthermore, the phenomena, striking as they often are, have not been used adequately in constructing theories of art. Finally, an underlying deep worry is that perhaps the entire effort is misguided. Art, by its very nature, might resist the kind of reduction insisted upon by science. Or, once filtered through the lens of science, art might lose the very qualities that make it a special human endeavor.

In this chapter, I suggest it is premature to make any final judgments about prospects for a neuropsychology of art. I focus specifically on visual arts. More progress has been made in visual art than in music or dance or literature. Thus, visual arts can better illustrate both the potential and pitfalls inherent in this line of inquiry. To begin with, I look backward at previous reports of artists with brain damage. I do so selectively, to underscore one approach (there are likely others) that in my view may prove to be fruitful. I will then discuss some limitations of the field and look forward at what needs to happen for the field to progress. One could speculate that artists, by virtue of their visuo-motor skills, might be relatively protected from the visuo-motor deficits commonly associated with brain damage. Such a speculation appears not to be true as is evident from reviews of the effects of brain damage on artistic production (Bogousslavsky & Boller, 2005; Chatterjee, 2004a, 2004b; Rose, 2006; Zaidel, 2005). Unilateral spatial neglect is a disorder in which patients are unaware of one side of space (Chatterjee, 2003). Artists with unilateral spatial neglect demonstrate neglect in their artwork (Jung, 1974). Visual agnosia is the inability to perceive or recognize objects visually. Artists with visual agnosias have difficulty depicting objects in their output (Wapner, Judd, & Gardner, 1978). Achromatopsia is the inability to apprehend color. Artists with achromatopsia may be unable to use color properly in their images (Sacks, 1995a). In these cases, the artwork illustrates the nature of neuropsychological deficits, sometimes in beautiful and captivating ways. But these works do not necessarily offer insight into the nature of artistic production itself.

How might we capitalize on cases of artists with brain damage more profitably? One strategy is to examine instances in which brain damage produces a paradoxical facilitation of artistic output. The effects of brain damage on the capacity to produce visual art can stand in sharp contrast to many other human capacities. Diseases of the brain can impair our ability to communicate information, coordinate movements, recognize objects, apprehend emotions, and make logical decisions. By contrast, while diseases of the brain can certainly alter the ability to produce art, the alterations are sometimes considered improvements. Cases of improved artistic abilities fall into a general class of paradoxical functional facilitations produced by brain damage (Kapur, 1996). Most other examples of such facilitation involve relatively simple sensory and motor abilities and automatic processes.

Implicit in this discussion is the view that there is no single art center in the brain. Nor is it the case that one hemisphere has some privileged role in art production per se. Rather, the production of art is highly complex, with many components mediated by different parts of the brain. The final artistic output emerges from a coordination of these different components. Brain damage alters which parts of the brain are available in the overall process, and the output becomes the result of a different coordination of components. In general, peripheral injuries, whether at input (blindness) or output (paralysis), are less likely to be revealing of the components involved in artistic production. By contrast, central disruptions, especially those in which there is a paradoxical facilitation of art, may offer greater insights into the nature of artistic production.

THE PARADOXICAL FACILITATION OF VISUAL ART

In what follows, I review four ways in which neurological disorders might improve art: the disposition to produce visual art, provision of a unique visual vocabulary, aids to descriptive accuracy, and changes in expressive powers.

Disposition to Produce Art

Fronto-temporal dementias (FTD) are a group of degenerative neurological diseases in which people undergo profound changes in their personalities. They can be socially disinhibited and disorganized, and they can have problems with their language, attention, and ability to make decisions. In addition to these alterations in comportment and cognition, a few people with FTD develop a propensity for producing art for the first time. Miller and colleagues (1998) note that their art tends to be realistic, not abstract or symbolic. It is most often visual and is highly detailed with an obsessive quality. The patients themselves seem intensely preoccupied with their art. The artistic output of people with FTD appears to be a consequence of the change in their personalities. That is, their acquired obsessive-compulsive traits find expression graphically, and they produce striking visual images as a consequence of their repetition and attention to detail.

Several other examples are consistent with the idea that obsessive-compulsive traits brought on by neurological diseases can predispose individuals to produce art. Sacks (1995b) described the case of the Italian painter Franco Magnani, living in San Francisco. Magnani painted hundreds of realistic scenes of an Italian town, Pontito, where he grew up. At the age of 31, Magnani had an illness, which was probably an encephalitic disease. Following that illness, he began to paint obsessively. Pontito was the only subject of his art and he painted compulsively. His obsession with Pontito preoccupied his thoughts and conversations. Sacks speculated that he had partial complex seizures and was in part demonstrating an obsessive "sticky" personality, which is sometimes associated with temporal lobe epilepsy (Waxman & Geschwind, 1975). Such patients are also sometimes "hypergraphic," meaning they write incessantly. However, instead of Magnani's hypergraphia being expressed verbally, he expressed himself visually.

Lythgoe, Polak, Kalmus, de Haan, and Chong (2005) reported the case of a builder with a subarachnoid hemorrhage. He had no interest in art premorbidly, but became an obsessive artist after recovery from the initial injury. After the hemorrhage, he had normal verbal and performance IQ and normal behavior except for some degree of verbal disinhibition. He did well on most neuropsychological tasks except for those that involved mental flexibility. He also began to draw hundreds of sketches, mostly faces. He then moved to large-scale drawings, sometimes covering entire rooms, while confining his art to a few themes.

Finally, about 10% of children with autism have savant-like abilities (Rimland & Fein, 1988). A subset of these children produce striking visual images (Sacks, 1995c). The most detailed description of such a case was Nadia, reported by Selfe (1977). As a baby, Nadia did not respond to her mother, and as she got older, she lacked social empathy. As a child, she had an obsessive concern with the presence of other children, without establishing any substantial interactions with them. Her acquisition of language was delayed. Despite these developmental abnormalities, she had remarkable drawing skills. By the age of 3 she was drawing life-like horses. She drew intensively for a few moments at a time, always copying images. She also focused on specific kinds of images like horses, of which she drew hundreds of examples. While Nadia's abilities were striking, she was not unique. Autistic children with these striking drawing skills seem to focus on specific subjects and draw them repeatedly.

Thus, several neurological disorders that produce obsessive-compulsive traits can also dispose people to produce art. These artists produce realistic images and tend to be preoccupied by a restricted range of themes. While the neural basis for obsessive-compulsive disorders is not completely understood, dopamine and alterations of reward circuits are probably involved. We recently reported a patient with Parkinson's disease who produced his art obsessively after being placed on dopamine agonists (Chatterjee, Amorapanth, & Hamilton, 2006). Interestingly, despite profound impairments in his motor control, which were evident when he wrote, he was able to make graceful, sinuous movements when drawing. Obsessive-compulsive traits are also associated with dysfunction of the orbitofrontal and medial temporal cortices and fronto-striatal circuits (Kwon et al., 2003; Saxena et al., 1999; Ursu, Stenger, Shear, Jones, & Carter, 2003). Notably, in the cases described in this section, these regions could have been damaged and posterior occipito-temporal cortices were presumably intact. The preservation of posterior cortices ensures that the neural substrate that represents faces, places, and objects are preserved and are thus available as subjects of these patients' obsessions.

We still do not know the details of how obsessive-compulsive trait changes results in the disposition to produce art. For example, why do only some patients with FTD or with autism develop these skills? Can the others be encouraged to produce art, and could such an "intervention" be therapeutic? What predisposes some individuals to produce visual art and others to obsess over other things?

Visual Vocabulary

Neurological disorders such as migraine and epilepsy can be associated with productive visual phenomena. Of over 200 entries submitted to the first National Art Competition sponsored by the British Migraine Association and WB Pharmaceuticals, 70% showed spectral appearances, 48% showed fortifications, 16% showed areas of visual loss, and 2.5% showed mosaic visions (Wilkinson & Robinson, 1985).

The artist Ignatius Brennan, reported by Podoll and Robinson (2000), eloquently expressed how migrainous auras inspired his own art. He experienced migraines at the age of 11 as frightening episodes of visual loss, often with a zigzag cloud obscuring much of his visual fields. As he got older, he saw triangles and rounded forms as well as mosaics. He also experienced visual distortions of things getting larger or smaller. He described the effects of migraines on his art as follows:

> I started with pictures of my migraine experiences unconsciously rather than deliberately, when I was in art school. I used to do a lot of drawings of landscapes at that time and often found that I would be drawing clouds not just in the sky, but everywhere, which I think was a reference to the visual voids experienced during visual loss. I also used serrated zigzag shapes in my drawings, symbolizing the experience of a whole being broken up. . . . Clouds, zigzags and other imagery are part of my own personal visual vocabulary, but which certainly has come out of migraine experiences. I'm absolutely sure. I don't tend to do that deliberately, but when it suits a particular subject, e.g., to represent a feeling or an emotion, I make use of these images in different ways. . . ." (Podoll & Robinson, 2000, p. 264)

Such patients may be able to offer insights into how artists use visual vocabulary in their productions. Greater analyses of these cases may even inform us about how artists develop this visual vocabulary and maybe even a visual grammar in concatenating visual primitives. Perhaps such analyses might provide insight into how individuals might be trained in "developing their eye."

Descriptive Accuracy

For centuries, visual artists have been preoccupied with accurately rendering objects and the environment. Underlying the problem of descriptive accuracy in drawing and painting are the roles of seeing and knowing when apprehending objects. Visual agnosias are a class of disorders in which patients have difficulty recognizing objects (Farah, 1990). Since Lissauer's classic descriptions of visual agnosias, object recognition deficits are recognized to lie on a continuum between perceptual and conceptual deficits (Lissauer, 1890). Perceptually based agnosias, called apperceptive agnosias, impair the ability to process the visual information into a coherent object. Conceptually based agnosias, called associative agnosias, involve impairments of semantic knowledge of the object (Farah, 1990).

Wapner et al. (1978) described an artist with an apperceptive agnosia who had difficulty copying images despite being able to convey depth and shading in drawings that were otherwise fragmented. His preserved semantic system was of little help in guiding his artistic production. Thus, when asked to draw a telephone, he would construct images by reasoning, "It needs a base for it to stand on, a place to speak into, something to hear with a wire to plug in for communication and a place to dial." This verbal strategy was not particularly effective in rendering accurate images. Thus, semantic knowledge by itself does not help render objects accurately.

This patient contrasts with two people with associative agnosias (Franklin, van Sommers, & Howard, 1992; Schwartz & Chawluck, 1990). In both cases, when asked to draw objects from verbal labels, these people drew crude, simplified images similar to those drawn by a young child. However, with complex visual images, the results were strikingly different. For example, one of these people could copy a portrait originally painted by Botticelli or draw a portrait of a staff worker beautifully (Franklin et al., 1992). Semantic knowledge of an object is by no means necessary to render it accurately.

Observations of a Polish aphasic artist are also consistent with this point (Kaczmarek, 1991). Profoundly influenced by the events of World War II, his premorbid paintings were antiwar statements, which often included numbers, letters, and ideograms. Following his stroke, he was nonfluent and only produced a few words. At its core, our semantic system has the ability to abstract and generalize. The use of abstracted symbols could be considered a marker for a preserved semantic system. Although his semantic system was not tested in detail, from the descriptions of his aphasia, one might infer that it was impoverished. His inability to make use of verbal symbols extended to his artwork. He was no longer able to produce paintings in his previous style. However, he was still able to draw realistic landscapes and portraits quite well, despite having lost his ability to manipulate symbols!

Does semantic knowledge of an object actually hinder artistic production? The art historian Ernst Gombrich (1960) observed that even trained artists impose knowledge of what they are looking at in their depictions in a way that can compromise their accuracy. Thus, impaired knowledge, provided visual-motor systems are intact, might aid in the ability to depict objects and scenes accurately. Perhaps such impaired knowledge accounts for cases of autistic children with savant-like artistic abilities.

Autistic artists need only to look at an object for a few minutes before drawing them rapidly and accurately (Sacks, 1995c; Selfe, 1977). Nadia's abilities were not an accelerated version of other children's drawing development. She did not first go through a phase of drawing simple schematic images before learning to draw realistically. Rather, her skills were developed at the outset and did not change much over time. Nadia initially drew horses repeatedly. She made lines deftly and without hesitation. Two observations suggest that Nadia treated these images differently than most people. First, she would start the drawing anywhere on the page. Rather than trying to squeeze the image into the page, she terminated the drawing when she came to the paper's edge even if it meant only drawing part of the horse. Second, most people draw horses by starting at the head. Nadia could start her drawing at the neck of the horse and seemed unaffected by critical features associated with a specific object, such as the head of a horse. Her remarkable skill at drawing horses and pelicans appear to have emerged from the obsessive focus on specific objects that were at the same time not obscured by semantic associations that interfere with the ability to "see" the visual object. As Nadia eventually acquired language, her drawings became more prosaic. Presumably, the acquisition of language reflected the development of a richer semantic system and detracted from her artistic skills.

Changed Expressivity

Visual art is of course not restricted to rendering objects and scenes accurately. Perhaps driven by the advent of photography, visual art has diverged into many forms. Among the most intriguing effects of brain damage on artists are a class of phenomena in which the inability to make accurate depictions results in surprisingly appealing stylistic changes in their art. These stylistic changes can occur in the use of color and form and in the content of images.

Sacks (1995a) described an artist with an acquired achromatopsia following a traumatic brain injury. His earlier paintings were colorful and quite abstract. After the accident, everything appeared "dirt gray" to him. His initial attempts to use color were haphazard, and he eventually resigned himself to black and white paintings. With time, he introduced a limited set of colors to his paintings. After an initial sense of helplessness, he began to consider his new way of seeing as a strange gift in which he saw the world as pure form, uncluttered by color. This new way of seeing introduced him to a new range of expressions. For example, when driving, he saw a sunrise in which blazing reds were seen as black. He described the scene as "The sun rose like a bomb, like some enormous explosion. Has anyone seen a sunrise like this before?" Inspired by this image, he produced a black and white painting called "Nuclear Sunrise."

Right hemisphere damage can produce left spatial neglect in which patients are unaware of the left side of space (Chatterjee, 2003). Artists with neglect omit the left side of images that they draw or paint (Blanke, Ortigue, & Landis, 2003; Cantagallo & Sala, 1998; Halligan & Marshall, 1997; Jung, 1974; Marsh & Philwin, 1987; Schnider, Regard, Benson, & Landis, 1993). As they recover from their neglect, their use of line may still be altered. Two examples show how this change in the use of line can produce art that comes to be regarded highly. Lovis Corinth, an important German artist, suffered a right hemisphere stroke in 1911. As he recovered, he resumed painting. His self portraits and portraits of his wife showed clear changes in style, with details on the left sometimes left out and textures on the left blended with the background. Alfred Kuhn characterized this work as follows (quoted in Gardner, 1975):

> He [Corinth] had become prescient for the hidden facets of appearance. . . . The contours disappear, the bodies are often as ript asunder, deformed, disappeared into textures . . . also the faithfulness of portraits had ceased almost entirely. . . . With wide stripes the person is captured in essence. Characterization is now exaggerated, indeed, often to caricature . . . Corinth always seems to be painting a picture behind the picture, one which he alone sees... at this point Corinth shifted from the ranks of the great painters into the circle of the great artists.

Heller (1994) reported the experience of the artist Loring Hughes, who, after a right hemisphere stroke, had difficulty coordinating the spatial relationship between lines. This forced her to abandon her premorbid style of depictive accuracy. Instead, she turned to her own imagination and emotions. Initially, she was too ashamed to display her paintings. Once she became comfortable with her new style, she began to show her work. The artistic community responded well to these distorted images. The critic Eileen Watkins described her work as now delivering "an emotional wallop" that was not present previously.

The stylistic changes, when they occur with left-brain damage, appear to be quite different from those observed with right-brain damage. The specific changes are the introduction of more vivid colors and a change in content. These changes are exemplified in the Bulgarian painter Zlatio Boiyadjiev, a Californian artist named Katherine Sherwood, and a Swiss painter reported by Annoni, Devuyst, Carota, Bruggimann, and Bogousslavsky (2004).

Boiyadjiev's premorbid artistic style was natural and pictorial, and he tended to use earth tones in his paintings. Following the onset of his aphasia, Boiyadjiev's paintings have been described as richer, more colorful and containing more fluid and energetic lines (Brown, 1977; Zaimov, Kitov, & Kolev, 1969). The imagery in his work became more inventive and at times even bizarre and fantastical. Similarly, Katherine Sherwood suffered a left-hemisphere hemorrhagic stroke, which left her with an aphasia and right-sided weakness (Waldman, 2000). She trained herself to paint with her left hand, and since then her career has flourished. Premorbidly, her images were described as "highly cerebral," incorporating a range of esoteric images such as cross-dressers, medieval seals, and spy photos. After her stroke, she felt that she could not produce such images if she wanted. Her new style is described as "raw" and "intuitive," with large irregular circular movements. She says her left hand enjoys an ease and a grace with the brush that her right hand never had, and describes it as "unburdened." Finally, Annoni and colleagues (2004) recently described a Swiss landscape painter whose art was described as being "figurative-impressionist." He had a small stroke in the left thalamus. His wife thought he had mild emotional dyscontrol after his stroke. He felt that he was more sensitive to the hidden beauty of images and used bolder colors. He switched from realistic to more impressionistic images. He thought that he was less likely to use lines, contours, and perspective clearly and was more creative when he used his left than his right hand. A final stylistic change rendered by brain damage is a move toward simplicity. Annoni and colleagues (2004) described a person with a left occipital lesion. A month after his stroke, he resumed drawing and painting. His new artwork was simplified, stylized, increasingly abstract, and confined to limited use of colors. It is not known if damage to visual association cortices would consistently result in simplification and abstraction. A few artists with Alzheimer's disease who have continued to paint (Crutch, Isaacs, & Rossor, 2001; Maurer & Prvulovic, 2004; Miller & Hou, 2004) seem to demonstrate a similar pattern. My clinical experience is that such patients are often too disorganized to bring an art project to completion. I have cared for several artist-patients who spend hours in their studio puttering around without producing much art. William Utermohlen painted a series of self-portraits several years into the course of his illness. As these portraits became increasingly simplified and distorted, they appear as haunting psychological self-studies.

The most prominent of artists with Alzheimer's disease is the expressionist Willem de Kooning (Storr, 1995). After the onset of his neurological disease, de Kooning's ex-wife and students provided the structure for him to continue to work. They stretched his canvases and mixed his colors. He was noted to be generally apathetic except in his studio, where he was engaged and lively. Experts generally agree that this late period represents a new and coherent style for de Kooning. His paintings became successively simpler, and he confined his palette to primary colors. Traces of shapes from earlier works are evident, but these are pared down. Garrels (1995), the senior curator at the San Francisco Museum of Modern Art, thought "the vocabulary of forms was retained, but clarified . . . the results are paintings of an openness and freedom not seen before, paintings that are extraordinarily lyrical, immediately sensual, and exhilarating."

LOOKING FORWARD

Despite the preliminary observations that I have recounted, much needs to be done if neuropsychology is to make substantive contributions to empirical aesthetics. For this field to mature, we need to do more than catalogue fascinating anecdotes. I suggest that three things are necessary (whether they are sufficient remains to be seen): greater in-depth study of cases, measurement, and the application of testable theories.

Case Studies

In the introduction, I mentioned that the data on which one might make inferences about the neuropsychology of art are sparse. When looking at the effects of brain damage on artistic production, group studies are probably impossible. Artists with neurological diseases are rare and too varied in their talents and styles to make group studies feasible (patients with migraines may be an exception). Thus, we are largely restricted to the analysis of single cases, an approach that has had a long and fruitful tradition in cognitive neuropsychology (e.g., Code, Wallesch, Joanette, & Lecours, 1996). Even though established artists with brain damage are rare, they are still probably underrepresented in the literature. Most clinicians view such cases as interesting oddities and not as potential probes for scientific inquiry. When such cases are published, the reports of their cognition and their art are sketchy and rarely analytic. At a minimum, we need more case studies that are studied well, if progress is to be made in the field.

Measurement

A major shortcoming of most of the cases reported thus far is the absence of measurement. How can one be certain about changes in artistic production rendered by brain damage without something measuring the artwork itself? Claims about changes in art after brain damage, such as those that I have reviewed, are usually *post hoc* interpretations. These interpretations are then supported by a few illustrative examples of artwork. We desperately need an instrument that can assess artistic change. Such an instrument should have at least two characteristics. First, it should assess artwork along a comprehensive set of attributes. These attributes should include formal properties (use of line, color, composition, etc.) and content properties (abstract, realisms, etc.). Second, it should distinguish between descriptive and evaluative judgments.

With such an instrument and a representative sample of works of art (such as those before or after brain damage), one could begin to impose quantitative structure to otherwise casual observations. Raters blinded to the status of individual artworks could assess these pieces in order to discern which attributes, if any, have changed. Ratings of these changes need to meet the most basic requirements of reliability and be subjected to statistics when testing hypotheses. Such an instrument need not be specific for neuropsychology. Rather, it would serve as a yardstick that could measure differences of any sort, whether rendered by brain damage or artistic styles or cultural traditions.

The kind of instrument I am advocating would have another very important use. We know nothing about the neuropsychology of the perception of art. One might expect that sensitivity to different attributes within a work of art would be affected by different kinds of brain damage. By establishing reliable ratings by normal subjects of these attributes in representative works of art, one could then begin to explore how brain damage impairs perception of different components of art and the preferences for these works.

Theory Construction

Finally, the field could use an infusion of conceptual clarity in moving forward. What are meaningful and tractable questions worth pursuing? For example, the question of whether aphasia affects art is probably ill-formed. Both art and aphasia are too varied to expect a direct mapping of one category onto the other. An analysis of the component processes of art (Chatterjee, 2004b) is needed to generate testable hypotheses about how brain damage alters the production and perception of art. Several overarching frameworks about the neural bases of art have been advanced. These frameworks vary in their emphasis in making links to principles of visual and cognitive processing (Livingstone, 2002; Ramachandran, & Hirstein, 1999; Zeki, 1999) and to evolutionary imperatives (Grammer, Fink, Moller, & Thornhill, 2003; Miller, 2000) underlying the experience of beauty and art. Such frameworks are critical in laying the initial groundwork for a neuroscience of art. But the initial groundwork should not be mistaken for its final construction. Unless broad theoretical claims can be distilled into prospectively testable hypotheses, they will remain just-so stories.

A FINAL CONSIDERATION

The kind of detailed analyses of patients and their artwork that I am advocating will require the cooperation of artists. Here lies a potential stumbling block. Artists might view the entire endeavor with suspicion. They and others might resist viewing art and its production as "brain phenomena." Discussions of their art, if simply reduced to the effects of brain damage, are likely to be off-putting. Katherine Sherwood and William Utermohlen's work have arguably garnered more attention after the onset of their neurological illnesses. There might be a danger of the art of individuals with neurological illnesses being idealized or used by the art market, recapitulating the role of "outsider art" (originally defined as art of individuals with mental illnesses) in the early twentieth century (Prinzhorn, 1972). Do we ascribe the acclaim of these artists' work, especially when considered better by critics, to their pathology? Undoubtedly, some public interest in their work is generated by the facts of their illness. But, how do we accept the assumption that brain damage can profoundly affect artistic output in principled ways (without this assumption, there is no neuropsychology of art) and at the same time not reduce the value of these works of art or the talents of individual artists to the effects of that brain damage?

One possible solution to this dilemma is to distinguish evaluative judgments across artistic styles from those within styles. For example, take the situation in which brain damage makes it difficult to render lines with descriptive accuracy. An artist with such brain damage might then adopt an expressionistic style. If one generally prefers expressionism to realism, then preference for the new work is more easily ascribed to the effects of brain damage. However, the fact that someone is guided to expressionism when habitual outlets to realism are interrupted by brain damage does not mean that the artist will be a *good* expressionist. Here the evaluation of the artwork and the talents of the artist working within an expressionist idiom are not easily reduced to their brain damage. Rather, instances in which such transitions are made effectively might speak to the talents and creative resilience of these individuals. Scientists will need to be sensitive to these distinctions if we want artists to willingly join our efforts.

CONCLUSIONS

In looking backward, I emphasized the putatively enhancing effects of brain damage on artistic production. Of course, these observations are based on very selected works. It is likely that many more artists are devastated by their brain injury, and these cases are not reported. We simply do not know the base rate of the kinds of effects I have outlined. And yet, the examples of changed and possibly improved art following brain damage point to the multifaceted nature of art. In my view, exploring the mechanisms underlying the alterations of and compensations for these facets is one way that neuropsychology can advance empirical aesthetics. Looking forward, unless the neuropsychology of art can incorporate the basic rigors of any experimental science, we will not get past the seduction of the striking artistic phenomenology under consideration. We can be guardedly optimistic about the prospects of a neuropsychology of art, but the "heavy lifting" remains ahead of us.

ACKNOWLEDGMENT

I would like to thank Lisa Santer, Sharon Gershoni, and Prin X Amorapanth for their helpful critiques of an earlier version of this chapter.

REFERENCES

Annoni, J., Devuyst, G., Carota, A., Bruggimann, L., & Bogousslavsky, J. (2004). Changes in artistic style after minor posterior stroke. *Journal of Neurology, Neurosurgery, and Psychiatry, 76*, 797-803.

Blanke, O., Ortigue, S., & Landis, T. (2003). Color neglect in an artist. *Lancet, 361*, 264.

Bogousslavsky, J., & Boller, F. (2005). *Neurological disorders in famous artists*. Basel: Karger.

Brown, J. (1977). *Mind, brain, and consciousness. The neuropsychology of cognition*. New York: Academic Press.

Cantagallo, A., & Sala, S. D. (1998). Preserved insight in an artist with extrapersonal spatial neglect. *Cortex, 34*, 163-189.

Chatterjee, A. (2003). Neglect. A disorder of spatial attention. In M. D'Esposito (Ed.), *Neurological foundations of cognitive neuroscience* (pp. 1-26). Cambridge, MA: The MIT Press.

Chatterjee, A. (2004a). The neuropsychology of visual artists. *Neuropsychologia, 42*, 1568-1583.

Chatterjee, A. (2004b). Prospects for a cognitive neuroscience of visual aesthetics. *Bulletin of Psychology and the Arts, 4*, 55-59.

Chatterjee, A., Amorapanth, P., & Hamilton, R. (2006). Art produced by a patient with Parkinson's disease. *Behavioural Neurology, 17*, 105-108.

Code, C., Wallesch, C.-W., Joanette, Y., & Lecours, A. (1996). *Classic cases in neuropsychology*. Hove: Psychology Press.

Crutch, S., Isaacs, R., & Rossor, M. (2001). Some workmen can blame their tools: Artistic change in an individual with Alzheimer's disease. *Lancet, 347*, 1096-1098.

Farah, M. J. (1990). *Visual agnosia*. Cambridge, MA: The MIT Press.

Franklin, S., van Sommers, P., & Howard, D. (1992). Drawing without meaning? Dissociations in graphic performance of an agnosic artist. In R. Campbell (Ed.), *Mental lives. Case studies in cognition* (pp. 179-198). Cambridge, MA: Blackwell.

Gardner, H. (1975). *The shattered mind. The person after brain damage*. New York: Alfred A. Knopf.

Garrels, G. (1995). Three toads in the garden: Line, color, and form. In *Willem de Kooning. The late paintings, the 1980s* (pp. 9-37). Minneapolis: San Franscisco Museum of Modern Art and Walker Arts Center.

Gombrich, E. (1960). *Art and illusion*. Princeton: Princeton University Press.

Grammer, K., Fink, B., Moller, A. P., & Thornhill, R. (2003). Darwinian aesthetics: Sexual selection and the biology of beauty. *Biological Review, 78*, 385-407.

Halligan, P. W., & Marshall, J. C. (1997). The art of visual neglect. *Lancet, 350*, 139-140.

Heller, W. (1994). Cognitive and emotional organization of the brain: Influences on the creation and perception of art. In D. Zaidel (Ed.), *Neuropsychology* (pp. 271-292). New York: Academic Press.

Jung, R. (1974). Neuropsychologie und neurophysiologie des konturund formsehens in zeichnerei und malerei. In H. Weick (Ed.), *Pyschopathologie mususcher gestaltungen* (pp. 27-88). Stuttgart: FK Shattauer.

Kaczmarek, B. (1991). Aphasia in an artist: A disorder of symbolic processing. *Aphasiology, 5*, 361-371.

Kapur, N. (1996). Paradoxical functional facilitation in brain-behavior research. *Brain, 119*, 1775-1790.

Kwon, J., Kinm, J., Lee, D., Lee, J., Lee, D., Kim, M., et al. (2003). Neural correlates of clinical symptoms and cognitive dysfunctions in obsessive-compulsive disorder. *Psychiatry Research, 122*, 37-47.

Lissauer, H. (1890). Ein fall von seelenblindheit nebst einem beitrage zur theori derselben. *Archiv fur Psychiatrie und Nervenkrankheiten, 21*, 222-270.

Livingstone, M. (2002). *Vision and art: The biology of seeing*. New York: Abrams.

Lythgoe, M., Polak, T., Kalmus, M., de Haan, M., & Khean Chong, W. (2005). Obsessive, prolofic artistic output following subarachnoid hemorrhage. *Neurology, 64*, 397-398.

Marsh, G. G., & Philwin, B. (1987). Unilateral neglect and constructional apraxia in a right-handed artist with a left posterior lesion. *Cortex, 23*(1), 149-155.

Maurer, K., & Prvulovic, D. (2004). Paintings of an artist with Alzheimer's disease: Visuoconstructive deficits during dementia. *Journal of Neural Transmission, 111*, 235-245.

Miller, B., & Hou, C. (2004). Portraits of artists: Emergence of visual creativity in dementia. *Archives of Neurology, 61*, 842-844.

Miller, B. L., Cummings, J., Mishkin, F., Boone, K., Prince, F., Ponton, M., et al. (1998). Emergence of artistic talent in frontotemporal dementia. *Neurology, 51*, 978-982.

Miller, G. (2000). *The mating mind: How sexual choice shaped the evolution of human nature.* New York: Doubleday.

Podoll, K., & Robinson, D. (2000). Migraine experiences as artistic inspiration in a contemporary artist. *Journal of the Royal Society of Medicine, 93*(5), 263-265.

Prinzhorn, H. (1972). *Artistry of the mentally ill.* Heidelberg: Springer-Verlag.

Ramachandran, V. S., & Hirstein, W. (1999). The science of art: A neurological theory of aesthetic experience. *Journal of Consciousness Studies, 6*(6-7), 15-51.

Rimland, B., & Fein, D. (1988). Special talents of autistic savants. In L. Obler & D. Fein (Eds.), *The exceptional brain* (pp. 474-492). New York: Guilford.

Rose, F. E. (2006). *The neurobiology of painting.* London: Academic Press.

Sacks, O. (1995a). The case of the color blind painter. In *An anthroplogist on mars* (pp. 3-41). New York: Alfred A. Knopf, Inc.

Sacks, O. (1995b). The landscape of his dreams. In *An anthropologist on mars* (pp. 153-187). New York: Alfred A. Knopf.

Sacks, O. (1995c). Prodigies. In *An anthropologist on mars* (pp. 188-243). New York: Alfred A. Knopf.

Saxena, S., Brody, A., Maidment, K., Dunkin, J., Colgan, M., Alborzian, S., et al. (1999). Localized orbitofrontal and subcortical metabolic changes and predictors of response to paroxetine treatment in obsessive-compulsive disorder. *Neuropsychopharmacology, 21*, 683-693.

Schnider, A., Regard, M., Benson, D. F., & Landis, T. (1993). Effect of a right-hemisphere stroke on an artist's performance. *Neuropsychiatry, Neuropsychology, & Behavioral Neurology, 6*(4), 249-255.

Schwartz, M., & Chawluck, J. (1990). Deterioration of language in progressive aphasia: A case study. In M. Schwartz (Ed.), *Modular deficits in Alzheimer-type dementia* (pp. 245-296). Cambridge, MA: The MIT Press.

Selfe, L. (1977). *Nadia. A case of extraordinary drawing ability in an autistic child.* New York: Academic Press.

Storr, R. (1995). At last light. In *Willem de kooning. The late paintings, the 1980s* (pp. 37-79). Minneapolis: San Franscisco Museum of Modern Art and Walker Arts Center.

Ursu, S., Stenger, V. A., Shear, M. K., Jones, M. R., & Carter, C. S. (2003). Overactive action monitoring in obsessive-compulsive disorder. *Psychological Science, 14*, 347-353.

Waldman, P. (2000, Friday, May 12). Master stroke: A tragedy transforms a right-handed artist into a lefty—and a star. *Wall Street Journal.*

Wapner, W., Judd, T., & Gardner, H. (1978). Visual agnosia in an artist. *Cortex, 14*, 343-364.

Waxman, S., & Geschwind, N. (1975). The interictal behavior syndrome associated with temporal lobe epilepsy. *Archives of General Psychiatry, 32*, 1580-1586.

Wilkinson, M., & Robinson, D. (1985). Migraine art. *Cephalalgia, 5*(3), 151-157.

Zaidel, D. (2005). *Neuropsychology of art.* New York: Psychology Press.

Zaimov, K., Kitov, D., & Kolev, N. (1969). Aphasie chez un peintre. *Encephale, 58*, 377-417.

Zeki, S. (1999). *Inner vision: An exploration of art and the brain.* New York: Oxford University Press.

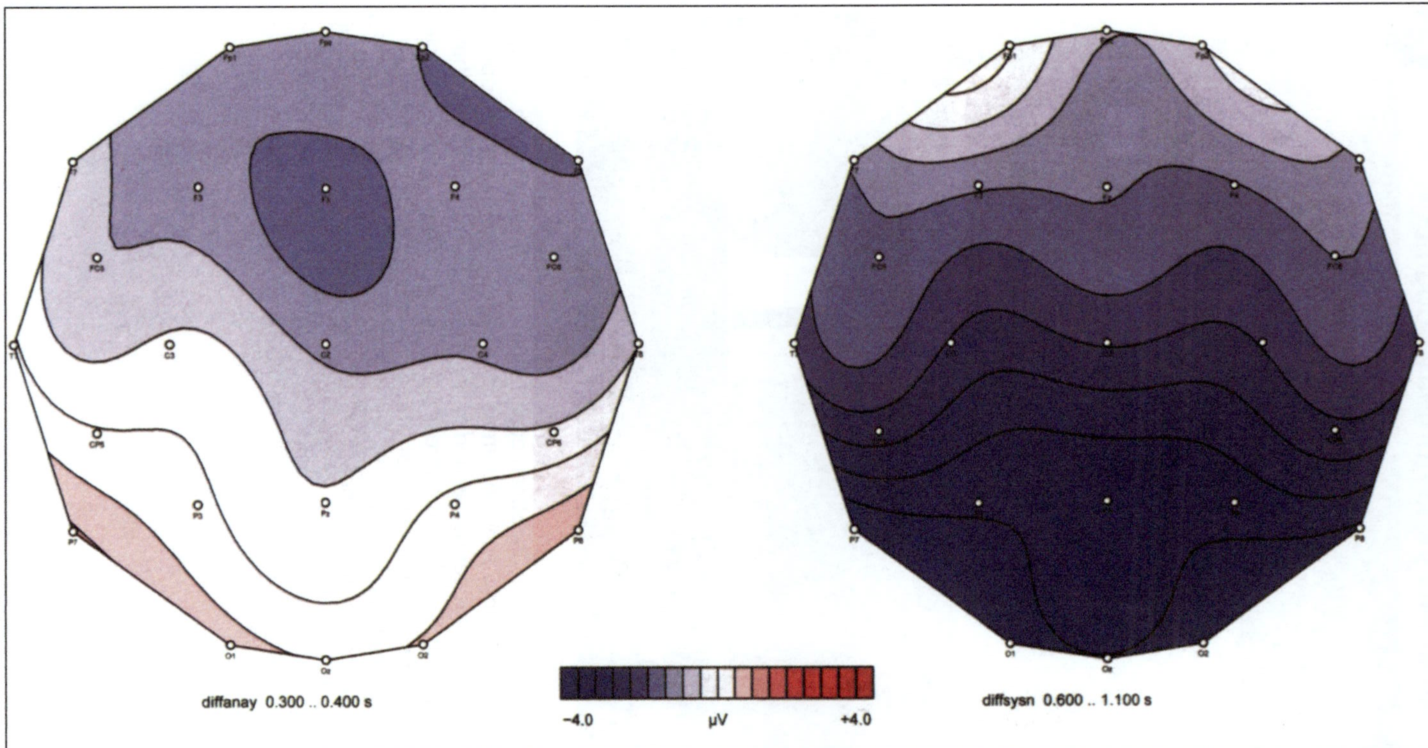

Figure 3. Event-related brain-potential data from Jacobsen and Höfel (2000, 2003). Potential maps. A frontal negativity elicited under the aesthetic judgment (left panel) and posterior sustained negativity elicited under the symmetry judgment task (right panel). Mean difference potentials were plotted. Not aesthetic minus aesthetic in the time window between 300 and 400 milliseconds for the frontal negativity and symmetrical minus nonsymmetrical in the time window between 600 and 1100 milliseconds after stimulus onset. (© Illustrations by Thomas Jacobsen.)

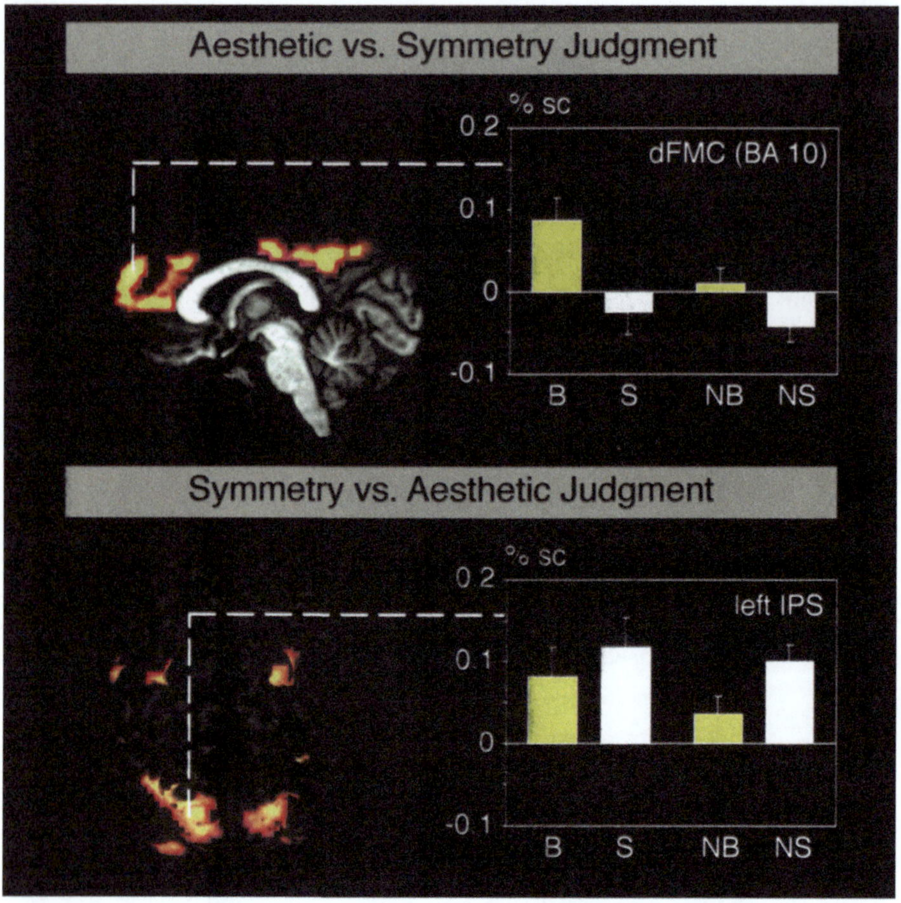

Figure 4. FMRI results from Jacobsen et al. (2006). Group-averaged (n = 15) statistical maps of significantly activated areas for aesthetic judgments as opposed to symmetry judgments (upper panel) and for symmetry as opposed to aesthetic judgments (lower panel). Z-maps were thresholded at $z = 3.09$ ($p < 0.05$ corrected for multiple comparisons). Bar charts show percentage signal changes in two regions of interest (dorsal frontomedian cortex, dFMC, and intraparietal sulcus, IPS) as measured during the judgments "beautiful" (B), "symmetric" (S), "not beautiful" (NB), and "not symmetric" (NS). (© Illustrations by Thomas Jacobsen.)

Figure 2. Monet (1891) poplars: **The Metropolitan Museum of Art, H. O. Havemeyer Collection, Bequest of Mrs. H. O. Havemeyer, 1929 (29.100.110). Image © The Metropolitan Museum of Art.**

Figure 6. *Tartuferi's retina*. Tartuferi, whose portrait is shown, applied Golgi's staining method to the retina. (© Illustration by Nicholas Wade.)

Figure 29. *Enigma variation.* A portrait of Semir Zeki in a pattern that produces apparent rotation around the annuli. He conducted neuroimaging studies of observers viewing a similar pattern by Isiah Leviant, called *Enigma.* (© Illustration by Nicholas Wade.)

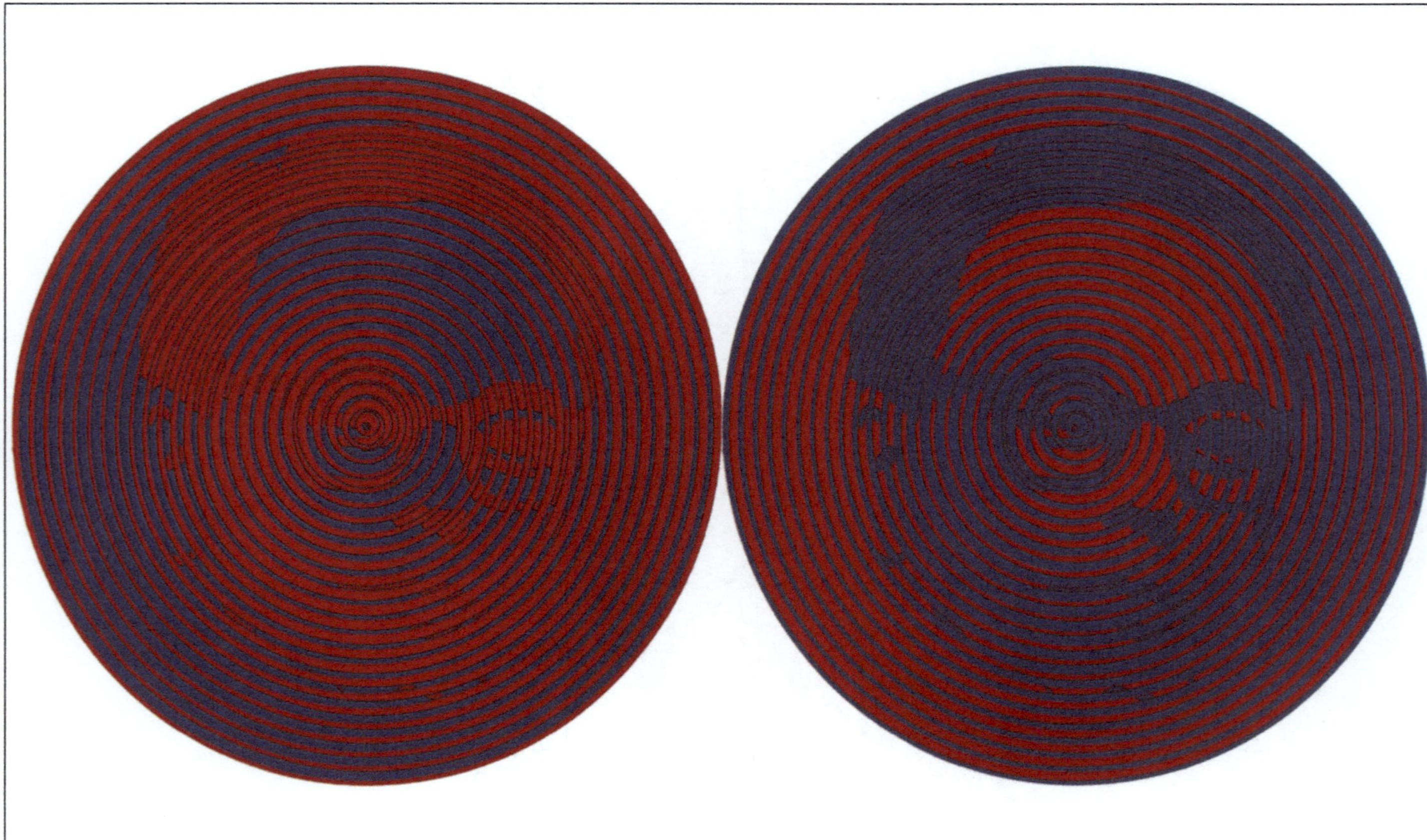

Figure 30. *Vasarely's vision.* (© Illustration by Nicholas Wade.)

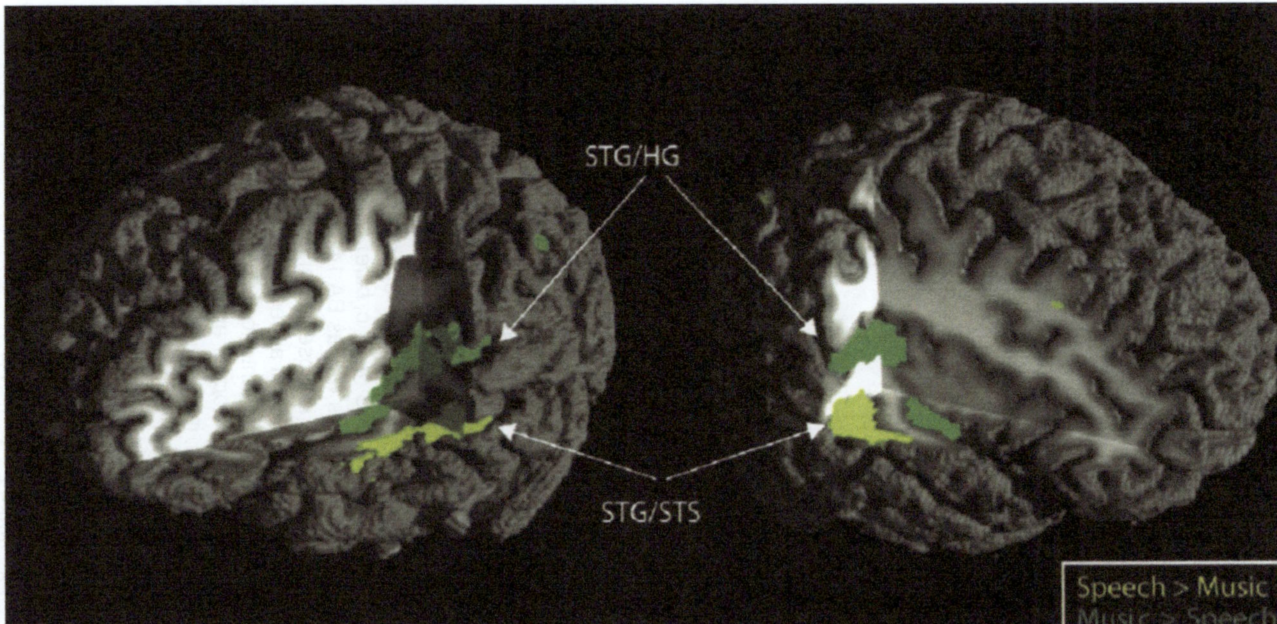

Figure 1. Brain areas selectively activated by speech sounds and music sounds. During the fMRI scanning, pseudowords /ba:ba/ and saxophone sounds with corresponding duration and pitch content were presented to the nonmusicians. The subjects were asked to indicate whether the sound sequences consisted of speech or music sounds. Brain regions showing significantly more activation during perception of speech vs. musical sounds are illustrated with yellow color and those activated more by music than speech sounds are illustrated with green color. STG = superior temporal gyrus, HG = Heschl's gyrus, STS = superior temporal sulcus. (© Illustration by Mari Tervaniemi.)

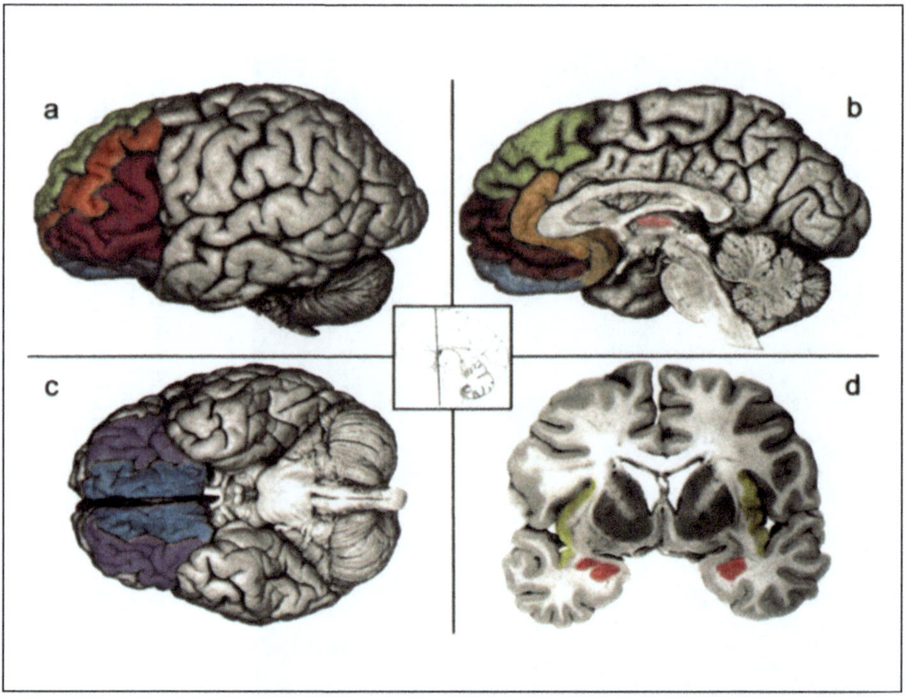

Figure 1. Key brain areas in the neural reference space for mental representations of emotion. The ventral system for core affect includes two closely connected circuits that are anchored in the orbitofrontal cortex (the entire ventral surface of the front part of the brain lying behind the orbital bone above the eye; Figure 1c). The more sensory system involves the lateral sector of the orbitofrontal cortex (OFC) and includes the lateral portions of BA 11 and 13, BA 47/12 (*a, c, purple*). It is closely connected to the anterior insula (*d, yellow*) and the basolateral (BL) complex in the amygdala (*d, rose,* ventral aspect). The visceromotor circuitry includes the ventral portion of the ventromedial prefrontal cortex (VMPFC), which lies in the medial sector of the OFC (a, b, c, *blue*) and includes medial BA 11 and 13 ventral portions of BA 10, as well as BA 14, where the medial and lateral aspects of OFC connect; VMPFC is closely connected to the amygdala (including the central nucleus, *d, rose*, dorsal aspect) and the subgenual parts of the anterior cingulate cortex involving the anterior aspects of BA 24, 25, and 32 on the medial wall of the brain (ACC; *b, copper* and *tan*). The dorsal system is associated with mental-state attributions, including the dorsal aspect of the VMPFC corresponding to the frontal pole in BA 10 (*b, maroon*), the anterior ACC (*peach*), and the dorsomedial prefrontal cortex (DMPFC) corresponding to the medial aspects of BA 8, 9, and 10 (*a, b, green*). Ventrolateral prefrontal cortex (VLPFC) is shown in *red* (*a*). Also shown for reference are the thalamus (*b, light pink*), the ventral striatum (*d, green*), and the middle frontal gyrus in the dorsolateral prefrontal cortex (*a, orange*). Reprinted, with permission, from the *Annual Review of Psychology*, Volume 58 ©2007 by Annual Reviews www.annualreviews.org

CHAPTER 8

Brain and Art: Neuro-Clues from Intersection of Disciplines

Dahlia W. Zaidel

Art is universally present in human societies, and its complex pairings of ideas, materials, methods, techniques, and skills express harmonious, meaningful, and symbolic representations. The practice is an integral feature of daily life in many non-Western cultures, where it is created in a multitude of ways for what seems to be countless reasons and occasions, by individuals possessing high talent as well as by the rest of the community (Dissanayake, 1988). People are able to derive meaning from art without being aware of its vocabulary and syntax. Clearly, it is a powerful communication tool. The ultimate significance of artistic compositions lies in knowing the cultural and ecological context in which the work was produced and experienced and, yet, even when we do not quite know that context, we do not fail to enjoy and be attracted to the art. The fact that European artists such as Van Gogh, Modigliani, Picasso, and many more produced works reflecting the influence and inspiration of art created in geographically and culturally distant societies illustrates not only art's wide appeal regardless of the epoch or culture in which it was created but also its biological basis. For these reasons alone, the neuroanatomical underpinning of art has long been intellectually and scientifically intriguing.

Human language relies on mechanisms that enable limitless pairings of vocabulary, sounds, and syntax to convey meaning and comprehension, but compared to art, it is exceptionally more efficient (Hauser, Chomsky, & Fitch, 2002; Pinker & Bloom, 1990). Both, however, are supported by neural computational mechanisms that likely took millions of years to evolve, an assumption derived from observations of animals (including bees, birds, fish, and nonhuman primates) using signals, symbols, sophisticated communication for sight and hearing, and referential cognition (Arnold & Zuberbuhler, 2006; de Waal & Tyack, 2003; Laland & Janik, 2006; Wilson, 2006). Still, while quite a bit is known and understood about the brain's support of language, scant little has been achieved in charting the relationship between art and the brain. This is mostly because the alphabetical primitives of art have not been fully deciphered, and also because some weak hypotheses have derailed fruitful research. An example of the latter is the sweeping notion that the right cerebral hemisphere specializes in art; being only a suggestion or a hypothesis in the first place, albeit with mesmerizing appeal, it inhibited for decades the art-brain relationship search. However, several sources can profitably shed light on the relationship and reverse the course. First and foremost are the neuroanatomical clues; they can be gleaned from established artists who acquired unilateral, focal brain damage well after launching their lifelong artistic careers. Such artists, though rare, can be found in the musical and visual arts. Similarly, insights on talent and creativity can be found in established artists with diffused, slowly evolving dementias as well as from autistic savants specializing in the arts. A critical source that should be studied in parallel is the universal practice of art; it invites inquiry after art's relationship to the evolution of the brain, its ancient origin, and its purpose and role in human existence. There is evidence that art's origins date back to well before the anatomically modern humans, *Homo sapiens*, first appeared. Thus, archaeology, anthropology, biology, evolutionary theories, neuropsychology, and neurology, collectively have something to contribute to the search. This is the approach developed in my book on brain and art (Zaidel, 2005), and this chapter explores these and additional issues. The adopted view is that with the convergence of interdisciplinary areas, the charting of the brain-art relationship can potentially be deciphered.

EMERGENCE OF EARLY ART IN HOMINID EVOLUTION

In the debate currently revolving around the origin of art, human language and art are discussed as intertwined, that art emerged when language emerged, that the two appeared on the human scene wrapped in the same bundle, particularly when sophisticated combinatorial language emerged (Corballis, 2004; Gentilucci & Corballis, 2006; Stringer, 2002). Since art is referential and symbolic and so is language, a similar brain transformation mediating both is argued. Moreover, the pivotal ancient adaptive event linked to language development is attributed to characteristic pharynx physiology, whereby the tongue, back of the throat, and voice box are juxtaposed uniquely to produce highly varied and subtle sounds (Lieberman, 2002). Of course, this would have had to be supported by some favorable genetic alteration, whether a mutation or an epigenetic aberration. The FOXP2 gene on chromosome 7 is currently viewed as that critical genetic alteration (Fisher & Marcus, 2006); the gene is found in many animals, but its pattern is reportedly different in humans, and its malfunctioning leads to language impairments (Vargha-Khadem, Gadian, Copp, & Mishkin, 2005; Vargha-Khadem et al., 1998). Language is currently associated only with the anatomically modern humans, *Homo sapiens*, who, according to current thinking, first evolved in Africa around 200,000 years ago, emerged from Africa around 100,000 years ago (Noonan et al., 2006), and meandered their way slowly toward the Middle East and Europe (and Asia as well; Carstairs-McCarthy, 2004). The precise timing continues to be discussed and debated and is likely to shift when more evidence is unearthed. Archaeological evidence for varied and abundant art, symbolic, representational, and nonfunctional, points to Western Europe, from about 35,000-45,000 years ago (Appenzeller, 1998; Lewis-Williams, 2002). The key here is not only that many artifacts were created at that period, but that much of it was ornamental and nonfunctional. This, in the view of some, clearly points to use of symbolism, representation, and cultural practices.

However, those dates are problematic for the association of art with the brains of the anatomically modern humans. There is a huge time gap between the time when anatomically modern *Homo sapiens* are said to have emerged and the appearance of abundant art (McBrearty & Brooks, 2000). There is certainly evidence for art-related activity in Africa going back to 70,000 years ago (Henshilwood, d'Errico, Vanhaeven, van Niekerk, & Jacobs, 2004; Henshilwood et al., 2002) and, more recently to the discovery by Sheila Coulson and her team in a Botswana cave of ritual practice, also as long ago 70,000 years ago. Why did the anatomically modern humans not produce abundant art 100,000 years ago, and what transpired neuroanatomically in the intervening years? These are natural questions to ponder. It is also important to understand that absence of archaeological evidence does not mean absence of a practice. The weather and geographical conditions of Africa are not identical to those of Western Europe, and this difference could contribute to difficulties in unearthing archaeological artifacts.

Then there is the issue of the Neanderthals (Harvati, Frost, & McNulty, 2004). They and modern humans are assumed to have shared a common ancestor from whom they diverged around 370,000 years ago (Noonan et al., 2006), and consequently, they each represent a separate Homo lineage (Delson & Harvati, 2006). The Neanderthals survived and lived in Europe from around 400,000 years up until about 25,000 years ago (having also originally migrated from Africa). They preceded the anatomically modern humans in Europe by hundreds of thousands of years, and yet there is only meager archaeological evidence for their symbol-related art productions for most of their European existence; whatever symbolic artifacts were found are attributed to learning from the *Homo sapiens* (Einwogerer et al., 2006). The following paragraphs discuss each one of these issues.

The relationship between the cognition of art and language is theoretically reasonable, but why the two should be so closely intertwined in the same evolutionary time window is not at all obvious. First, it is difficult to conceive of a *sudden* alteration in the brain initiating symbolic and referential representation, given the fact that primates and hominids have used sound and visual communication strategies to interact and survive successfully for millions of years. The pharynx-language relationship also could not have developed suddenly and independently of other cognitive developments. Second, art artifacts are associated with hominids, not with nonhuman primates, so this pushes the symbolic-referential capabilities to about six millions ago, a time when the first bipedal ancestors of *Homo sapiens* appeared. Third, the reliance of both art and language on abstraction invites the possibility of long-evolving neural substrates to support both of these forms of communication. On the other hand, it is not unreasonable to assume that in the course of human brain evolution, art expression preceded language development, possibly even predicting language specialization following prolonged use of nonlanguage types of symbolism and representation.

To complicate matters, recent evidence from archaeological sites in France suggests the need for serious reexamination of the original dating of the abundant early art (Zilhao, d'Errico, Borders, Lenoble, & Texier, 2006). The critical consideration concerns sites occupied by the Neanderthals and the anatomically modern humans. Apparently poor excavation techniques used in the nineteenth century, particularly by fossil hunters, misplaced sediment layers, something that misled subsequent archaeologists. One such site is the Grotte des Fées in France, where evidence supporting abundant art production by the anatomically modern humans was dated to around 40,000 years ago. But the Neanderthals who occupied the same site apparently were there earlier than that and produced personal ornaments such as pierced fox teeth and other sophisticated artifacts. Not long ago, other important archaeological evidence was unearthed in the Gorham's Cave in Gibraltar (Finlayson et al., 2006): Neanderthal-related artifacts suggest that they lived there 25,000 years ago and thus overlapped quite substantially with the abundant art-producing *Homo sapiens*—more overlap than had been supposed earlier (for review, see Delson & Harvati, 2006). Another important recent discovery is the grave of two Neanderthal infants in Austria who were decorated with ivory beads (Einwogerer et al., 2006); the grave is dated to around 27,000 years ago. The Neanderthals are not associated with language because they lack the presumptive critical anatomical apparatus for speech production. Yet, musical flutes from bone and antlers made by them have been found in several locations in Europe. To attribute art capability to the Neanderthals implies symbolic and referential thinking. Such a conclusion would force the reconsideration of the art and language relationship, as well as cultural practices. Finally, the art-language-*Homo sapiens* theory is bogged down by evidence for production by early hominids of art as far back as 300,000 years ago (Brooks, Nevel, Yellen, & Hartman, 2006; Dennell, 1997; McBrearty & Brooks, 2000; McBrearty & Tryon, 2006).

While communication exists virtually in all living organisms, both art and human language are unique in scope, versatility, and effectiveness. Both rely on abstract cognition to communicate ideas, facts, intentions, emotions, and so on. It is reasonable to suppose that art and language cognition share computational and neuroanatomical arrangements, but there is no need to assume that in the millions of years it took for the underpinnings of both to evolve that art and language evolved in tandem.

BIOLOGY OF ART

Art is a connecting tool leading to interpersonal interaction and to bonding (Turner, 2006), as well as to the social practice of culture (Ikegami, 2005). Some of the fundamental questions ask what is the biological purpose of art, why do humans create art, and how does it all fit with the evolution and growth of the human brain? Anthropologists, biologists, philosophers, and evolutionists debate the answers (Dissanayake, 1988, 1995; Gottschall & Wilson, 2005). An appealing explanation is proposed and discussed by Geoffrey Miller (Miller, 2000, 2001a, 2001b). He posits that creating art is linked to its display, which in turn is associated with judgment by others; and the display along with the judgment hark back to biological mate-selection strategies where display is emphasized so that mate choosing for procreation can take place. In nature, fitness quality is judged early on in the mate-selection stage; animals display their prowess and physical appearance with the goal of exposing the quality of their genes and thereby the potential of their progeny to survive. The better the genes, the better the heritability fitness. Art production is meant to show quality of physical strength plus intelligence, both of which are critical for survival of the species. Art, in Miller's sexual-selection view, is an extension of this selection strategy, and this applies to all forms of art.

The wide variety of displays by animals for mating purposes (described by Gould & Gould, 1989) draws labels usually applied to human creations: to wit, creativity, cleverness, ingenuity, and inventiveness. Here we will discuss one critical example: birds known as bowerbirds, after the bowers created by the males of the species that live mostly in Australia and New Guinea (Diamond, 1982). The bowers come in different shapes and forms, and range from simple to complex, small to large, elaborate, highly decorative, with and without colors, and even use decorations taken from humans. The male bowerbird builds his constructions solely for the purpose of attracting a female. They are not nests. The intended goal is to show the builder's talent and skill, fitness and heritability, cleverness, and strength. Once attracted, the females and males do not mate in the bower nor do they care for or feed their chicks there. But there is evidence that the size of the brain in bowerbirds correlates with the architectural complexity of the bower (Madden, 2001)! This is true in both members of the species: in the males who build and the females who observe. So the mental cognition needed to create and judge such artistic constructions has neuroanatomical underpinnings.

A common mate-selection strategy with many animals consists of males in contests. In a herd of mountain bighorn sheep, males fight each other off until the winner emerges and it is he who gets the females. When they fight, they bang their curved thick horns against each other repeatedly, hoping to topple the other. The skull underneath is particularly thick, having evolved to minimize damage. The brain, on the other hand, is small, the space in the head having been taken over by the thickness of the skull. Unlike the repeated creations of the bowerbird, this type of fighting to win the females only lasts for about a year since the expansion of energy is enormous; it is not possible to repeat the ordeal year in and year out. There does not appear to be too much female choice here; she has to mate with whoever wins (Gould & Gould, 1989). There is skill, cleverness, and strength in contest displays, but not nearly as much flexibility, talent, creativity, memory, and inventiveness as in the case of the bowerbird.

NEURO-CLUES FROM ARTISTS WITH BRAIN DAMAGE

It is important to distinguish between art style and technique: style is defined here as the genre adopted by the artist (impressionism, realism, surrealism, abstract expressionism, and so on) while technique implies the personal characteristic of the production (the adopted manner in which the artist expresses the genre). Not all the impressionists, for example, painted as Claude Monet and not all of the surrealists painted as Salvador Dali or René Magritte. Within a given genre (or art movement), then, there is variability in technique.

Regional functional localization in the brain is traditionally accomplished through the study of patients with focal, circumscribed brain lesions in the left or the right cerebral hemispheres. Inferences regarding functional localization for art can potentially be obtained from established artists who have suffered brain damage, and the principal questions regarding the effects of the damage concern the appearance of any alterations in the art, in general, and how style, technique, skill, talent, or creativity fared the onslaught of the damage, specifically. Obviously, artists with brain damage are rare. However, in my book on brain and art (Zaidel, 2005), over 15 nondemented visual artists with unilateral damage are reviewed and discussed. They continued to express artistic competence despite the presence of neurological conditions, regardless of etiology. This is so regardless of the laterality of the damage. The artists maintained their creativity, retained their talent and their skills, which demonstrates that individual artistic style (see my definition of art style above), perfected and worked out prior to the damage, is by and large unaltered. This suggests that neither cerebral hemisphere specializes in these aspects of art, and no specific localized region within the hemispheres controls the production. In addition, published cases of established artists with slowly encroaching brain degeneration have also been reviewed (Zaidel, 2005) and here, too, been found to retain their artistic skills, style, and creativity long into their illness. The various etiologies studied include Parkinson's disease, Alzheimer's disease, fronto-temporal dementia, dementia with Lewy Bodies, and corticobasal degeneration. Extensive neuronal death and loss of connectivity is what characterizes these neurological conditions, albeit with differing loss rate, and yet artistic abilities were retained. Final deterioration of artistic skills in these dementing conditions paralleled severe cognitive decline in many domains of their existence. In all, presently multiple components of art defy functional localization in the brain.

An artist who painted with realism prior to the damage continued to do so afterwards. The alterations in technique that do occur on occasion postdamage can be explained as adjustments to the motoric or visual, or both, limitations inflicted by the damage itself. An artist with right-hand paralysis (the damage is in the left hemisphere) creates works postdamage with the left hand; neglect of the left half of visual space in an artist with right-hemisphere damage produces art shifted to the right half of the canvas. These are the principal causes for technique alterations. Many other features of the artistic endeavor proceed unchanged, as mentioned above, including the motivation to create.

Such preservation illustrates resilience of highly-practiced skills as well as, of course, absence of specific functional artistic localization. Preservation probably reflects the effects of damaged tissue in combination with healthy tissue. Both mechanisms interact with each other in the art of such artists. In addition, preserved functions are assumed to reflect redundancy of representation in multiple neuronal circuits, and the preservation is attributed to the sparing of some of these circuits (Carmichael, 2006; Jenkins & Merzenich, 1987). Currently, active research in anatomical reshaping consequent to brain damage is focused on language recovery (Knecht et al., 2002; Saur, Baumgaertner, Schraknepper, Willmes, Rijntjes, & Weiller, 2006), but the findings can be generalized to other types of cognition (Kapur, 1996).

Established artists with brain damage appear to retain their motivation and expressive capabilities independently of their linguistic competence. Indeed, the brain damage evidence points to dissociation between linguistic and artistic expression, but this does not necessarily stem from left-right hemispheric specialization issues (the left specializes in the main language functions, the right in visuo-spatial functions). One mode of expression need not interfere with the other, need not exclude the other, and the two need not be mutually antagonistic. Although visual art requires normal visuo-spatial perception and cognition, the absence or degradation of such cognition does not seem to interfere with production of aesthetic, creative, and skilled artworks. In Western art, depiction of space includes line convergence and vanishing lines. Accurate realistic depictions of the world are facilitated with these techniques. But artistic genres in non-Western societies do not always emphasize 3-D space in their depictions. Consider, for example, Chinese and Japanese art. Consider, too, abstract art and surrealistic art; such genres are either devoid of any depth depictions or the depth is distorted to create imaginary worlds. Thus, visuo-spatial cognition need not be the dominant cognition in visual art.

Background issues in the hemispheric role in art production and perception should be elaborated. Since approximately the 1960s, when the Roger W. Sperry commissurotomy ("split-brain") studies at Caltech, Pasadena, were published, hypotheses were proposed regarding right-hemisphere specialization in art; but this was with the idea that as hypotheses they would be modified as additional research shed further light on hemispheric differences. With regard to art, the hypothesis rested on the need to distinguish art from language, where the latter was definitely confirmed over and over again to be principally specialized in the left hemisphere, from cognition that was nonverbal in nature, namely art. The subsequent years never yielded robust empirical evidence for exclusive or even main right-hemisphere-art connection. Assertions that the right hemisphere is "creative, artistic, emotional" have little empirical basis in the commissurotomy studies, or in studies of other groups of brain-damaged patients. Besides, art consists of many kinds of cognition (production, reception, techniques, styles, memory), and those have never been parsed out to explain how art could be specialized in the right more than in the left hemisphere (Zaidel & Kasher, 1989). Unfortunately, in time, this speculative hypothesis turned into an appealing and popular metaphor that too many began to believe as a substantiated fact.

PICTURES, DRAWINGS, AND THE BRAIN

Communication through pictures and drawings is relatively easy, it is universal, cuts across age and culture, applies to realistic and abstract depictions, and is even observed in neurological patients who have lost the ability to communicate verbally or emotionally. Indeed, pictures are commonly used as stimuli in neuropsychological tests following left- or right-hemisphere damage. Notwithstanding widespread diffuse brain disease, seldom if ever is there apictoria, the inability to understand all pictures, following unilateral brain damage. In some patients with visual object agnosia, there is selective impairment in deriving the meaning of specific classes of pictured objects (De Renzi, 1999; Farah, 1990), but even agnosic patients are not impaired across the board in deciphering all pictorial representations. Drawing is produced even when language and memory are severely compromised: patients suffering from Alzheimer's Disease can go on drawing objects, with realism or as abstractions, despite serious failure in language and memory (Kirk & Kertesz, 1991, 1993). Characteristic drawing techniques are displayed sometimes by neurological patients where, following damage in the right parietal and occipital lobes, the drawings lack the contour frame, emphasizing instead the details of the drawn objects; drawings by left-hemisphere-damaged patients can show the reverse; that is, of contour frames lacking in inside details (Lezak, 1995; Warrington & James, 1966). The idea of piecemeal and analytic thinking in the left hemisphere and gestalt thinking in the right hemisphere was initially derived from observations of drawing patterns by patients with different brain-damage laterality (Ettlinger, Warrington, & Zangwill, 1957; Paterson & Zangwill, 1944; Zangwill, 1964). However, even with characteristic styles of representing objects, drawing can be conceptualized and executed with the control of neural substrates in each hemisphere.

Drawings by professional artists suffering from aphasia (a language disorder that follows brain damage, typically in the left hemisphere) address the issue of language and art. The findings with such artists highlight dissociation between the two modes of expression. But this does not have to imply accomplishment through right-hemisphere control. Intact regions within the left hemisphere can control execution of the drawings, and there may even be bihemispheric control in the execution. The role of the inferior temporal lobe in the left hemisphere in deriving pictorial meaning from pictorial objects has been reported (Whatmough, Chertkow, Murtha, & Hanratty, 2002); with regard to scenes, this is evident in the neurological condition known as simultanagnosia (Clavagnier, Berger, Klockgether, Moskau, & Karnath, 2006; Kinsbourne & Warrington, 1962; Levine & Calvanio, 1978), the inability to describe the central theme of a scene. In sum, cognition in each hemisphere contributes something to symbolic representation in drawings.

COLORS IN VISUAL ART

Colors are but one special dimension invoking aesthetic sensation in art; achromatic manifestations bring forth a strong aesthetic reaction as well. Think of photography, lithographs, etchings, architecture, and so on. Film is an exceptionally good example of art that does not need color to convey meaning and aesthetic pleasure (Arnheim, 1958). It is amply demonstrated in theatrical stage performances as well, but even more so in films. In the cinema, degrees of illumination as well as light and dark manipulations are a dimension of the aesthetic experience. Movies such as *Casablanca, The Third Man, The Seventh Seal,* and many, many more illustrate the point. Watching a noncolor movie in a darkened theater brings out effects unlike viewing black-and-white still photography, where the ambient environment is highly illuminated with light. For many years, even after color film became available to filmmakers, well-known film artists preferred creating motion pictures in grayscale. Ingmar Bergman, the film director, and Sven Nykvist, the cinematographer, are but two such artists (Nykvist, 2003).

Cataracts and normal age-related alterations in the eye affect the way colors and objects are depicted artistically (Ravin, 1997). Not seeing well because of cataracts means not depicting realistic images (Nathan, 2002). For example, it has been suggested, not unreasonably, that the Impressionists' hazy style reflects in part the artists' compromised vision by disease due to excessive exposure to sunlight or due to other etiological reasons such as cataracts. One such artist was Claude Monet. Similarly, artists such as Leonardo da Vinci and Rembrandt painted darker paintings as they aged because of naturally occurring age-related alterations in the eyeball (Marmor & Lanthony, 2001). Color-blind artists produce art despite their retina-specific impairment. Thus, in individual artists, it is useful to explore sensory visual processing (Marmor & Lanthony, 2001). Neuropsychologists have traditionally separated sensory deficits from central (brain) impairments in order to be sure that the behavior under study is due to brain rather than to sensory alterations. Clarifications of sensory deficits in artists further inform the relationship between neuroscience, the brain, and art.

NEURO-CLUES FROM MUSICAL ARTISTS WITH BRAIN DAMAGE

With the visual arts, pictorial and visual symbols are presumed to have eventually led to written symbols, and with music, mimicry of animal sounds (as in deception, communication, or celebration) could have contributed greatly to language speech as well as to music production, vocally and through instruments. While the visual arts leave traceable archaeological evidence, we can only speculate about the origins of the musical arts.

With the musical arts, both the composing and the performing aspects should be included in the discussion on art and brain. Currently, findings with extensive neuroimaging techniques reveal that widely spaced brain structures are activated in musical artists, and no single "music center" has thus far been identified (Altenmüller, 2001; Peretz, 2002). Early on, neurologists did not fail to observe that musical disorders followed unilateral damage in the left or right hemisphere (Basso, 1999). The temporal lobes are predominantly involved with musical perception and the frontal lobes in musical output and expression (Baeck, 2002). The attempt to distinguish between music and language stemmed from observations that patients suffering from language deficits (damage in the left hemisphere) sometimes had spared musical abilities, although both language and music can become impaired in some cases with left-hemisphere damage (Basso, 1999). The general hemispheric picture is that while the left hemisphere specializes in the perception of timing and rhythm, the right hemisphere specializes in pitch and timbre perception.

However, training sculpts musical memory and reactions to music in non-brain-damaged individuals. Musical training plays a crucial role in hemispheric involvement, with the left hemisphere being maximally involved in trained musicians while the right is maximally involved in nonmusicians (Bever & Chiarello, 1974), and there is evidence for structural brain differences between musicians and nonmusicians (Münte, Altenmüller, & Jäncke, 2002). Neuroimaging results reveal that professional musicians have slightly different activated brain regions than nonmusicians, especially in music execution regions (Pantev, Oostenveld, Engelien, Ross, Roberts, & Hoke, 1998). Noninvasive brain-imaging studies of nonmusicians and musicians alike suggest that music triggers multiple neural regions, which further complicates pinpointing responsible neural regions (centers), while at the same time highlighting the broad spectrum of musical reactions (Patel, 2003).

Most of the published cases of composers with degenerative disease or with localized damage involve the left hemisphere. Scarcity of published cases of composers with localized right hemisphere damage prevents balanced conclusions regarding the contribution of each hemisphere's cognition to musical composition (Wieser, 2003). The composers reviewed in Zaidel (2005) were able to compose despite neurological complications. Some examples are the Russian composer Vissarion Shebalin, the French composer Jean Langlais, and the British composer Benjamin Britten. Extensive training, skill overlearning, exceptional musical talent, as well as inherited musically conducive conditions are all factors that enhance preserved abilities of composers following brain damage (Bentivoglio, 2003; Zatorre, 2003). Functional representation of well-rehearsed musical habits (often from early childhood) and neuronal plasticity contribute to these spared skills. This is particularly true in slow, progressive neurodegenerative brain disease, where functional reorganization in a brain reacting to loss of neurons and connections is highly likely; Maurice Ravel was one such composer who continued to compose well into his slowly evolving illness (Amaducci, Grass, & Boller, 2002).

Similarly, neurosyphilis, a devastating sexually transmitted disease before the discovery of penicillin, took a heavy toll on composers such as Robert Schumann, Bedrich Smetana, and Franz Schubert, which did not prevent them from composing, although one should wonder what music would have been produced by them had they not suffered from the disease. In addition, sensory deficits causing deafness in Smetana and Beethoven could have influenced the nature of their work if it were not for their skills, craft, and talent. When all is considered, the neuroanatomical underpinning of the artistic feature of musical composition is attributed to multiple neural regions controlling skills, which might have a strong genetic basis, and the brain's plasticity in reaction to damage.

BEAUTY IN ART AND BIOLOGY

Art is yet another format of idea conceptualization generated by the uniqueness of the human brain. The fact that art elicits pleasure is an added dimension, or a bonus. Beauty reactions are independent of the degree to which reality is represented in art, thereby suggesting beauty's anchor in biology and neuroanatomy. It is hard to tease apart the aesthetic value of art from its communicative value. Where does beauty come from in art? Does the artist consciously put it there, and if so, how, exactly? I propose that beauty in art is an emergent property, not deliberately constructed by the artist but rather something that is extracted by the viewer's brain upon perceiving the work of art.

In explaining the neural basis of beauty, first and foremost it should be stressed that aesthetic-relevant reactions are not limited to art nor do they originate with art. We need only contemplate the myriad reactions to nature vistas seen from mountain tops, flying airplanes, or reactions to sunsets, rainbows, cloud formations, full moons, curved dunes, colorful birds, mists across lakes, and many other natural phenomena, to realize that aesthetic reactions are rather commonplace. Early on, Darwin discussed this issue of aesthetics in animals and humans (see Welsch, 2004). To this list we should add reactions to attractiveness and beauty in human faces, in paintings (Zaidel & FitzGerald, 1994), or in photographs (Chen, German, & Zaidel, 1997; Zaidel, Chen, & German, 1995; Zaidel & Cohen, 2005). It is thus reasonable to suggest that elicitation of the aesthetic reactions existed well before humans started to produce art. It is also logical to wonder, as Darwin did, whether or not animals experience aesthetic-relevant reactions.

Sensing a distinct physiological reaction spelling "beautiful" upon gazing at a painting is a common experience. Frequently, the painting elicits similar reactions across viewers regardless of who painted it and independently of the epoch in which it was created. Indeed, emotional reactions to life events are not diametrically opposite to reactions to art. Since art represents the context and environment of the artist, it is reasonable to expect great similarity or, at the very least, a natural continuum between emotional reactions to art and nonart stimuli.

One interesting notion regarding artworks is that the brain's reaction to visual aesthetics rises from the visual system's search for components of form primitives in perceived shapes. Presumably, a good match between what is seen, say, edges and feature detectors, could explain reactions to art. Findings described in the literature regarding the oblique effect lay bare this notion (Appelle, 1972; Latto & Russell-Duff, 2002; McMahon & MacLeod, 2003). The effect is based on countless observations over the past 150 years that specialized performance is obtained for horizontally or vertically oriented stimuli than for obliquely oriented stimuli (McMahon & MacLeod, 2003). This is true in some animals as well as in children (Appelle, 1972). Further study of these effects and of their components could provide fruitful data for localizing neural substrates of aesthetic reactions.

BRAIN ACTIVITY AND ART AESTHETICS

Recently, a few studies attempted to explore brain functional activation in the perception of art material in terms of aesthetics (Cela-Conde et al., 2004). Multiple brain areas were activated in response to task instructions and decisions regarding viewed paintings, as follows: In an important study, Vartanian and Goel (2004) asked their subjects to rate paintings according to their aesthetic preferences, and the findings revealed a relationship between decreased preference and degree of right caudate nucleus activation (the less preference, the less activity) as opposed to increased activation for increased preference in the occipital lobe and fusiform gyrus bilaterally and left cingulate. Kawabata and Zeki (2004) asked their subjects, while they were being scanned, to view paintings that previously received aesthetically related categories (ugly, beautiful, or neutral); they, too, found multiple brain regions to be engaged and no specific regions to be associated with the specific categories of ugly, beautiful, or neutral. In other words, no specific differentiation among categories was replicated in brain areas. Jacobsen, Schubotz, Hofel, and Cramon (2006) showed their subjects laboratory-constructed graphic geometrical patterns and asked them for aesthetic judgments while their brains were scanned; they found that diverse brain regions were activated, both unilaterally and bilaterally. Taken together, these studies show absence of circumscribed area/region in art aesthetics and, in addition, confirm the notion that hemispheric specialization per se does not explain aesthetic art judgments.

NEUROPSYCHOLOGICAL CONSIDERATIONS OF CREATIVITY, TALENT, AND SKILLS

Art production by established artists represents the activities of several systems of neural substrates. Artistic success rests on multiple factors including talent, practice, and creativity. Elucidating the roles of skill, technique, and talent presents a major challenge to researchers. What is creativity exactly? The best definitions ascribe creativity to that which is brand new and positive for society, something that did not exist previously, or has been modified so as to be labeled innovative, inventive, or original. Creativity calls for flexibility and the ability to conceptualize ideas in ways diametrically opposed to that which is taken as a given, established, known, rehearsed, stereotyped, and accepted. Creativity is not confined to the arts. Scientists and business people are creative as well, as are medical doctors, nurses, gardeners, and countless other members of society (see Rose, 2004).

The best neural clues that creativity is bilaterally represented in the brain come from its intactness in established artists with damage in either cerebral hemisphere (as reviewed in a previous section of this chapter). The evidence from these artists points to the involvement of several brain regions and to cooperation between the two hemispheres. Further clues are observed in atypical artists: autistic savants typically suffer from severe language and social communication problems (DeLong, 1999; Freitag, 2006; Frith & Hill, 2003); left-hemisphere dysfunction is often assumed to be mainly responsible for the communication disorder, principally because of the observed severe language deficits. The savant artists seem to possess innate drawing and exceptional graphic talent despite their extensive neuronal brain disorder. But their productions are by and large realistic representations with little or no abstraction, and there is not much to see by way of creativity (Sacks, 1995). Interestingly, little benefit, if any, is gained by most of them from art training (Sacks, 2004). Moreover, such artists represent but a small fraction of individuals with autism. Compared with the population as a whole, however, their productions can be matched by a select few. The natural conclusion is that talent and skill are dissociable from creativity, and can be functional despite extensive neuronal disorder.

Artistic production by few neurological patients who have not produced art prior to the start of a dementing process, fronto-temporal dementia or Alzheimer's disease, for example, could imply that selective atrophy in neuronal connectivity in such cases leads to emergence of new expressions; such conclusions have been proposed (Miller et al., 1998; Miller & Hou, 2004; Miller, Ponton, Benson, Cummings, & Mena, 1996). An alternative explanation is that artistic talent and creativity have always been present, but due to economic reasons such as societal pressures on obtaining a reliably paying job, the art talents went unpracticed. When the life-long profession could no longer be practiced due to specialized work-related deteriorating cognition, time became available for the practice of art. If art production is the natural consequence of a brain-dementing disease, we would expect millions of patients suffering from dementia to produce art. Since this is not the case, it is reasonable to conclude that only those with long-standing talent display artistic abilities upon disease onset.

In all artists, raw artistic talent denotes abilities and skills with probable strong genetic components. The talent is expressed through interaction with creativity in different forms of art, as well as in other fields of human endeavors. Skill preservation, together with inventiveness and ingenuity, are remarkable in some neurological cases given the extent and nature of the brain alterations. Talent, extensive practice, and skill all suggest redundancy in their functional representation and the basis for spared artistic capacity following brain or sensory damage.

CONCLUDING REMARKS

Art, as language, is a form of communication. Types of communication exist practically in all living organisms, and it is reasonable to assume that neuroanatomical underpinnings of art-relevant behaviors in humans such as symbolism and referential representation have been evolving adaptively for millions of years. Extensive cultural practices serve to enhance the practice of art and feed these evolutionary pressures. In any case, it is not obvious that art co-evolved with language, or that the two "appeared" on the human scene as a single packaged bundle, nor is it reasonable to assume that where there is no archaeological evidence for abundant art, there is no extensive language practice.

For the link to the neuroanatomy, it is useful to seek clues from brain damage in established artists. Upon reviewing the relevant literature, my observation is that unilateral focal brain damage and extensive neuronal damage due to dementing diseases do not obliterate the ability to communicate through art, and the artists do retain creativity, talent, skill, and motivation. Even with extensive brain damage and severe language or other cognitive impairments, the ability to depict in symbolic referential manner persists. All of this suggests that the neuronal basis of art is diffusely represented in the brain, unlike language where there is distinct regional localization. The pattern of preserved artistic abilities in established artists with brain damage supports the notion that art and language have not co-evolved; the evolution and adaptation could well have been staggered, with art expression preceding language.

Moreover, brain damage itself does not enable art creation, even as it leads to some modification in technique. Innate artistic talent contributes greatly to the sparing of skills in brain disease. The ways in which the damage selectively influences artistic output remain a major challenge to deciphering the brain-art relationship.

The aesthetic nature of a work of art is not necessarily something "embedded" deliberately by the artist, but rather, as proposed here, it can be viewed as an emergent property formed in the observer's mind, albeit with neuroanatomical underpinning. Aesthetic reactions could be viewed as adaptive attention-getting means to the communicative message in art, being closely linked to attachment, possessiveness, and pleasure. Beauty-related reactions themselves are not limited to art since they exist in a wide variety of contexts and may well have been generated by the mind in the brain as "attraction for attachment" much before humans began producing art, or engaged in art-relevant behaviors. After all, evolution utilizes preexisting anatomical mechanisms through adaptation, rather than abruptly generating them. It is thus reasonable to wonder whether or not animals experience aesthetic reactions, as suggested by Darwin. Future research should not view the issue as epistemological but rather address the issue empirically.

REFERENCES

Altenmüller, E. O. (2001). How many music centers are in the brain? *Annals of the New York Academy of Sciences, 930*, 273-280.

Amaducci, L., Grass, E., & Boller, F. (2002). Maurice Ravel and right-hemisphere musical creativity: Influence of disease on his last musical works? *European Journal of Neurology, 9*, 75-82.

Appelle, S. (1972). Perception and discrimination as a function of orientation: The 'oblique effect' in man and animals. *Psychological Bulletin, 78*, 266-278.

Appenzeller, T. (1998). Art: Evolution or revolution? *Science, 282*, 1451.

Arnheim, R. (1958). *Film as art.* Berkeley: University of California Press.

Arnold, K., & Zuberbuhler, K. (2006). Language evolution: Semantic combinations in primate calls. *Nature, 441*, 303.

Baeck, E. (2002). The neural networks of music. *European Journal of Neurology, 9*, 449-456.

Basso, A. (1999). The neuropsychology of music. In *Handbook of clinical and experimental neuropsychology*. Hove, UK: Psychology Press.

Bentivoglio, M. (2003). Musical skills and neural functions. The legacy of the brains of musicians. *Annals of the New York Academy of Science, 999*, 234-243.

Bever, T. G., & Chiarello, R. J. (1974). Cerebral dominance in musicians and nonmusicians. *Science, 185*, 137-139.

Brooks, A. S., Nevel, L., Yellen, J. E., & Hartman, G. (2006). Projectile technologies of the African MSA: Implications for modern human origins. In E. Hovers & S. L. Kuhn (Eds.), *Transitions before the transition: Evolution and stability in the middle paleolithic and middle stone age* (pp. 233-256). New York: Springer.

Carmichael, S. T. (2006). Cellular and molecular mechanisms of neural repair after stroke: Making waves. *Annals of Neurology, 59*, 735-742.

Carstairs-McCarthy, A. (2004). Language: Many perspectives, no consensus. *Science, 303*, 1299-1300.

Cela-Conde, C. J., Marty, G., Maestu, F., Ortiz, T., Munar, E., Fernandez, A., et al. (2004). Activation of the prefrontal cortex in the human visual aesthetic perception. *Proceedings of the National Academy of Sciences, USA, 101*, 6321-6325.

Chen, A. C., German, C., & Zaidel, D. W. (1997). Brain asymmetry and facial attractiveness: Beauty is not simply in the eye of the beholder. *Neuropsychologia, 35*, 471-476.

Clavagnier, S., Fruhmann Berger, M., Klockgether, T., Moskau, S., & Karnath, H. O. (2006). Restricted ocular exploration does not seem to explain simultanagnosia. *Neuropsychologia, 44*, 2330-2336.

Corballis, M. C. (2004). The origins of modernity: Was autonomous speech the critical factor? *Psychology Reviews, 111*, 543-552.

De Renzi, E. (1999). Agnosia. In G. Denes & L. Pizzamiglio (Eds.), *Handbook of clinical and experimental neuropsychology*. Hove, UK: Psychology Press.

de Waal, F. B. M., & Tyack, P. L. (Eds.). (2003). *Animal social complexity: Intelligence, culture, and individualized societies*. Cambridge, MA: Harvard University Press.

DeLong, G. R. (1999). Autism: New data suggest a new hypothesis. *Neurology, 52*, 911-916.

Delson, E., & Harvati, K. (2006). Palaeoanthropology: Return of the last Neanderthal. *Nature, 443*, 762-763.

Dennell, R. (1997). The world's oldest spears. *Nature, 385*, 767.

Dissanayake, E. (1988). *What is art for?* Seattle: University of Washington Press.

Dissanayake, E. (1995). *Homo aestheticus: Where art comes from and why*. Seattle: Washington University Press.

Einwogerer, T., Friesinger, H., Handel, M., Neugebauer-Maresch, C., Simon, U., & Teschler-Nicola, M. (2006). Upper palaeolithic infant burials. *Nature, 444*, 285.

Ettlinger, G., Warrington, E. K., & Zangwill, O. L. (1957). A further study of visual-spatial agnosia. *Brain, 80*, 335-361.

Farah, M. J. (1990). *Visual agnosia: Disorders of object recognition and what they tell us about normal vision*. Cambridge, MA: MIT Press.

Finlayson, C., Pacheco, F. G., Rodriguez-Vidal, J., Fa, D. A., Gutierrez Lopez, J. M., Santiago Perez, A., et al. (2006). Late survival of Neanderthals at the southernmost extreme of Europe. *Nature, 443*, 850-853.

Fisher, S. E., & Marcus, G. F. (2006). The eloquent ape: Genes, brains and the evolution of language. *Nature Reviews Genetics, 7*, 9-20.

Freitag, C. M. (2007). The genetics of autistic disorders and its clinical relevance: A review of the literature. *Molecular Psychiatry, 12*, 2-22.

Frith, U., & Hill, E. (Eds.). (2003). *Autism: Mind and brain*. Oxford: Oxford University Press.

Gentilucci, M., & Corballis, M. C. (2006). From manual gesture to speech: A gradual transition. *Neuroscience & Biobehavioral Reviews, 30*, 949-960.

Gottschall, J., & Wilson, D. S. (Eds.). (2005). *The literary animal: Evolution and the nature of narrative*. Chicago: Northwestern University Press.

Gould, J. L., & Gould, C. G. (1989). *Sexual selection*. New York: Scientific American Library.

Harvati, K., Frost, S. R., & McNulty, K. P. (2004). Neanderthal taxonomy reconsidered: Implications of 3D primate models of intra- and interspecific differences. *Proceedings of the National Academy of Sciences, USA*, *48*, 647-652.

Hauser, M. D., Chomsky, N., & Fitch, W. T. (2002). The faculty of language: What is it, who has it, and how did it evolve? *Science, 298*, 1569-1579.

Henshilwood, C., d'Errico, F., Vanhaeren, M., van Niekerk, K., & Jacobs, Z. (2004). Middle stone age shell beads from South Africa. *Science, 304*, 404.

Henshilwood, C. S., d'Errico, F., Yates, R., Jacobs, Z., Tribolo, C., Duller, G. A. T., et al. (2002). Emergence of modern human behavior: Middle stone age engravings from South Africa. *Science, 295*, 1278-1280.

Ikegami, E. (2005). *Bonds of civility: Aesthetic networks and the political origins of Japanese culture*. New York: Cambridge University Press.

Jacobsen, T., Schubotz, R. I., Hofel, L., & Cramon, D. Y. (2006). Brain correlates of aesthetic judgment of beauty. *NeuroImage, 29*, 276-285.

Jenkins, W., & Merzenich, M. (1987). Reorganization of neocortical representations after brain injury: A neurophysiological model of the bases of recovery from stroke. *Progress in Brain Research, 71*, 249-266.

Kapur, N. (1996). Paradoxical functional facilitation in brain-behaviour research. A critical review. *Brain, 119*, 1775-1790.

Kawabata, H., & Zeki, S. (2004). Neural correlates of beauty. *Journal of Neurophysiology, 91*, 1699-1705.

Kinsbourne, M., & Warrington, E. K. (1962). A disorder of simultaneous form perception. *Brain, 85*, 461-486.

Kirk, A., & Kertesz, A. (1991). On drawing impairment in Alzheimer's disease. *Archives of Neurology, 48*, 73-77.

Kirk, A., & Kertesz, A. (1993). Subcortical contributions to drawing. *Brain and Cognition, 21*, 57-70.

Knecht, S., Floel, A., Drager, B., Breitenstein, C., Sommer, J., Henningsen, H., et al. (2002). Degree of language lateralization determines susceptibility to unilateral brain lesions. *Nature Neuroscience, 5*, 695-699.

Laland, K. N., & Janik, V. M. (2006). The animal cultures debate. *Trends in Ecology and Evolution, 21*, 543-547.

Latto, R., & Russell-Duff, K. (2002). An oblique effect in the selection of line orientation by twentieth century painters. *Empirical Studies of the Arts, 20*, 49-60.

Levine, D. N., & Calvanio, R. (1978). A study of the visual defect in verbal alexia-simultanagnosia. *Brain, 101*, 65-81.

Lewis-Williams, D. (2002). *The mind in the cave: Consciousness and the origins of art*. London: Thames and Hudson.

Lezak, M. D. (1995). *Neuropsychological assessment*. Oxford: Oxford University Press.

Lieberman, P. (2002). On the nature and evolution of the neural bases of human language. *American Journal of Physical Anthropology, 119*, 36-62.

Madden, J. (2001). Sex, bowers and brains. *Proceedings of the Royal Society of London B, 268*, 833-838.

Marmor, M. F., & Lanthony, P. (2001). The dilemma of color deficiency and art. *Survey of Ophthalmology, 45*, 407-415.

McBrearty, S., & Brooks, A. S. (2000). The revolution that wasn't: A new interpretation of the origin of modern human behavior. *Journal of Human Evolution, 39*, 453-563.

McBrearty, S., & Tryon, C. (2006). From acheulean to middle stone age in the Kapthurin formation, Kenya. In E. Hovers & S. L. Kuhn (Eds.), *Transitions before the transition: Evolution and stability in the middle paleolithic and middle stone age* (pp. 257-277). New York: Springer.

McMahon, M. J., & MacLeod, D. I. A. (2003). The origin of the oblique effect examined with pattern adaptation and masking. *Journal of Vision, 3*, 230-239.

Miller, B. L., Cummings, J., Mishkin, F., Boone, K., Prince, F., Ponton, M., et al. (1998). Emergence of artistic talent in frontotemporal dementia. *Neurology, 51*, 978-981.

Miller, B. L., & Hou, C. E. (2004). Portraits of artists: Emergence of visual creativity in dementia. *Archives of Neurology, 61*, 842-844.

Miller, B. L., Ponton, M., Benson, F. D., Cummings, J. L., & Mena, I. (1996). Enhanced artistic creativity with temporal lobe degeneration. *Lancet, 348*, 1744-1745.

Miller, G. F. (2000). *The mating mind: How sexual choice shaped the evolution of human nature*. New York: Doubleday.

Miller, G. F. (2001a). Evolution of human music through sexual selection. In N. L. Wallin, B. Merker, & S. Brown (Eds.), *The origins of music* (pp. 329-360). Cambridge, MA: MIT Press.

Miller, G. F. (2001b). Aesthetic fitness: How sexual selection shaped virtuosity as a fitness indicator and aesthetic preferences as mate choice criteria. *Bulletin of Psychology and the Arts, 2*, 20-25.

Münte, T. F., Altenmüller, E., & Jäncke, L. (2002). The musician's brain as a model of neuroplasticity. *Nature Reviews Neuroscience, 3*, 473-478

Nathan, J. (2002). The painter and handicapped vision. *Clinical and Experimental Optometry, 85*, 309-314.

Noonan, J. P., Coop, G., Kudaravalli, S., Smith, D., Krause, J., Alessi, J., et al. (2006). Sequencing and analysis of Neanderthal genomic DNA. *Science, 314*, 1113-1118.

Nykvist, S. (2003). The director of photography. In IMAGO (Ed.), *Making pictures: A century of European cinematography*. New York: Harry N. Abrams.

Pantev, C., Oostenveld, R., Engelien, A., Ross, B., Roberts, L. E., & Hoke, M. (1998). Increased auditory cortical representation in musicians. *Nature, 392*, 811-814.

Patel, A. D. (2003). Language, music, syntax and the brain. *Nature Neuroscience, 6*, 674-681.

Paterson, A., & Zangwill, O. L. (1944). Disorders of visual space perception associated with lesions of the right cerebral hemisphere. *Brain, 67*, 331-358.

Peretz, I. (2002). Brain specialization for music. *Neuroscientist, 8*, 372-380.

Pinker, S., & Bloom, P. (1990). Natural language and natural selection. *Behavioral and Brain Sciences, 13*, 707-784.

Ravin, J. G. (1997). Artistic vision in old age. In M. F. Marmor & J. G. Ravin (Eds.), *The eye of the artist*. St. Louis: Mosby-Year Book, Inc.

Rose, M. (2004). *The mind at work: Valuing the intelligence of the American worker*. New York: Viking.

Sacks, O. (1995). *An anthropologist on Mars*. New York: Alfred A. Knopf.

Sacks, O. (2004). Autistic geniuses? We're too ready to pathologize. *Nature, 429*, 241.

Saur, D., Baumgaertner, A., Schraknepper, V., Willmes, K., Rijntjes, M., & Weiller, C. (2006). Dynamics of language reorganization after stroke. *Brain, 129*, 1371-1384.

Stringer, C. (2002). Modern human origins: Progress and prospects. *Philosophical Transactions of the Royal Society B: Biological Sciences, 357*, 563-579.

Turner, C. (2006). Through art to association in Japanese politics. *Science, 313*, 1575-1576.

Vargha-Khadem, F., Gadian, D. G., Copp, A., & Mishkin, M. (2005). FOXP2 and the neuroanatomy of speech and language. *Nature Review Neuroscience, 6*, 131-138.

Vargha-Khadem, F., Watkins, K. E., Price, C. J., Ashburner, J., Alcock, K. J., Connelly, A., et al. (1998). Neural basis of an inherited speech and language disorder. *Proceedings of the National Academy of Sciences, USA, 95*, 12695-12700.

Vartanian, O., & Goel, V. (2004). Neuroanatomical correlates of aesthetic preference for paintings. *NeuroReport, 15*, 892-897.

Warrington, E. K., & James, M. (1966). Drawing disability in relation to laterality of cerebral lesion. *Brain, 89*, 53-82.

Welsch, W. (2004) Animal aesthetics. *Contemporary Aesthetics, 2*, 56-62.

Whatmough, C., Chertkow, H., Murtha, S., & Hanratty, K. (2002). Dissociable brain regions process object meaning and object structure during picture naming. *Neuropsychologia, 40*, 174-186.

Wieser, H. G. (2003). Music and the brain. Lessons from brain diseases and some reflections on the "emotional" brain. *Annals of the New York Academy of Sciences, 999*, 76-94.

Wilson, D. O. (2006). Genomics: How to make a social insect. *Nature, 443*, 919-920.

Zaidel, D. W. (2005). *Neuropsychology of art: Neurological, cognitive, and evolutionary perspectives*. Hove, UK: Psychology Press.

Zaidel, D. W., & Cohen, J. A. (2005). The face, beauty, and symmetry: Perceiving asymmetry in beautiful faces. *International Journal of Neuroscience, 115*, 1165-1173.

Zaidel, D. W., Chen, A. C., & German, C. (1995). She is not a beauty even when she smiles: Possible evolutionary basis for a relationship between facial attractiveness and hemispheric specialization. *Neuropsychologia, 33*, 649-655.

Zaidel, D. W., & FitzGerald, P. (1994). Sex of the face in Western art: Left and right in portraits. *Empirical Studies of the Arts, 12*, 9-18.

Zaidel, D. W., & Kasher, A. (1989). Hemispheric memory for surrealistic versus realistic paintings. *Cortex, 25*, 617-641.

Zangwill, O. L. (1964). Neurological studies and human behaviour. *British Medical Bulletin, 20*, 43-48.

Zatorre, R. J. (2003). Absolute pitch: A model for understanding the influence of genes and development on neural and cognitive functions. *Nature Neuroscience, 6*, 692-695.

Zilhao, J., d'Errico, F., Borders, J.-G., Lenoble, A., & Texier, J.-P. (2006). Analysis of Aurignacian interstratification at the Chatelperronian-type site and implications for the behavioral modernity of Neanderthals. *Proceedings of the National Academy of Sciences, USA, 103*, 12643-12648.

CHAPTER 9

Allusions to Visual Representation

Nicholas Wade

The beauty of vision has not been adequately expressed by those who typically describe its processes. That is, visual scientists have not represented the subject matter of their enquiry with a feeling for the aesthetics it possesses. Visual artists have taken on this role, and they have often provided some of the most alluring examples of the visual phenomena studied experimentally by visual scientists. Someone wishing to discover more about aesthetics and its visual underpinnings is unlikely to go first to a textbook on vision. Despite the fact that visual artists and visual scientists are often concerned with examining similar phenomena, the methods they adopt differ radically. Scientists generally try to discover new facts regarding old phenomena. Artists are concerned with arranging phenomena in a manner that has not been seen before or perhaps to increase the viewers' awareness of the phenomena. Often this involves complicating the effects rather than simplifying pattern elements. Thus, scientists rarefy and isolate phenomena to control them in the laboratory, whereas artists embrace complexity and manipulate phenomena intuitively, often exposing aesthetic aspects that have been hidden from scientists. Not only have artists provided more engaging examples of visual phenomena, but they have also enhanced their range in ways that are scientifically novel (see Wade, 2007b).

I will try to present some basic aspects of the visual process in a manner that is unconventional but with the hope that it might capture an element of the aesthetic dimension of vision. That is, I will try to convey the ideas presented verbally in graphical form, too. The starting point will be the stimulus for vision, followed by the anatomy and physiology of processing light, a variety of visual phenomena, and ending with a nod toward experimental aesthetics.

LIGHT AND THE EYE

For much of its long history, the study of sight has been intimately entwined with the nature of light. Some Greek thinkers believed it was emitted from the eye and others considered that it was received by the eye (see Park, 1997; Wade, 1998a, 2007a). Indeed, light and sight were virtually synonymous until Johannes Kepler (1571-1630) described how images were formed in the eye. His analysis of the dioptrics of the eye resulted in a distinction between the physics of light and the psychology of sight. However, the nature of light presented its own problems for physics being considered either as particles or waves—a duality that still remains. Isaac Newton (1642-1727; Figure 1, left) championed the former, whereas Christiaan Huygens (1629-1695; Figure 1 right) favored the latter. Up to this period, the science of vision was divided into three parts: optics, dioptrics, and catoptrics (see Cohen & Drabkin, 1958). An additional phenomenon, diffraction, was demonstrated by Franciscus Maria Grimaldi (1665), who suggested that light might act like a liquid, flowing in waves. Wave theory was supported and extended by Huygens (1690): he proposed and illustrated the wave fronts that could be produced by points on luminous sources. He made an analogy between light and sound; diffraction was analyzed in terms of the wave fronts originating at an aperture or edge. In contrast, Newton proposed that light consisted of small corpuscles that collided with one another. However, Newton did not rule out the operation of light as waves. Thereafter, the theoretical contrast was between Huygens' wave theory and Newton's corpuscular theory of light. The balance was tipped in favor of wave theory with Thomas Young's (1802) demonstration and analysis of interference phenomena.

Figure 1. Left, *Visionary*; a perceptual portrait of Newton combining his face with his diagrams for the formation of the visible spectrum and for the partial decussation of the visual pathways (from Wade, 1995). Right, *Wave theorist*; Huygens embedded in a pattern of waves. (© Illustrations by Nicholas Wade.)

Color compounds the physical and psychological dimensions of optics, although an appreciation of this was only possible when the physical properties of light had been elucidated. In his *Opticks* (1704), Newton illustrated and interpreted the spectrum produced by sunlight passing through a prism: differences in color were related to differences in the amount they were refracted by the prism. He also noted that color was a subjective experience rather than a property of light: "For the Rays to speak properly are not coloured. In them there is nothing else than a certain power and disposition to stir up a sensation of this or that Colour" (Newton, 1704, p. 90). That power was dependent in part on the degree to which sunlight was refracted when passing through a prism. A wide range of color phenomena was available to Newton before he conducted his prismatic experiments, including the prismatic colors themselves. The phenomena concerned color mixing, after-images, color contrasts, and color shadows; they had accumulated over centuries and spawned competing theories. Most theories were based on the Aristotelian view that color was a property of bodies, and that it was carried by light through the transparent medium to the eye. Newton provided a unified theory of light and colors: white light was not unitary but compounded, in precise proportions, of many components that differed in their refraction. He was able to analyze the prismatic colors with an armory of subtle experimental procedures. For example, small sections of the prismatic spectrum could be isolated and mixed with other parts, so that the rules of their mixture could be determined.

With the appreciation that light could be considered as a physical property, and that its reflections and refractions followed physical principles, its study became the province of physicists, whereas the examination of sight was pursued by physiologists and philosophers. The separation of the physics of light from the philosophy of sight was to reflect the ancient schism between materialists and idealists: light was an external, material phenomenon, whereas sight was internal and subjective.

The long-lasting problem with regard to sight has concerned the nature of images. Visual images have always been based on light, whether it was emitted by or received by the eye. Both of these positions were consistent with the fact, described by Euclid (ca. 323-283 BC), that light travels in straight lines. This fact, more than any other, informed the early theories of images and their formation. Euclid's optics were both physical and psychological; the rays in his diagrams represented not only light but also sight. For example, Euclid's book entitled *Optics* is concerned with describing visual space in terms of visual angles, so that the perception of space was analyzed geometrically (see Burton, 1945). From Euclid's time onward, the vision problem has been illustrated by ray diagrams drawn between objects and the eye. Euclid realized that the size of the image at the eye varies with the distance of the object. Thus, an object of a given size will project a smaller angle at the eye with increasing distance from the eye (Figure 2, upper). Put another way, the rectilinear propagation of light enabled students of vision to describe objects in terms of visual angles, the trigonometry of which was simple. This was typically represented using an arrow as the object that would be imaged. Arrows are still used as pictorial devices in optics, as in the formation of focused images by lenses.

Figure 2. Upper, *The arrow in the eye*; all the letters in the words (apart from the "e" which is an eye) subtend the same angle. Lower, *Shifted perspective*; the letters are arranged in a grid that will appear rectangular if viewed from the extreme right side, the word that describes the effect will be recognized. (© Illustrations by Nicholas Wade.)

Artists also utilized the concept of visual angle, and progress was most evident in defining how images are formed in front of the eye rather than in the eye itself. In the early fifteenth century, Fillipo Brunelleschi (1377-1446) invented practical methods for harnessing visual angles on the picture plane. Explicit rules for representing three-dimensional space on a two-dimensional surface were formulated by Leon Battista Alberti (1404-1472), which were eagerly adopted by the artists of the day (see Kemp, 1990). Linear perspective provided a theory for the formation of images on a surface before the eye.

Alberti described the picture plane as a window through which the subject to be painted is seen. Light could then travel like an arrow along the Euclidean rays to reach the eye or from the eye to meet the object. The direction in which light traveled had no effect on the line diagrams drawn. No such ambiguity was associated with the flight of the arrow; it traveled from bow to object. This was delightfully depicted in the fresco *Martyrdom of St. Christopher,* painted around 1450-1457 by Andrea Mantegna (see Kubovy, 1986). It celebrates a Greek legend based on a third C saint who was condemned by the Roman emperor Decius to die if he did not renounce his faith. On refusing, St. Christopher was tied to a stool and the archers took aim. All the arrows missed the saint, but one passed through the eye of the emperor. Before St. Christopher was killed, he told the emperor that his eye would be healed with the blood of the saint. When the emperor's sight returned, he converted to Christianity. Mantegna depicted the arrow passing through Alberti's window to enter the eye of Decius. In practice, however, the arrow of perspective stopped at the picture plane. Although the visual artists of the fifteenth and sixteenth centuries were also the visual scientists of their day, they added little to our understanding of the eye as an optical instrument. This was so even when they used optical instruments, like the *camera obscura,* to assist in the production of pictures in perspective.

Linear perspective was rapidly and widely adopted by artists in the fifteenth century. It was also distorted in the form of accelerated and decelerated perspective architectures and anamorphic paintings. Leonardo da Vinci (1472-1519) also made anamorphoses—distorted perspectives (Figure 2, lower). The letters in the figure were drawn using the same principles employed in the sixteenth and seventeenth centuries to produce anamorphoses: a pictorial image in central perspective was initially drawn within a regular rectangular grid. The grid was then transformed with regard to some eccentric station point, and the contents of the original grid cells were transposed to them. The first anamorphoses probably came to the West from China (Baltrušaitis, 1977). These were analyzed mathematically and optically by Jean-François Niceron (1646) in his book on curious perspectives. He produced linear, conical, and cylindrical anamorphoses. The principles behind these are essentially the same ones that Adelbert Ames (1880-1955) applied in his famous perceptual demonstrations (see Behrens, 1993; Ittelson, 1952).

Several artists drew parallels between the operation of a camera and the eye, but the arrow of perspective took two centuries to penetrate the eye itself! Kepler (1604) (Figure 3), described how light was refracted by the various transparent surfaces of the eye to form a retinal image. This established the retina as the receptive surface rather than the lens, as had previously been thought. However, it reinforced the pictorial metaphor in the analysis of vision. This was particularly so because the optical image on the retina was inverted and reversed, and this did not correspond with perceptual experience. It was thought that the retinal image was a picture, and that this representation required reversing and inverting in some way. Kepler was reluctant to entertain speculation as to how this might come about, considering it beyond the realm of physics:

> I say that vision occurs when the image (*idolum*) of the whole hemisphere of the world which is in front of the eye, and a little more, is formed on the reddish white concave surface of the retina (*retina*). I leave it to natural

Figure 3. *Kepler's dioptrics*. Kepler's portrait is embedded in retinal structures that are contained within the words "RETINAL IMAGE" (presented both upright and inverted). (© Illustration by Nicholas Wade.)

> philosophers to discuss the way in which this image or picture (*pictura*) is put together by the spiritual principles of vision residing in the retina and in the nerves. (Kepler, 1604, translated in Crombie, 1964, pp. 147-148)

That is, Kepler made an explicit distinction between the physical optics of image formation and the psychological optics of vision. In so doing, he posed the problem that students of vision have struggled with ever since (Smith, 2004).

Another astronomer, Christoph Scheiner (1573-1650; Figure 4), was soon to provide an accurate representation of the gross anatomy of the eye based on dissections of the eyes of many animals, but not of a human: the lens and its curvatures are appropriately represented, and the optic nerve leaves the eye nasally. Scheiner (1619) appreciated that an equation of artificial and natural image formation could be made, and he described how an artificial eye could be constructed. Some years later, Scheiner (1630) presented a pictorial analysis of optical-image formation in the camera and the eye, with both inverted and upright images due to the addition of convex and concave lenses (see Daxecker, 2004). He noted that an upright retinal image resulted in inverted vision. Furthermore, Scheiner described how an image could be seen on the exposed surface of an excised animal's eye—an experiment he "had often performed." The demonstration of an inverted and reversed image cast on the retina of an animal's eye, together with those from artificial eyes hastened optical analyses of vision.

Kepler and Scheiner set the scene for an integration between image and eye, and this union was forged by René Descartes (1596/1650; Figure 5, left). He amplified the diagrams of the eye following Scheiner, and he made an artificial eye, suggesting that eggshell was a suitable substitute for the retina. The impact of Descartes' analysis was represented potently by his illustrations. The most familiar representation of image formation in an excised eye is that from Descartes's *Dioptrique* (1637/1902, 1965), in which the cosmic observer ponders on the spatial arrangement of the inverted and reversed retinal image. Descartes was able to provide a more precise analysis of image formation than Kepler because he could apply Snell's law to the refractions taking place (Wade, 1998b). Use of artificial eyes brought the problem of focusing to the fore: objects at different distances required lenses of different strength in order to form a focused image. Descartes also speculated about the brain processes associated with the processes of perception and particularly those that could mediate binocular single vision.

Following these advances in understanding the gross anatomy of the eye, interest shifted from the lens to the retina. Nonetheless, some physiologists raised doubts about assigning a receptive function to the retina. These were based on a compelling phenomenon, first described by Edmé Mariotte (1620-1684), namely the blind spot. Mariotte (1668) found that the image of a small object falling on the base of the optic nerve is invisible when one eye alone is used. The phenomenon enabled Mariotte and others to locate the entrance point of optic nerve with precision, either in terms of visual angles or retinal dimensions. There remained considerable controversy concerning the interpretation of the phenomenon. Mariotte contended that the retina extended over the whole inner surface of the eye, including the optic nerve,

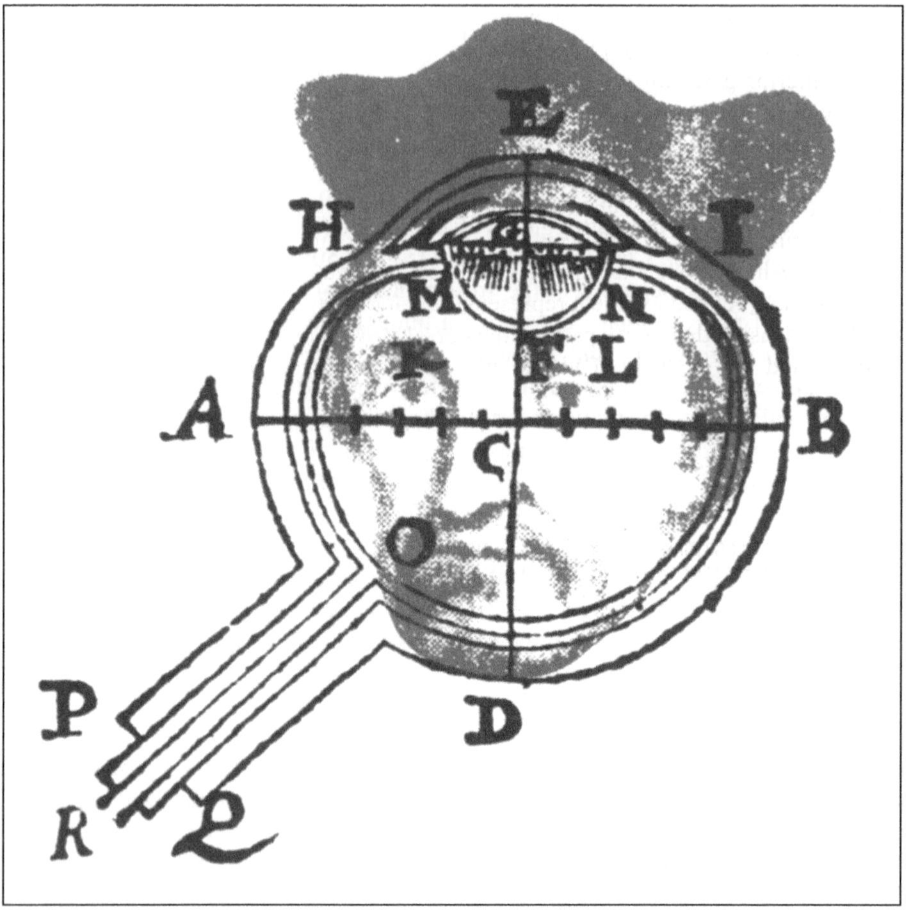

Figure 4. *Scheiner's Oculus*. The diagram of the eye is taken from Scheiner (1619). (© Illustration by Nicholas Wade.)

and so the retina could not be the receptive organ. Almost everyone else disagreed on the grounds that other obstructions to light in the eye do not disrupt vision, that the blind spot is not seen with pressure images, or that comparative studies indicate that the retina undergoes fewer species differences than the choroid. The dispute was instructive because it stimulated studies of the retina. Perhaps the pinnacle of direct observation of the retina was reached by Samuel Thomas von Soemmerring (1755-1830; Figure 5, right). He produced beautiful engravings of sections of the eye and also described the yellow spot.

von Soemmerring (1801) was skeptical about microscopic studies of the retina because of the potential artifacts that sectioning could induce, and because the simple microscopes were prone to optical aberrations. Such studies had been conducted since van Leeuwenhoek directed his microscope to the optic nerve of the

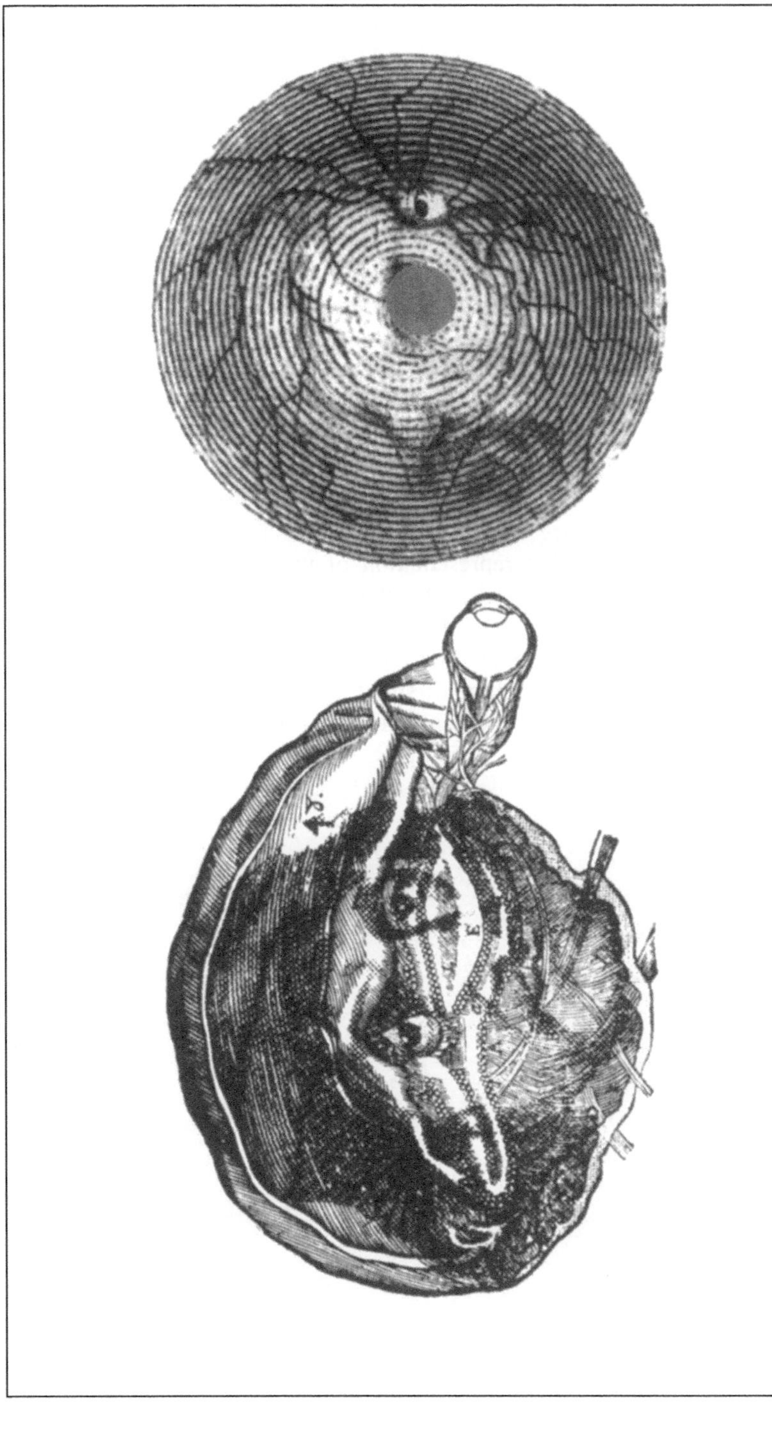

Figure 5. Left, *Descartes' brain*. Descartes' diagram of the brain is taken from his *Traité de l'Homme* (1664/1909). Right, *Gelbe Flecke*. von Soemmerring within his diagram of the retina to which the yellow spot has been added. (© Illustrations by Nicholas Wade.)

cow in the seventeenth century, but the power of the achromatic microscope was only brought to bear after von Soemmerring's death. Achromatic microscopes were introduced in the 1820s, and the years following 1840 saw rapid advances in fixing, sectioning, and staining microscopic preparations (see Wade, 2007a).

PHYSIOLOGY OF VISION

A major problem faced by microscopists was that of rendering the nerve fibers more readily visible. The solution came with the "black reaction" devised by Camillo Golgi (1843-1926) in 1873; it consisted of hardening the preparation in potassium bichromate and then impregnating it with silver nitrate. The subsequent black reaction (*reazione nera*) exposed the networks of nerves in grey matter in a manner that had not been possible previously. The power of the procedure was initially demonstrated on the arborizations of Purkinje cells in the cerebellum, but interest soon shifted to the retina. It was one of Golgi's students, Ferrucio Tartuferi (1887), who first applied the silver staining technique to this structure, and his portrait is contained in his beautiful illustration of the retina (Figure 6). The horizontal and amacrine cells are clearly represented, as are the rods, cones, and bipolar cells. Despite the detailed representation of the constituent parts of the retina, Tartuferi retained his teacher's view that the nervous system was a connected and continuous unit—a reticulum (see Wade & Piccolino, 2006).

Golgi's staining method was adopted and adapted by Santiago Ramón y Cajal (1852-1934) to investigate a broad range of structures within the nervous system, including the large cells in the cerebellum. The retina was the second structure

Figure 6. See p. 148 for full color.

studied by Cajal (1893), and it was seen by him as providing strong evidence in favor of the neuron doctrine, enunciated by Wilhelm Waldeyer in 1891. However, Cajal did not represent the retina with the same precision displayed by Tartuferi. Cajal took the principal distinction between the rods and cones to support duplicity theory: that rods and cones have different functions. He also sought to retain the distinction for the fibers in connection with the receptors. The presence of lateral connections from the horizontal and amacrine cells presented a problem for Cajal's conception of the manner in which vision operated. He considered that there was a point-to-point analysis of the retinal image, with the punctate pattern being retained at central sites. Lateral connections in the visual pathways could disturb this pattern of projection, and Cajal sought to see in his histology the evidence for such a sequence.

Much of the research in the twentieth century followed the direction charted by Cajal. His histological studies provided support for the neuron doctrine, which has dominated neurophysiology ever since. It could be argued that it is mainly due to his work that the photographic paradigm of point-to-point stimulation and coding dominated physiological investigations of the retina for the first half of the twentieth century. This was so despite the clear psychophysical demonstration of lateral interactions within visual channels and also the pioneering physiological studies of Hartline (1928) in *Limulus*, of Barlow (1953) in the frog, and of Kuffler (1953) in mammalian eye: a new conception of retinal processing slowly emerged. Their studies demonstrated that lateral and recurrent interactions, occurring in a complex network of neuronal circuits, were considered fundamental mechanisms for visual information processing. Hartline, together with Granit and Wald, shared the Nobel Prize for Medicine or Physiology in 1967 for their researches on the retina (Figure 7). Thus, modern conceptions of retinal function seem to correspond more closely to the reticularist scheme advocated by Tartuferi (under Golgi's influence) than to Cajal's photographic paradigm.

The physiological dimension was also pursued with Nobel aims by Hubel and Wiesel (Figure 8). Technological advances led to the recording of electrical activity in single nerve cells using microelectrodes and amplifiers, not only in the retina but also at more central sites. By recording the receptive fields of single cells in the visual cortex, Hubel and Wiesel (1962, 1968) were able to determine the stimuli that most strongly excited them. Contrary to the conception of Cajal and others, points of light were not the most effective trigger features; the cortical cells were more selective to lines and edges, particularly if they were moving in a direction perpendicular to their orientation. These orientation-selective neurons were once considered to make up the majority of cells in the visual cortex. Indeed, such was the interest elicited after their discovery that they were called feature detectors. This was because the cortical neurons were selectively tuned to extract certain features contained in the pattern of retinal stimulation, in this case orientation. Direction of edge motion is another feature extracted, as are binocular disparity and color. The orientation-selective neurons have a highly ordered organization over the visual cortical area known as V1, both perpendicular to the cortical surface and parallel to it. If a microelectrode is inserted at right angles to the surface and all

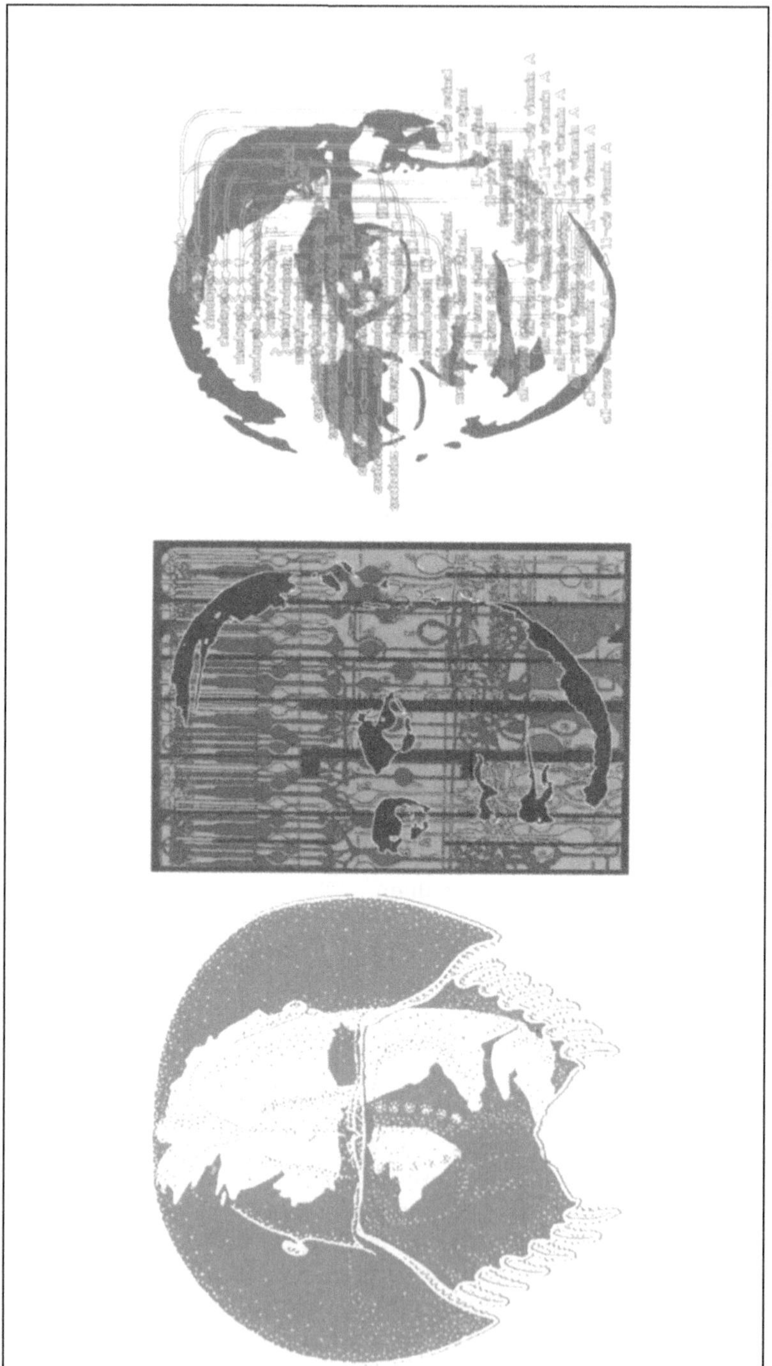

Figure 7. The Nobel retina. Perceptual portraits of the Nobel laureates for Medicine or Physiology in 1967: Left, *Limulus*, Haldan Keffer Hartline (1903-1993). Center, *Nobel colours*, Ragnar Granit (1900-1991) in the structure of the retina. Right, *Visual purple*, George Wald (1906-1997) with the rhodopsin reaction. (© Illustrations by Nicholas Wade.)

orientation cells encountered are recorded, then they will have the same preferred orientation. This has been called a cortical column. An equivalent insertion in the neighboring column will record a slightly different orientation selectivity; the next column would have cells displaying a preferred orientation of around 15 degrees, and so on, each column differing by about 15 degrees from its immediate neighbor. In fact, the orientation selectivity of the cortical cells is not quite as precise as might have been suggested here; there is a particular orientation that will produce the maximum response from each neuron, but it will also respond, though with decreasing intensity, to lines within 10 to 20 degrees either side of the preferred orientation. Accordingly, a given line falling on the retina will excite a range of orientation-selective neurons, but to varying extents. Area V1 has a vertical organization in terms of orientation selectivity and a horizontal organization in terms of orientation change. This results in all orientations being represented for a given retinal region.

The wavelength characteristics of the stimulus are coded in what are called cortical blobs; the cells are non-orientation-selective and they have double opponency. The receptive fields have a center-surround organization with the center, say, being excited by long wavelengths and inhibited by medium ones (denoted by R+G-) with the reverse influence on the surround (R-G+). These cell types are more common than those coding for B+Y- center and B-Y+ surround or the converse. These feature detectors have an orderly representation in the visual cortex and they project to clearly defined eye-dominance regions. The patterns displayed in Figure 8 are of the alternating patterns of eye-dominance regions over the visual cortex, and the visual scientists are represented in different ones, Hubel on the left and Wiesel on the right.

Single-unit recordings have greatly extended our understanding of how light striking the retina is processed at subsequent stages. This is represented schematically and metaphorically in Figure 9. The central radiating lines are like light rays that enter the eye through a small aperture and then strike the retina. Within the retina there are three neural levels consisting of receptors, bipolar cells, and retinal ganglion cells, all of which have lateral connections. The axons from the ganglion cells travel to the visual cortex, undergoing partial separation so that the left and right hemiretinae project to opposite hemispheres; however, there is some projection to both hemispheres for fibers from the vertical midline of the retina. At the level of the visual cortex, there is an organization in terms of vertical columns, within which are six horizontal layers. In the central region, the circles represent the two overlapping monocular visual fields, in which there is binocular brightness enhancement.

As the functional specialization of visual areas of the cortex became better understood, so there were suggestions that different regions of the visual brain are organized into two rather different kinds of processing pathway or stream. An early idea was that of "two visual systems" (Ungeleider & Mishkin, 1982), which developed the distinction drawn in the 1960s between the "what" and "where" systems of the cortex and superior colliculi, respectively. Their proposal was that there were two distinct cortical streams of processing, the inferotemporal pathway or "ventral" route, allowing the detailed perception and recognition of an object (its size, shape, orientation, and color) with the posterior parietal or "dorsal" route,

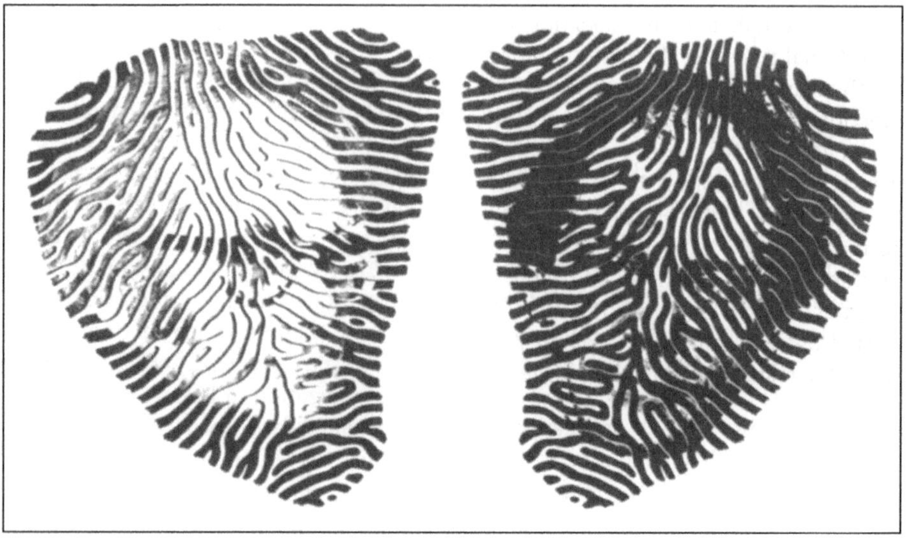

Figure 8. *Feature detectives*. Hubel and Wiesel were jointly awarded the Nobel Prize for Physiology or Medicine in 1981 in recognition of their neurophysiological studies of the visual system. They are depicted in the alternating ocular dominance columns of monkey visual cortex. (© Illustration by Nicholas Wade.)

allowing the perception of an object's location. Milner and Goodale (1995; Goodale & Milner, 2003) produced an important development of this theory by suggesting that these two parallel streams of visual processing are actually separately specialized for action (dorsal stream) and for visual experience of the world (ventral stream). The dorsal route is said to be the evolutionarily older visual system that enables a creature to navigate through the world and catch prey. The ventral route is developed particularly in primates to allow the detailed perception and interpretation of objects and, they contended, a conscious awareness of these.

The concept of channels or spatial filters emerged after that for single unit recordings, and it was applied with particular rigor by Fergus Campbell (1924-1993; Figure 10, right) and his colleagues to the detection of and adaptation to sine-wave gratings (see Campbell & Robson, 1968). The attraction of gratings was that they provided at one and the same time a definition of the stimulus and theory of the response to it. Kenneth Craik (1914-1945, Figure 10, left) characteristically foresaw the principle behind these developments:

> the action of various physical devices which 'recognize' or respond identically to certain simple objects can be treated in terms of such [mathematical] transformations. Thus the essential part of physical 'recognizing' instruments is usually a filter—whether it be a mechanical sieve, an optical filter, or a tuned electrical circuit—which 'passes' only quantities of the kind it is required to identify and rejects all others. (Craik, 1966, pp. 44-45)

Figure 9. *Eye and brain.* The schematic visual system representing the stages from rays of light to cortical columns. (© Illustration by Nicholas Wade.)

Craik, as well as Alan Turing (1912-1954), anticipated that the computer would be a powerful tool to simulate theories of perception, as well as providing a metaphor for the processes of perception and cognition themselves (see Millican & Clark, 1996). Since the late 1960s, the study of visual perception had been profoundly influenced by computers. As well as allowing scientists to collect or to analyze data

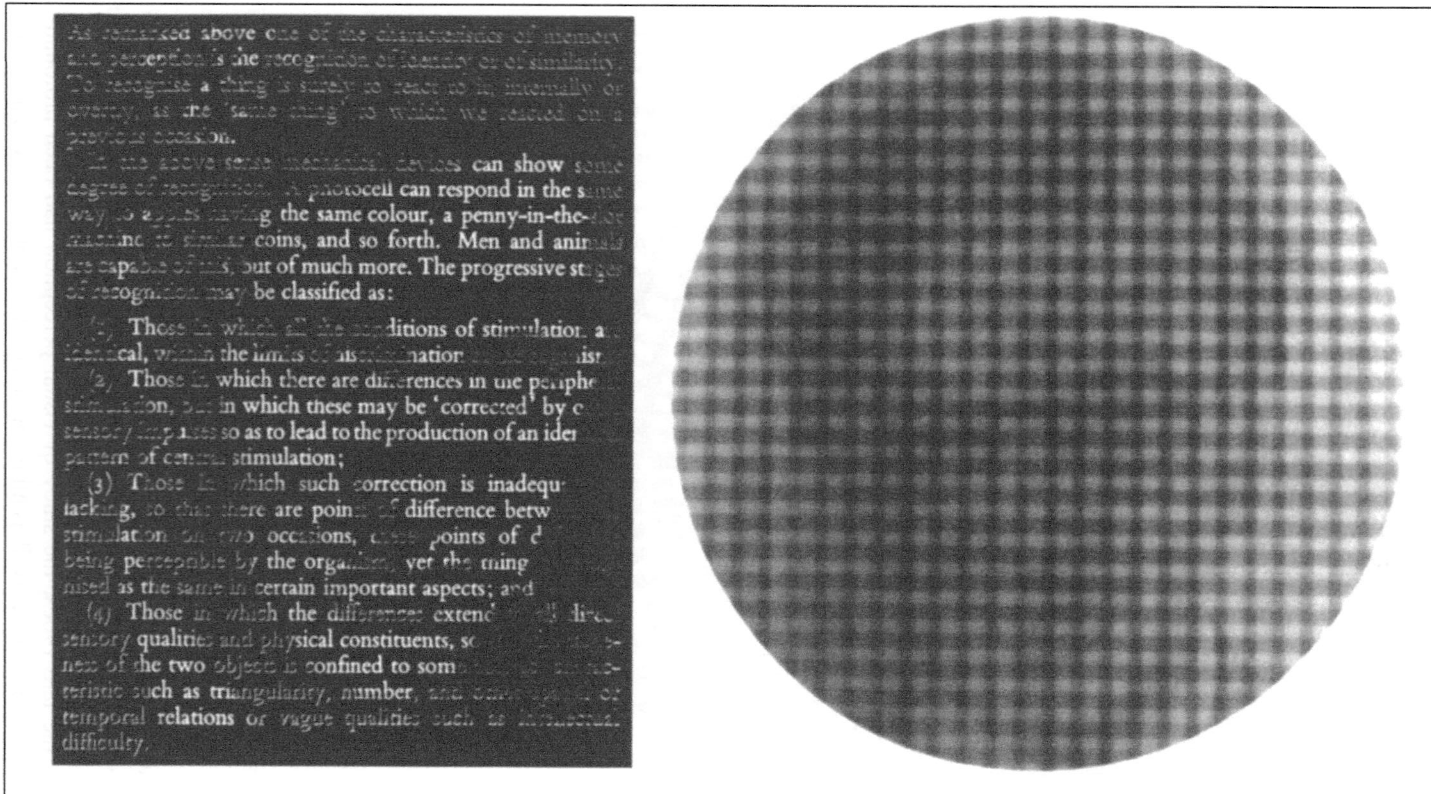

Figure 10. Left, *Recognition of identity*; a portrait of Kenneth Craik in text from his book on the nature of explanation (Craik, 1943). Right, *Campbell tartan*; crossed sine-wave gratings incorporate the smiling face of Fergus Campbell. (© Illustrations by Nicholas Wade.)

more quickly, the digital computer provided a tool for the laboratory scientist to develop new ways of testing the visual system with novel kinds of visual displays. The move away from reliance on oscilloscopes to present sine-wave gratings and other simple patterns facilitated the increasing use of more naturalistic patterns, as well as those that can be constructed and manipulated in controlled ways. Computer developments also enabled the better recording of eye movements and the linkage of eye movements to changes in display features, allowing a number of groups to conduct ingenious experiments into the control of eye movements in reading (see Findlay & Gilchrist, 2003; Wade & Tatler, 2005). Nonetheless, some of the shortcomings of computer modeling should also be voiced (Wade & Heller, 1997).

The computer provides a useful metaphor for the brain because both can perform many different functions with the same structures. Despite these similarities, we have to be careful not to take the metaphor too far. It has, in fact, proved very difficult to create anything resembling perception in a machine, despite the advances of recent years. There are several reasons for this, one of which may be the unsuitability of current computer architectures for the simulation of biological information processing. Human vision relies on an extremely large number of relatively simple computations, occurring in parallel. Many of the computing elements are interconnected in a complex manner, which can alter as the result of experience. Since nerve impulses travel slowly compared with electronic signals, and nerve cells take time to recover from activity, biological computation is also slow. A typical electronic computer uses serial processing, in which only one computation at a time can be performed, but at very high speed. There are rapid developments both in parallel computing and in the organization of processes in the form of connected networks, but the scale of these is at present very far from that of even quite simple organisms. In addition, it is possible that we simply do not have a clear enough idea about the way in which perceptual processes operate to be able to re-create them in a computer.

The machine metaphor was to prove particularly attractive to experimental psychologists, although only relatively simple machines were enlisted initially. For example, Craik (1966) worked with analog devices because the digital computer was still embryonic. Nonetheless, he did formalize the input, processing, and output components of servo systems in a manner that could be applied to digital computers. When computing machines increased in speed and complexity, the tasks that they could simulate became more complex. Concepts from engineering, like information and self-organization, were also integrated with a growing knowledge of neurophysiology resulting in the computer becoming a metaphor for the brain (see Wade & Bruce, 2001).

The computers mounted initially for the metaphorical odyssey to mind were digital and serial, but at around the same time, the ground was being laid for principles of parallel processing. McCulloch and Pitts's (1943) model of the neuron provided the foundation for later connectionist models of pattern recognition, and the networks connecting perception to its underlying physiology were further woven by Donald Hebb (1904-1985; Figure 11) in his speculative synthesis of perception and learning. Hebb (1949) proposed that perceptual learning takes place when

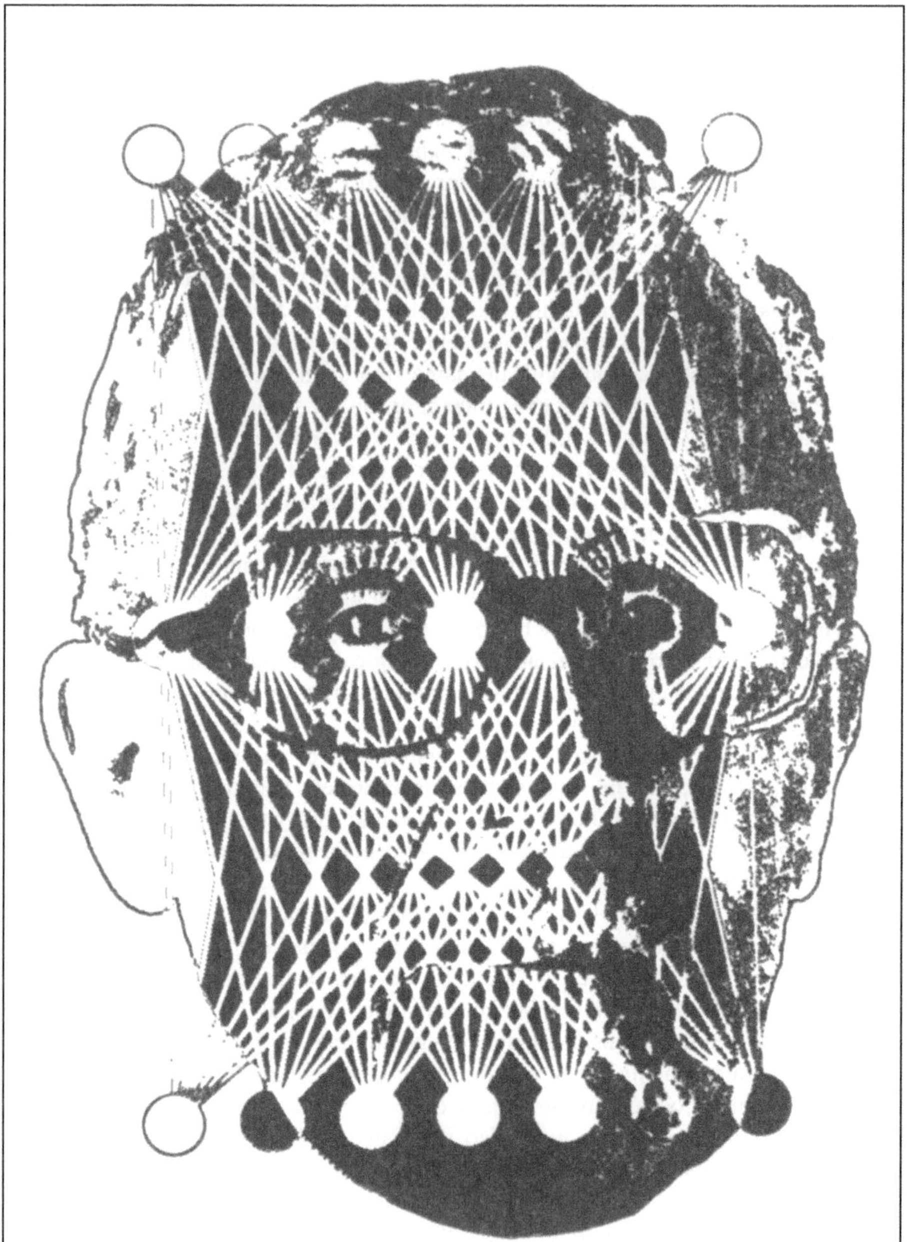

Figure 11. *Hidden units*. The face of Donald Hebb can be seen in the middle layer of a three-level network: each cell in the middle layer is connected to every other one in the levels above and below it. (© Illustration by Nicholas Wade.)

assemblies of cells fire together; their reverberating activity resulted in synaptic changes that further increased the probability of the nerves firing together. The functions of cell assemblies and phase sequences were based on his neurophysiological postulate: "When an axon of cell A is near enough to excite cell B and repeatedly or persistently takes part in firing it, some growth process or metabolic change takes place in one or both cells such that A's efficiency, as one of the cells firing B, is increased" (Hebb, 1949, p. 62). Hebb's postulate is taken as providing the foundation for current connectionist models of recognition and learning. Hebb later applied the concepts to account for a wide range of phenomena, from stabilized retinal images to sensory deprivation. The rapid development of computers has resulted in the design of more complex neural networks, involving more hidden layers, the activity of which cannot be determined from either the input or the output layers.

David Marr (1945-1980; Figure 12) set out to develop a computational framework for vision, spanning the very lowest-level processes within the retina up to the process of visual object recognition. Marr (1982) defined three levels at which any information processing system, including the visual system, can be understood. At the top level is the description of computational theory. This involves stating the purpose and goal of the process, why it is appropriate in the context of other functions, and the general logic of the strategy needed to carry it out. Below this is the algorithmic level of representation. This level requires statements about the actual sequence of processes that take place, so that the computation is achieved via various logical procedures, called algorithms. There will generally be a number of algorithms for any given computation. That is, the computational theory does not specify a particular means of achieving a goal, which must be determined independently. Marr referred to the first level as the "what" and "why" of the computation, and to the second as the "how" of it. Independent of both computational theory and representation is the level of hardware implementation. Just as a given computational function can be carried out by a number of algorithms, so a given algorithm can be instantiated by various alternative physical devices. An algorithm for multiplication can be implemented in an electronic computer, a mechanical calculator, a brain or even an abacus. In terms of visual perception, Marr's analysis suggests that we should be careful not to confuse the different levels of explanation.

Marr argued that the starting point for the analysis of vision must be a proper description at the level of computational theory, because only this can provide a framework for understanding the operations at lower levels. If we lack a good general description of the purpose of a perceptual process, we are unlikely to understand its underlying logic or the physiological hardware in which it takes place. Marr argued that "For the subject of vision, there is no single equation or view that explains everything. Each problem has to be addressed from several points of view—as a problem in representing information, as a computation capable of deriving that representation, and as a problem in the architecture of a computer capable of carrying out both things quickly and reliably" (Marr, 1982, p. 5). While many vision scientists still adopt Marr's general approach, the details of his models have been superceded.

Figure 12. *2½ D sketch*. David Marr's portrait is presented, rather like a difference of Gaussian functions, within a representation of a cube. There are slight differences in pattern properties for the three faces of the cube, so that it takes on the characteristics of a 2½-dimensional sketch. That is, the elements within the two dimensional pattern provide pointers to the three-dimensional characteristics of the object represented. (© Illustration by Nicholas Wade.)

VISUAL PHENOMENA

The range of visual phenomena is legion, making it necessary to restrict those here presented. As in many aspects of vision, it is wise to consult one of its greatest exponents, Hermann Helmholtz (1821-1894). He addressed visual phenomena, or the sensations of vision as he called them, in the second and third volumes of his *Handbuch der physiologischen Optik*, published in 1867. He presented his analysis of color vision in the second volume, where he extended Thomas Young's hypothesis that color could be perceived through the action of three mechanisms, and he presented three speculative curves showing the respective wavelength sensitivities of nerves with these specific energies. Helmholtz (1873) also differentiated between additive and subtractive color mixing and wrote on the relationship between the science of vision and the practice of painting in his *Popular Lectures* (Helmholtz, 1873). In Figure 13, a youthful Helmholtz is shown in combination with the curves depicting the specific energies for nerves responding to three regions of the visible spectrum.

Helmholtz acknowledged that little he wrote on the theories of vision was novel, but he marshalled the arguments over a wider range of phenomena than others had done before. He summarized his position succinctly:

> The sensations of the senses are tokens for our consciousness, it being left to our intelligence to learn how to comprehend their meaning. . . . Evidently, any other sensations, not only of sight but of other senses also, produced by a visible object when we move our eyes or our body so as to look at the object from different sides or to touch it, etc., may be learned by experience. The content of all these possible sensations united in a total idea forms our idea of the body; and we call it perception when it is reinforced by actual sensations. The only psychic activity required for this purpose is the regularly recurrent association between two ideas which have often been connected before. (1925, 2000, pp. 533-534)

By adopting a starkly empiricist interpretation of perception, and by contrasting it so sharply with nativism, he reopened a debate that has reverberated throughout perception ever since. The debate was personified in the conflict between Helmholtz and Ewald Hering (1834-1918), and the main battle-grounds were color vision and stereoscopic depth perception (see Turner, 1994).

Hering was a physiologist whose psychology was in the tradition of Wolfgang Goethe (1749-1832). Hering (1931) represented the phenomenological and nativist position in studying perception. His work in vision concerned space perception, color vision, and contrast phenomena. Like Goethe, Hering stressed the subjective dimension of color, and he based his opponent-process theory on color appearances rather than on mixing lights of different wavelengths after the manner of Young and Helmholtz. Hering adopted the procedure of presenting colored papers to observers and asking them to name the colors from which they were mixed. Red, green, blue, and yellow were not said to be mixtures of any other colors, nor were black and white. He also examined simultaneous and successive color-contrast

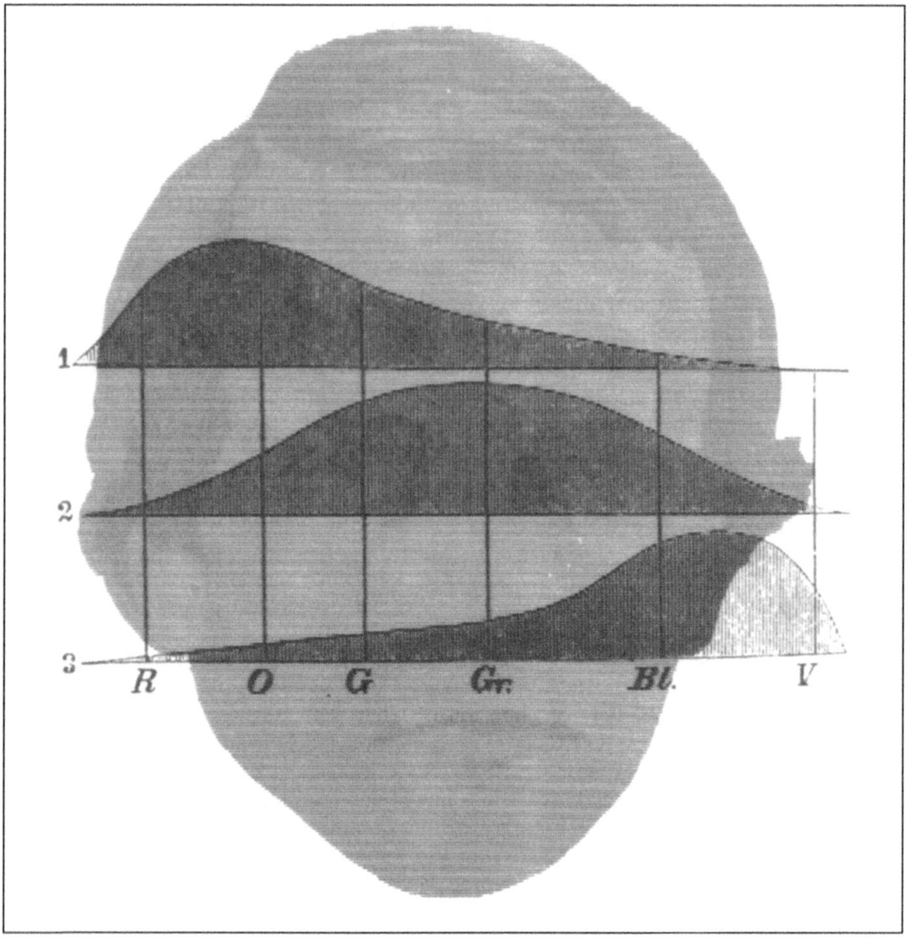

Figure 13. *Young Helmholtz*. The perceptual portrait is derived from a Daguerreotype of Helmholtz taken in 1847. The curves represent the speculated sensitivity functions of nerves responding to red, green, and blue regions of the visible spectrum given in his *Handbuch*. (© Illustration by Nicholas Wade.)

phenomena. Together, these led him to propose a theory of color vision based on three oppositional pairs: red-green, blue-yellow, and white-black. He speculated that there are three retinal pigments that are either built up or broken down by light to yield the six elements. Modern color theory has shown both Helmholtz and Hering to be correct in principle, but wrong in detail: the initial stage involves three cone pigments (not three kinds of fibers), the signals from which combine neurally (not in the action of the pigments) to produce opposing pairs of red-green, blue-yellow and white-black.

Their other major area of dispute was binocular vision. The problem of single vision with two eyes was an ancient one, but it had been transformed during Helmholtz's lifetime with the invention of the stereoscope by Charles Wheatstone (1802-1875; Figure 14); he demonstrated that slightly different images to each eye can yield depth rather than double vision. The critical issue in the dispute between Helmholtz and Hering was whether retinal local signs were adaptable or fixed and how they served stereoscopic vision. Helmholtz believed they were learned, whereas Hering argued that each retinal point has local signs for the space values of height, breadth, and depth, and that binocular fusion was physiological. Helmholtz considered that each monocular view was available to consciousness and that fusion was a psychical act. The stereoscope proved to be the critical instrument for examining the predictions from the two theories. It is not surprising that Helmholtz concluded "The invention of the stereoscope by Wheatstone made the difficulties and imperfections of the Innate Theory of sight much more obvious than before" (1873, p. 274).

The stereoscope opened a new world for the study of binocular vision. That world was the laboratory, and with the aid of the stereoscope, the methods of physics could be applied to the investigation of spatial vision. Wheatstone was able to manipulate

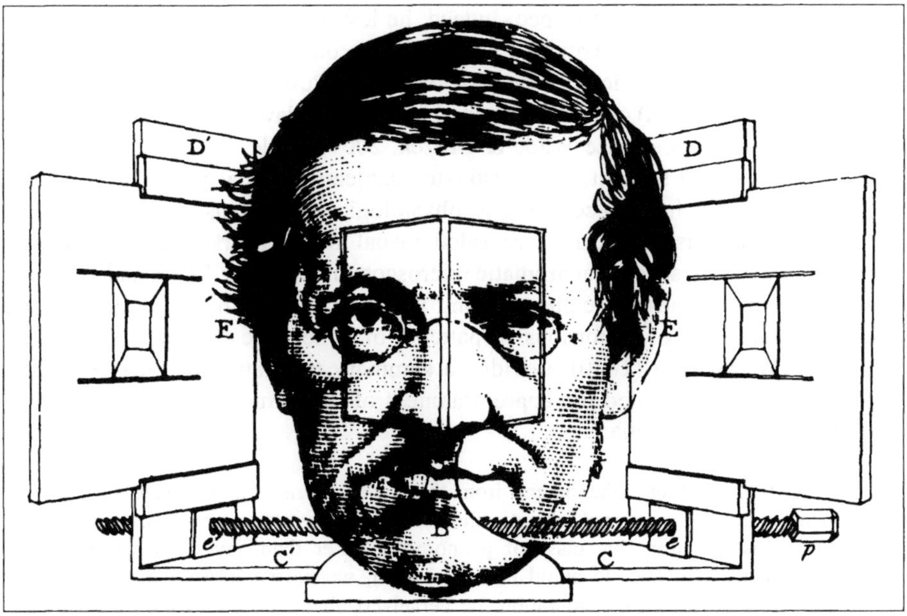

Figure 14. *Mirror stereoscopist*. Charles Wheatstone in the mirror stereoscope that he invented in the early 1830s. Slightly different images mounted on the lateral boards (E' and E) were reflected by the mirrors to enter the left and right eyes. (© Illustration by Nicholas Wade.)

the pictures presented to each eye and observe the depth that was produced. Having established that dissimilar pictures, when viewed in the stereoscope, produce the appearance of depth, Wheatstone conducted a series of systematic manipulations of the figures in order to discover the nature of the relationship. In his first article (1838) he demonstrated that the sign of disparity (crossed or uncrossed) determined the relative depth seen (nearer or farther), that there was a limit to the disparity yielding singleness of vision, that eye movements were not involved (because depth was seen in disparate afterimages), and that radically different pictures or colors resulted in binocular rivalry.

In 1839, the year after Wheatstone's first article on the stereoscope appeared, his friend William Henry Fox Talbot (1800-1877) made public his negative-positive photographic process. This friendship led to a marriage between the stereoscope and photography. However, it was not Wheatstone's mirror version that proved so popular, but the model using half-lenses, invented by David Brewster (1781-1868) in 1849, that took the Victorian world by storm (see Wade, 1983).

Subjective visual phenomena held an interest for both Brewster and Wheatstone, although their rivalry was expressed in this area as well as in their interpretations of binocular vision. Brewster (1825) described the subjective colors that can be seen in the fine lines of engravings. However, the term "subjective visual phenomena" belongs to Jan Evangelista Purkinje (1787-1869; Figure 15), who applied a more systematic approach to Goethe's phenomenology. Purkinje is best known for the microscopic structures he described. Indeed, he left his mark throughout the body: there are Purkinje cells in the brain, Purkinje fibers around the heart, Purkinje images are reflected from the optical surfaces of the eye, a Purkinje tree (the shadows of the retinal blood vessels) can be rendered visible, and at dawn and dusk the Purkinje shift can be experienced (see Wade & Brožek, 2001; Wade, Brožek & Hoskovec, 2002). As a medical student, he investigated subjective visual phenomena in part because he did not have access to any physiological apparatus, but also because he believed that visual illusions revealed visual truths (Purkinje, 1823, 1825). Purkinje gained access to an achromatic microscope in the early 1830s and made his histological discoveries thereafter. Among the simple phenomena he investigated was the observation of distortions in patterns of concentric circles, like those in Figure 15. Wheatstone (1830) provided a summary translation of Purkinje's first book, although he disputed the appropriateness of the term "subjective" in distinguishing visual phenomena:

> To distinguish these phenomena from those which arise on the presence of their appropriate external objects, the author employs the term subjective, which, as denoting this class of phenomena better than any other we are acquainted with, and, to avoid circumlocution, we have purposely retained; it will, however, on consideration, be perceived, that the term is not strictly proper, as, correctly speaking, all phenomena, *as such*, are subjective, i.e., in the mind; and were we, without qualification, to admit the classification of phenomena into objective and subjective, we should be unable to determine, with any degree of accuracy, where the objective ends or the subjective begins. (Wheatstone, 1830, p. 102)

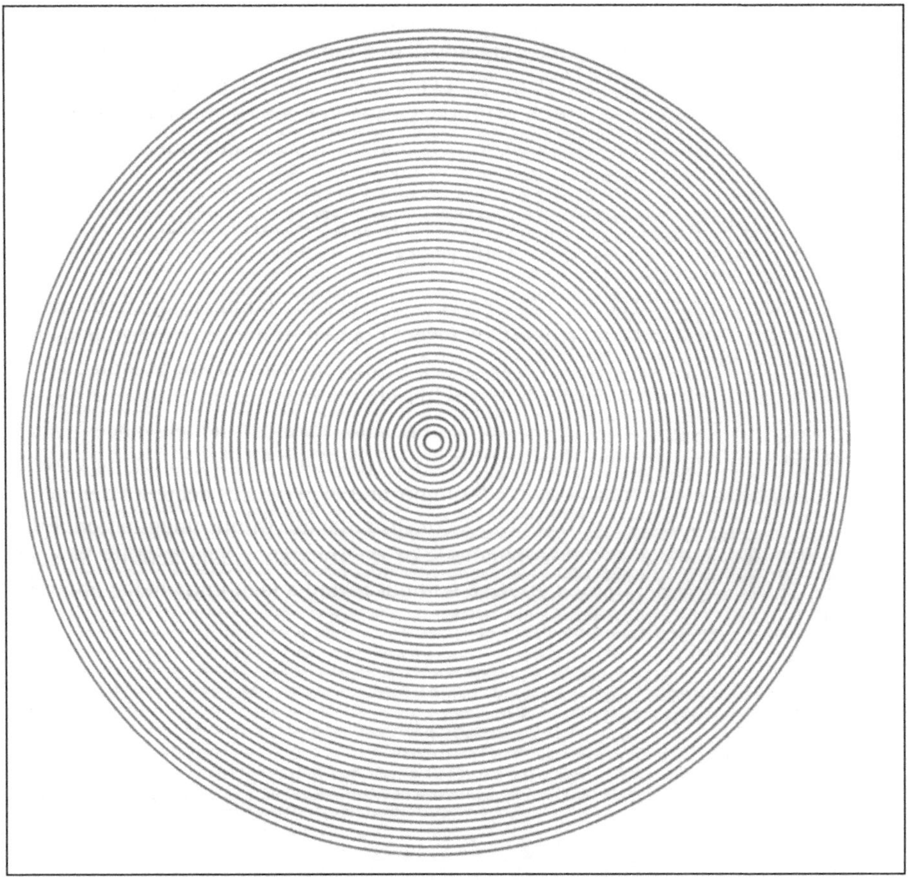

Figure 15. *Sehen in subjektiver Hinsicht*. Purkinje is partially hidden in a pattern of concentric circles; if the pattern is observed for some seconds, the circles themselves will appear to distort, and spokes will seem to radiate from the center and rotate. When the whole pattern is out of focus, his face can be seen. Purkinje considered that the distortions were due to the overlap of the image with its afterimage, but it is probably caused by transient astigmatic changes in the crystalline lens. (© Illustration by Nicholas Wade.)

Wheatstone not only gave a summary of selected sections from Purkinje's book, but he also added novel methods for observing some phenomena, particularly the visibility of retinal blood vessels.

Helmholtz was not sympathetic to the methods of phenomenology and cast Goethe in the role of a poet rather than a scientist. Helmholtz did, however, adopt eye movement interpretations of many phenomena, including illusions. His views were in turn opposed by Ernst Mach (1838-1916; Figure 16), who outlined a positivist approach to science by arguing that all sciences reduce to sensations. Mach (1886) defined a new area of form perception by correlating the appearance of

Figure 16. *Mach bands.* Ernst Mach can be dimly defined within the light and dark bands that surround him. The design was drawn to match the borders of his head, the details of which can be discerned from afar. Some artistic license has been taken in defining the facial features since they are not, strictly speaking, due to Mach bands, but they can be seen with an adequate analysis of the sensations. (© Illustration by Nicholas Wade.)

contours with physical variables. In studying the complexes of sensations that are involved in the perception of forms, he prepared the ground for the Gestalt psychologists in the twentieth century. However, one striking contrast phenomenon could not be defined so readily: a uniform gradient of luminance from light to dark does not appear uniform: a light band flanks the light border, while a dark band is visible to the side of the dark border. These are now called Mach bands, and he described them mathematically in terms of the second derivative of luminance change (see Ratliff, 1965).

Illusions as departures from veridical perception have been a constant source of enquiry throughout the recorded history of vision (see Wade, 2005a). Nonetheless, they were imbued with increased significance in the late nineteenth century. On the one hand, they liberated psychology from physiology, and on the other, they were considered to hold the key to unlock the secrets of perception. Moreover, they could be readily visualized via simple outline drawings, which induced compelling contrasts. Paradoxically, some of the first illusions displayed in this form were of phenomena that could be experienced in the natural environment, like the moon and waterfall illusions. Helmholtz (1867) was able to see the start of this illusory movement, and he also added a static illusion that is called Helmholtz squares (Figure 17). It is basically an example of the horizontal-vertical illusion: the area defined by horizontal lines appears smaller than that made up of vertical lines.

The illusions that attracted the interests of many nineteenth-century visual scientists were those labeled "geometrical optical" by Oppel (1856). They consist of relatively small but reliable distortions of visual space, mostly in the domains of size or orientation. Many novel forms were devised and depicted in the final decades of the century, and they often bear the names of those who first drew and described them. Geometrical optical illusions are quintessentially phenomena of the late nineteenth century, when the likes of Ponzo, Poggendorff, Mach, and Müller-Lyer described their eponymous phenomena. It is, however, instructive to examine why there should have been this burst of illusory activity in the late nineteenth century. Put another way, why did outline drawings assume such a central role in the study of perception? It could have been due to the combination of two powerful strands of thinking about vision. The first stems from the seventeenth century, when Kepler and later Descartes elucidated the dioptrical properties of the eye. They thereby set in train the idea that the problem of perception has as its starting point the static, two-dimensional retinal image. The retinal image was considered as static, and the problem was seen as restoring the missing dimension of distance from the ambiguous projection. However, this is both a physical and a physiological fiction. The static retinal image is a convenient physical fiction because it allows us to draw ray diagrams that describe the dioptrical properties of the eye. It is a physiological fiction because the eye is never still and the receptors collect energy at differential rates. Nonetheless, these fictions continue to drive our models of vision. The second strand relates to the experimental approaches to the study of perception introduced in the mid-nineteenth century. Wheatstone and Helmholtz argued that the experimental rigor of the physical sciences should be brought to bear on the study of perception. Thus, stimulus variables should be isolated and manipulated in quite unnatural ways in order to determine how perception is modified. It is difficult to manipulate solid objects, but it is exceedingly easy to create novel pictures. Moreover, Wheatstone himself showed that the perception of three-dimensional space can be synthesized from the use of two appropriate flat drawings. So pictures became the accepted stimuli for the study of vision. Once accepted, the psychologists then rediscovered tricks that had been a part of the artist's armory for centuries and they devised some novel ones, too.

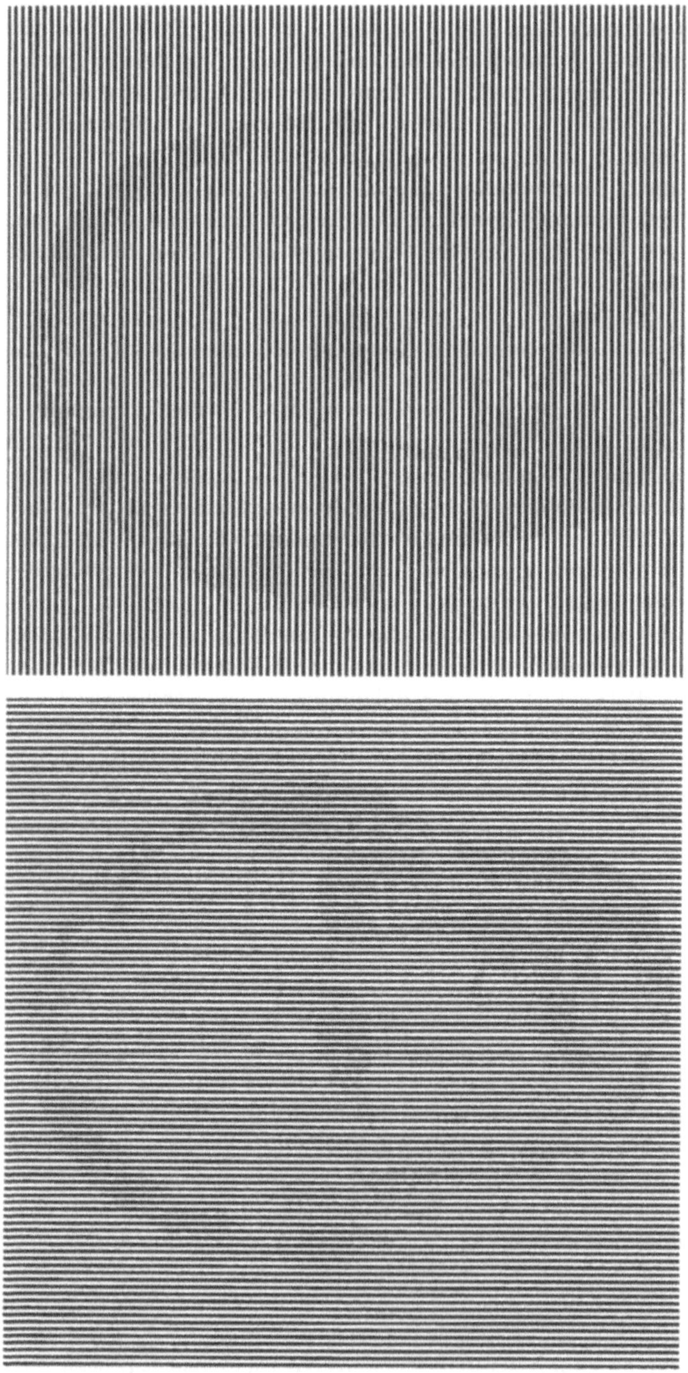

Figure 17. *Helmholtz's squares*. Helmholtz is enclosed twice within squares like those he printed, defined by either vertical or horizontal lines. (© Illustration by Nicholas Wade.)

The Helmholtz squares illusion is based on the distortions of space in the cardinal orientations. It is now called the horizontal-vertical illusion and it is usually represented as single lines in an inverted T shape. It incorporates both orientation and extent, whereas most others involve one of these dimensions alone. Two orientation illusions are shown in Figure 18; one is associated with Helmholtz's erstwhile assistant (Wundt) and the other with his antagonist (Hering).

Illusions of length were represented somewhat later, but they have been subject to more intense experiment and interpretation than those of orientation. Perhaps the best known is the Müller-Lyer illusion (Figure 19). Geometrical optical illusions have an important place in the history of psychology, because they were among the factors that led Wundt to establish his Psychological Institute at Leipzig in 1879—he

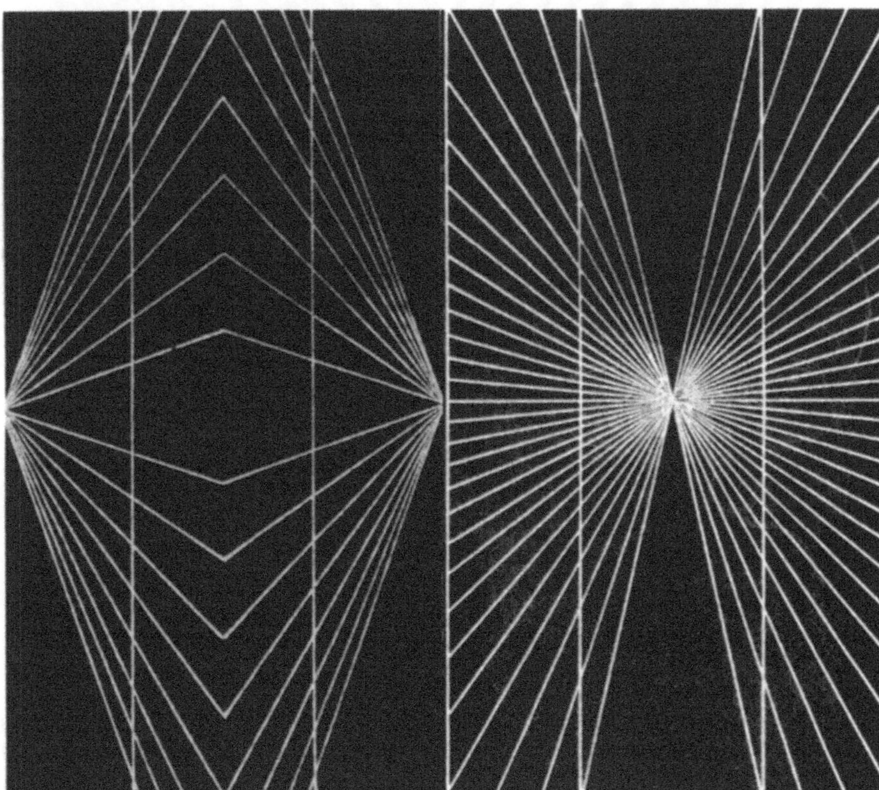

Figure 18. *Wundt and Hering Illusions*. Wilhelm Wundt is shown in a pattern of inclined lines that make the two verticals appear curved inward; it is called the Wundt illusion. The orientation illusion eponymously linked with Ewald Hering consists of radiating lines resulting in the verticals appearing curved outward. The illusion figures were printed with white lines on a black background in Wundt (1898). (© Illustration by Nicholas Wade.)

Figure 19. *Illusionist*. The two horizontal lines are the same physical length but they appear different: the upper one appears longer. This was described by Franz Carl Müller-Lyer (1857-1916), whose bearded features are present in the illustration. (© Illustration by Nicholas Wade.)

could not envisage how illusions could be accounted for in physiological terms, and so they, along with consciousness, required a separate discipline. Wundt took as his yardstick the proximal stimulus (the retinal image), and he could not accept that, say, two linear extents (like the horizontal lines in Figure 19) that produced equivalent retinal extents could yield perceptual inequality due to physiological processes. Thus, geometrical optical illusions are important in the context of establishing psychology as an independent discipline: there was considered to be no physiological correlate of perception. Psychologists like Wundt sought to determine correlates, and the one most favored at that time was in terms of eye movements, although other higher level alternatives were also entertained.

Contrast phenomena provided another potent source of visual illusion. Although the influence that a surrounding color can have on an enclosed one had long been known, subtle effects of brightness contrast were described in the nineteenth century (see Wade, 2005b). For example, Ludimar Hermann (1838-1914) gave an account of the effects that can be seen in the grid on the left of Figure 20—dark dots appear at the intersection of the white lines. He related the illusory dots to the operation of simultaneous contrast. The converse, where light grey dots are seen at the intersections of the black lines was described later by Hering. The Hermann grid on the left contains the face of Hermann, and the Hering grid on the right contains Hering's portrait.

The Hermann and Hering grids have assumed a position of considerable importance in contemporary visual science, as they have provided a means by which receptive fields recorded physiologically can be related to "perceptive fields" determined psychophysically (see Lingelbach & Ehrenstein 2002; Spillmann 1994). The dimensions of concentric receptive fields are smallest in the retinal ganglion cells receiving their input from the central fovea, and they increase in size with increasing distance from the fovea. This is probably the reason why the Hermann-Hering dots are not visible at the fixated intersection: both the center and surround

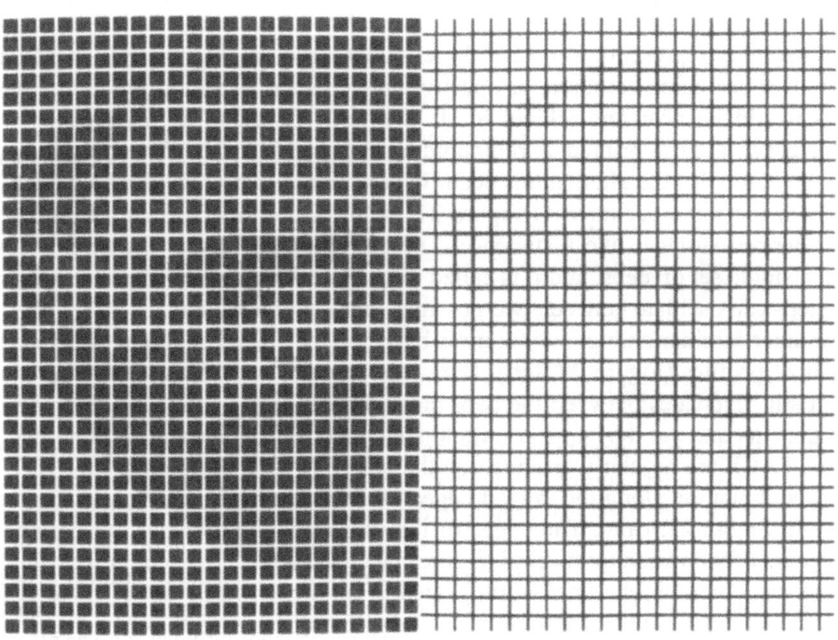

Figure 20. *Hermann-Hering grids*. The grid on the left contains the face of Ludimar Hermann, whereas the grid on the right contains the face of Hering. The faces will be seen more easily if the figure is viewed from several meters. (© Illustration by Nicholas Wade.)

would fall between the squares and within the intersections, so that there would be no differential response from them, and no illusory dots. If the separations are made sufficiently small then the dots can be seen at the fixated intersections. It is by this means that measuring the limiting dimensions of grids yielding the illusory dots has been used to estimate the sizes of "perceptive fields" at different eccentricities in human vision.

Yet another area rich in aesthetic potential is that involving perceptual ambiguities. Manipulations of perceptual ambiguity have a long history in both visual art and visual science (see Alais & Blake, 2005; Gombrich, 1960; Piccolino & Wade, 2007). One theme that has been played for centuries is the reversing figure. Ambiguity is inevitably involved in compressing three dimensions to two, which is the nature of pictorial images. Cameos and intaglios provided a source of reports of ambiguous depth (Wade, 1998a), and the anamorphoses mentioned previously systematically distorted pictorial depth. Ambiguity can be amplified in simple outline figures that fluctuate in allusory depth, like those shown literally in Figure 21. On the left, the letters spell the name of the man after whom the reversing pattern is named; Louis Albert Necker (1832) noticed that outline drawings of crystals appeared to fluctuate in depth. Despite the letters being clearly flat, their appearance flips between the impression of a cube with the left and lower face closer or the right and upper face closer. It is difficult to prevent the perceptual fluctuations occurring, even with the full knowledge that the pattern is flat. The picture is interpreted as representing a three-dimensional structure, but there is insufficient detail (for occluding contours, perspective convergence, or texture) to define which parts would be near and which far. It is often referred to as the Necker cube, but Necker (1832) printed a rhomboid rather than a cube. Wheatstone (1838) demonstrated that the alternations occur with a three-dimensional skeleton cube.

Much the same occurs with Figure 21, right, but in this case the impression is of a stepped surface, like a staircase. The conventional way of presenting this is with a single set of steps, and it is called the Schroeder staircase. The orientation of the steps can oscillate between two possible depth interpretations.

Another familiar ambiguous figure is based on the shared contours of a vase and a pair of profiles (Figure 22, left). Here it is produced by illusory contours alone, but it still fluctuates between the two: there is no continuous line dividing the two components and yet they appear quite distinct and sharply separated. Note that the words FACE are regularly arranged on the left-hand side, but not on the right. The good continuation along the ragged edges of the letters is shown with even greater force in Figure 22, right. The edges of the illusory white triangles are defined by the letters of the varied terms used to describe them—subjective, cognitive, illusory, and virtual contours; the final word, shared by all the terms, is shown in the center. Illusory contours can be produced in several different ways, as shown in Figure 23.

Pictures provide allusions to objects, and some of the tricks that can be played with the transition from three to two dimensions have been mentioned above. Indeed, this is grist to the artistic mill: pictures incorporate ambiguities and impossibilities that are rarely or never present in objects. Pictorial impossibilities of the type shown in Figure 24 have been dissected psychologically (Penrose & Penrose, 1958) and

Figure 21. Literal pictures of *Necker's cube* (left) and *Stairway to chevron* (right), with the Schroeder staircase. (© Illustrations by Nicholas Wade.)

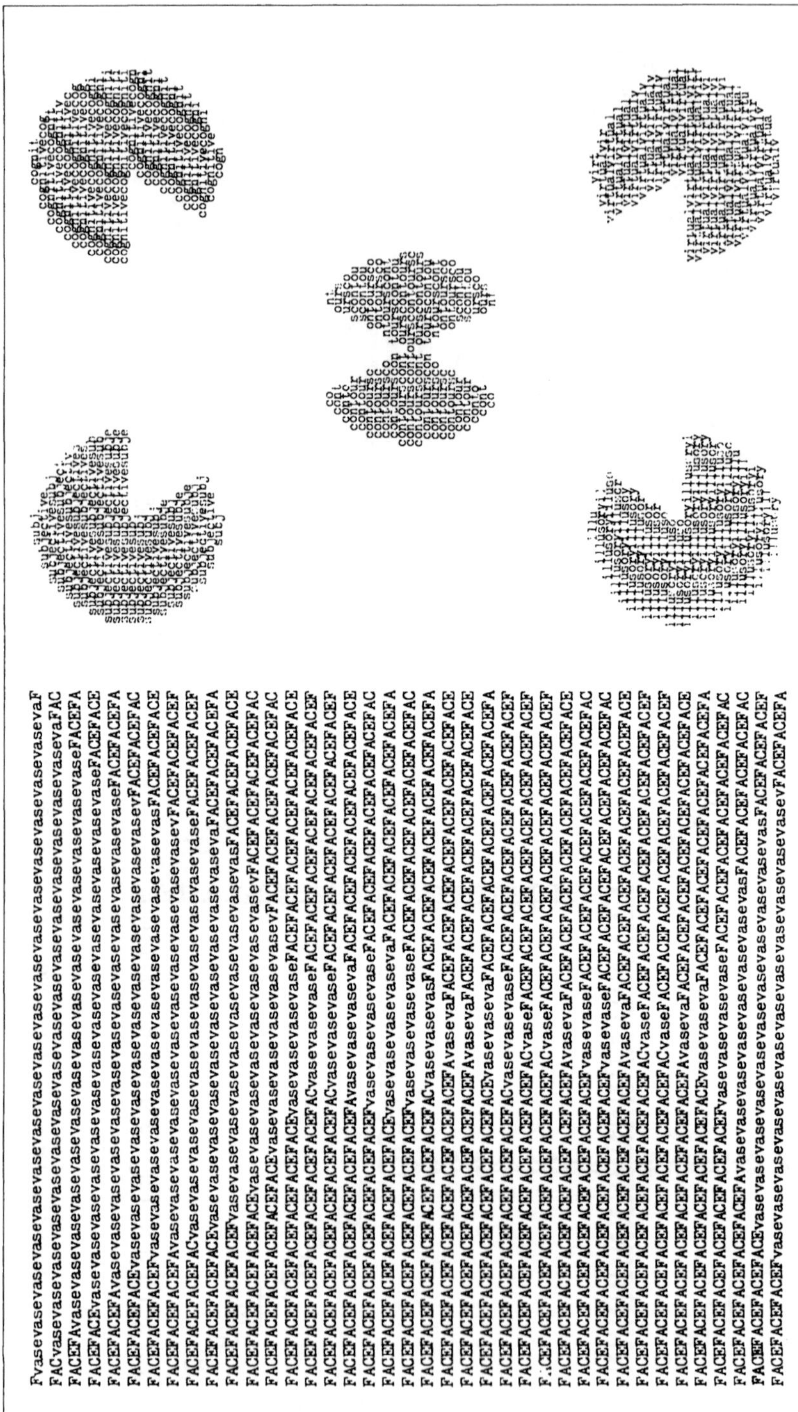

Figure 22. Left, *Facing faces*, the vase/face motif spelled out. Right, *One phenomenon or many?* giving the various names for the phenomenon of completing the sides of the "triangles." (© Illustrations by Nicholas Wade.)

Figure 23. Upper, *Fooling the I*, incomplete words describing the phenomenon. Lower, *Undulations*. (© Illustrations by Nicholas Wade.)

displayed graphically by Maurits C. Escher (Ernst, 1986). For example, a rectangular rod can be depicted by three lines and a quadrilateral, whereas a cylinder can be described by only two lines and an ellipse. The "impossible" triangle has four rectangular rods extending from each side which are transformed into six cylinders at the extremities of the lines. These two principles are combined in Figure 24.

Visual phenomena provide the bedrock for science and art. Both disciplines revel in the license allowed by pictorial manipulation. Natural vision is dynamic, binocular, and yields the perception of depth. Pictures are static and flat. Perceptual ambiguities, which feed on these features, involve alternating depth interpretations of flat drawings. Ambiguities reflect the failure of depth perception in the monocular domain. In both vision and aesthetics, pictorial patterns are paramount. In vision,

Figure 24. *Double impossibility*. (© Illustration by Nicholas Wade.)

they provide a ready means of stimulus manipulation, whereas in aesthetics they remove the troublesome dimensions of depth and motion that attend natural objects.

AESTHETICS

Ever since marks were made on surfaces by humans, they must have elicited preferences from those who viewed them (see Wade & Melcher, 2006). With more formalized representations in Greek art, the aesthetic appeal of pictures was a constant source of discussion. An experimental dimension was added to aesthetics by a major figure in the history of vision. Gustav Theodor Fechner (1801-1887; Figure 25) is best known as the founder of psychophysics—the relationship between the physical domain of the stimulus and the psychological dimensions of sensory experience (Fechner, 1860). Fechner's insight was that the mental and material worlds could be united mathematically in the domains of sensory and stimulus

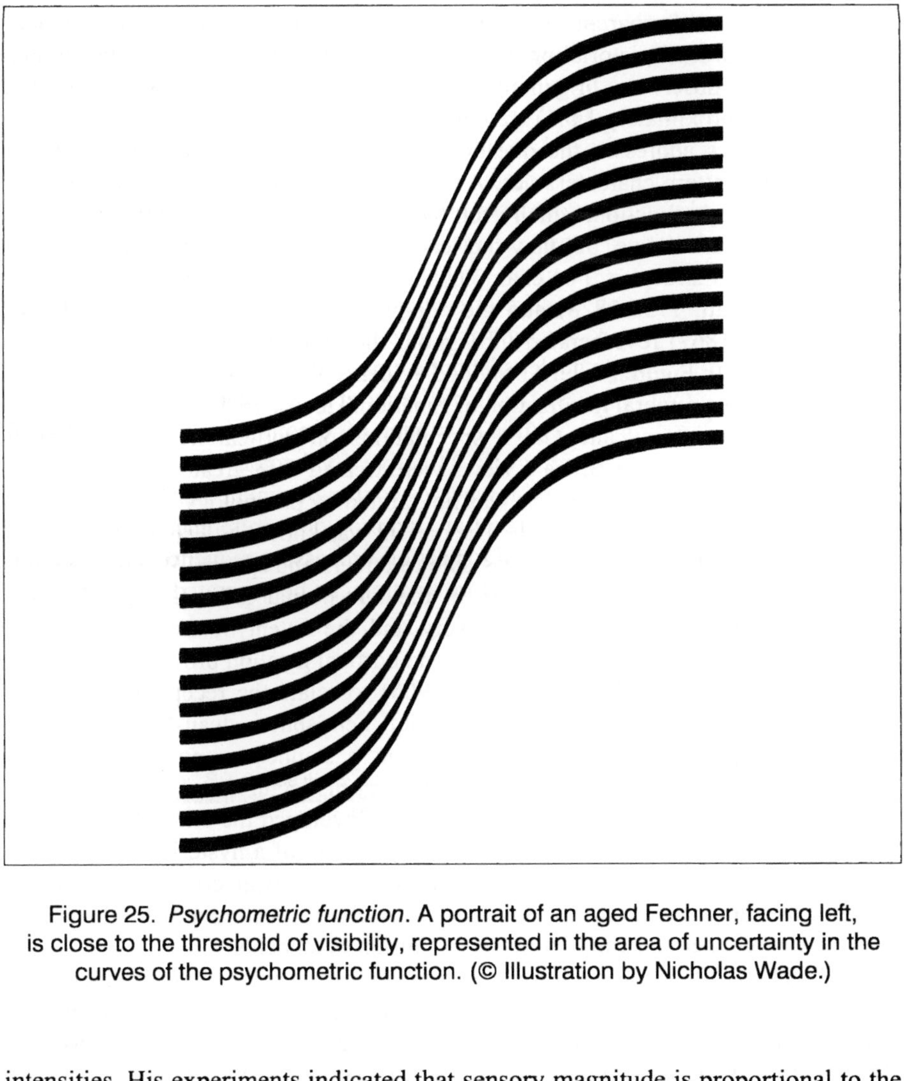

Figure 25. *Psychometric function*. A portrait of an aged Fechner, facing left, is close to the threshold of visibility, represented in the area of uncertainty in the curves of the psychometric function. (© Illustration by Nicholas Wade.)

intensities. His experiments indicated that sensory magnitude is proportional to the logarithm of stimulus magnitude—the lawful relationship that bears Fechner's name. The curves in Figure 25 in which he is just noticeable represent psychometric functions, and Fechner's portrait is to be found in the area of uncertainty. The logarithmic relationship between stimulus and sensation was challenged by Stanley Smith Stevens (1961), who proposed an alternative power law. The essential difference between the laws was the assumptions on which each was based: for Fechner, equal stimulus differences produced equal sensory differences, whereas for Stevens, equal stimulus ratios led to equal ratios of sensory magnitude (see Wade & Swanston (2001).

In his eighth decade, he applied his quantitative approach to the study of beauty and founded the subject of experimental aesthetics (Fechner, 1876). The topic he examined was the time-honored one of the golden ratio or section. The attraction of the golden ratio was apparent to Euclid, and it was often said to be incorporated in art. Fechner probed pictorial proportions in a novel way by eliciting preference judgments from observers. In general, rectangles with sides in the vicinity of the golden ratio (approximately 1.6:1) were preferred.

Neuroaesthetics addresses the question of how the various measures of brain activity reflect pattern characteristics. As such, it is intimately concerned with the localization of brain function, which itself has a fascinating history. Initial enquiries were distinctly speculative, but they did lead to an appreciation that specialization existed within its structure. For example, the debate between the localizers (like Franz Joseph Gall, 1758-1828) and the equipotentialists (like Marie Jean Pierre Flourens, 1794-1867) reverberated throughout the nineteenth century. Pierre Paul Broca (1824-1880; Figure 26, left) provided evidence from clinical examination and autopsy to support cerebral localization of function. He was initially influenced both by comparative anatomy and Gall's speculations on cortical localization. Such evidence was not new, but Broca's views were treated with greater seriousness by the scientific community because he was not tainted by phrenology. Broca treated a patient suffering from loss of speech. The patient was known as Tan, since this was the only utterance he made, but he was able to understand speech. When Tan died, his brain was found to have a cavity in the left frontal lobe. Despite disputes regarding the priority of Broca's discovery and the extent of the lesions in his patients, the link forged between language and cortical location proved very fruitful and led others like Carl Wernicke (1848-1905) to relate the receptive aspects of language to more posterior locations in the left hemisphere. Jean-Martin Charcot (1825-1893; Figure 26, right), with Broca, was a staunch supporter of cerebral localization, and he dealt with aphasia at length in his lectures and books. Charcot related clinical symptoms to brain autopsies and developed the clinical-anatomical method. His portrait is shown together with a drawing of a hysterical patient in a classical posture—*l'arc de cercle*. It is the same hysterical crisis that is represented in the famous painting by Brouillet of "A clinical lecture at the Salpêtrière" in which Charcot demonstrates hypnosis to a group of students.

The functions of the brain were investigated theoretically by Alexander Bain (1818-1903; Figure 27, left). He integrated sensory physiology with philosophy to espouse an independent discipline of psychology "conceiving that the time has now come when many of the striking discoveries of Physiologists relative to the nervous system should find a recognised place in the Science of Mind" (Bain, 1855, p. v). The perceptual portrait reflects the importance of Bain's *Mind*, which was initially edited by one of his former students; it also incorporates a model of a neural processing designed by Bain (1873) to give differential output with input of varied intensities. Bain proposed a connectionist account of learning 70 years before Hebb (see Wilkes & Wade, 1997).

Whereas Bain founded *Mind*, David Ferrier (1843-1928; Figure 27, right) was a founding editor of the journal *Brain* in 1878. Ferrier electrically stimulated the brains of many species and mapped areas of the cortex into sensory and motor regions. The long-held view that the brain was unaffected by direct stimulation had been overturned by Gustav Theodor Fritsch (1838-1927) and Eduard Hitzig

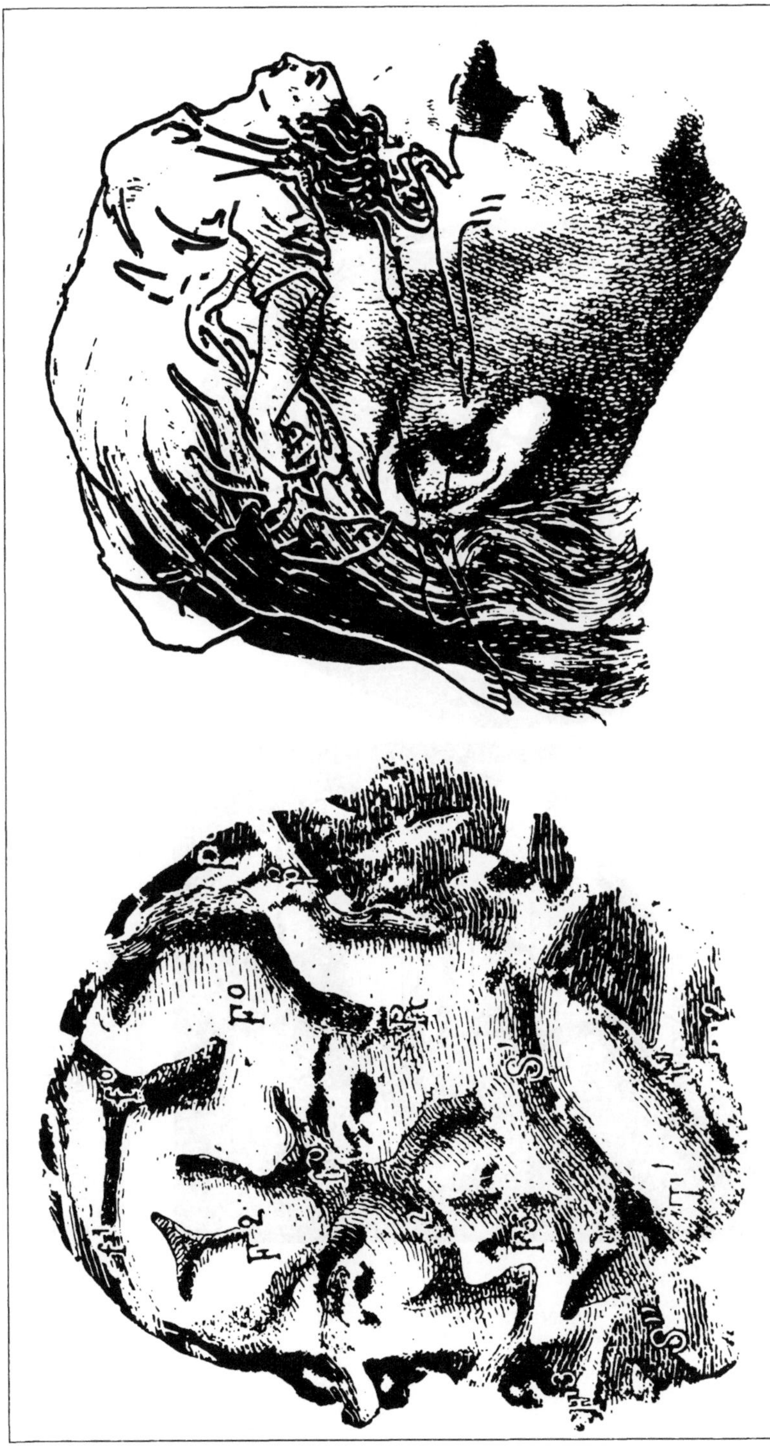

Figure 26. Left, *Broca's area* showing Broca in a diagram of Broca's area (taken from an illustration in Broca, 1888). Right, *L'arc de cercle*, a portrait of Charcot after the frontispiece engraving in Charcot (1892). Motif was derived from a drawing of a hysterical patient adopting *l'arc de cercle* in Charcot, & Richer (1887). (© Illustrations by Nicholas Wade.)

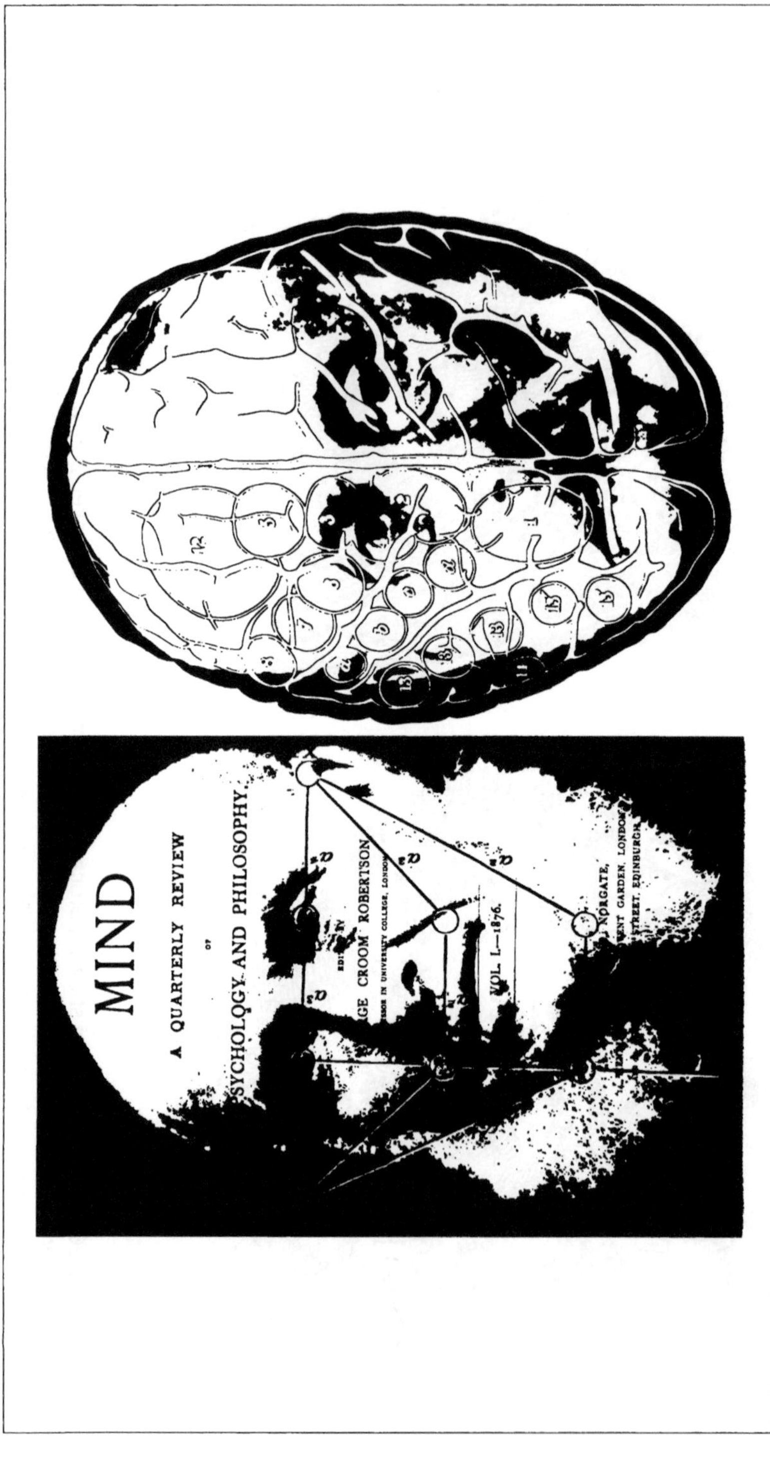

Figure 27. Left, *Mind reader;* Bain, together with the title page of the first issue of *Mind* and a diagram of a neural network model derived from Bain (1873). Right, *Brain stimulator;* Ferrier is enclosed in a diagram of the human brain (from Ferrier, 1876). (© Illustrations by Nicholas Wade.)

(1838-1907) in 1870. They electrically stimulated the exposed brains of unanaesthetized dogs and found specific precentral areas that resulted in muscular contractions: they divided the cortex into two parts: motor and not motor. The involvement of certain cortical regions in motor control had been proposed by John Hughlings Jackson (1835-1911) on the basis of his studies of epilepsy and these, too, were the stimulus for Ferrier's investigations. In 1873, Ferrier commenced a series of experiments on anaesthetized frogs, pigeons, guinea pigs, rabbits, cats, dogs, and monkeys in which he applied electrical stimulation to localized areas of the cortex; he also carried out ablations of the same areas. These studies demonstrated large species differences and pointed to the dangers of extrapolating broadly. Ferrier is represented in his illustration of the human brain that is marked with the motor map of monkey cortex: the numbers specify localized movements with the letters representing movement areas for the hand and wrist.

Ferrier did much to shift the center of gravity of nineteenth-century neuroscience toward the English language, and this movement was reinforced by Charles Scott Sherrington (1857-1952; Figure 28, left). Electrical stimulation of the brain represented a novel technique that could disclose functions of the brain. Many others were based on the emerging concept of the nerve cell as the building block of the nervous system. The neuron doctrine was firmly established by evidence about the synapse, the term introduced by Sherrington, who proposed a mode of chemical transmission across the synaptic junctions. Sherrington's early work was concerned with the kneejerk reflex and then the scratch reflex, and he found similar integrating principles in operation. In his *Integrative Action of the Nervous System* (1906), he mapped out what was known about reflex action and signed the way ahead.

The techniques available to Ferrier and Sherrington for studying brain activity in humans were very limited. Small cortical potentials had been recorded from the exposed brains of rabbits, cats, and monkeys as early as 1875 by Richard Caton (1842-1926), but no success had been achieved with recordings from humans. This was to change radically when Hans Berger (1873-1941; Figure 28, right) recorded electrical potentials on the surface of the human scalp and plotted the electroencephalogram. His life-long search was for an objective index of subjective experience. He initially measured variations in brain circulation and temperature in an attempt to capture the essence of psychic energy, but he abandoned that approach. After many vain attempts on his patients, Berger achieved success with recordings from his teenage son and from himself, as he was able to report in 1929. Berger is shown together with the first tracing of the alpha rhythm, published in his second report of 1930. The record has been graphically multiplied and is accompanied by those for the heart rate and time base.

The EEG was an early and important tool for diagnosing brain damage, but also provided a research tool for examining electrical responses to events (event-related potentials, or ERPs). Productive research using ERPs to map cognitive activity in the brain was conducted in the last decades of the twentieth century, but there have always been problems of interpretation due to limited information about the spatial origins of ERP components. Subsequent developments of dense-mapped ERP and the related technique of using a magnetometer to record the magnetoencephalogram

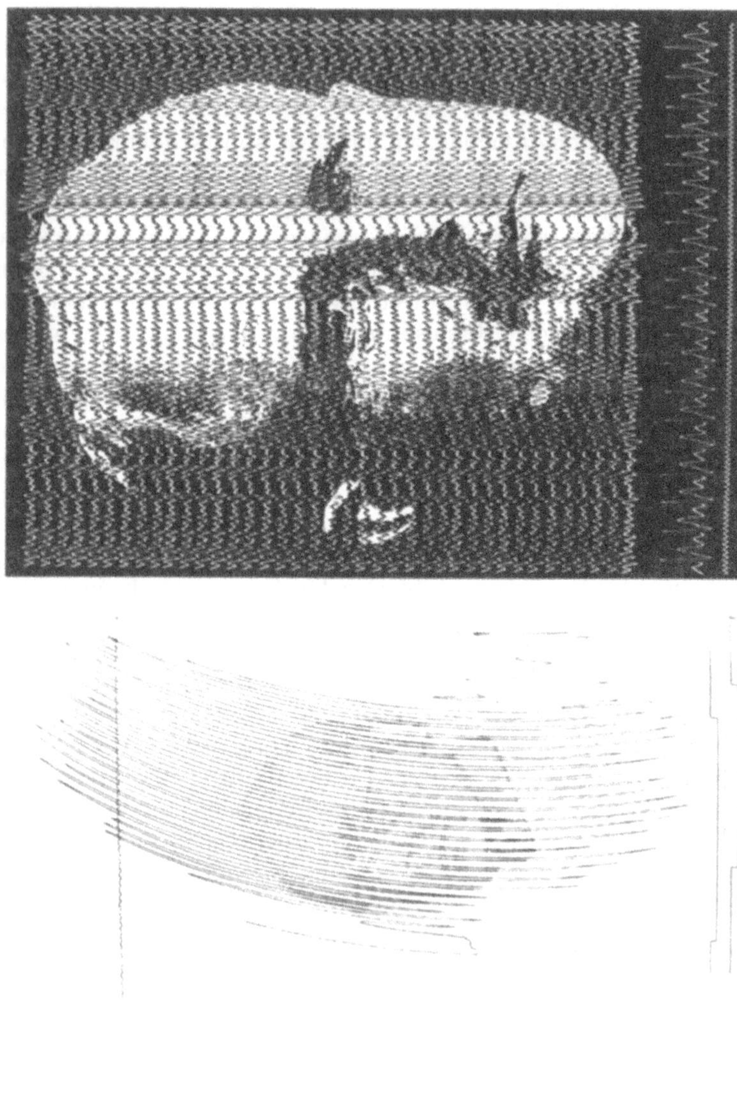

Figure 28. Left, *Scratch reflex*; Sherrington's portrait is enclosed within a tracing of the scratch reflex (from Sherrington, 1906). Right, *Alpha rhythm*; Berger's face is captured within his first published EEG pattern (derived from Berger, 1930). (© Illustrations by Nicholas Wade.)

(MEG) and detect magnetic event-related fields (ERFs) attracted much more attention. In part, this was because the precise temporal information gained by these techniques could complement the spatial precision achieved with newer techniques of brain imaging.

Another technique based on magnetic fields generated in the cortex is called transcranial magnetic stimulation (TMS). Following the lead of Silvanus Thompson (1910), alternating magnetic fields can be applied to restricted regions of the head in order to stimulate or to disrupt neural activity in some way. In TMS, a magnetic coil is positioned over a particular area of a subject's head and a current is briefly passed through the coil. The magnetic field so produced induces an electrical current in a specific part of the subject's brain (see Walsh & Cowey, 1998). The timing of such TMS is very precise, so it can be applied at known intervals after some visual stimulation has taken place. It is as if the technique produced virtual patients because the disruption is temporary.

The armory of techniques for probing the workings of the visual system has been extended so that the operation of the whole working brain can now be imaged. Initially, positron emission tomography (PET) scans were used to examine the regional cerebral blood flow when volunteers looked at different kinds of visual patterns. For example, a colored pattern produced activation in regions corresponding to V1, V2, and V4; when the same pattern was shown in shades of grey, the activation in V4 was much reduced, suggesting that V4 was an area for the analysis of color in humans. Similarly, a moving compared with a static pattern produced specific activation of "human V5"; illusory motion seen in static patterns has also been attributed to this area (see Zeki, 1999). Semir Zeki (Figure 29) is one of the pioneers of neuroaesthetics. He has argued that we are at the threshold "of learning something about the neurobiological basis of one of the most noble and profound of human endeavours" (Zeki, 1999, p.2).

There are sophisticated ways of examining human brain activity during perceptual processing, but all techniques have drawbacks, and experiments must be designed with great care if they are to be clearly interpretable. In comparison with PET scans, magnetic resonance imaging (MRI) yields more precise spatial resolution. Developments in functional MRI (fMRI) allow activity to be temporally as well as spatially mapped. It will be work using fMRI combined with developments in other technologies with more temporal precision such as TMS and MEG, which will likely hold the key to understanding the neural processing of visual information by people. These imaging techniques now form the cornerstone of neuroaesthetics.

CONCLUSIONS

The study of vision has been the study of images, although one particular type of image has taken precedence over others: the pictorial image. Art has been produced by humans for thousands of years, and it involves distilling aspects of perception and re-presenting them in ways that can be recognized by others. Perhaps it is this universality of the pictorial image that has proved so attractive to both observers and theorists of vision. When it was combined with the principles of image

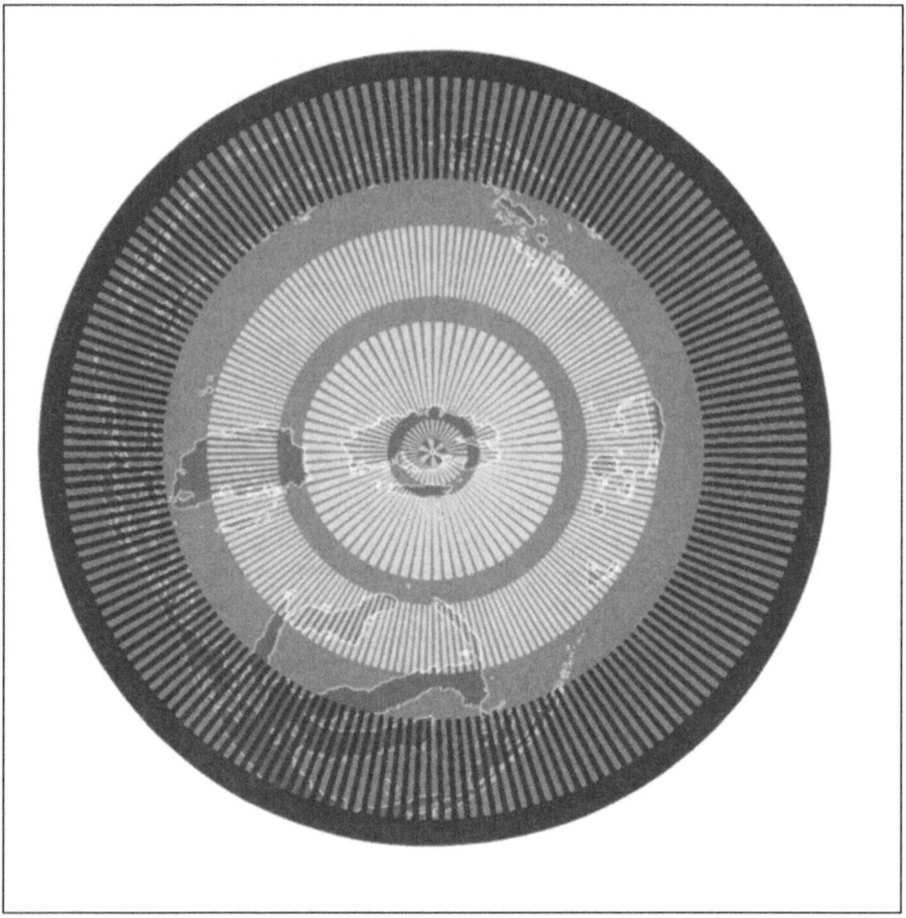

Figure 29. See p. 149 for full color.

formation in the eye, its appeal was overwhelming. The metaphor of the picture-in-the-eye drives contemporary visual science in much they same way it did students in the seventeenth century. I have referred to this as the "legacy of Kepler" (Wade, 2005a). We now know much more about the optics of the eye and the physiology of vision, but the conceptual problem posed remains essentially unchanged. This enchantment with pictorial images has been enhanced with the introduction of computer graphics. More complicated pictures can be produced, and can be manipulated in ways that were previously impossible.

Kepler formulated the problem that generations of students of vision have since attempted to resolve: how do we perceive the world as three-dimensional on the basis of a two-dimensional retinal image? Indeed, this legacy can be considered as having defined the problem in terms of single, static retinal images rather than considering the starting point as binocular and dynamic. The seductive allure of the pictorial image has amplified the belief that the first stage of vision is a two-dimensional image in the eye. The task of the theorist is then seen as restoring the third dimension. An impressive array of neurophysiological results can be brought to bear on this problem: single cells in the visual cortex are excited by particular stimulus features, and different visual modules process those features further. Most of the information is derived from the ideal assay for Kepler's legacy: an anaesthetized animal with a nonmoving eye. Neuroimaging techniques for studying human perception have generally supported these conclusions. Of course, the stimuli used in the constrained confines of the devices are pictorial. Much has been learned from the use of two-dimensional stimuli, but sight must not be lost of the goal of perceptual research—understanding our interactions with a world of solid structures.

Are pictures so central to understanding vision and aesthetics? What is the relationship between the perception of pictures and of the objects they portray? Will understanding pictures facilitate our interpretations of vision, or vice versa? And how do those peculiar pictures—geometrical optical illusions—relate to other forms of pictorial representation? It could well be argued, as Gibson (1966, 1979) has, that the study of perception will not be furthered by the examination of pictures.

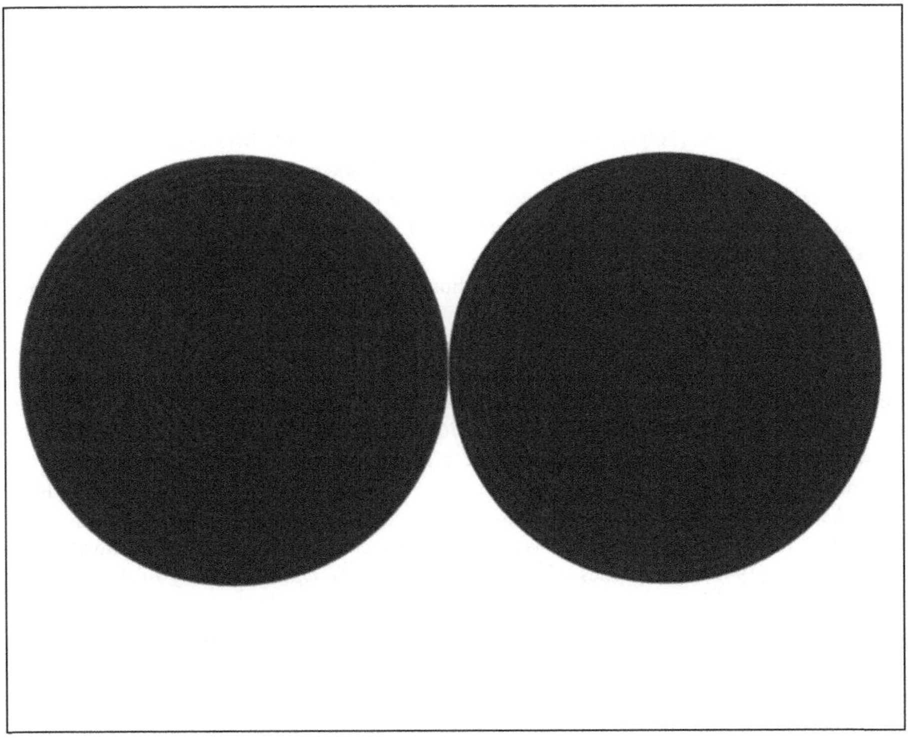

Figure 30. See p. 150 for full color.

When Purkinje remarked that "visual illusions reveal visual truths," he was not referring to geometrical optical illusions. To question the appropriateness of pictures as the stimuli for vision is more subversive than it might at first appear, because it is attacking the experimental basis of much of the discipline.

Rather than concluding on a negative note, a salute is made in Figure 30 to an artist who revelled in the delights of design. Victor Vasarely (1908-1997) employed a variety of simple visual phenomena in his works (see Holzhey, 2005; Vasarely, 1965; Wade, 1982, 1990, 2007c). Indeed, Vasarely provides a fitting finale to this allusory survey of vision: he manipulated pattern elements, like circles and squares, in a skilful manner so as to expose processes of perception that often pass by unnoticed. He even added to the range of visual phenomena that can be studied scientifically (see Tronscoso, Macknik, & Martinez-Conde, 2005). Moreover, he was keenly aware of the subtleties of sight and played upon the aesthetic dimension of designs with considerable skill. One of the manipulations common to many of his works was that of reversing the contrast relations of the elements in his designs—so, black shapes would be transformed into white ones in symmetrical parts of the pictures. In Figure 30, the contrast reversal involves colour and the perceptual transformation is rather like that of shifting from negative to positive in a photographic process. Perhaps it is time for visual scientists to pay a little more heed to the activities of their artistic colleagues.

REFERENCES

Alais, D., & Blake, R. (2005). *Binocular rivalry*. Cambridge, MA: MIT Press.

Bain, A. (1855). *The senses and the intellect*. London: Parker.

Bain, A. (1873). *Mind and body. The theories of their relation*. London: King.

Baltrušaitis, J. (1977). *Anamorphic art*. W. J. Strachan (Trans.). Cambridge, UK: Chadwyck-Healey.

Barlow, H. B. (1953). Summation and inhibition in the frog's retina, *Journal of Physiology* (Lond.) *119*, 69-88.

Behrens, R. R. (1993) *The man who made distorted rooms: A chronology of the life of Adelbert Ames Jr.* University of Northern Iowa: published by the author.

Berger, H. (1930). Über das Elektrenkephalogramm des Menschen. Zweite Mitteilung. *Journal für Psychologie und Neurologie, 40,* 160-179.

Brewster, D. (1825). On some remarkable affections of the retina, as exhibited in its insensibility to indirect impressions, and to the impressions of attenuated light. *Edinburgh Journal of Science, 3,* 288-293.

Broca, P. (1888). *Mémoires sur le cerveau de l'homme et des primates*. Paris: Reinwald.

Burton, H. E. (1945). The Optics of Euclid. *Journal of the Optical Society of America, 35,* 357-372.

Cajal S. R. y, (1893). La rétine des vertebras, *La Cellule, 9,* 119-257. (English edition 1972: *The structure of the retina*, S. A. Thorpe & M. Glickstein (Trans.), Springfield, IL: Charles C Thomas.)

Campbell, F. W., & J. G. Robson. (1968). Application of Fourier analysis to the visibility of gratings. *Journal of Physiology, 197,* 551-566.

Caton, R. (1875). The electric currents of the brain. *British Medical Journal, 2,* 278.

Charcot, J.-M. (1892). *Oeuvres complètes de J. M. Charcot. Lecons sur les maladies du système nerveux*. Paris: Baittaille.

Charcot, J.-M., & P. Richer. (1887). *Les démoniaques dans l'art*. Paris: Delahaye and Lecrosnier.

Cohen, M. R., & Drabkin, I. E. (1958). *A source book in Greek science*. Cambridge, MA: Harvard University Press.

Craik, K. J. W. (1943). *The nature of explanation*. Cambridge, MA: Cambridge University Press.

Craik, K. J. W. (1966). *The nature of psychology. A selection of papers, essays and other writings by the late Kenneth J. W. Craik*. S. L. Sherwood (Ed.). Cambridge, MA: Cambridge University Press.

Crombie, A. C. (1964). Kepler: De Modo Visionis. In *Mélange Alexandre Koyré I. L'Aventure de la Science* (pp. 135-172). Paris: Hermann.

Daxecker, F. (2004). *The physicist and astronomer Christopher Scheiner. Biography, letters, works*. Innsbruck: Leopold-Franzens-University of Innsbruck.

Descartes, R. (1637/1902). *La Dioptrique*. In *Oeuvres de Descartes* (Vol. 6, pp. 81-228). C. Adam & P. Tannery (Eds.). Paris: Cerf.

Descartes, R. (1664/1909). *Traité de l'Homme*. In *Oeuvres de Descartes* (Vol. 11, pp. 119-215). C. Adam & P. Tannery (Eds.). Paris: Cerf.

Descartes, R. (1965). *Discourse on method, optics, geometry, and meteorology*. P. J. Olscamp (Trans.). Indianapolis: Bobbs-Merrill.

Ernst, B. (1976). *Het begoochelde oog. Onmogelijkeen meerzinnige figuren*. Utrecht: Meulenhoff/Landshoff.

Fechner, G. T. (1860). *Elemente der Psychophysik*. Leipzig: Breitkopf and Härtel.

Fechner, G. T. (1876). *Vorschule der Aesthetik*. Leipzig: Breitkopf and Härtel.

Ferrier, D. (1876). *The functions of the brain*. London: Smith, Elder.

Findlay, J. M., & Gilchrist, I. D. (2003). *Active vision: The psychology of looking and seeing*. Oxford: Oxford University Press.

Gibson, J. J. (1966). *The senses considered as perceptual systems*. Boston: Houghton Mifflin.

Gibson, J. J. (1979). *The ecological approach to visual perception*. Boston: Houghton Mifflin.

Golgi, C. (1873). Sulla struttura della sostanza grigia del cervello. *Gazzetta Medica Italiana (Lombardia), 6,* 244-246

Goodale, M. A., & Milner, A. D. (2003). *Sight unseen. An exploration of conscious and unconscious vision*. Oxford: Oxford University Press.

Gombrich, E. H. (1960). *Art and illusion. A study in the psychology of pictorial representation*. London: Phaidon.

Grimaldi, F. M. (1665). *Physico-mathemis de lumine coloribis et iride*. Bologna.

Hartline, H. K. (1928). A quantitative and descriptive study of the electric response to illumination of the arthropod eye. *American Journal of Physiology, 83,* 466-483.

Hebb, D. O. (1949). *The organization of behavior*. New York: Wiley.

Helmholtz, H. (1867). *Handbuch der physiologischen Optik*. In G. Karsten (Ed.). *Allgemeine Encyklopädie der Physik* (Vol. 9). Leipzig: Voss.

Helmholtz, H. (1873). *Popular lectures on scientific subjects. First series*. E. Atkinson (Trans.). London: Longmans, Green.

Helmholtz, H. (1925). *Helmholtz's treatise on physiological optics* (Vol. 3). J. P. C. Southall (Trans.). New York: Optical Society of America.

Helmholtz, H. (2000). *Helmholtz's treatise on physiological optics* (3 Vols.). J. P. C. Southall (Trans.). Bristol: Thoemmes.

Hering, E. (1931). *Wissenschaftliche Abhandlungen* (Vol. 1). Leipzig: Thieme.

Holzhey, M. (2005). *Victor Vasarely (1906-1997); Pure vision*. Taschen: Köln.

Hubel, D. H., & Wiesel, T. N. (1962). Receptive fields, binocular interaction and functional architecture in the cat's visual cortex. *Journal of Physiology, 166,* 106-154.

Hubel, D. H., & Wiesel, T. N. (1968). Receptive fields and functional architecture of the monkey visual cortex. *Journal of Physiology, 195,* 215-243.

Huygens, C. (1690). *Traité de la lumiere*. Leiden: Vander Aa.

Ittelson, W. H. (1952). *The Ames demonstrations in perception*. Princeton: Princeton University Press.

Kemp, M. (1990). *The science of art. Optical themes in Western art from Brunelleschi to Seurat*. New Haven, CT: Yale University Press.

Kepler, J. (1604). *Ad Vitellionem paralipomena*. Frankfurt: Marinium and Aubrii.

Kubovy, M. (1986). *The psychology of perspective and Renaissance art*. Cambridge, MA: Cambridge University Press.

Kuffler, S. W. (1953). Discharge patterns and functional organization of mammalian retina. *Journal of Neurophysiology, 16,* 37-68.

Lingelbach, B., & Ehrenstein, W. H. (2002). Das Hermann-Gitter und die Folgen. *Deutsche Optikerzeitung, 5,* 14-20.

Mach, E. (1886). *Beiträge zur Analyse der Empfindungen*. Jena: Fischer.

Mariotte, E. (1668). A new discovery touching vision. *Philosophical Transactions of the Royal Society 3,* 668-669.

McCulloch, W. S., & Pitts, W. H. (1943). A logical calculus of the ideas immanent in nervous activity. *Bulletin of Mathematical Biophysics, 5,* 115-133.

Marr, D. (1982). *Vision. A computational investigation into the human representation and processing of visual information*. New York: Freeman.

Millican, P. J. R., & Clark, A. (Eds.). (1996). *Machines and thought. The legacy of Alan Turing* (Vol. 1). Oxford: Clarendon Press.

Milner, A. D., & Goodale, M. A. (1995). *The visual brain in action*. Oxford: Oxford University Press.

Necker, L. A. (1832). Observations on some remarkable phenomena seen in Switzerland; and an optical phenomenon which occurs on viewing a figure of a crystal or geometrical solid. *London and Edinburgh Philosophical Magazine and Journal of Science, 1,* 329-337.

Newton, I. (1704). *Opticks: Or, a treatise of the reflections, refractions, inflections and colours of light*. London: Smith and Walford.

Niceron, J.-F. (1646). *Thaumaturgus Opticus*. Paris.

Oppel, J. J. (1856). Neue Beobachtungen und Versuche über eine eigentümliche, noch wenig bekannte Reaktionsthätigkeit des menschlichen Auges. *Annalen der Physik und Chemie, 99,* 540-561.

Park, D. (1997). *The fire within the eye. A historical essay on the nature and meaning of light*. Princeton: Princeton University Press.

Penrose, L. S., & Penrose, R. (1958). Impossible objects: A special type of illusion. *British Journal of Psychology, 49,* 31-33.

Piccolino, M., & Wade, N. J. (2007). *Insegne ambiguë. Percorsi obliqui tra storia, scienza e arte, da Galileo a Magritte.* Pisa: Edizioni ETS.

Purkinje, J. (1823). *Beobachtungen und Versuche zur Physiologie der Sinne. Beiträge zur Kenntniss des Sehens in subjectiver Hinsicht*. Prague: Calve.

Purkinje, J. (1825). *Beobachtungen und Versuche zur Physiologie der Sinne. Neue Beiträge zur Kenntniss des Sehens in subjectiver Hinsicht*. Berlin: Reimer.

Ratliff, F. (1965). *Mach bands: Quantitative studies on neural networks in the retina*. San Francisco: Holden-Day.

Scheiner, C. (1619). *Oculus, hoc est fundamentum opticum*. Innsbruck: Agricola.

Scheiner, C. (1630). *Rosa Ursina*. Bracciani: Phaeum.

Sherrington, C. S. (1906). *The integrative action of the nervous system.* New York: Scribner.

Smith, A. M. (2004). What is the history of medieval optics really about? *Proceedings of the American Philosophical Society, 148,* 180-194.

Spillmann, L. (1994). The Hermann grid illusion: A tool for studying human perceptive field organization. *Perception, 23,* 691-708.

Stevens, S. S. (1961). To honor Fechner and repeal his law. *Science, 133,* 80-86.

Tartuferi, F. (1887). Sulla anatomia della retina. *Archivio per le Scienze Mediche, 11,* 335-358.

Thompson. S. P. (1910). A physiological effect of alternating magnetic field. *Proceedings of the Royal Society of London. Series B, 82,* 396-398.

Tronscoso, X. G., Macknik, S. L., & Martinez-Conde, S. (2005). Novel illusions related to Vasarely's 'nested squares' show that corner salience varies with corner angle. *Perception, 34,* 409-420.

Turner, R. S. (1994). *In the eye's mind. Vision and the Helmholtz-Hering controversy.* Princeton: Princeton University Press.

Ungeleider, L. G., & Mishkin, M. (1982). Two cortical visual systems. In D. J. Ingle, M. A. Goodale, & R. J. W. Mansfield (Eds.), *Analysis of visual behaviour* (pp. 549-586). Cambridge, MA: MIT Press.

Vasarely, V. (1965). *Vasarely*. Neuchatel: Editions Griffon.

von Soemmerring, S. T. (1801). *Abbildungen des menschlichen Auges*. Frankfurt: Varrentrapp and Wenner.

Wade, N. (1982). *The art and science of visual illusions*. London: Routledge and Kegan Paul.

Wade, N. J. (Ed.). (1983). *Brewster and Wheatstone on vision*. London: Academic Press.

Wade, N. (1990). *Visual allusions: Pictures of perception*. Hove, UK: Lawrence Erlbaum Associates.

Wade, N. (1995). *Psychologists in word and image*. Cambridge, MA: MIT Press.

Wade, N. J. (1998a). *A natural history of vision*. Cambridge, MA: MIT Press.

Wade, N. J. (1998b). Light and sight since antiquity. *Perception, 27,* 637-670.

Wade, N. J. (2005a). *Perception and illusion: Historical perspectives*. New York: Springer.

Wade, N. J. (2005b). Sound and sight: Acoustic figures and visual phenomena. *Perception, 34,* 1275-1290.

Wade, N. J. (2007a). Image, eye and retina. *Journal of the Optical Society of America A, 24,* 1229-1249.

Wade, N. J. (2007b). Artful visions. *Spatial Vision, 21,* 27-53.

Wade, N. J. (2007c). *Circles. Science, sense and symbol.* Dundee: Dundee University Press.

Wade, N. J., & Brožek, J. (2001). *Purkinje's vision. The dawning of neuroscience.* Mahawa, NJ: Erlbaum.

Wade, N. J., Brožek, J., & Hoskovec, J. (2002). Images of Purkinje's vision. *History & Philosophy of Psychology, 4,* 1-9.

Wade, N. J., & Bruce, V. (2001). Surveying the seen. 100 years of British vision. *British Journal of Psychology, 92,* 79-112.

Wade, N. J., & Heller, D. (1997). Scopes of perception: The experimental manipulation of space and time. *Psychological Research, 60,* 227-237.

Wade, N. J., & Melcher, D. (2006). Cave art interpretation. I. *Perception, 35,* 577-580.

Wade, N. J., & Piccolino, M. (2006). Nobel stains. *Perception, 35,* 1-8.

Wade, N. J., & Swanston, M. T. (2001). *Visual perception: An introduction* (2nd ed.). Hove, UK: Psychology Press.

Wade, N. J., & Tatler, B. W. (2005). *The moving tablet of the eye: The origins of modern eye movement research*. Oxford: Oxford University Press.

Walsh, V., & Cowey, A. (1998). Magnetic stimulation studies of visual cognition. *Trends in Cognitive Sciences, 2,* 103-110.

Wheatstone, C. (1830). Contributions to the physiology of vision. No I. *Journal of the Royal Institution of Great Britain, 1,* 101-117. (Published over the initials C. W.).

Wheatstone, C. (1838). Contributions to the physiology of vision—Part the first. On some remarkable, and hitherto unobserved, phenomena of binocular vision. *Philosophical Transactions of the Royal Society, 128,* 371-394.

Wilkes, A. L., & Wade, N. J. (1997). Bain on neural networks. *Brain and Cognition, 33,* 295-305.

Wundt, W. (1898). Die geometrisch-optischen Täuschungen. *Abhandlungen der mathematisch-physischen Classe der Königlichen Sächsischen Gesellschaft der Wissenschaften, 42,* 55-178.

Young, T. (1802). On the theory of lights and colours. *Philosophical Transactions of the Royal Society, 92,* 12-48.

Zeki, S. (1999). *Inner vision. An exploration of art and the brain*. Oxford: Oxford University Press.

CHAPTER 10

Musical Sounds in the Human Brain

Mari Tervaniemi

In Western society, music surrounds us in a number of different forms. It is respected as a professional accomplishment and as a deliberate hobby. Moreover, it is present in our daily life via radio, TV, and recordings in multiple forms without us being necessarily consciously aware of its presence or its content. Yet, it affects our mood and can even alter our pragmatic actions such as choices in the supermarket (North, Hargreaves, & McKendrick, 1997).

Due to its complexity as an acoustic, cognitive, and cultural phenomenon, music and its neural processing offer a great challenge for modern cognitive neuroscience. In this chapter, two traditional empirical approaches to neural music encoding are described, the first dealing with sound novelty and the second with the relationship between music and speech processing. In addition, recent endeavors in revealing the neural basis of musical emotions are introduced.

DETECTION OF SOUND NOVELTY

In general, sensitivity in detecting novel events and modifying behavior according to the demands set by these events is essential to the survival of any human or nonhuman being. In music, the existence of novel, unexpected sound events is in a key position to keep the listener alert and, if present in an appropriate degree, also important in creating positive emotions (Meyer, 1956). Due to their relevance, these viewpoints strongly influenced the first investigations in the cognitive neuroscience of music. These early studies mainly relied on electric brain potentials (event-related potentials, ERPs), which allow one to track on a millisecond basis the information flow in the human brain, from the brain stem to the cortical levels.

Besson, Faïta, & Requin (1994) and Besson and Faïta (1996) used the P600 component of the ERPs to probe the higher-level expectancies created while listening to a melody. Previously, P600 was used as an index of the degree of unexpectancy encountered in linguistic context (Hahne & Friederici, 1999). Besson and colleagues found that unexpected ending notes of auditorily presented melodies, were they either in melody, harmony, or rhythm, evoked the P600. Moreover, the P600 was stronger when the unexpectancy occurred in a familiar rather than unfamiliar melody. Also, the P600 was stronger and earlier in musicians than in nonmusicians when the unexpectancy occurred in a melodic or harmonic domain. However, the P600 evoked by a delayed (rhythm violated) ending tone did not differ between musicians and nonmusicians. These data thus suggest that obvious rhythm violations are usually equally processed by musicians and nonmusicians while melodic and harmonic violations are more readily processed by musicians.

In several studies, the neural determinants of the subjective expectancies created by chord cadencies were also probed. The unexpected chords, presented within otherwise traditional cadences, were either dissonant or in a wrong mode (Janata, 1995), nearby- or distant-key chords instead of the same-key chords (Patel, Gibson, Ratner, Besson, & Holcomb, 1998), or Neapolitan chords (Koelsch, Gunter, Friederici, & Schröger, 2000; Koelsch, Schröger, & Gunter, 2002; Maess, Koelsch, Gunter, & Friederici, 2001; for a review, see Koelsch & Siebel, 2006). Depending on the stimulation and the task given to the subject, different brain indices were found. The earliest responses, only after 200 ms from the chord onset, followed the presentation of Neapolitan chords (Koelsch et al., 2000, 2002; Maess et al., 2001). According to Western music theory, these chords are incongruous when placed in such a musical cadence. In these studies, the subjects were not informed about the existence of the Neapolitan chords; instead, they were instructed to detect timbre-violated tones within the stimulation. While subjects were asked to detect the "wrong" chords, dissonant or wrong-mode chords evoked strong responses at about 300 ms (Janata, 1995) and wrong-key chords at about 600 ms after the chord onset (Patel et al., 1998). In all studies, the degree of unexpectancy was reflected in the subjects' neural responses, so that the chords most strongly violating the subjects' expectancies evoked earliest and largest responses. Based on these findings, it has been proposed that the human brain is tracking the musical syntax, resembling the syntax of the language (Koelsch & Siebel, 2006).

It has also been investigated whether the human brain, and more specifically, the auditory cortex, encodes musically relevant sounds or sound features while the subjects perform a task outside the auditory modality (e.g., the participants in the experiments are reading a book or watching a movie; see Näätänen, 1992; Tervaniemi & Huotilainen, 2003). These studies illuminate the ability of the human brain to monitor and execute several activities in parallel. Here, the presence of a mismatch negativity (MMN) brain component is taken as evidence of the presence of a short-term memory trace in the auditory cortex for the sounds. The MMN is expected to be generated when a repetitively presented sound (e.g., piano sound of 440 Hz) is suddenly replaced by a different sound, be it lower, higher, louder, or performed by a different timbre, and so on.

As for musically relevant sounds, it was found that the MMN is evoked by sounds deviating from the majority of the tones in their timbre (Caclin et al., 2006; Toiviainen, Tervaniemi, Louhivuori, Huotilainen, Saher, & Näätänen, 1998). Also, the MMN elicited by harmonically rich sounds is stronger than the MMN elicited by pure sinusoidal tones (Novitski, Tervaniemi, Huotilainen, & Näätänen, 2004;

Tervaniemi, Alho, Paavilainen, Sams, & Näätänen, 1993). This suggests a hardwired facilitation to process spectrally complex, natural sound signals above artificially pure "laboratory-made" sounds. Finally, since the MMN parameters closely correlated with the subjects' behavioral accuracy in timbre discrimination (Toiviainen et al., 1998) and pitch discrimination (Novitski et al., 2004), preattentively formed memory traces seem to provide the basis for subsequent conscious discrimination of the music sounds.

Increasingly, not only single sounds but also combinations of sounds flowing in time have been used as stimulation in MMN studies to determine the extent of complex musical material that we can preattentively encode. For instance, direction of the pitch change within a tone pair (Saarinen, Paavilainen, Schröger, Tervaniemi, Näätänen, 1992), continuous pitch change such as a Shepard-tone sequence (Tervaniemi, Maury, & Näätänen, 1994) as well as the contour of transposed melody-like sound patterns (Tervaniemi, Rytkönen, Schröger, Ilmoniemi, & Näätänen, 2001) are automatically encoded by the auditory cortex. Recently, also a relatively large set of unfamiliar melodies has been used as experimental stimulation (Brattico, Tervaniemi, Näätänen, & Peretz, 2006). Some of the melodies contained wrong notes, the notes being either out of tune or out of key. The subjects, who lacked formal training in music, displayed brain responses closely resembling the MMN to the wrong notes of both types. Thus, these findings indicate that the human auditory cortex encodes relatively invariant, abstract sound information without the subjects' attentive listening (see also Näätänen, Tervaniemi, Sussman, Paavilainen, & Winkler, 2001). Consequently, with regard to music, the invariances in melodic, harmonic, and rhythmic aspects seem to be encoded to a large extent without the listener being actively aware of these.

SPEECH vs. MUSIC PERCEPTION

Behavioral testing of neurological patients with brain damage in the cortical areas underlying auditory functions (for reviews, see Dalla Bella & Peretz, 1999; Samson 1999) led to a model differentiating the roles of the left and right hemispheres in audition. According to this model, the left auditory cortex has a dominating role in speech perception, while the right auditory cortex is more important in music perception. These views received support from several studies utilizing brain research techniques. Some of these will be briefly introduced in the following section.

The first evidence was obtained by Mazziotta, Phelps, Carson, and Kuhl (1982). They presented the subjects with monaural and binaural verbal (detective story) and nonverbal (single musical sounds, sound pairs, and chord pairs) stimulation during positron-emission tomography (PET) scanning. It was found that while verbal stimulation activated more widespread areas in the left than in the right hemisphere, the opposite was true for nonverbal stimulation. In addition, the pattern of activity observed during tone-pair stimulation reflected the subjects' listening strategy: The subjects, who reported to have listened to the sounds analytically or by using visual imagery, obtained more pronounced activity in the left hemisphere. By contrast, in subjects who listened to the sounds without any specific strategies, stronger activity in the right hemisphere was observed. Although the experimental paradigm and also the size of the subject pool leave some doors open for criticism, the work by Mazziotta and his colleagues can still be regarded as pioneering in the field since it was the first brain-mapping study to employ musical stimulation and concepts.

More recently, the complementary roles of the left vs. right hemispheres in processing speech vs. music sounds have received further support. In a within-subject design, Zatorre, Evans, Meyer, and Gjedde (1992) showed that while keeping the stimulation constant, the pattern of brain activity could also vary as a function of the task given to the subjects. In their study, the subjects were asked in separate blocks to either categorize the phonemes or to discriminate between the pitch contents of two subsequent sounds. The results displayed a left-sided activation during phoneme categorization, whereas a right-sided pattern of activity was found during the pitch-discrimination task. However, the right-hemispheric activity was located in the frontal areas, denoting the importance of working-memory systems guided by the frontal lobe in the musical pitch-comparison task rather than the modulation of the temporal-lobe (auditory-cortex) activity.

In PET recordings, Hugdahl, Brönnick, Kyllingsbaek, Law, Gade, and Paulson (1999) used a dichotic-listening paradigm in which subjects were presented with speech and musical sounds in a similar sequence with an instruction to detect a predefined target. The data indicated a left-hemispheric dominance for speech sounds and a tendency toward a right-hemispheric dominance for musical sounds. The behavioral data on dichotic-listening response accuracy indicated a significant left-hemispheric dominance for speech sounds and right-hemispheric dominance for musical sounds. These data thus suggest that during a sound-detection task, left- and right-hemispheric areas adopt a different role in processing speech vs. music sounds.

In magnetoencephalographic (MEG) and PET recordings using a MMN paradigm in which the subjects are concentrating on a task unrelated to the sounds (see above), it was shown, first of all, that chord discrimination (A major vs. A minor) evoked a stronger right- than left-hemispheric activity (Tervaniemi, Kujala, Alho, Virtanen, Ilmoniemi, & Näätänen, 1999; Tervaniemi et al., 2000). However, the hemispheric asymmetry for vowel discrimination was less replicable and subject to manipulation, at least in the vowel duration. Yet, these data indicate that the seat of MMN generation differs within each hemisphere for vowel vs. chord changes (Tervaniemi et al., 1999). The chord-MMN loci were located more superior than vowel-MMN loci. This suggests that in addition to a tonotopical arrangement of the cortical neurons as a function of pitch (Pantev, Hoke, Lütkenhöner, & Lehnertz, 1989a; Tiitinen, Alho, Huotilainen, Ilmoniemi, Simola, & Näätänen, 1993), duration (He, Hashikawa, Ojima, & Kinouchi, 1997) and intensity (Heil, Rajan, & Irvine, 1994; Pantev, Hoke, Lehnertz, & Lütkenhöner, 1989b), there are spatially distinct areas within both hemispheres representing sounds of different informational content (speech, music). Moreover, it seems plausible that subjects' conscious attention toward the sounds is not necessary for activating these neural representations.

Recently, functional magnetic resonance imaging (fMRI) was used to further test the hypothesis that different brain areas are involved in time and frequency encoding in music and speech sounds (Tervaniemi et al., 2006). Like PET, fMRI can be used to monitor metabolic changes in the brain related to neuronal activation. The data obtained by Tervaniemi and colleagues (2006) indicated that speech and music sound patterns activate separate brain areas in the temporal and frontal lobes (Figure 1). Parameter-specific activations were observed in the auditory areas so that duration modifications in speech sounds were predominantly encoded in the left hemisphere and in music sounds in the right hemisphere. Frequency modifications in music sounds were predominantly encoded in the right auditory cortex, while in speech sounds, they activated the auditory areas bilaterally. Additionally, duration and frequency modifications in speech sounds activated thalamic structures. Thus, not only areas in the auditory cortex (as in Tervaniemi et al., 1999, 2000) but also in the frontal cortex and subcortical (thalamic) structures can be selectively activated by speech or music sounds.

A different approach to investigate the existence of separate neural representations for speech vs. music processing was adopted by Besson, Faïta, Peretz, Bonnel, and Requin (1998). Instead of anatomically localizing the speech- and music-related processes in the brain, they employed functional ERP indices N400 and P600. These components reflect the degree of unexpectancy encountered in language-semantic (N400) and music-syntactic (P600) information (Besson et al., 1998; Kutas & Hillyard, 1980). Besson and colleagues provided professional opera-singer subjects with opera excerpts with either a congruent or incongruent ending note. If the last note was incongruent, the incongruence occurred either in the lyrics, in the tune, or simultaneously in both. According to Besson and colleague's hypothesis, if lyrics and melody had separate neural representations, then both N400 and P600 should emerge when the last note violated the subjective expectancies in both domains.

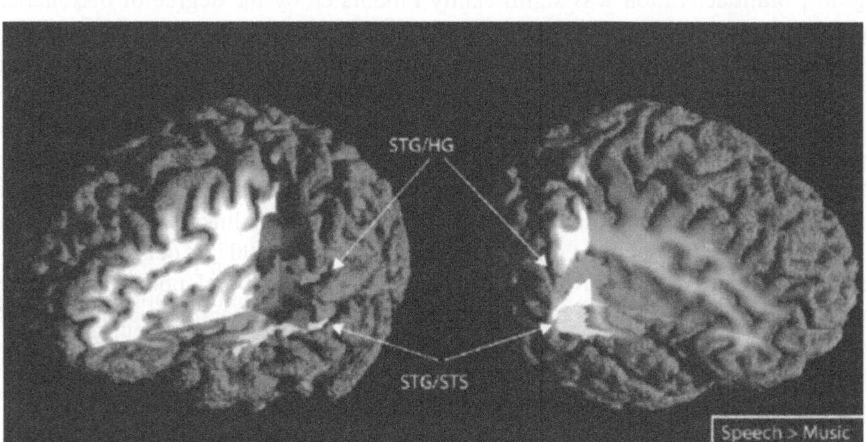

Figure 1. See p. 151 for full color.

Indeed, this was the pattern of the data obtained (see Figure 2). In fact, the ERP data recorded in the "both incongruent" condition was a close match to that summed from "lyrics" and "tune" incongruencies. These data thus strongly support the existence of the speech- vs. music-specialized neuronal networks even at the high-level (cognitive) processing.

To summarize, the existing empirical evidence supports the specialization of the right and left auditory cortices to differentially process music vs. speech material. However, according to the most recent views, this specialization is not caused by informational content of the auditory information per se, but rather by the existence and importance of rapid temporal changes, especially in speech sounds (Zatorre, 2001). Anatomical and physiological constraints (Zatorre, 2001; Zatorre, Belin, & Penhune, 2002) are in favor of these views, but these findings need further confirmation.

MUSIC AND EMOTIONS

During the past decade, pioneering studies on the neuronal correlates of music-induced emotions have started to appear. In these studies, PET and fMRI methods allowing reliable sources that also allow localization in subcortical brain regions have been employed. From previous studies on emotional brain functions conducted in visual modality (e.g., Lane & Nadel, 1999), subcortical structures were predicted to be involved.

In the first of these studies, unpleasantness of music was systematically manipulated by varying the degree of consonance vs. dissonance between the melody and the accompanying chords (Blood, Zatorre, Bermudez, & Evans, 1999). According to the ratings made by the subjects, these musical phrases did not differ from each other in sad/happy—dimension, but they did differ in their perceptual pleasantness (e.g., in terms of feeling tension, irritation, anger). In several subcortical brain regions, brain activation was significantly modulated by the degree of dissonance: right parahippocampal gyrus and the precuneus were more activated by increased dissonance while areas in the cingulate cortex were related to decreased dissonance. We should point out that these areas were distinct from those activated by mere music listening. In this pioneering study, those areas also differed from the brain regions commonly activated by negative emotions; in other words, no activation in the amygdala was observed. However, in recent fMRI and neuropsychological investigations, effects of dissonant music have also been linked to the functions of the amygdala (Gosselin, Peretz, Johnsen, & Adolps, 2007; Koelsch, Fritz, von Cramon, Muller, & Friederici, 2006), hippocampus, temporal poles, and, corresponding to original findings of Blood et al. (1999), also to parahippocampal gyrus. Interestingly, the strength of the activations increased during the experimental session (Koelsch et al., 2006), indicating that music emotions are not necessarily observable in the brain signal immediately but rather they need time to develop.

In a second study, the brain regions underlying pleasant music-induced emotions were investigated (Blood & Zatorre, 2001). To this end, musically trained subjects were instructed to choose musical excerpts that would reliably induce positive

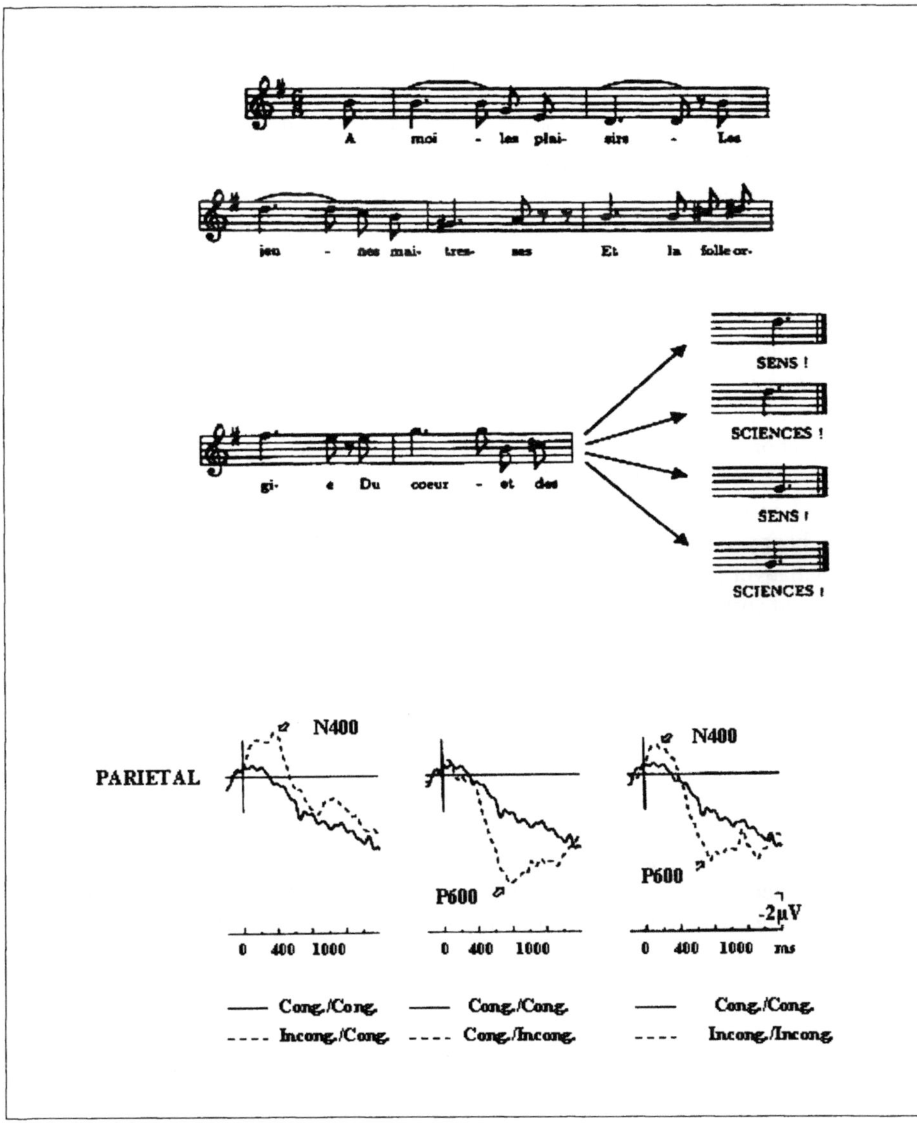

Figure 2. Brain potentials elicited by incongruent melody endings. Upper panel: Examples of different endings of opera excerpts. Both lyrics and pitch were congruent or incongruent in three different manners: the lyrics were incongruent, the pitch was incongruent, or both were incongruent. Bottom panel: The ERPs elicited by these melody endings (average across 16 musicians). Incongruent lyrics elicited the N400 when presented without or with pitch incongruency (left, right). Correspondingly, incongruent pitch elicited the P600 when presented without or with inconsistency in lyrics (middle, right). The data support independent processing of harmony and semantic information in music. (© Illustration by Mari Tervaniemi.)

emotions as indexed by the presence of chills. The chosen excerpts did not include lyrics and were minimally associated with episodic memories. The brain activity elicited during listening to these pleasant excerpts was compared to brain activity elicited by listening to neutral excerpts. It was found that the chill-evoking musical excerpts co-occurred with activity changes in cortical and subcortical structures underlying emotional and vigilance changes (ventral striatum, midbrain, amygdala, orbitofrontal cortex, and ventromedial prefrontal cortex). Interestingly, some of these regions have previously been related to basic biological fulfillment (food, sex), or to positive feelings produced by pharmacological substances. This link between neural substrates underlying music-induced emotions and biologically determined emotions led the authors to highlight the importance of music as a general source of pleasure and reward.

The third example of research on the brain basis of musical emotions is inspired by quite elaborate and replicable mood-manipulation effects of music: Music in minor keys (especially when in slow tempo) is often connected to sad emotions while music in major keys (especially when in fast tempo) is predominantly connected to happy emotions (e.g., Peretz et al., 1998). Khalfa, Schon, Anton, and Liegeois-Chauvel (2005) found excerpts in minor keys to activate cingulate cortex and prefrontal cortex (left orbito- and mid-dorsolateral cortex) more than excerpts in major keys, again areas which are known to be involved in more generalized processing of emotions as well.

Taken together, the picture of the brain system involved in musical emotion will become more complete in coming years. It is now rather generally agreed that despite methodological challenges and high intersubject variation, the emergence of the music emotions in the brain can be tracked using the current research paradigms and facilities. Moreover, novel approaches to combine experimental paradigms from cognitive and emotional research traditions have been recently developed (Steinbeis, Koelsch, & Sloboda, 2006). In the long run, such initiatives will most likely also broaden our thinking of the motivational basis of our involvement in musical activities.

CONCLUDING REMARKS

In this chapter, I have tried to describe two traditional empirical approaches to neurocognitive music research and their findings on cortical music-sound encoding, as well as the first attempts to investigate the brain basis of musical emotions. As the descriptions illustrate, there are several theoretical and conceptual frameworks in the field that are fostering the ongoing experimental work in parallel. Part of the research efforts is motivated by the theories and models in psychology, while some others are mainly motivated by physiological and anatomical questions. In both viewpoints, music and musicians offer a fruitful means for investigating human behavior at a very high cognitive and creative level in a well-controlled setting.

REFERENCES

Besson, M., & Faïta, F. (1996). An event–related potential (ERP) study of musical expectancy: Comparison between musicians and non-musicians. *Journal of Experimental Psychology: Human Perception and Performance, 21,* 1278-1296.

Besson, M., Faïta, F., & Requin, J. (1994). Brain waves associated with musical incongruities differ for musicians and non-musicians. *Neuroscience Letters, 168,* 101-105.

Besson, M., Faïta, F., Peretz, I., Bonnel, A. M., & Requin, J. (1998). Singing in the brain: Independence of lyrics and tunes. *Psychological Science, 9,* 494-498.

Blood, A. J., Zatorre, R. J., Bermudez, P., & Evans, A. C. (1999). Emotional responses to pleasant and unpleasant music correlate with activity in paralimbic brain regions. *Nature Neuroscience 2,* 382-387.

Blood, A. J., & Zatorre, R. J. (2001). Intensely pleasurable responses to music correlate with activity in brain regions implicated in reward and emotion. *Proceedings of the National Academy of Sciences, 98,* 11818-11823.

Brattico, E., Tervaniemi, M., Näätänen, R., & Peretz, I. (2006). Musical scale properties are automatically processed in the human auditory cortex. *Brain Research, 1117,* 162-174.

Caclin, A., Brattico, E., Tervaniemi, M., Näätänen, R., Morlet, D., Giard, M.-H., et al. (2006). Separate neural processing of timbre dimensions in auditory sensory memory. *Journal of Cognitive Neuroscience, 18,* 1959-1972.

Dalla Bella, S., & Peretz, I. (1999). Music agnosias: Selective impairments of music recognition after brain damage. *Journal of New Music Research, 28,* 209-216.

Gosselin, N., Peretz, I., Johnsen, E., & Adolps, R. (2007). Amygdala damage impairs emotion recognition from music. *Neuropsychologia, 45,* 236-244.

Hahne, A., & Friederici, A. D. (1999). Electrophysiological evidence for two steps in syntactic analysis: Early automatic and late controlled processes. *Journal of Cognitive Neuroscience, 11,* 194-205.

He, J., Hashikawa, T., Ojima, H., & Kinouchi, Y. (1997). Temporal integration and duration tuning in the dorsal zone of cat auditory cortex. *Journal of Neuroscience, 17,* 2615-2725.

Heil, P., Rajan, R., & Irvine, D. R. (1994). Topographic representation of tone intensity along the isofrequency axis of cat primary auditory cortex. *Hearing Research, 76,* 188-202.

Hugdahl, K., Brönnick, K., Kyllingsbaek, S., Law, I., Gade, A., & Paulson, O. B. (1999). Brain activation during dichotic presentation of consonant-vowel and musical instrument stimuli: A ^{15}O-PET study. *Neuropsychologia, 37,* 431-440.

Janata, P. (1995). ERP measures assay the degree of expectancy violation of harmonic contexts in music. *Journal of Cognitive Neuroscience, 7,* 153-164.

Khalfa, S., Schon, D., Anton, J. L., & Liegeois-Chauvel, C. (2005). Brain regions involved in the recognition of happiness and sadness in music. *NeuroReport, 6,* 1981-1984.

Koelsch, S., Fritz, T., von Cramon, D. Y., Muller, K., & Friederici, A. D. (2006). Investigating emotion with music: An fMRI study. *Human Brain Mapping, 27,* 239-250.

Koelsch, S., Gunter, T. C., Friederici, A. D., & Schröger, E. (2000). Brain indices of music processing: 'Non-musicians' are musical. *Journal of Cognitive Neuroscience, 12,* 520-541.

Koelsch, S., & Siebel, W. A. (2006). Towards a neural basis of music perception. *Trends in Cognitive Sciences, 10,* 195-196.

Koelsch, S., Schröger, E., & Gunter, T. C. (2002). Music matters: Preattentive musicality of the human brain. *Psychophysiology, 39,* 38-48.

Kutas, M., & Hillyard, S. A. (1980). Reading senseless sentences: Brain potentials reflect semantic incongruity. *Science, 207,* 203-205.

Lane, R. D., & Nadel, L. (1999). *Cognitive neuroscience of emotion*. Oxford, UK: Oxford University Press.

Maess, B., Koelsch, S., Gunter, T. C., & Friederici, A. D. (2001). Musical syntax is processed in Broca's area: An MEG study. *Nature Neuroscience, 4,* 541-545.

Mazziotta, J. C., Phelps, M. E., Carson, R. E., & Kuhl, D. E. (1982). Tomographic mapping of human cerebral metabolism: Auditory stimulation. *Neurology, 32,* 921-937.

Meyer, L. B. (1956). *Emotion and meaning in music*. Chicago: The University of Chicago Press.

Näätänen, R. (1992). *Attention and brain function*. Hillsdale, NJ: Lawrence Erlbaum Publishers.

Näätänen, R., Tervaniemi, M., Sussman, E., Paavilainen, P., & Winkler, I. (2001). 'Primitive intelligence' in the auditory cortex. *Trends in Neurosciences, 24,* 283-288.

North, A. C., Hargreaves, D. J., & McKendrick, J. (1997). In-store music affects product choice. *Nature, 390,* 132.

Novitski, N., Tervaniemi, M., Huotilainen, M., & Näätänen, R. (2004). Frequency discrimination at different frequency levels as reflected by electrophysiological and behavioral indices. *Cognitive Brain Research, 20,* 26-36.

Pantev, C., Hoke, M., Lütkenhöner, B., & Lehnertz, K. (1989a). Tonotopic organization of the auditory cortex: Pitch versus frequency representation. *Science, 246,* 486-488.

Pantev, C., Hoke, M., Lehnertz, K., & Lütkenhöner, B. (1989b). Neuromagnetic evidence of an ampliotopic organization of the auditory cortex. *Electroencephalography and Clinical Neurophysiology, 72,* 225-231.

Patel, A. D., Gibson, E., Ratner, J., Besson, M., & Holcomb, P. J. (1998). Processing syntactic relations in language and music: an event-related potential study. *Journal of Cognitive Neuroscience, 10,* 717-733.

Peretz, I., Gagnon, L., & Bouchard, B. (1998). Music and emotion: Perceptual determinants, immediacy, and isolation after brain damage. *Cognition, 68,* 111-141.

Saarinen, J., Paavilainen, P., Schröger, E., Tervaniemi, M., & Näätänen, R. (1992). Representation of abstract attributes of auditory stimuli in human brain. *NeuroReport, 3,* 1149-1151.

Samson, S. (1999). Musical function and temporal lobe structures: A review of brain lesion studies. *Journal of New Music Research, 28,* 217-228.

Steinbeis, N., Koelsch, S., & Sloboda, J. A. (2006). The role of harmonic expectancy violations in musical emotions: Evidence from subjective, physiological and neural responses. *Journal of Cognitive Neuroscience, 18*, 1380-1393.

Tervaniemi, M., Alho, K., Paavilainen, P., Sams, M., & Näätänen, R. (1993). Absolute pitch and event-related brain potentials. *Music Perception, 10,* 305-316.

Tervaniemi, M., & Huotilainen, M. (2003). The promises of change-related brain potentials in cognitive neuroscience of music. *Annals of the New York Academy of Sciences, 999,* 29-39.

Tervaniemi, M., Kujala, A., Alho, K., Virtanen, J., Ilmoniemi, R. J., & Näätänen, R. (1999). Functional specialization of the human auditory cortex in processing phonetic and musical sounds: A magnetoencephalographic (MEG) study. *NeuroImage, 9,* 330-336.

Tervaniemi, M., Maury, S., & Näätänen, R. (1994). Neural representations of abstract stimulus features in the human brain as reflected by the mismatch negativity. *NeuroReport, 5,* 844-846.

Tervaniemi, M., Medvedev, S. V., Alho, K., Pakhomov, S. V., Roudas, M. S., van Zuijen, T. L., et al. (2000). Lateralized automatic auditory processing of phonetic versus musical information: A PET study. *Human Brain Mapping, 10,* 74-79.

Tervaniemi, M., Rytkönen, M., Schröger, E., Ilmoniemi, R. J., & Näätänen, R. (2001). Superior formation of cortical memory traces for melodic patterns in musicians. *Learning & Memory, 8,* 295-300.

Tervaniemi, M., Szameitat, A. J., Kruck, S., Schröger, E., Alter, K., De Baene, W. et al. (2006). From air oscillations to music and speech: Functional magnetic resonance imaging evidence for fine-tuned neural networks in audition. *Journal of Neuroscience, 26,* 8647-8652.

Tiitinen, H., Alho, K., Huotilainen, M., Ilmoniemi, R. J., Simola, J., & Näätänen, R. (1993). Tonotopic auditory cortex and the magnetoencephalographic (MEG) equivalent of the mismatch negativity. *Psychophysiology, 30,* 537-540.

Toiviainen, P., Tervaniemi, M., Louhivuori, J., Huotilainen, M., Saher, M., & Näätänen, R. (1998). Musical timbre: Convergence of neural, behavioral, and computational approaches. *Music Perception, 16,* 223-241.

Zatorre, R. J. (2001). Neural specializations for tonal processing. *Annals of the New York Academy of Sciences, 930,* 193-210.

Zatorre, R. J., Belin, P., & Penhune, V. (2002). Structure and function of auditory cortex: Music and speech. *Trends in Cognitive Sciences, 6,* 37-46.

Zatorre, R. J., Evans, A. C., Meyer, E., & Gjedde, A. (1992). Lateralization of phonetic and pitch discrimination in speech processing. *Science, 256,* 846-849.

CHAPTER 11

Neuroaesthetics of Literary Reading

David S. Miall

LITERARINESS

Literary reading is an experience that most people probably recognize implicitly. However, it is not easy to say what characterizes it. Are there properties that make it distinctive? Can we, in fact, demarcate it from other kinds of reading, such as our response to a Harlequin romance or a narrative in an advertisement? In this chapter, I focus on the implications of this question for empirical studies of literary reading. This will serve to identify several key processes that appear to be implicated in the experience of "literariness." A comparison with the findings of neuropsychological research helps to define the processes and indicate directions for further inquiry. While there is, as yet, no explicit body of neuropsychological research on literary reading, a number of studies provide suggestive parallels: these focus on questions about memory, insight, empathy, feeling, and language, and provide a framework for examining some of the constituents of the aesthetic response to literary narrative and poetic language.

For a preliminary sketch of literary reading, I consider the opening two paragraphs of the following short story, by the Irish writer Seán O'Faoláin, "The Trout," which has been the focus of several of our empirical studies of reading (Miall & Kuiken, 1994; Kuiken & Miall, 2001). The text is divided into segments, indicated by the numerals in square brackets.

> [1] One of the first places Julia always ran to when they arrived in G—was The Dark Walk. [2] It is a laurel walk, very old, almost gone wild, a lofty midnight tunnel of smooth, sinewy branches. [3] Underfoot the tough brown leaves are never dry enough to crackle: there is always a suggestion of damp and cool trickle.
>
> [4] She raced right into it. [5] For the first few yards she always had the memory of the sun behind her, [6] then she felt the dusk closing swiftly down on her so that she screamed with pleasure and raced on to reach the light at the far end; [7] and it was always just a little too long in coming so that she emerged gasping, clasping her hands, laughing, drinking in the sun. (O'Faoláin, 1980-1982)

The text is amenable to two main types of analysis, linguistic and narrative. At the linguistic level, certain stylistic features tend to stand out: these include the unusual abbreviation "G---," the consonance created in phrases such as "damp and cool trickle," the repeated "ah" sounds in "gasping, clasping . . . laughing," and the figurative expression "lofty midnight tunnel." Readers tend to take account of such features, although they may not do so consciously. Typically, readers take longer to read segments that contain a number of such stylistic features, and when asked to judge their effects they report that the segments are striking and that they experience elevated levels of feeling (Miall & Kuiken, 1994).

As narrative, readers recognize the presence of the character named in the first segment and appear to construe the story, at least in part, from her point of view. The story provides indications of place and time, and a consistent sequence of events relating the character's actions within the world she inhabits. Thus, in the terminology of discourse processing, readers construct a situation model through which they track the unfolding events of the story (Zwaan & Radvansky, 1998). Over the course of a narrative (i.e., beyond the opening two paragraphs reproduced here), readers follow the unfolding plot, experiencing the vicissitudes of the main characters' actions and desires, often empathizing with a character; they may feel suspense, curiosity, or surprise. In addition, readers tend to form an implicit relationship with the narrator (Bortolussi & Dixon, 2003, pp. 72-77). During the reading or after it is over, readers may reflect on ways in which the meaning of the story resonates with their own experiences, such as their autobiographical memories, their values, or the narrative's cultural significance.

The influence of some of the linguistic and narrative features can be seen in the following protocol, collected from a reader whom we asked to think aloud while reading the story, segment by segment. I reproduce her response to the opening segments.

1. Oh, I like the name Julia. I wonder why they have dashes after the G. Why don't . . . why don't they tell us the name? The Dark Walk sounds very ominous.
2. "Smooth, sinewy branches." That's very poetic, I like that.
3. I like the adjectives. They make me think of the forest.
4. That seemed so abrupt, "She raced right into it."
5. I can picture the sun being behind me when I read that too.
6. And the dusk like, something like a blanket closing around me when I read.
7. Makes me feel happy to read "laughing, drinking in the sun." That's really nice.

The reader's references to her feelings are a prominent constituent of her comments. The poetic qualities of the language seem to evoke at least two comments (segments 2 and 3), while it seems probable that at segment 7 the assonance that includes "laughing" and the metaphor "drinking in the sun" contribute to her feeling of happiness. In response to these segments, she repeats two phrases from the story, which suggests that she has found them striking and by repeating them aloud is better able to savor their poetic qualities. In previous empirical studies, we have found that the tendency to repeat phrases correlates with a higher frequency of stylistic effects. This reader also appears to have a positive association to the name "Julia"; this may indicate a positivity bias to the character, a willingness to endorse the view of reality that the character's perspective suggests. This seems evident by segments 5 and 6, since here the reader aligns her perspective to that of Julia: she reports experiencing the sun and the dusk as though she were Julia. As Green has shown, readers transported to the narrative world show increased positivity toward sympathetic characters (Green, 2004, p. 248), and they are likely to accept the validity of what they read (Green & Brock, 2000, p. 703).

The only negative feelings in the response occur at segment 1, where the reader questions the narrator's stance in withholding the full name of G--- (the narrator is referred to as "they"), followed by her immediate response that the Dark Walk "sounds very ominous." The reader seems surprised at segment 4, "That seemed so abrupt": probably the segment disrupts the mood instilled in the reader by the previous two segments; at that moment, Julia's behavior may seem anomalous (the reader may not yet have appreciated that Julia is a child: later in the story we are told she is 12).

There are two standard claims about what makes our reading literary: that it is triggered, first, by our encounter with a rich, organized array of stylistic features (Miall & Kuiken, 1999), or, second, by the (usually empathic) engagement with characters in literary narratives (Oatley & Mar, 2005). This short section of a reader's response thus illustrates several features that have been considered characteristic of literary response. Given these basic features, we can theorize several other features that will be required for a more complete aesthetic response, including to the story as a whole.

One potential development lies in the contrast of feelings reported by the reader in response to the Dark Walk: it is "ominous" at first, then appears pleasant when the poetic description reminds the reader of a forest. In fact, the contrast motivates this reader's understanding of the main character at several points later in the story, in particular at the climax of the story when Julia visits the Dark Walk at night. Conflicts of feeling often seem central to the aesthetic complexity of literary texts: they focus the reader's attention in successive episodes and organize the reader's understanding of the issues at stake (Miall, 2004). In addition, readers may experience insight into the meaning of their feelings and undergo a shift in understanding as a result (Kuiken, Miall, & Sikora, 2004). Although this may not be a frequent occurrence while reading, such gains in self-understanding can be the most valuable experiences we acquire from literary reading.

Another, shorter-term development of the feelings evoked during reading is what we have termed the *defamiliarization-reconcepualization* cycle (Miall & Kuiken, 2001). At the encounter with a stylistically rich passage that is found striking, the reader's accustomed schemata may be inadequate for comprehension; we surmise that the feelings evoked by the passage provide an alternative perspective directing the reader's search for a new understanding. The resulting reconcepualization occurs downstream from the initial encounter (perhaps several segments further on).

A feeling experienced during reading, such as the response to striking passages, often contains a surplus of meaning; it prompts more thought than can be considered within the frame of working memory (readers' think-aloud comments, of the kind reproduced previously, capture only a part of what the reader is actually experiencing). This may indicate that a prototypical feeling has been evoked, linking the present response both to the reader's previous experiences of the feeling and to the laws within which the feeling typically operates. As I will mention later, this may underlie the so-called disinterested aspect of aesthetic response.

On the narrative side, readers have been shown to track character's feelings (De Vega, Leon, & Diaz, 1996; Gernsbacher, Goldsmith, & Robertson, 1992) and knowledge (Graesser, Bowers, Olde, White, & Person, 1999). A literary text, unlike other narratives, can provide privileged access to the minds of characters, building on the capacity that we possess for reading others' minds (Zunshine, 2006). Literary reading thus facilitates investigation of Theory of Mind, providing support for the simulation account rather than the theory-theory account (Carruthers & Smith, 1996). This capacity also provides an important framework for considering empathy, our ability to experience another's feelings as though they were our own.

It is these aspects of literary reading—defamiliarization, feelings, empathy—that I will discuss in relation to a number of neuropsychological studies. The model of reading I have outlined presents an aesthetics that builds in important respects on several previous essays in this area, including recent neuropsychological contributions by Julie Kane (2004) and Raymond Mar (2004). Kane argues that the right hemisphere (RH) controls a distinctive set of language processes that are characteristic of poetry. These include imagery, alliteration, synaesthesia, synecdoche and metonymy, paradox, irony, prosody (i.e., emotional tone), and story relationships. As I suggested in an earlier review (Miall, 1995), feeling appears to be a central component of such RH phenomena; the unresolved issue is how feeling in this context participates in or evokes a distinctively literary experience, since all the features that Kane cites can also be found occurring without literary effect in nonliterary language. Kane itemizes an essential part of the literary toolkit, but the aesthetic power that incorporates them into a literary experience remains to be demonstrated. Mar (2004) outlines the components of narrative and examines a range of candidate neuropsychological mechanisms that might instantiate them. For instance, Baddeley's episodic working memory model provides a framework for developing the hypothetical scenarios of narrative (see Miall, 2006, pp. 148-150); the work of Beeman and his colleagues demonstrates RH "coarse" semantic coding, appropriate for the poetic features examined by Kane; the Theory of Mind that allows inferences about characters in narrative appears localized to several RH structures. Mar also points to the sensitivity of brain scanning, which can demonstrate differences in response (mostly RH) between a story presented either with or without a title (Mar, 2004, p. 1421), a finding that suggests the fine discrimination of literary from nonliterary experience should now be within reach of brain-scanning technology. Again, however, Mar's work, while illuminating a range of narrative features and showing their probable neuropsychological mechanisms, stops short at the boundary beyond which the distinctive experience of literary narrative occurs.

How to go beyond this limitation is another question. The primary problem in pursuing the topic (as with empirical studies more generally) is a theoretical one: how to specify what is distinctive to literary response, and to do so in sufficient detail that we can isolate the psychological processes that are implicated. If we find a difference due to literary processing, can we understand what it means, that is, how it contributes to a conception of literariness? Here, neuropsychology provides what may be reliable grounds for research, since the resolution with which scanning occurs should enable us to discriminate the structures that distinguish a literary from a nonliterary response. In contrast, empirical methods that call for an explicit response from the reader, such as a rating or a verbal comment, are liable to distortions of the literary experience when participants provide socially desirable responses or because the task of verbalizing interferes with the experience. While brain-scanning technology itself is intrusive and may militate against the absorption typical of a powerful literary experience, the measures it provides are not liable to direct influence by the participant, nor are they limited to the verbal domain. In the remaining sections of this chapter, I outline two approaches to the issue of literariness and point to neuropsychological studies that may help illuminate its components.

FOREGROUNDING

Foregrounding, as I noted earlier, appears to initiate a cycle that begins with the response to stylistic features: for instance, the alliteration and metaphor that occur in this phrase about the Dark Walk near the beginning of "The Trout": "a lofty midnight tunnel of smooth, sinewy branches." These are found striking (i.e., defamiliarizing), and arouse feeling; feeling, in turn, provides a context within which over time the unfamiliar aspects of the phrase are recontextualized. In response to the term "midnight" in this phrase, for example, a reader might go on to experience a Gothic atmosphere in the Dark Walk; or the bodily hint of "smooth, sinewy branches" might suggest the animation of the Walk (either of these connotations provides a valid context for understanding what will occur later in the story). This sequence of responses is undoubtedly dependent on right-hemisphere processes, as Kane (2004) shows; what makes it distinctively literary appears to be the richness of response—the number of potential meanings sensed within the short timespan of normal reading—and the evocation of feeling with the power to instantiate a subsequent shift in meaning for the reader (the reconceptualization process). Several neuropsychological studies provide support for this interpretation of the response to foregrounding.

It seems probable that the initial response to a foregrounded passage will activate the amygdala (as Robinson has proposed: 2005, p. 71). As Davidson, Pizzagalli, Nitschke, and Kalin (2003) observe, in a comment that corresponds well to the challenge of foregrounding, the amygdala plays a critical role in "co-ordinating cortical arousal and vigilant attention for optimizing sensory and perceptual processing of stimuli associated with underdetermined contingencies, such as novel, 'surprising' or 'ambiguous' stimuli" (p. 15). This first, rapid response (the "low road" rather than the slower "high road" of cognitive processing: LeDoux, 1996,

p. 161) may then connect to emotional memories (Hogan, 2003, p. 156) that provide alternative frameworks for assigning significance to the experience. These first responses need not be "primitive," as Robinson (2005, p. 151) suggests, as the studies I will mention next help to show.

The richness of meaning evoked by foregrounding appears to occur early in the response. As Posner and DiGirolamo (2000) have shown, while awareness of an object depends on processes occurring in the first 100 msec following input, they note that the "difference between the activation caused by novel and familiar objects can be shown in ventral visual areas within 155 msec after input." Moreover, they show that processing of unattended stimuli may occur to a high level: "Selecting one stimulus over others does not mean that unselected items will not produce a reorienting of attention." In other words, the richness of meaning in foregrounding need not be apprehended consciously in order to influence subsequent processing. As Eckstein and Friederici (2006) found, the prosodic aspects of language, which would include foregrounded aspects, are taken up early in processing: they report that incongruities in prosody are detected 300-500 msec after word onset, which suggests "the immediate influence of phrasal prosody during the initial parsing stage in speech processing." Their findings demonstrate an early interaction of syntactic (LH) and prosodic (RH) features.

To compare these response times with readers of "The Trout" (data from Miall & Kuiken, 1994): mean reading times per syllable are 258 msec with a standard deviation of 96 msec; thus, responses within the normal range vary from 354 msec for passages high in foregrounding to 162 msec for passages low in foregrounding (response to highly foregrounded passages thus takes roughly twice as long). These times indicate that complex processing of stylistic aspects is likely to be occurring prior to the window of consciousness. As Damasio (1999) puts it, "We are probably late for consciousness by about five hundred milliseconds" (p. 127). Since one syllable can embody several foregrounded features, the initial occurrence of feelings outside of awareness may often be rich and complex (i.e., far from the initial "quick and dirty" processing on which Robinson [2005, p. 50] bases her response model; see Hogan [2003, p. 176], who rules out the possibility for literature of the "low road" of "direct emotive stimulation"). At the same time, this initial response is likely to be unreportable. Fiore and Schooler (1998) report a study with two problem-solving tasks, one an incremental, logic task, the other an insight task. It was found that verbalizing interfered with the insight task but not the logic task, suggesting that "insight problems may rely more on nonreportable processes that are vulnerable to verbalization" (p. 352), and (paradoxically, since foregrounding is a linguistic phenomenon) "depend on the ability to avoid the inherent constraints of language-based thought" (p. 368).

Thus, once the response to foregrounding becomes consciously available to the reader at around 500 msec, a reader will experience a richness of felt meaning already in train, yet one that may have evoked unfamiliar meanings that remain to be resolved. In the terms of Owen Barfield (1964), the "*interior* significance" of defamiliarization "must be felt as arising from a different plane or mode of consciousness" (pp. 170-171). This, in itself, is a recognizable and characteristic effect of literariness. A literary reader often has the sense that the literary text is in control of the self and directs response from some intimate yet strange quarter of the mind. The further development of the response toward reconceptualization may be compared with the process of resolving insight problems, studied by Beeman and his colleagues.

The work of Beeman is based on the premise that the right hemisphere provides coarse semantic coding in contrast to the left hemisphere. Thus, the more distant associations of words are better recognized when presented to the left visual field (RH) (Beeman, 1998, p. 267). The interesting aspect of this research, however, and its relevance for understanding the processes of literary response, is that while the LH tends to select close associations early in processing, RH capacity for more remote associations only shows its advantages over time in relation to insight problems of a kind for which LH processes are unsuited. Bowden and Beeman (1998) asked participants to solve insight problems in which three words were presented; participants then had to find a fourth word that would pair with each of the three to create familiar phrases. For example, given *high, district*, and *house*, the solution word was *school*. After 7 or 15 seconds, it was found that the RH had greater priming than the LH for the solution word: participants pronounced the solution word faster when it was presented in the left visual field; at earlier intervals (1.25 or 2 secs) no RH advantage appeared. They suggest that in initial processing, LH interpretive processes dominate, while after several seconds the more connotative RH processing shows its advantage. This research also argues for the greater predictive powers of RH processing during connected discourse, such as a narrative: "When a coherence break is encountered, a [RH] search ensues for potentially connecting information that has been previously activated by explicit mention, by close relation to input words, or by overlap from distantly related input words" (Beeman, Bowden, & Gernbacher, 2000, p. 328). As Grafman (2002) puts it, the RH may thus be "adept at integrating or synthesizing information across events in time," such as finding the moral of a story (p. 301). The role of the RH in insight problems is confirmed by an imaging study: Bowden, Jung-Beeman, Fleck, & Kounios (2005) report that "fMRI results revealed an increased signal in the right anterior superior temporal gyrus for insight relative to non-insight solutions" (p. 325). In a parallel study, Coulson and Wu (2005) studied responses to jokes and found a "frame shifting" response attributable to RH processing, suggesting RH facilitation of distantly related meanings. Such shifts in meaning are more characteristic of literary than nonliterary texts, as an empirical study of readers by Meutsch and Schmidt (1985, p. 566) demonstrated.

The neuropsychological work reported here supports the theorized function of foregrounding in literary response, suggesting that RH processes facilitate a reconceptualization, analogous to the solution of an insight problem, that occurs downstream from the initial response. We (Miall & Kuiken, 2001) previously described this model in three phases: the neuropsychological studies discussed here provide evidence for phases one (defamiliarization) and three (reconceptualization). We proposed that in phase two, feeling directs a search for an appropriate context to locate the unfamiliar aspects of foregrounding (such as the "midnight" metaphor or the *s*-alliteration). Our empirical findings suggested that shifts in meaning were inhibited during this phase. Preliminary support for this proposal is also provided by Beeman's studies. Beeman (1998) reported that during response to narrative, immediately following the point where an inference was possible, the RH may have been inhibited since "participants did not show priming in reaction time for inference-related targets in the lvf-RH at the time when the inference should be selected for incorporation," while "they did show priming in accuracy at this same time, suggesting that the information was activated above baseline, but not easily (rapidly) available for output." This is evidence for what he calls a "tentative inhibition hypothesis" (p. 276). We might speculate that the temporal interval indicated here allows feeling some scope for hypothesis testing, enabling it to locate the most appropriate context for interpretation. In literary reading, the most dramatic example of such an interval occurs during response to the sublime: here we might suggest that LH processing is disabled while the temporary RH inhibition corresponds to the experience of the momentary suspension of thought and feeling often reported—what one witness referred to as "a sort of annihilation of self" (Williams, 1798, I, p. 60).

Confirmation of the significance of feeling in phase two is provided by a study of narrative response. In a functional magnetic resonance imaging (fMRI) study, Ferstl, Rinck, and von Cramon (2005) showed that RH activation in response to affective incongruities in short stories lasted up to 14 secs from word onset. Their mapping of responses to the stories showed a nonverbal, emotional dimension of response: "Elicited by the emotional target information, the orbitofrontal and ventromedial prefrontal activations, including the extended amygdala complex, clearly show that the affective component of the stories directly induced processes beyond language comprehension. Thus, the situation model for these stories includes a nonverbal, nonpropositional representation of the affective dimension" (pp. 733-734). In a literary context, such as the encounter with foregrounding, it seems likely that feeling would provide the primary vehicle for developing an interpretation of foregrounded elements.

Foregrounding thus appears to initiate a rich response prior to awareness: as early as 155 msec, the detection of unfamiliar stylistic features may initiate a response process that includes prosodic, affective, as well as semantic aspects. This is followed by an inhibitory phase during which feeling is contexualizing the unfamiliar, leading to emergence of new meanings or shifts in perspective a number of seconds downstream from foregrounding onset. Several neuropsychological studies, such as those on coarse coding, help elaborate the mechanisms required for this model. In the next section, I examine some bodily and affective aspects that are also central to literary response.

EMPATHY AND IMMERSION

Among the more salient features of our response to narrative, perhaps the most prominent is the sense of "being there" or "transport" (Green, 2004). The absorption we experience while reading may occur in relation to a vividly imagined setting (e.g., the moorland in *Wuthering Heights*) or the sense of a character's presence (e.g., Heathcliff), and at times it may enable us to empathize with the feelings and motives of a character and to share his or her goals. This effect was first described in the eighteenth century by Lord Kames: he termed it "ideal presence" and characterized it as a "waking dream" (Kames, 1762, I, pp. 108-112). Such experience, as if we saw and felt events unfolding before us, can be powerful enough at times to cause bodily symptoms, influencing heart rate, sweating, or muscular tension (Auracher, 2006). It has also been a problematic issue, since it is hard to explain how we can experience what feels like real emotion in relation to fictional events and characters (Walton, 1990). Nevertheless, it is a familiar response not only to literary texts, but also to subliterary and other art forms such as movies. I will describe first the neuropsychological work that enables us to understand the efficacy of texts in this respect, then offer a view of how this provides the basis for a distinctively literary experience.

The main proposal I discuss here is that brain regions responsible for interpreting perceptual input are also those that represent an imagined perception. For example, the primary visual areas are activated when an object is merely imagined, a process that involves "running perception backward," or top-down, as Behrmann (2000) put it. Behrmann points out that there is also evidence that the size or distance of an image is also represented; for instance, when a participant imagines a larger image, relatively more parts of the visual area are activated (p. 51). In the light of such evidence, Zwaan (2004) put forward the proposal that a reader is an "immersed experiencer," using descriptions of situation and characters in order to construct an experiential simulation. Thus, "comprehension is the vicarious experience of the described events through the integration and sequencing of traces from actual experience cued by the linguistic input" (p. 38). Zwaan is describing reading in general. Aesthetic experience during reading may involve more vivid imagery or more intense feeling, but probably requires an additional dimension, as I will suggest shortly.

Related to Zwaan's model of reading is the discovery of mirror neurons. First observed in the monkey, single neurons were found to fire either when the monkey carried out a specific action (e.g., reaching out the hand to grasp an object) or when the monkey observed another monkey performing the same action. The neurons were found to be quite specific: if the hand reached without grasping an object, the neuron was not activated. More recently, mirror neurons, including neurons performing a wider range of functions, were also found in humans. Gallese and Goldmann (1998) suggest that the function of mirror neurons is to facilitate "mind reading," that is, they enable an observer to represent another's goals and purposes, helping us to anticipate whether the other's intentions are friendly or hostile. Rizzolatti (2005) points out that the monkey's mirror neurons in the superior temporal sulcus are responsive to various bodily movements; this region is also linked to the amygdala and other emotion centers. This suggests that simulation of emotional responses can also occur.

The mirror-neurons finding thus also provides a mechanism for helping to understand social cognition, the Theory of Mind module that enables us to read others' minds. Of the two standard explanations of Theory of Mind, mirror-neuron activity supports a simulation view in contrast to the theory-theory view (Gallese & Goldmann, 1998). The theory-theory approach argues that we use causal and explanatory laws to relate external events to inner states, that we reason in relation to tacitly understood causal laws. Simulation theory argues that people use their own mental mechanisms to calculate and predict what others think, feel, or do; that is, we put ourselves in the place of the other person and figure out what their experience means. If this is correct, the mirror-neuron system also underlies the experience of empathy, which is often an important component of our response to narrative (Keen, 2006, p. 211).

Evidence for the role of mirror neurons during reading, and their activation of empathic and other affective responses, is available from several studies. Boulenger, Roy, Paulignan, Deprez, Jeannerod, and Nazir (2006) report an interaction between reading and the motor system within 200 msec of word onset. In their study, when a particular reaching movement was taking place while the participant concurrently processed an action verb, interference occurred when the movement called on different effector muscles than implied by the action verb. This finding suggests that "the perception of an action word and not the perception of the action per se would be sufficient to trigger the mirror-neuron system" (p. 1607). The language and motor systems thus appear to share neuronal representations. Hauk and Pulvermuller (2004) found that while reading words relating to actions by face, arm, or leg, topographical, location-specific neuronal activity occurred within 210 to 230 msec. This finding also points to mirror neurons in the premotor cortex. They propose that "action-related neurons are activated early when words are being processed and that they play a crucial role for identifying these words" (p. 199). Similar findings, relating response to language to mirror-neuron systems for specific motor actions are reported by Garbarini and Adenzato (2004), Grafton, Fadiga, Arbib, and Rizzolatti (1997), Oliveri, Finocchiaro, Shapiro, Gangitano, Caramazza, and Pascual-Leone (2004), and Tettamanti and colleagues (2005). Iacoboni (2005) points out that mirror neurons occur in humans in area BA 44, representing hand and mouth movements, an area that is also part of Broca's area, responsible for language (p. 89). This area in humans thus plays an important role in imitation, in addition to responsibility for language, suggesting "an evolutionary continuity between action recognition, imitation, and language" (p. 91).

Mirror neurons also appear to underlie our capacity to simulate the experiences of touch, feeling, and emotion. Keysers, Wicker, Gazzola, Anton, Fogassi, and Ballese (2004), in a fMRI study, showed activation of the secondary somatosensory area (SII) both when participants observed another person being touched (on the leg) and when they were touched in the same place. A previous study also found a response in SII when participants only had the expectation of being touched (p. 341). Gallese, Keysers, and Rizzolatti (2004) show that a mirror mechanism also underlies understanding and experience of emotion. For example, the human insula is activated by the sight of the face of another person experiencing disgust; electrical stimulation of the insula also produces feelings of nausea and disgust. Through simulation, mirror neurons thus appear to provide experiential knowledge of others' emotions, not just a conceptual knowledge of them. A physiological basis for empathy is discussed by Iacoboni (2005). An fMRI study found substantially similar activation in anterior sectors of the insula during both observation and imitation of emotion, although in several areas, activation was higher during imitation; this emotional response also correlated with increased activity in the amygdala. Iacoboni notes that anterior insula also appears responsible for monitoring agency, that is, the ownership of actions (p. 97). Other studies demonstrating a mirror-neuron system for empathy are described by Singer, Seymour, O'Doherty, Kaube, Dolan, and Frith (2004) and de Vignemont and Singer (2006).

Empathy in literary response thus may involve not only simulating the feeling experienced by a character about which we are reading, but also such embodied experiences as touch or motor activation. The responses of the reader I cited earlier suggest such a response: she experiences the same visual imagery as the character she is re-creating: "I can picture the sun being behind me when I read"; she appears to experience the setting kinaesthetically, since the dusk of the Dark Walk is "something like a blanket closing around me when I read"; and the character's emotion appears to be contagious, making her "feel happy to read 'laughing, drinking in the sun.' That's really nice." The mirror-neuron system thus appears to support a wide array of empathic responses during reading.

A study by Becchio and Bertone (2005), also involving mirror neurons, suggests that the initial response during reading involves a type of disinterest, where the experience portrayed is considered in its own right, independent of agency. Aesthetic disinterest, a concept that originates with Kant, is described by Iris Murdoch (1970) as a response that points "away from self" (p. 66), is "impersonal" (p. 75) and "unselfing" (p. 84); bad art in comparison is like a "selfish daydream" (p. 86). Murdoch's account would be modified in an important direction if the Becchio and Bertone study is correct. These authors report that certain mirror neurons are amodal, activated whether the event in question is visual or aural; that is, they are activated whether watching, performing, or merely imagining doing an action. They go on to claim that these "audiovisual mirror neurons not only discriminate between actions in all modalities, but map actions in a *multisubjective* neural format neutral with respect to the agent." How would this apply to reading? "When two agents socially interact with one another, the activation of mirror networks creates shared representation, i.e. representations simultaneously activated in the brains of the two agents" (p. 23). In the asymmetric case of reading, while a character is not physically present but imagined, mirror neurons represent the character's experience in the reader, replicating his feelings or motor actions. But, Becchio and Bertone ask, if the same representation is active in two brains, how do we distinguish the "I"? (p. 24)—a question that also applies to the situation of reading. They suggest that "Motor intentions are first shared, and only in the second place attributed" (p. 28). This perspective suggests that as readers, we experience, even if only momentarily, a schema for action or feeling that makes its own demands on us for understanding. Its status as a vehicle for reflection and anticipation orients us, independently of the self, toward the implications of the narrative we are reading, although it may subsequently be linked to our own intentions, goals, or feelings.

The mirror-neuron framework thus helps provide an account not only of how the body is implicated while reading, or how empathic responses to character are possible (thus pointing to a solution of the problem of how we can have real feelings for fictional characters), but also seems to provide a foundation for the disinterested response to literary art, not by explicitly pointing away from the self, as Murdoch claims, but by presenting experience without agency. Experience only later, downstream, becomes a token for explicit self-reference through activating the reader's feelings, and (perhaps) the reader's autobiographical memory. While the implications of disinterestedness remain to be worked out in more detail, they provide another avenue for considering how literary response may be distinctive. Moments of foregrounding, or surprising turns in a narrative, provide the grounds for disinterest, situating the experience in question as a prototype with its own distinctive laws of being and development. The two claims to literariness I have made in this chapter thus come together in such moments. Although their topics are familiar from aesthetic theory—stylistic aspects and disinterest both have a long critical history—recent neuropsychological studies provide fruitful grounds not only to reaffirm but also to reconceptualize them.

REFERENCES

Auracher, J. (2006, August). *Biological correlates of suspense—An empirical investigation.* Paper presented at the 10th Conference of the International Society for the Empirical Study of Literature and Media (IGEL), Frauenchiemsee, Germany.

Barfield, O. (1964). *Poetic diction: A study in meaning.* Toronto: McGraw-Hill.

Becchio, C., & Bertone, C. (2005). Beyond Cartesian subjectivism: Neural correlates of shared intentionality. *Journal of Consciousness Studies, 12,* 20-30.

Beeman, M. (1998). Coarse semantic coding and discourse comprehension. In M. Beeman & C. Chiarello (Eds.), *Right hemisphere language comprehension: Perspectives from cognitive neuroscience* (pp. 255-284). Mahwah, NJ: Erlbaum.

Beeman, M. J., Bowden, E. M., & Gernbacher, M. A. (2000). Right and left hemisphere cooperation for drawing predictive and coherence inferences during normal story comprehension. *Brain & Language, 71,* 310-336.

Behrmann, M. (2000). The mind's eye mapped onto the brain's matter. *Trends in Psychological Science, 9,* 50-54.

Bortolussi, M., & Dixon, P. (2003). *Psychonarratology: Foundations for the empirical study of literary response.* Cambridge, MA: Cambridge University Press.

Boulenger, V., Roy, A. C., Paulignan, Y., Deprez, V., Jeannerod, M., & Nazir, T. A. (2006). Cross-talk between language processes and overt motor behavior in the first 200 msec of processing. *Journal of Cognitive Neuroscience, 18,* 1607-1615.

Bowden, E., & Beeman, M. J. (1998). Getting the right idea: Semantic activation in the right hemisphere may help solve insight problems. *Psychological Science, 9,* 435-440.

Bowden, E. M., Jung-Beeman, M., Fleck, J., & Kounios, J. (2005). New approaches to demystifying insight. *Trends in Cognitive Sciences, 9,* 322-328.

Carruthers, P., & Smith, P. K. (Eds.). (1996). *Theories of theories of mind.* Cambridge, MA: Cambridge University Press.

Coulson, S., & Wu, Y. C. (2005). Right hemisphere activation of joke-related information: An event-related brain potential study. *Journal of Cognitive Neuroscience, 17,* 494-506.

Damasio, A. (1999). *The feeling of what happens: Body and emotion in the making of consciousness*. New York: Harcourt Brace.

Davidson, R. J., Pizzagalli, D., Nitschke, J. B., & Kalin, N. H. (2003). Parsing the sub-components of emotion and disorders of emotion: Perspectives from affective neuroscience. In R. J. Davidson, K. R. Scherer, & H. H. Goldsmith (Eds.), *Handbook of affective sciences* (pp. 8-24). Oxford: Oxford University Press.

De Vega, M., Leon, I., & Diaz, J. M. (1996). The representation of changing emotions in reading comprehension. *Cognition and Emotion, 10,* 303-321.

de Vignemont, F., & Singer, T. (2006). The empathic brain: How, when and why? *Trends in Cognitive Sciences, 10,* 435-441.

Eckstein, K., & Friederici, A. D. (2006). It's early: Event-related potential evidence for initial interaction of syntax and prosody in speech comprehension. *Journal of Cognitive Neuroscience, 18,* 1696-1711.

Ferstl, E. C., Rinck, M., & von Cramon, D. Y. (2005). Emotional and temporal aspects of situation model processing during text comprehension: An event-related fMRI study. *Journal of Cognitive Neuroscience, 17,* 724-739.

Fiore, S. M., & Schooler, J. W. (1998). Right hemisphere contributions to creative problem solving: Converging evidence for divergent thinking. In M. Beeman & C. Chiarello (Eds.), *Right hemisphere language comprehension: Perspectives from cognitive neuroscience* (pp. 349-371). Mahwah, NJ: Lawrence Erlbaum.

Gallese, G., & Goldmann, A. (1998). Mirror-neurons: In reflection. *Trends in Cognitive Sciences, 2,* 493-501.

Gallese, V., Keysers, C., & Rizzolatti, G. (2004). A unifying view of the basis of social cognition. *Trends in Cognitive Sciences, 8,* 396-403.

Garbarini, F., & Adenzato, M. (2004). At the root of embodied cognition: Cognitive science meets neurophysiology. *Brain and Cognition, 56,* 100-106.

Gernsbacher, M. A., Goldsmith, H. H., & Robertson, R. R. W. (1992). Do readers mentally represent characters' emotional states? *Cognition and Emotion, 6,* 89-111.

Graesser, A. C., Bowers, C., Olde, B., White, K., & Person, N. K. (1999). Who knows what? Propagation of knowledge among agents in a literary story world. *Poetics, 26,* 143-175.

Grafman, J. (2002). The Structured Event Complex and the human prefrontal cortex. In D. T. Stuss & R. T. Knight (Eds.), *Principles of frontal lobe function* (pp. 292-310). New York: Oxford University Press.

Grafton, S. T., Fadiga, L., Arbib, M. A., & Rizzolatti, G. (1997). Premotor cortex activation during observation and naming of familiar tools. *Neuroimage, 6,* 231-236.

Green, M. C. (2004). Transportation into narrative worlds: The role of prior knowledge and perceived realism. *Discourse Processes, 38,* 247-266.

Green, M. C., & Brock, T. C. (2000). The role of transportation in the persuasiveness of public narratives. *Journal of Personality and Social Psychology, 79,* 701-721.

Hauk, O., & Pulvermuller, F. (2004). Neurophysiological distinction of action words in the fronto-central cortex. *Human Brain Mapping, 21,* 191-201.

Hogan, P. C. (2003). *Cognitive science, literature, and the arts*. New York & London: Routledge.

Iacoboni, M. (2005). Understanding others: Imitation, language, and empathy. In S. Hurley & N. Chater (Eds.), *Perspectives on imitation: From neuroscience to social science* (Vol. 1): *Mechanisms of imitation and imitation in animals* (pp. 77-99). Cambridge, MA: MIT Press.

Kames, H. H., Lord. (1762). *Elements of criticism*. Edinburgh: A. Miller.

Kane, J. (2004). Poetry as right-hemispheric language. *Journal of Consciousness Studies, 11,* 21-59.

Keen, S. (2006). A theory of narrative empathy. *Narrative, 14,* 207-236.

Keysers, C., Wicker, B., Gazzola, V., Anton, J-L., Fogassi, L., & Gallese, V. (2004, April 22). A touching sight: SII/PV activation during the observation and experience of touch. *Neuron, 42,* 335-346.

Kuiken, D., & Miall, D. S. (2001). Numerically aided phenomenology: Procedures for investigating categories of experience. *FQS. Forum: Qualitative Social Research*, 2.1, February 2001. Retrieved February 27, 2007, from http://qualitative-research.net/fqs-texte/1-01/1-01kuikenmiall-e.htm

Kuiken, D., Miall, D. S., & Sikora, S. (2004). Forms of self-implication in literary reading. *Poetics Today, 25,* 171-203.

LeDoux, J. (1996). *The emotional brain: The mysterious underpinnings of emotional life.* New York: Simon & Schuster.

Mar, R. A. (2004). The neuropsychology of narrative: Story comprehension, story production and their interrelation. *Neuropsychologia, 42,* 1414-1434.

Meutsch, D., & Schmidt, S. J. (1985). On the role of conventions in understanding literary texts. *Poetics, 14,* 551-574.

Miall, D. S. (1995). Anticipation and feeling in literary response: A neuropsychological perspective. *Poetics, 23,* 275-298.

Miall, D. S. (2004). Episode structures in literary narratives. *Journal of Literary Semantics, 33,* 111-129.

Miall, D. S. (2006). *Literary reading: Empirical and theoretical studies.* New York: Peter Lang.

Miall, D. S., & Kuiken, D. (1994). Foregrounding, defamiliarization, and affect: Response to literary stories. *Poetics, 22,* 389-407.

Miall, D. S., & Kuiken, D. (1999). What is literariness? Three components of literary reading. *Discourse Processes, 28,* 121-138.

Miall, D. S., & Kuiken, D. (2001). Shifting perspectives: Readers' feelings and literary response. In W. van Peer & S. Chatman (Eds.), *New perspectives on narrative perspective* (pp. 289-301). Albany, NY: State University of New York Press.

Murdoch, I. (1970). *The sovereignty of good.* London: Routledge and Kegan Paul.

Oatley, K., & Mar, R. A. (2005). Evolutionary pre-adaptation and the idea of character in fiction. *Journal of Cultural and Evolutionary Psychology, 3,* 179-194.

O'Faoláin, S. (1980-1982). The trout. In *The collected stories of Seán O'Faoláin* (Vol. I, pp. 383-386). London: Constable.

Oliveri, M., Finocchiaro, C., Shapiro, K., Gangitano, M., Caramazza, A., & Pascual-Leone, A. (2004). All talk and no action: A transcranial magnetic stimulation study of motor cortex activation during action word production. *Journal of Cognitive Neuroscience, 16,* 374-381.

Posner, M. I., & DiGirolamo, G. J. (2000). Cognitive neuroscience: Origins and promise. *Psychological Bulletin, 126,* 873-889.

Rizzolatti, G. (2005). The mirror neuron system and imitation. In S. Hurley & N. Chater (Eds.), *Perspectives on imitation: From neuroscience to social science.* Vol. 1: *Mechanisms of imitation and imitation in animals* (pp. 55-76). Cambridge, MA: MIT Press.

Robinson, J. (2005). *Deeper than reason: Emotion and its role in literature, music, and art.* Oxford: Clarendon Press.

Shklovsky, V. (1965). Art as technique. In L. T. Lemon & M. J. Reis (Eds. and Trans.), *Russian formalist criticism: Four essays* (pp. 3-24). Lincoln, NE: University of Nebraska Press. (Original work published 1917.)

Singer, T., Seymour, B., O'Doherty, J., Kaube, H., Dolan, R. J., & Frith, C. D. (2004, February 20). Empathy for pain involves the affective but not sensory components of pain. *Science, 203,* 1157-1162.

Tettamanti, M., Buccino, G., Saccuman, M. C., Gallese, V., Dannal, M., Scifo, P., et al. (2005). Listening to action-related sentences activates fronto-parietal motor circuits. *Journal of Cognitive Neuroscience, 17,* 273-281.

Walton, K. L. (1990). *Mimesis as make-believe: On the foundations of the representational arts*. Cambridge, MA: Harvard University Press.

Williams, H. M. (1798). *A tour in Switzerland; or, A view of the present state of the government and manners of those cantons: With comparative sketches of the present state of Paris*. London: G. G. & J. Robinson.

Zunshine, L. (2006). *Why we read fiction: Theory of mind and the novel.* Columbus: Ohio State University Press.

Zwaan, R. A. (2004). The immersed experiencer: Toward an embodied theory of language comprehension. In B. H. Ross (Ed.), *The psychology of learning and motivation* (Vol. 44, pp. 35-62). New York: Academic.

Zwaan, R. A., & Radvansky, G. A. (1998). Situation models in language comprehension and memory. *Psychological Bulletin, 123,* 162-185.

CHAPTER 12

Film Aesthetics and the Embodied Brain

Torben Grodal

Films have a special position within aesthetics due to the fact that film is "total art." Films may use those visual sophistications of color, perspective and so on that characterize visual art. Film uses music extensively as well as a range of other sounds. Films, like theater, are able to portray nonverbal communication and surpass theater in its ability to provide close-ups of the human face and body to make aesthetic use of those modules that analyze and emotionalize interpersonal communication. Films often include architecture-like sculpturing of space and objects enhanced by film lighting. Film is based on storytelling, like literature. Furthermore, as pointed out by the Harvard psychologist Hugo Münsterberg in 1916, films have invented sophisticated techniques of their own to simulate human attention by means of, for instance, camera focus and camera movements, just as superimpositions and montage of images provides powerful tools for creating associative links and networks. Thus, moving pictures are (in tandem with video games and certain virtual reality applications) the most sophisticated simulation of humans experience by the interaction of the embodied brain and the world (see Anderson, 1996). This complexity demands and makes possible a series of higher-order integrative processes to make a unified aesthetic experience out of these different fields. The most important tools of integration are narrative, emotions, and feelings.

The drive for inventing films was to make a medium that was able to mimetically simulate the visual world in motion. This does not mean that all aesthetic effects of films are necessarily based on realism. Films may enhance and boost or tone down any of the effects of the thousands of mental devices that support a realist world representation. The classical film scholar Rudolf Arnheim (1957, 1974/1954), who was inspired by Gestalt psychology, thought that what made film art possible was all the ways in which film could use its deviations from natural vision to create emphasis, for instance by using lack of depth or lack of color. Fantasy films create effects by dispensing with some or many fundamental aspects of reality. Films manipulate the natural coupling of perceptual features to make "impossible" experiences. Thus, in *Vertigo,* Hitchcock produced the famous vertigo shot by tracking in on a stairwell and at the same time continual changing the lens from tele to wide angle. Some elements in the picture (object size) then suggest approach, whereas the transformation from tele to wide angle increased the visual field that in real life would indicate increased distance, and this short-circuiting of perceptual processes creates vertigo.

FILM EXPERIENCE AND BRAIN ARCHITECTURE

Films need not employ all these capabilities in all circumstances. For example, by focusing on basic perceptual processes, certain art and experimental films may make stimuli that are abstract or only rudimentarily mimetic and figurative. This has the effect of foregrounding the basic processes in the visual cortex, and thereby not allowing the stimuli to be integrated into a larger "realist" framework. The brain is built for guiding the body around and to perceive objects and spaces, not to focus on abstract forms, colors, and such. I have (Grodal, 1997) called such experiences that activate perception in relative isolation from other experiences and in relative isolation from distinct emotional content *intense*. Intense feelings may often seem to indicate some hidden meanings, because built-in mechanisms are preset to try to find some figurative meaning and recruit some meaningful associations down the line.

Other films, like many music videos and lyrical sequences in narrative films, foreground images and rudimentary scenes as part of associative processes and networks (probably predominantly in the temporal and parietal cortex). Such associations are always tagged with some emotional values that provide crude but rich emotional charge and markers to such associations (Damasio, 1999), such as associations linked to feelings of fear, lust, happiness, and so on. To the extent that such associations are unable to be linked to (frontal) structures that are associated functionally to agencies that may act out such emotions in unambiguous settings, I have called them *saturated* (see Grodal, 1997). The reason is that there are no action patterns available that can transform the feelings into action-oriented emotions. Such saturated associations may be felt as possessing very deep meaning.

Some films and most television sitcoms may narrowly focus on social intelligence in tandem with verbal and nonverbal communication. Most films, however, are mainly focused on narrative action and portray people moving through space and time in pursuit of some goals. The visual and associative material becomes linked to motor actions. Thus, the emotions evoked by matching the incoming images with stored emotion-charged memories become *tense* (see Grodal, 1997), because the motor activation in premotor and motor cortex is felt as tensity, as an urge to act.

To a certain degree then, individual types of film may be characterized by what brain region's activity they foreground because this will characterize specific dimensions in the aesthetic experience, like the difference between intense, saturated, and tense experiences. The typical film is dominantly narrative, and the basic perceptual processes are soaked up as raw material for the actions and forward-directed expectations of outcomes, so that the average viewer is unable to remember the details of the visual style elements. Especially during fast cutting or quick camera movements, capacity limitations will narrowly focus our conscious experience on these action-relevant elements. Thus, films typically integrate the perceptual, the cognitive, and the emotional elements that may also exist in other arts by means of narrative.

Before TV and home movie theaters film was consumed in dark cinemas by projecting images and sounds that the spectator is forced to perceive. A visitor to a museum and gallery is free to walk around, focus on different paintings; the time used on a given painting is controlled by the visitor. In contrast, the outline of the viewer's attention and the temporal order and the speed of the progression of the film are outside the viewer's control, and the screen covers large parts of the viewers' central field of vision. The viewer is even unable to pause or to go back to a previous scene, whereas reading a story may provide some freedom. Films, therefore, need to be strongly fascinating to compensate for the lack of freedom and the way in which viewers cannot interact with their physical surroundings. Hence, films for mass audiences have exclusively been narrative films, based on very strong emotional involvement to glue viewers to the screen. The films have furthermore typically been told in a way that was close to one or a few characters' point of view. The visual and acoustic elements, the nonverbal communication of film acting, and especially the film music have been subordinated to or integrated in the narrative. Thus, mainstream films are strongly narrative, whereas art films often diminish the narrative elements and may focus on the visual elements. Let us therefore start to look at how narratives function and then analyze how art films cater to more acquired tastes.

The basic story-creating emotions are those that are supported by the sympathetic nervous system aimed at active coping, like in fight or flight. Even quests for mates as in romantic comedies often presuppose active coping. The endings may, however, be situations that evoke parasympathetic reactions that support relaxation, food intake, and sex, because stories typically end when some major goals are achieved. Muscle tension as measured by EMG also rises through a fascinating story and drops after the conclusion (see Malmo, 1975), creating pleasant feelings of closure. Parasympathetic reactions are linked to relaxation, and also food intake and sex.

STORYTELLING AND PRIMITIVE SELF-EMOTIONS

The central feature of the most basic and simple stories in films is that they derive their focus and interest from a living being that feels, perceives, and acts (the hero, the main character). This is not unique to films; folktales, for instance, always focus on stories that have one main character, the hero. This hero-agency's concerns are the source of interest, value, and emotions for everything in the story. Only for short periods will basic storytelling dwell on something that is not the very explicit concern of some living being. The hero-agencies need not be a human being; basic storytelling for children abounds in animal heroes like fish, deer, or mice. But the hero needs to be able to perceive, to feel basic emotions, and to act and communicate.

It is reasonable to believe that the hero is in some dimension a vicarious representative of the viewer and her or his core self. Panksepp (1999) described how the core self is supported by structures that he locates in the periaqueductal gray. Panksepp states that "The extended PAG elaborates a visceral type map of the body along with basic neural representations of pain, fear, anger, separation-distress, sexual and maternal behavior systems" (p. 121). The primitive self integrates valorizations deriving from basic (limbic) emotion systems with incoming perceptual information, and with primitive response schemas (action schemas). Panksepp emphasizes that the self is more closely related to the motor system than to the incoming sensory information. This is in accordance with, for instance, Frijda's (1986) statement that emotions are action tendencies and with Nöe and O'Regan's (2001) emphasis on the motor basis of perception. Ramachandran and Hirstein (1999) further emphasize that the temporal cortex has an important function for welding together perception, emotion, and action, for instance by providing a feeling of a body image.

The descriptions of how basic self-structures and body image structures weld together perceptions, basic emotions and action fit perfectly with how canonical stories work (see Bordwell, 1986; Greimas, 1983; Grodal, 1997; Propp, 1968). Such stories are, in a fundamental manner, software for the superior integration of the basic agency functions. A canonical narrative is focused on a hero that sees this, feels this, thinks that, and does that—what I have called the PECMA flow, an abbreviation of Perception, Emotion, Cognition, Motor Action (see Grodal, 1997, 2006, 2009). Strong physical self-feelings are activated when the hero fights dragons, searches for princesses or princes and anticipates upcoming dangers or opportunities. All the daily trivia are peeled away. In the animated film *Finding Nemo,* Nemo's father, the clown fish, loses his son, which makes him engage in a series of actions to regain his son. It does not matter that the agent is a clown fish because the strong basic emotions related to separation, fear, and anger, in tandem with the appropriate actions, anchor the experience.

As soon as a salient agent appears on the screen, viewers will start to try to model its intentions, feelings, and actions to the degree of course that the story supports such a modeling. Due to the viewing (or listening) conditions the concrete self-awareness of the viewer (or listener), the empirical I of the viewer, is not relevant for the actions on the screen, and thus the film is free to "hijack" the viewer's self-functions. The more intense action presented and the more fundamental the emotional motives implicated, the stronger the viewer's involvement (all other factors being equal). More than a hundred years of filmmaking has very much been aimed at welding together some primal emotions and actions that can modulate such emotions (chase scenes, horror scenes, love scenes, detection scenes, etc.). Those techniques linked to creating strong emotional involvement by actions like the basic mammalian play-chase scenarios of hiding or chasing (see Steen & Owens, 2001) have been linked to techniques that, via close-ups of facial expressions, enhance the simulation of emotions through the facial recognition modules in the ventral part of the temporal lobe and their limbic connections. To be able to simulate other beings makes functional and adaptive sense because this provides an easy way to learn by imitative simulation (see Bandura 1994; Gibbs Jr., 2006).

Imitative simulation theory (ST) fits with aspects of the so-called mirror-neuron theory (Rizzolati, Craighero, & Fadiga, 2002). When observing basic actions such as grasping, mirror neurons in the pre-motor cortex fire in a way similar to how they will fire if the observer performs the grasping. Thus, the understanding of some types of behavior can be apprehended in a simulation of that behavior. Simple simulation is probably not the whole truth about understanding other peoples' minds, and one of the simplest reasons for that is that the self-agency is often confronted with other agencies so that there would be no capacity, no circuits to model those others, just as the close connection between emotions and action tendencies in simulations would create problems. Especially in cases of confronting "villains" involving opponents with emotions and motives quite opposite to "self-agencies" simulations would be difficult and confusing. For instance, in simulating the fear of a possible victim of Dracula, the viewer should also be forced to simulate Dracula's lustful aggression.

A rival theory hypothesizes that we have special brain functions with some built-in theories and inference rules (a la folk psychology) that are used to infer what other people think (as in the Theory of Mind (ToM) (see Baron-Cohen, 1995). In order to compare simulation theories with Theory of Mind theories, Vogeley and Newen (2002) made some experiments with people reading different stories. Two types aimed at evoking self, close to basic film story telling; one was a "physical" story told in the third person about how a burglar performed his job, thus integrating self-supported actions; the other was a story in the first person about going to London without an umbrella when it starts to rain. Two story types were designed to evoke ToM functions and contained several actors; one consisted of a story of a burglar and a policeman; another of a person who had been robbed by a burglar who is then confronted by a policeman. Self-stories activated the right temporoparietal cortex and the anterior cingulate cortex, but further led to a significant increase in the right pre-motor and motor cortex, and bilaterally in the precuneus. Vogeley describes the function of the right inferior temporoparietal cortex as important for navigating through virtual-reality scenes, and that the activation of this brain structure may be important for a body representation as a center of egocentric experiential space. It is furthermore highly interesting that self-centered stories provide a significant increase of activation in the motor and pre-motor cortex, providing support for the idea that the basic story experience consists of welding together emotions with body images and motor actions. ToM stories activated the right anterior cingulate cortex and left temporopolar cortex. It makes sense that the brain has developed mechanisms, predominantly located in the anterior cingulate cortex, to deal with the more advanced task of dealing with other minds.

THE PECMA FLOW AND VISUAL AESTHETICS OF MENTAL LIFE

Those stories that Vogeley and Newen (2002) analyzed were induced by reading. Watching film in addition relies on numerous audiovisual skills. The general mechanisms that mold film watching are a continuous flow of audiovisual stimuli entering the ears and the eyes, and analyzed in the visual and acoustic cortices. The association cortices make provisions in processing preliminary form and semantic meaning, as does the limbic system for processing emotional charge in connections to self-functions. Furthermore, prefrontal structures are involved in providing causal structures and intentionality, just as pre-motor (and motor) cortices are activated to simulate actions. The forward processing is supplemented with feedback cascades (see Edelman et al., 2000). As mentioned, I have called the forward processing flow for the PECMA flow. Microsituations will be a series of small PECMA-PECMA-PECMA . . . cycles, because motor actions, including those actions that serve to pick up information, will produce new perceptual situations.

For normal adults, vivid qualia are something that is an aspect of the perception of the exterior world, which is intimately linked to the way in which the exterior world is a possible object for motor actions. It has even been hypothesized by (among others) Noë and O'Regan (2001) that qualia are ways in which those phenomena that are possible objects for motor actions are flagged. In contrast, the inner world of thoughts, feelings, and imaginations only has vague or nonexistent qualia. Films, however, may try to provide a subjective tone to visualize how the exterior world may be colored by or is imagined in the embodied brain. A series of visual effects are linked to tampering with the PECMA flow to produce special experiences that you might describe as a kind of blend between what is experienced as the interior mental space and what is experienced as the exterior physical space.

Films are able to simulate and manipulate our natural vision in time, and this time dimension provides a series of effects unique to films. Films are able to simulate characters that interact, feel, and intend in relation to a world that is vividly perceived and illusionistically experienced as a world that enables interaction. As emotions are action tendencies, the viewer is cued into simulating strong emotions by situations that not only cue emotions but also allow for goal-directed actions to release the emotions. Further, because the film world is a simulation of a live world, films have unique tools for evoking strong subjective emotions by impeding, blocking, or otherwise filtering the perceptual access to such a live world, because this is experienced in a context of time and motion. Thus, the film world may freeze, slow, or speed up to fast motion. Slow motion (as in scenes in *Elvira Madigan*) and freeze frames (as the famous last frame in Truffaut's *The 400 Blows*) provide a strong lyrical emphasis. A painting is, by definition, a dead world, and at the same time an object in space that you may actively scrutinize so spectators do not have the same vivid feeling of a frozen world. However, when the film world suddenly freezes in a strongly emotional situation for a character, the brain may experience the freeze as an expression of some brain-internal, emotion-induced deviation, a subjective feeling, analogous to unclear vision when you are dizzy. Because the film activates all those mental capacities that we use to experience the real world, viewers strongly feel visual modifications as mental, brain-interior processes.

Other mood-enhancing and lyrical devices are linked to synaesthesia. Prominently, film uses film lighting to represent the action potentials of the visual field and thus also to provide some tactile synaesthetic qualities to the images (Grodal, 2005). The main tool is to control the relation between the ambient (diffuse) and the directed light. The directed light (like sunlight directly from the sun) casts shadows, and shadows are very important for the visual brain's analysis of three-dimensional objects to provide contours and such. Directed light is therefore called "sharp" to indicate how it provides very solid tactile qualities to an object. In order for the texture of the object to be visible, you also need some ambient light that may soften the shadows. The directed light may, for instance, make the nose ridge stand out to provide a sculptural, solid quality; whereas the ambient light prevents one side of the head from being dark or invisible. In contrast, very ambient light, as that created by fog or by thick clouds, prevents shadows and thus makes the objects soft and nearly two-dimensional. Strongly directed light also destroys our perception of solid, sculptural objects, but here the reason is that the shadows distort our object recognition, as when one side of the face is totally dark. Backlight will deprive objects of their three-dimensionality and therefore provide them with a "mental," spiritual feel, whereas underlighting is uncanny, because the brain is preset to assume that light comes from above, from the sun. Thus, our vision has built-in links to the tactile qualities of objects that represent some standard assumptions, because the tactile qualities of an object do not change because of a change of lighting. Filmmakers may therefore make soft, lyrical, and mental images by playing with the visual system's innate architecture.

Even if a narrative film shows scenes in which nothing happens for a prolonged period of time and in which there are no vivid protagonist concerns, the viewer may, after a short period of time, feel that the emotional tenseness typical of a setting imbued with action tendencies disappears and is transformed into saturated feelings. The reason might be that the brain's processing of visual input is preset for supporting actions performed by agencies, or to perform "pseudoactions," like making propositions that may also be supported by pre-motor and motor cortex and thus provide focus to the experience. The psychologist Malmo (1975) describes an experiment with giving patients curare that blocked out any feedback from the muscular neurons. The result was that the patients were unable to have focused thoughts and were reduced to having streams of consciousness. The language center of Broca is part of the pre-motor cortex, and propositions may be seen as motor acts. So if there are no actions to perform in a film scene, no propositions to make, just perceptions that an alien agency (the filmmaker) let stay on the screen, the brain may return to a "temporal-parietal" associative default mode underpinned by saturated feelings in which it performs an unfocused search for some (hidden) meaning. In real life, we will ourselves feel responsible for finding some meaning when we watch a particular scene. However, films are ambiguous in the sense that on one hand the images may be real-life scenes, on the other hand if their meaning is not obvious (as they would be if they for instance showed a tiger attacking a protagonist), the viewer may feel that the images are communications from the director that somehow guarantee that there are some hidden meanings.

Art film directors like Tarkovsky, Lynch, or Antonioni often show such scenes that have no obvious narrative sense. The effect will be even more complicated if the scenes have some recurrent salient images without any obvious meaning, like Tarkovsky's use of fire and also water in a film like *The Mirror [Zerkalo]*. Associations may build up, the nodes connecting fire with an increasing number of scenes in the film will provide saturated feelings of importance and meaning, although there is no way that these feelings can be transformed into a propositional and unambiguous content, like fire equals love, or fire equals death. Such feelings of depth and meaning due to saturated associations may even go in tandem with religious feelings that are also thought partly to be effects of the temporal cortex (see Newberg & D'Aquili, 1998).

The many different types of saturated mood modulations described above may be used for short periods of time in mainstream films to support action-induced feelings. However, an extensive use of such devices only takes place in art films (see Grodal, 2000), which have a much smaller audience than mainstream narrative films. It seems that the mental processes involved in blocking the flow and focusing on associations are more difficult to perform than to simulate actions motivated by basic needs. It is much more difficult than to activate primitive self-emotions, and furthermore the viewers have to perform mental metaoperations by taking an analytical stance on their experiences. The stories in art films are furthermore often metastories, in the sense that they often focus on an effort to bring cohesion in one's life and to find one's true identity (Bergman, Tarkovsky, Wenders, and Lynch are filmmaker who often focus on such "metaquestions"). Antonio Damasio (1999) sketched a model of the self with three steps: a basic level, a core self, and an autobiographical self. The core self organizes those basic emotions that Panksaap also described, whereas the autobiographical self consists of those higher mental functions that try to achieve consistency in values and understanding over extended periods of time in a person's life. Such processes are of course much more abstract and demand more mental energy than what is related to basic situations.

THE BRAIN'S REALITY STATUS, EVALUATIONS, AND FILM

The fact that images may be felt as aspects of inner life points to the issue of the status of reality. The brain must tag the current content of consciousness in such a way that its reality status and its relevance for ongoing actions are obvious. If we confused dreams, thoughts, or memories with what is our current environment, we would have some troubles; but if we were not able to represent the relevance of such "offline" perceptions, emotions, and actions, we would not be able to let our current behavior be properly influenced by the thoughts and experiences accumulated in the brain, and we would not be able to have a constructive use of our imagination. Film viewing demands very complex evaluations of reality status. The activity as such demands that you engage in the narrative without losing a tacit knowledge about its fictitiousness. Within that frame, there are multiple levels of reality from subjective states like dreams and lyrical streams of consciousness, via pretended real actions and pretended actions (like in comedies where it is important that you know that some of the characters pretend, to metafictions that watch the narrative from a point outside the narrative, as in many of Greenaway's films).

The evolutionary root of our ability to distinguish several levels of reality and also to enjoy fiction is probably to be found in the mammalian ability to chase play. To play demands that you are able to perform a given behavior, say to chase or be chased, in two different modes, a serious mode and a pretend mode. The chaser as well as the chased needs to feel some of the emotions that are appropriate for their roles, but at the same time they need some other markers that inhibit a full role-identification and that allow them to feel some kind of gratification even when they, for instance, play the chased. Brain structures invented for the mammalian training mode chase play have then been reused for new purposes, like an advanced ability to plan and hypothesize. Storytelling is a latecomer that allows us to watch fiction films.

A special development of the play modes that has great importance for films is laughter and humor, as such reactions are dominant in a large group of those films that are not directly chase play (as action, thriller, etc.). Laughter and different forms of humor are special modes to modify the reality status of the actions and emotions involved. Provine (2000) traces aspects of the laughter-humor development back to mechanisms that allowed our ancestors to accept and to be pleased by being touched by others during playing, expressed in tickle pleasure. Our smile goes back to the play faces that monkeys have used when engaging in playful activities, including pretend activities. Humor appreciation appears to be based in the lower frontal lobes of the brain, a location associated with social and emotional judgment and planning (for an overview of neural correlates of laughter and humor see Wild, Rodden, Grodd, & Ruch, 2003). Laughter and humor activate the limbic pleasure center the nucleus accumbens.

There are many causes of comic reactions, but the common denominator is that they are triggered by arousal (see Grodal, 1997). Besides lack of motor control (falling, clumsiness, for instance), cognitive paradoxes and obsessive behavior, a very important group of causes of humor in film is a series of negative social emotions like shame. Comic reactions transform such strongly negative reactions to pleasure by redefining the reality status: we do not need to take these experiences for real (although the situations that provide the negative arousal that is transformed to pleasure are often very real). Laughter is therefore a safety valve that allows us to escape from negative experiences and soften social communication by discontinuing coping. However, those decision-making processes that allow us to decide whether we want to laugh or not are very complicated and very context sensitive. Often we even must choose between two bail-out mechanisms that have two opposing hedonic valences: sad crying or pleasurable laughter. Both reactions supplant world-directed coping with self-modification. Sadness and laughter to a degree share the same neuronal support, and there is a kind of brain damage that will make the patients laugh or cry due to damage to links between frontal cognitive centers that analyze causes and eliciting conditions for laughter and crying and those centers in the cerebellum and brainstem that control crying and laughter (Parvizi et al., 2001). And both reactions presuppose some mental mechanisms that determine when to give up coping. Thus, mechanisms to evaluate reality status are used to provide aesthetic effects in four dimensions. The first dimension relates to distinguishing between whether something takes place in the exterior world or in the mind, articulating tenseness vs. saturation (or intensity). The second dimension relates to modifications of the hedonic valence (the place of emotions on a positive/negative scale) and strength of the emotions induced by film events by modifications of its felt reality. The third dimension relates to the degree of seriousness vs. pretend and playing, and this dimension is often used, as in the case of humor and laughter, to modify the second dimension. The fourth dimension consists of playing with the relation between the real and the supernatural (as in horror films or fairy tales). Modulating or subverting reality-status mechanisms often evokes strong feelings that can be used for aesthetic purposes in mainstream films as well as in art films.

BRAIN ARCHITECTURE AND FILM AESTHETICS

Most films will generally represent the exterior world. Often, therefore, films are described in relation to what they are telling about the exterior world, including persons inhabiting this world. Alternatively, art may be described as culturally produced ways to stimulate and modulate innate features of the brain. This is especially pertinent with regard to the question of the relation between feelings and meaning in films. It is often suggested that art in general is a vehicle of deep meanings about life and the world, and that a brain approach would be reductionist. My position is that the obvious and banal meanings like love, death, friendship, illness, quest for safety, and such, are also the most profound. Operas and films often have ultrabanal storylines, and even complicated art films like *Last Year in Marienbad* or *Memento* (that was actually inspired by Damasio's work) are only complicated because the directors scrambled the narratives. The distinctive mark of art is therefore the ability to make such common human experiences highly salient. The fundamental question in relation to (film) art is therefore not *what* they mean but *how* they mean.

The salience is sometimes provided by imitating and enhancing our natural perceptual, emotional, and cognitive capabilities, such as by providing close-ups, optimal lighting conditions, easy-to-understand facial expressions, perceptual contrasts, and so on. But often the salience is provided by short-circuiting mental functions. As mentioned, one way films do this is by blocking or impeding the PECMA flow, for instance, by providing unfocused chains of saturated images. Another way to short-circuit is, as described previously, to provide vertiginous experiences by short-circuiting our ability to establish an unambiguous reality status, for instance in films about unusual mental states, supernatural phenomena, or comic manipulation of emotional responses.

Damasio pointed out (1999, p. 188) that the closest match to the working of consciousness is the storytelling in film. Thus, the study of film aesthetics is a two-way street. On the one hand, knowledge of brain architecture provides insights into the reasons for storytelling in film, and on the other hand, film is a model example of how different mental functions cooperate and how those schemata that control storytelling function as the superior integrative mechanisms for coordinating the basic PECMA flow. In contrast to lab experiments, films often show human interaction with each other and the world in a naturalistic setting as a continuous flow of perceptual, emotional, cognitive, and enactive processes.

REFERENCES

Anderson, J. D. (1996). *The reality of illusion: An ecological approach to cognitive film theory.* Carbondale: Southern Illinois University Press.

Arnheim, R. (1957). *Film as art.* Berkeley, CA: University of California Press.

Arnheim, R. (1974/1954): *Art and visual perception: A psychology of the creative eye.* Berkeley, CA: University of California Press.

Bandura, A. (1994). Social cognitive theory of mass communication. In J. Bryant & D. Zillmann (Eds.), *Media effects. Advances in theory and research.* Hillsdale, NJ: Lawrence Erlbaum Associates.

Baron-Cohen, S. (1995). *Mindblindness.* Cambridge, MA: MIT Press.

Bordwell, D. (1986). *Narration in the fiction film.* London: Methuen.

Damasio, A. (1999). *The feeling of what happens. Body and emotion in the making of consciousness.* New York: Harcourt, Brace & Co.

Frijda, N. (1986). *The emotions.* Cambridge: Cambridge University Press.

Greimas, J. A. (1983/1966). *Structural semantics: An attempt at a method.* Lincoln: University of Nebraska Press.

Grodal, T. (1997) *Moving pictures. A new theory of film genres, feelings and cognition.* Oxford: Clarendon/Oxford University Press.

Grodal, T. (2000). Art film, the transient body and the permanent soul. *Aura, 6*, 33-53

Grodal, T. (2005). Film lighting and mood. In J. Anderson & B. Anderson (Eds.), *Motion picture theory: Ecological considerations* (pp. 152-163). Carbondale: Southern Illinois University Press.

Grodal, T. (2006, Summer). The PECMA flow. A general theory of visual aesthetics. *Film Studies, 8*, 1-11.

Grodal, T. (2009). *Embodied visions. Evaluation, emotion, culture and film.* New York: Oxford University Press.

Malmo, R. B. (1975). *On emotions, needs, and our archaic brain.* New York: Holt, Rinehart and Winston.

Newberg, A. B., & D'Aquili, E. G. (1998). The neuropsychology of religious experience. In H. G. Koenig et al. (Eds.), *Handbook of religion and mental health* (pp. 75-94). San Diego: Academic Press.

Noë, A., & O'Regan, K. (2001). A sensori-motor account of vision and visual consciousness. *Behavioral and Brain Sciences, 24*, 5.

Panksepp, J. (1999). The periconscious substrates of consciousness. Affective states and the evolutionary origins of the self. In S. Gallagher & J. Shear (Eds.), *Models of the self* (pp. 113-130). Exeter: Imprint Academic

Propp, V. (1968). *Morphology of the folktale.* Austin, TX: University of Texas Press.

Provine, R. R. (2000). *Laughter. A scientific investigation.* New York: Penguin.

Rizzolati, G., Craighero, L., & Fadiga, L. (2002). The mirror systems in humans. In M. Stamenov & V. Gallese (Eds.), *Mirror neurons and the evolution of brain and language* (pp. 37-59). Amsterdam/Philadelphia: John Benjamins.

Stamenov, M., & Gallese, V. (Eds.). (2002). *Mirror neurons and the evolution of brain and language*. Amsterdam/Philadelphia: John Benjamins.

Steen, F. F., & Owens, S. A. (2001). Evolution's pedagogy: An adaptiationist model of pretense and entertainment. *Journal of Cognition and Culture, 1*, 289-321.

Vogeley, K., & Newen, A. (2002). Mirror neurons and the self construct. In M. Stamenov & V. Gallese (Eds.), *Mirror neurons and the evolution of brain and language* (pp. 135-150). Amsterdam/Philadelphia: John Benjamins.

Wild, B., Rodden, F., Grodd, W., & Ruch, W. (2003). Neural correlates of laughter and humour. *Brain, 126*, 2121-2213.

CHAPTER 13

Conscious Experience of Pleasure in Art

Oshin Vartanian

Aesthetic experiences are common phenomena. We have them when we consciously engage in paradigmatic aesthetic acts such as viewing movies, listening to music, or reading a book, but also when we embrace a loved one or smell the scent of food in a good restaurant. The extent to which such experiences have been attributed to relative contributions of "cold" cognition and "hot" emotion has been a source of constant debate in psychology and philosophy, and despite some recent claims to the contrary (see Freedberg & Gallese, 2007) remains a contentious issue. For example, an astonishingly large number of aesthetic phenomena can be accounted for using purely cognitive models of aesthetic experience that do not explicitly evoke emotion in the process at all (see Martindale, 2001). At the very least, such evidence suggests that emotional engagement may not be a necessary precondition for aesthetic experiences.

The aim of this chapter is not to engage in this debate, but to achieve a different goal altogether. I will present a neural theory for the conscious experience of pleasure in art that is founded on recent insights from the neuroscience of emotion. I agree with others in this volume (Brown & Dissanayake) that we need more sophisticated theories of emotion to account for the role of emotion and pleasure in the aesthetic experience, and I think that one such theory has emerged recently. Then, I will discuss how recent findings from neuroaesthetics map onto this model of emotion, and what the findings tell us about the role of pleasure in the aesthetic experience. By definition, this discussion will be relevant only for those aesthetic experiences that involve felt pleasure. I will leave it to others to determine how widespread this category of aesthetic experience is.

Pleasure in Aesthetic Experience

When we observe and interact with artworks, we can become conscious of the experience of pleasure. Although few would disagree that this sensation involves cognitive and visceral processes (see Zaidel, 2005), to date no theory has successfully accounted for the role that the conscious experience of pleasure plays in such aesthetic experiences. In the context of this chapter, I will leave out the role of unconscious affective states in experiencing pleasure (but see Berridge & Winkielman, 2003; Winkielman & Berridge, 2004). This pragmatic decision is based on the fact that because most studies in aesthetics ask subjects to generate evaluations, currently more data are available for addressing the question of conscious rather than unconscious processing. Having limited the discussion to the conscious experience of pleasure, there is a good chance that findings from neuroscience can contribute to constructing better psychological models of aesthetic experience in at least two ways. First, we must consider neuroscientific research on the *subjective experience of emotion*, at least insofar as it concerns the experience of pleasant and unpleasant affective states, and set boundary conditions for testing its involvement in the aesthetic experience. Note that I am not equating the experience of pleasure with the experience of emotion. Rather, because I will argue that emotions are evoked upon conscious awareness of core affect (Barrett, Mesquita, Ochsner, & Gross, 2007), it would seem that a theory of conscious experience of pleasure must make contact with a theory on the experience of emotion.

In addition, I take it for granted that the mechanisms that are evoked leading to the conscious experience of pleasure in relation to art are no different than those evoked by the conscious experience of pleasure while evaluating other stimuli (see also Zaidel, 2005). This is in the spirit of evidence in the neurosciences that has emphasized the role of *process* over that of the *stimulus* (Stephan et al., 2003), as well as the evolutionary unlikelihood that the brain would rely on different neural circuitries for instantiating conscious pleasure as a function of the stimulus under consideration.

Part of the problem in determining the place of conscious pleasure in the aesthetic experience is related to our current level of knowledge about the precise sequence of processes that lead to affective states associated with viewing artworks. Although recently promising models have been proposed that can shed light on this issue (e.g., Chatterjee, 2003; Leder, Belke, Oeberst, & Angustin, 2004), some of their critical aspects have yet to be tested. Testing such models is critical because the sequencing question speaks to cause-and-effect relations in the overall experience mechanism, beginning with exposure to the artwork and culminating in the formation of an evaluation about the artwork. In fact, whether the act of forming an evaluation about the artwork is integral to having an aesthetic experience is open to debate, regardless of the cognitive or emotional nature of that evaluation (see Chatterjee, 2003). Even allowing that it may be, it has yet to be determined whether affective evaluative judgments follow or precede cognitive evaluative judgments, a question that I will address in the last part of this chapter.

Second, although the focus in this chapter will be on visual art in the form of paintings, we need not limit our scope to only those studies that have used paintings as stimuli. For example, many studies have investigated the role of various brain structures in viewing faces that vary in attractiveness, or rating faces on attractiveness in the scanner. Many such studies have found that rating faces on attractiveness activates reward and emotion circuitries in the brain that are also activated during pleasurable experiences (see Senior, 2003). Results from these studies can shed light on the key question under consideration here: Is the conscious experience of pleasure related to the conscious experience of emotion in aesthetic experience?

Outline

This chapter will be organized as follows: First, because I have argued that a theory about the conscious experience of pleasure must make contact with a theory on the experience of emotion, I will sketch out the basic tenets of a recently proposed neurobiological theory of emotional experience that I believe is amenable to such a "bridging" approach (see Barrett et al., 2007). Second, I will sketch out and review an information-processing model of aesthetic experience that has discussed the role of affect and emotion in the process (i.e., Leder et al., 2004) and will show how Barrett et al.'s (2007) model of emotion can form the neurobiological basis for the role of affect and emotion in Leder et al.'s (2004) model of aesthetic experience. Third, I will review some of the available literature on the aesthetic evaluation of paintings and faces in the fMRI scanner to highlight what the results can contribute to the question of emotion and pleasure in aesthetic experience. Finally, I will sketch out a basic scheme for studying the contribution of pleasure to aesthetic experience.

NEUROSCIENCE OF EMOTION EXPERIENCE

Three large meta-analyses of neuroimaging studies of emotion have appeared recently in the literature (Barrett & Wager, 2006; Murphy, Nimmo-Smith, & Lawrence, 2003; Phan, Wager, Taylor, & Liberzon, 2002). Two main conclusions can be drawn from the overall pattern of results: First, although emotion engages a distributed network of structures in the brain, a preliminary sketch can be made of a number of structures that form a relatively consistent core of this system. Second, no dissociable activation pattern can be mapped out for discrete emotions such as fear, anger, happiness, or sadness. Rather, the experience of these emotions seems to be correlated with the activation of a largely overlapping network of areas. While this finding may be problematic for certain programs of research that seek to highlight dissociable cortical systems corresponding to dissociable (basic) emotions, it is strongly supportive of a research program that views emotion as the mental representation of core affect as it interacts with the environment (Russell, 2003). This program of research is discussed below.

Core Affect and Emotion

Barrett et al.'s (2007) model of the experience of emotion takes at its departing point John Searle's (2000) biologically grounded philosophical framework for the study of emotion. Briefly, "biological naturalism" has three tenets. First, an adequate account of an emotional experience requires not only a specification of its cause(s), but also a specification of its content (i.e., what is felt by the person). Second, and related to the first tenet, the content of an emotional experience can not be reduced to its cause(s). This tenet states that although an emotion can be linked to features of brain activity, the experience of that emotion encompasses more than the brain activity alone. The experience of emotion is an emergent property that has phenomenological as well as neurobiological features, and although the two features are related, they denote different entities. Third, because the experience of emotion is a conscious state, it only exists from a first-person point of view. This means that to study the experience of emotion, it is necessary to ask people what they feel. The flipside of this statement implies that to study the experience of emotion, reliance on third-person measures will not be sufficient.

Starting from the vantage point of biological naturalism, Barrett et al. (2007) have developed a model of emotional experience that encompasses both its phenomenological and its neurobiological features. The key feature of Barrett et al.'s (2007) model is the concept of core affect (Russell, 2003) is a state of pleasure or displeasure that has content. It encompasses knowledge about whether an object or event is good or bad, helpful or harmful, rewarding or threatening. In turn, the experience of emotion constitutes the mental representation of such core affective states. In support of this view, they cite a large body of evidence that places states of pleasure or displeasure as the core of the mental representation of emotions. Naturally, Barrett et al. (2007) do not claim that emotional experiences can be reduced to states of pleasure or displeasure, but that a state of pleasure or displeasure is a necessary building block for the experience of emotion. They argue that an emotion is experienced when a person forms a mental representation of a core-affective state that involves a state of pleasure or displeasure, but the emotion can also involve other assessments or evaluations of the relationship between the organism and the environment. The key idea here is that the experience of emotion is a state of mind that has affective and conceptual components. The affective component is a state of pleasure or displeasure encapsulated by core affect. The conceptual component is the mental representation of the affective state that informs the organism about his or her relationship to the environment. Because core affect is a dynamic state, our psychological construal of the environment changes as a function of variations in the state of core affect.

Brain Substrates of Core Affect

As mentioned above, although it is true that neuroimaging studies of emotion have not linked discrete or basic emotions (fear, anger, etc.) to dissociable neural signatures (Barrett & Wager, 2006; Murphy et al., 2003; Phan et al., 2002), the ventral portion of the human brain includes two neural systems that in conjunction appear to mediate core affect. There is much evidence supporting the role of the ventral portion of the human brain in the computation of value (Bechara, Damasio, & Damasio, 2000; Kringelbach & Rolls, 2004), where value is understood as the mental representation of how the sensory properties of an object or an event affect the organism's state. In turn, this allows for the adjustment of the organism's core affect in relation to prior experiences with the object or event. This appears to be achieved through the function of two dissociable but interdependent neural systems.

The first neural system is composed of the basolateral complex of the amygdala, the central and lateral aspects of the orbitofrontal cortex, and the anterior insula (Figure 1). This system generates a value-based representation of the object, including its sensory properties and its impact on the organism. In this integrated system, the basolateral complex of the amygdala codes the original value of the stimulus, the central and lateral aspects of the orbitofrontal cortex code the context-dependent value of the stimulus, and the anterior insula codes for interoceptive cues. In combination, these three structures generate an initial value-based representation of the stimulus that includes information about its sensory properties and what this information means to the organism.

The second neural circuit involves the ventromedial prefrontal cortex and its links with the anterior cingulate cortex and the amygdala (Figure 1). Receiving value-based input from the first circuit, the second circuit provides what Barrett et al. (2007) refer to as an "affective working memory" such that its content can form the basis for choices, decisions, and judgments. In other words, the representations formed by the second circuit, in particular the ventromedial prefrontal cortex, enable the organism to make choices, decisions, and judgments that are based on feelings and intuitions rather than abstract rules.

CORE AFFECT AND AESTHETIC EXPERIENCE

There is much evidence in support of the specific functions that Barrett et al. (2007) have ascribed to the structures in the two neural circuits involved in core

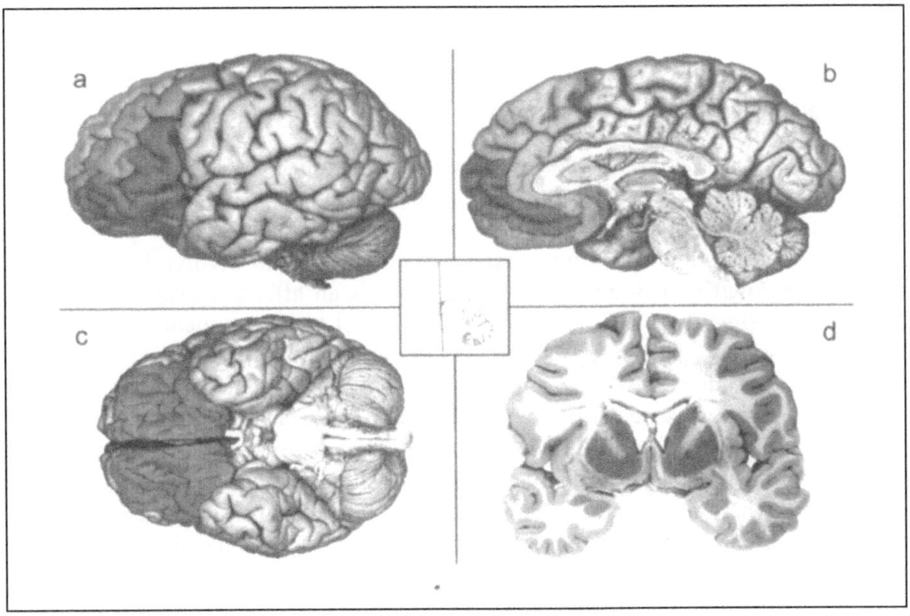

Figure 1. See p. 152 for full color.

affect (e.g., Bechara et al., 2000; Kringelbach & Rolls, 2004; Phelps, 2006). What concerns us here, however, is how this model can be used to understand the role of the conscious experience of pleasure in aesthetic experience. I believe that despite the rudimentary neural architecture sketched out, this model can form the basis for testing hypotheses about the conscious experience of pleasure in art, insofar as it relates to the experience of emotion in general. Specifically, when interacting with a visual object *as an artwork* (Leder et al., 2004), the viewer is bound to form a first-person mental representation of its value. This value will be influenced by previous experiences with concepts that are represented symbolically by the visual object. This mental representation will have content, in that it will contain information about what is felt by the person. This mental representation may change in the course of interacting with the artwork as a function of the changing nature of the extracted information. If Barrett et al. (2007) are correct, and given that I take it as given that the neural mechanisms that are evoked leading to the conscious experience of pleasure in relation to art will be the same as those that are evoked by conscious experience of pleasure while evaluating other stimuli (see also Zaidel, 2005), we can test to see whether structures that form part of the two neural circuits in Barrett et al.'s (2007) model of emotional experience have been implicated in aesthetic experience in relation to visual objects such as paintings or faces. Before doing that, however, I will briefly review Leder et al.'s (2004) model of aesthetic experience, which has explicitly discussed the roles of affect and emotion in the aesthetic experience. Elsewhere, Marcos Nadal and I have already discussed and stated specific hypotheses about various aspects of the aesthetic experience that can be derived from this model and tested at a biological level (Vartanian & Nadal, 2007). Here the focus will be on what this model can offer in terms of the conscious role of pleasure in the aesthetic experience.

A Model of Aesthetic Experience

Leder et al.'s (2004) model of aesthetic experience is composed of five information-processing stages that are connected in sequence, as well as through several feedback loops. Information flow is unidirectional in some parts of the model and bidirectional in others, such that certain phases involve bottom-up as well as top-down processing. In addition, there is an affective evaluation stream (*Continuous Affective Evaluation*) that runs parallel to this sequential stream and receives its output. The input into the system is the artwork itself, which for the purpose of this chapter will be limited to visual stimuli. Then, at each stage, a particular operation is performed on the artwork to extract various characteristics from it. The first stage involves *perceptual analyses*. At this stage, features such as complexity or symmetry are distilled. The second stage involves *implicit memory integration*, where the perceptual information is related to past experience. At this stage, people compare what they see with what they know, and this affects their responses to it. The third stage involves *explicit classification*, by the analysis of content information and explicit information about the style of the artwork. The fourth stage is referred to as *cognitive mastering*, the moment at which interpretation or meaning is imposed on the artwork. Thus, having already distilled its perceptual properties and placed it within a self-referential (implicit memory integration) and explicit (explicit classification) context, we make sense of what it is that we see. In the final stage, referred to as *evaluation,* we appraise the meaning or interpretation that was placed on the artwork during mastering. This evaluative stage generates two outputs: aesthetic judgment and aesthetic emotion. If cognitive mastering is successful and the subject has successfully interpreted the artwork, the artwork will be evaluated as either a good or poor work of art. Those aesthetic judgments will be accompanied by positive and negative aesthetic emotions, respectively. On the other hand, if cognitive mastering is unsuccessful and the subject has failed to interpret the artwork, then it will likely be evaluated as a poor work of art, accompanied by negative aesthetic emotion.

As described, Leder et al.'s (2004) model is remarkably congruent with two key features of Barrett et al.'s (2007) model of emotional experience outlined above. Leder et al.'s (2004) model distinguishes between affect as registered by Continuous Affective Evaluation and aesthetic emotion, which is one of the two end products of the aesthetic experience. Continuous Affective Evaluation runs parallel to the sequential information-processing stream and receives input from it on a continuous basis. This is conceptually similar to Barrett et al.'s (2007) description of core affect, which is construed as a dynamic reading of the value of environmental inputs that impinge on the organism. Of course, whereas in Barrett et al.'s (2007) model core affect is conceptualized as the critical building block in the experience of emotion in general, in Leder et al.'s (2004) model Continuous Affective Evaluation is conceptualized in relation to aesthetic experience in particular. Nevertheless, at this stage, both emphasize affect and not emotion. However, in the final stage of Leder et al.'s (2004) model, one of the two outputs generated is aesthetic emotion. If cognitive mastering is successful and the subject has successfully interpreted the artwork, it will be evaluated as either a good or poor work of art. Those aesthetic judgments will be accompanied by positive and negative aesthetic emotions respectively. On the other hand, if cognitive mastering is unsuccessful, the artwork will likely be evaluated as a poor work of art, accompanied by negative aesthetic emotion. Again, this definition of aesthetic emotion is congruent with Barrett et al.'s (2007) definition of an aesthetic experience, in which emotional experience involves the mental representation of core affect. Neither model considers emotional experience complete unless a meaningful mental representation of affective state has been formed.

NEUROBIOLOGY OF AESTHETIC EXPERIENCE

Recall that Barrett et al.'s (2007) model rests critically on the following assumption: Given that the experience of emotion is a conscious state, it only exists from a first-person point of view. This implies that we can only gain access to people's subjective states of experience by asking them what they feel. No third-person account will suffice. I will extend the same principle to neuroscientific studies of aesthetics that can shed light on the role of pleasure in the aesthetic experience. Also recall that not all aesthetic experiences need involve conscious pleasure. Some aesthetic judgments can be accounted for quite successfully using models of aesthetic experience that place greater emphasis on perceptual analysis and subsequent visual processing (e.g., Chatterjee, 2003). Therefore, here I will limit our discussion to two sets of studies. First, I will review the results of studies in visual aesthetics of artworks in which subjects were instructed explicitly to focus on subjective preferences or beauty, both of which involve cognitive as well as affective states (Leder, Augustin, & Belke, 2005). Second, I will discuss a study in which subjects were instructed explicitly to focus on subjective preferences (attractiveness) while viewing faces in the scanner. I will then compare the results of these two sets of studies to discover overlaps that may tell us something interesting about the role of pleasure in both acts.

Visual Aesthetics of Artworks

As stated above, no neuroimaging study to date has instructed subjects to indicate subjective levels of pleasure in response to viewing works of art. However, three fMRI studies have investigated the neural correlates of subjective preference or beauty judgments. Because preference and beauty judgments have affective as well as cognitive components (Leder et al., 2005), both can shed light on the role of emotion in aesthetic experience. After discussing the findings of each study, I will relate them to Leder et al.'s (2004) model of aesthetic experience and Barrett et al.'s (2007) model of emotion experience.

Vartanian and Goel (2004) instructed their subjects to rate paintings on aesthetic preference as they viewed them in the scanner. Preference was defined as the degree of liking for a painting. By allowing subjects to indicate preference from a first-person point of view, the design allowed one to gain access to people's subjective states of experience by asking how much they liked the paintings. The authors were interested in determining whether aesthetic preference toward works of art is characterized by a "disinterested" or cognitive stance, or whether is it underwritten by an emotional response toward properties of artworks. They hypothesized that if aesthetic preference was mediated by emotion, then it should involve brain structures that have been implicated in processing emotion. Otherwise, if aesthetic preference was primarily a cognitive process, then it should involve brain structures that have been implicated in evaluation under emotionally neutral conditions. The results demonstrated that activation in several cortical structures that were implicated in processing emotion or reward covaried as a function of preference ratings, including the visual cortex, the caudate nucleus, and the cingulate sulcus.

Let us consider how well these results fit Leder et al.'s (2004) model of aesthetic experience and Barrett et al.'s (2007) model of emotional experience. Recall that Leder et al.'s (2004) Continuous Affective Evaluation runs parallel to the information-processing stream, and it receives continuous input from it. This means that a subject interacting with a work of art can provide a preference rating for that artwork at any given point along the information-processing sequence, and need not have mastered the work cognitively before a rating can be generated. Therefore, the results of Vartanian and Goel (2004) probably shed light on the cortical and subcortical structures that mediate Continuous Affective Evaluation and indicate the areas that one should expect to see activated when subjects are asked to indicate their liking for given artworks. Also, recall that in Barrett et al.'s (2007) model value—understood as the mental representation of how the sensory properties of an object or an event affect the organism's state—is computed through the integrated function of two dissociable but interdependent neural systems. As already noted, the second system in this model provides what Barrett et al. (2007) refer to as an "affective working memory," which enables the organism to make choices, decisions, and judgments that are based on feelings and intuitions rather than abstract rules. This circuit involves the anterior cingulate cortex. Given that Vartanian and Goel's (2004) task required subjects to make preference judgments and that the cingulate sulcus was one of the areas activated, the results suggest that making first-person preference judgments in response to works of art may be mediated by the neural system that subserves core affect.

Two fMRI studies used judgments of beauty (rather than liking) as the dependent variable of choice. Kawabata and Zeki (2004) presented their subjects with paintings that they had already rated as beautiful or ugly prior to viewing in the scanner, and instructed them to rate the paintings again inside the scanner. Their results demonstrated that activity in the orbital frontal cortex was greater for stimuli classified as beautiful: the authors argued that this activation in the orbital frontal cortex was due to the reward value of beautiful paintings. In contrast, Skov, Christensen, Roule, and Paulson (2005) presented their subjects with stimuli from the International Affective Picture System (IAPS). The IAPS is an inventory of pictures that have been categorized as emotionally positive, negative, or neutral. Subjects were asked to view and rate each stimulus as beautiful, ugly, or neutral inside the scanner. Compared to ugly pictures, beautiful pictures activated a wide network of areas including the occipital, parietal, and frontal lobes. However, when subjects rated pictures as beautiful despite the fact that they were emotionally negative (e.g., a scene that exhibits death or injury), there was activation in a network including the occipital, temporal, and the frontal lobes, but in particular bilateral orbital frontal cortex. Note that both Kawabata and Zeki (2004) and Skov et al. (2005) allowed subjects to indicate judgments from a first-person point of view, thus allowing one to access subjective states of experience.

Despite methodological differences, the studies by Kawabata and Zeki (2004) and Skov et al. (2005) attempted to isolate those cortical structures that were activated relatively more by stimuli evaluated as beautiful. According to Leder et al.'s model of aesthetic experience, evaluations of beauty tap aesthetic judgment, and therefore its computation can only occur following processing along all five stages of the model. Thus, activation in the orbital frontal cortex in both studies is likely not in relation to Continuous Affective Evaluation. Rather, it is more likely that certain affective properties of beauty are computed in the orbital frontal cortex. Activation in the orbital frontal cortex has, in turn, been linked to a wide array of processes, but in particular to complex reward, hedonic, and emotion interactions (Kringelbach, 2005; Kringelbach & Rolls, 2004). According to Barrett et al.'s (2007) model, the first system involved in the computation of value is composed of the basolateral complex of the amygdala, the central and lateral aspects of the orbitofrontal cortex, and the anterior insula. This system generates a value-based representation of the object, including its sensory properties and its impact on the organism. In this system, the central and lateral aspects of the orbitofrontal cortex code the context-dependent value of the stimulus, contributing to an initial value-based representation of the stimulus that includes information about its sensory properties and what this information means to the organism. Given that the task in both studies required subjects to make beauty judgments and that the orbital frontal cortex was one of the areas activated in both studies in relation to subjective judgments of images as "beautiful"—especially when this judgment contradicted the emotional state of the image in Skov et al. (2005)—the results suggest that making first-person beauty judgments in response to visual images may be mediated by the neural system that subserves core affect, and that beauty judgments code for value at a relatively early stage in the sequence of processes leading to a mental representation of value.

In summary, the findings of Vartanian and Goel (2004), Kawabata and Zeki (2004), and Skov et al. (2005) fit the models of aesthetic experience and emotional experience quite well. They suggest that first-person aesthetic experiences involve an emotional component that is, in turn, linked to core affect, coding for basic states of pleaure or displeasure. It is important to mention that Cela-Conde et al. (2004) have also conducted a magnetoencephalography (MEG) study of beauty judgment. MEG's superior temporal resolution enabled Cela-Conde et al. (2004) to analyze data at very short latencies (< 1000 ms) compared with what is possible with fMRI. Their results demonstrated that during late latencies (400-1000ms), activity in the left dorsolateral prefrontal cortex was significantly greater when participants judged stimuli as beautiful as compared with nonbeautiful. The very short time window within which these results were obtained suggest that this activation can be attributed to early monitoring and initiation of top-down information flow in the service of decision making (Davidson & Irwin, 1999; Heekeren, Marrett, Bardettini, & Ungerleider, 2004; Herrington et al., 2005; Krawczyk, 2002; Wallis & Miller, 2003).

Visual Aesthetics of Faces

The literature on the neuroscience of processing beauty in faces is very large (for review, see Senior, 2003), and a thorough review of its findings falls beyond the scope of this chapter. However, recall that our approach in this chapter has been focused on studies that have investigated first-person approaches to visual aesthetics, and if that criterion is established, then the field of studies involving faces narrows considerably. Nakamura et al. (1998) conducted one of the few studies of this kind. In their study, six male participants were shown female faces in Positron Emission Tomography (PET) scanner and asked to rate them as attractive, neutral, or unattractive. The results showed that compared with a color-discrimination task, rating faces on attractiveness resulted in increased regional cerebral blood flow (*r*CBF) in the left anterior and middle frontal cortex, left fronto-temporal junction, orbitofrontal cortex, caudate nucleus, and the visual cortex. The authors argued that the involvement of the aforementioned regions in attractiveness ratings is a specific example of their more general involvement in evaluative judgments that involve an affective component. In other words, the authors considered attractive faces as rewarding stimuli that can elicit emotional responses. The role of the orbitofrontal cortex in Barrett et al.'s (2007) model involves generating a value-based representation of the object, including its sensory properties and its impact on the organism. The central and lateral aspects of the orbitofrontal cortex code the context-dependent value of the stimulus, contributing to an initial value-based representation of the stimulus, which includes information about its sensory properties and what this information means to the organism. This description fits nicely with the task that participants were asked to do in Nakamura et al.'s (1998) study, as it involved male subjects making attractiveness judgments based on female faces. Here again, the results suggest that making first-person aesthetic (attractiveness) judgments in response to visual images (faces) may be mediated by the neural system that subserves core affect at a relatively early stage in the sequence of processes leading to a mental representation of value.

A MODEL OF PLEASURE IN AESTHETIC EXPERIENCE

In this chapter, I sketched out the basic tenets of Barrett et al.'s (2007) theory of emotional experience and outlined how it can form the neurobiological basis of affect and emotion in Leder et al.'s (2004) model of aesthetic experience. I then reviewed some of the literature on the aesthetic evaluation of paintings and faces in the fMRI scanner to highlight how the results contribute to the question of emotion and pleasure in aesthetic experience. In the process, I tried to sketch out a basic scheme for studying the contribution of pleasure to aesthetic experience.

Currently, the field of neuroaesthetics lacks a framework that can bridge the gap between emotion and cognition and, in the process, account for the role of pleasure in aesthetic experience. To achieve this framework, two models are necessary, namely a psychological model of aesthetic experience that accounts for the differential roles of affect and emotion, and a neurobiological theory of emotional experience that can link states of felt pleasure and displeasure to emotion and, in the process, incorporates mental representations of core affect. I believe that the models proposed by Leder et al. (2004) and Barrett et al. (2007) can fulfill these two requirements respectively. Because Nadal and I have proposed a detailed set of hypotheses that can be derived from Leder et al.'s (2004) model and tested at a biological level (Vartanian & Nadal, 2007), I will not repeat the exercise here. However, I do hope that the framework sketched here is sufficiently clear to motivate further research. In essence, it can be reduced to these axioms: First, core affect forms the physiological basis for emotion experience. Second, mental representations of core affect give rise to emotions. Third, because mental representations of core affect involve cognitive mastery of their content, they form the bridge between emotion and cognition. Fourth, to the extent that core affect forms the physiological underpinning of states of felt pleasure and displeasure, there is a theoretical link between core physiological states, the emotions that arise from them, and the cognitions that give them meaning. All the "joints in this system" await experimental scrutiny in the context of aesthetic experience.

REFERENCES

Barrett, L. F., Mesquita, B., Ochsner, K. N., & Gross, J. J. (2007). The experience of emotion. *Annual Review of Psychology, 58*, 373-403.

Barrett, L. F., & Wager, T. (2006). The structure of emotion: Evidence from the neuroimaging of emotion. *Current Directions in Psychological Science, 15*, 79-85.

Bechara. A, Damasio, H., & Damasio, A. R. (2000). Emotion, decision making and the orbitofrontal cortex. *Cerebral Cortex, 10*, 295-307.

Berridge, K. C., & Winkielman, P. (2003). What is an unconscious emotion: The case for unconscious 'liking.' *Cognition and Emotion, 17*, 181-211.

Cela-Conde, C. J., Marty, G., Maetsu, F., Ortiz, T., Munar, E., Fernandez, A., et al. (2004). Activation of the prefrontal cortex in the human visual aesthetic perception. *Proceedings of the National Academy of Sciences USA, 101*, 6321-6325.

Chatterjee, A. (2003). Prospects for a cognitive neuroscience of visual aesthetics. *Bulletin of Psychology and the Arts, 4*, 55-60.

Davidson, R. J., & Irwin, W. (1999). The functional neuroanatomy of emotion and affective style. *Trends in Cognitive Sciences, 3*, 11-21.

Freedberg, D., & Gallese, V. (2007). Motion, emotion, and empathy in esthetic experience. *Trends in Cognitive Sciences, 11*, 197-203.

Heekeren, H. R., Marrett, S., Bandettini, P. A., &. Ungerleider, L. G. (2004). A general mechanism for perceptual decision-making in the human brain. *Nature, 431*, 859-862.

Herrington, J. D., Mohanty, A., Koven, N. S., Fisher, J. E., Stewart, J. L., Banich, M. T., et al. (2005). Emotion-modulated performance and activity in left dorsolateral prefrontal cortex. *Emotion, 5*, 200-207.

Kawabata, H., & Zeki, S. (2004). Neural correlates of beauty. *Journal of Neurophysiology, 91*, 1699-1705.

Krawczyk, D. C. (2002). Contributions of the prefrontal cortex to the neural basis of human decision making. *Neuroscience and Biobehavioral Reviews, 26*, 631-664.

Kringelbach, M. L. (2005). The human orbitofrontal cortex: Linking reward to hedonic experience. *Nature Reviews Neuroscience, 6*, 691-702.

Kringelbach, M. L., & Rolls, E. (2004). The functional neuroanatomy of the human orbitofrontal cortex: Evidence from neuroimaging and neurophysiology. *Progress in Neurobiology, 72*, 341-372.

Leder, H., Belke, B., Oeberst, A., & Augustin, D. (2004). A model of aesthetic appreciation and aesthetic judgments. *British Journal of Psychology, 95*, 489-508.

Leder, H., Augustin, D., & Belke, B. (2005). Art and cognition: Consequences for experimental aesthetics. *Bulletin of Psychology and the Arts, 5*, 11-20.

Martindale, C. (2001). How does the brain compute aesthetic experience? *The General Psychologist, 36*, 25-35.

Murphy, F. C., Nimmo-Smith, I., & Lawrence, A. D. (2003). Functional neuroanatomy of emotions: A meta-analysis. *Cognitive, Affective, & Behavioral Neuroscience, 3*, 207-233.

Nakamura, K., Kawashima, R., Nagumo, S., Ito, K., Sugiura, M., Kato, T., et al. (1998). Neuroanatomical correlates of the assessment of facial attractiveness. *Neuroreport, 9*, 753-757.

Phan, K. L., Wager, T., Taylor, S. F., & Liberzon, I. (2002). Functional neuroanatomy of emotion: A meta-analysis of emotion activation studies in PET and fMRI. *Neuroimage, 16*, 331-348.

Phelps, E. A. (2006). Emotion and cognition: Insights from studies of the human amygdala. *Annual Review of Psychology, 57*, 27-53.

Russell, J. A. (2003). Core affect and the psychological construction of emotion. *Psychological Review, 110*, 145-172.

Searle, J. R. (2000). Consciousness. *Annual Review of Neuroscience, 23,* 557-578.

Senior, C. (2003). Beauty in the brain of the beholder. *Neuron, 38*, 525-528.

Skov, M., Christensen, M. S., Rowe, J. B., & Paulson, O. B. (2005, June). *Specific activations underlie aesthetic judgment of affective pictures.* Poster presented at the 11th annual meeting of Human Brain Mapping, Toronto, Ontario, Canada.

Stephan, K. E., Marshall, J. C., Friston, K. J., Rowe, J. B., Ritzl, A., Zilles, K., et al. (2003). Lateralized cognitive processes and lateralized task control in the human brain. *Science, 301*, 384-386.

Vartanian, O., & Goel, V. (2004). Neuroanatomical correlates of aesthetic preference for paintings. *NeuroReport, 15*, 893-897.

Vartanian, O., & Nadal, M. (2007). A biological approach to a model of aesthetic experience. In L. Dorfman, C. Martindale, & V. Petrov (Eds.), *Aesthetics and innovation* (pp. 429-444). Cambridge, MA: Cambridge Scholars Press.

Wallis, J. D., & Miller, E. K. (2003). Neuronal activity in primate dorsolateral and orbital prefrontal cortex during performance of a reward preference task. *European Journal of Neuroscience, 18*, 2069-2081.

Winkielman, P., & Berridge, K. C. (2004). Unconscious emotion. *Current Directions in Psychological Science, 13,* 120-123.

Zaidel, D. W. (2005). *Neuropsychology of art: Neurological, cognitive, and evolutionary perspectives*. Hove, UK: Psychology Press.

CHAPTER 14

The Origins of Aesthetic Pleasure: Processing Fluency and Affect in Judgment, Body, and the Brain*

Troy Chenier and Piotr Winkielman

This chapter concerns what we take to be the *sin qua non* of the aesthetic experience: aesthetic pleasure—the immediate hedonic experience elicited by the perception of an object. Many research traditions seek to understand this experience by focusing on either the semantic aspects (associative meanings) or the formal features (colors or shapes) of objects. In contrast, here we suggest that aesthetic pleasure may sometimes derive from another source: the fluency of information processing. In what follows, we begin by defining what we mean by the term "processing fluency." We then review research showing the hedonic consequences of high processing fluency as expressed in judgments of liking and attractiveness and in psycho-physiological reactions indicative of positive affect. Finally, we conclude with a consideration of the neural basis of fluency and affect. Throughout, we endeavor to show that the concept of processing fluency provides us with a parsimonious explanation for a broad range of aesthetic phenomena: from those originating in the cognitive and social sciences—mere exposure, structural relation preferences, proto-typicality, and priming-based preferences—to those most often associated with experimental aesthetics—amount of information, symmetry, and contrast and clarity.

THE CONCEPT OF PROCESSING FLUENCY

Processing fluency is a general term used to characterize the relative speed or ease of mental operations occurring at both the perceptual (see Jacoby, Kelley, & Dywan, 1989) and conceptual (see Winkielman, Schwarz, Fazendeiro, & Reber, 2003) levels. The concept assumes that in addition to the content of information ("what"

*This research was supported by NSF grant BCS-0217294 (P.W.).

the stimulus is), perceivers also have access to the quality of the processing itself ("how" fast or easy it is to process the stimulus). Evidence for this assumption comes from numerous studies showing that despite no alteration in content, stimuli may vary in the speed of their identification (see Jacoby, 1983; Roediger, 1990; Tulving & Schachter, 1990) or classification (see Posner & Keele, 1968; Winkielman et al., 2006). There is a great deal of evidence that this fluency signal serves as an input into judgment and decision making. Thus, for example, memory researchers have shown that despite no change in stimulus content, enhancing the fluency with which a stimulus is processed leads to higher claims that it has been seen before (see Whittlesea, Jacoby, & Girard, 1990). Presumably, this occurs because participants believe that high fluency (fast identification speed) indicates some prior practice with processing the stimulus. Other research has shown that fluency contributes to judgments as diverse as truth, fame, and frequency (Schwarz, 2004).

Here, we propose that just as fluency may be used as a cue to infer the historical or truth status of a stimulus, it may also be used to make evaluative judgments—to arrive at a decision about the likeability or pleasantness of a stimulus. Importantly, while we acknowledge that in some contexts fluency may be used to evaluate a stimulus in a "cold" manner (via either implicit or explicit inference), we argue throughout this chapter that fluency may also influence evaluative judgments through a "hot" route, namely, by engendering genuine, positive affect.

The basic idea behind this hot proposal is that high fluency can function as a signal of a positive state of affairs, either within the cognitive system or in the world. More specifically, high fluency can signal (a) good progress in processing and likelihood of achieving the current cognitive goal, (b) availability of appropriate knowledge structures to interpret the stimulus, (c) previous experience with the stimulus and, thus, lower likelihood that the stimulus is harmful, and (d) greater degree of harmony or lower conflict within the cognitive system. Given that highly fluent processing is characterized by these properties, we believe this signal to have an intrinsic "warm glow" (for a more comprehensive discussion, see Reber, Schwarz, & Winkielman 2004; Winkielman et al., 2003).

Critical for the viability of our hedonic fluency proposal, and central to the topic of this book, is evidence from psychophysiology and neuroscience. Accordingly, in what follows, we discuss several studies using these methods. Most of the relevant studies were conducted using facial electromyography (EMG), which indexes affect by measuring the amount of electrical activity in facial muscles (Cacioppo, Petty, Losch, & Kim, 1986). Specifically, positive affect is associated with an increase in activity of the zygomaticus major (smiling muscle), whereas negative affect is associated with an increase in activity of the corrugator supercillii (frowning muscle). Indexing affective responding in this way provides us with a means of unobtrusively measuring positive affect and therefore with obtaining convergent support for our proposal that high processing fluency is hedonically marked. We also discuss relevant studies using neuroimaging techniques, such as positron emission tomography (PET) and functional magnetic resonance imaging (fMRI), though few of these studies have directly linked fluency and affect.

THE LINK BETWEEN HIGH PROCESSING FLUENCY AND PREFERENCE

Research into aesthetic phenomena may be divided into two traditions. On the one hand, there is the cognitive and social psychological tradition where the focus has been on understanding how the learning experiences of the perceiver shape his or her preferences. On the other hand, there is the experimental aesthetics tradition where the concern has been primarily with identifying hedonic properties of aesthetic objects (see Jacobsen, this volume). In this section, we endeavor to demonstrate that both the learning experiences of the perceiver and the properties of aesthetic objects influence behavioral measures of aesthetic responsiveness (liking and pleasantness ratings) through one and the same mechanism: by enhancing processing fluency.

The Learning Experiences of the Perceiver

Research on preferences in psychology has focused on how a prior experience with a domain may influence the subsequent appeal of the same or related items from that domain. In this tradition, four related phenomena have received much attention: mere exposure, structural relation preferences, prototypicality, and priming-based preferences. As we show, these preference phenomena might reflect hedonic reactions to high processing fluency.

Mere Exposure

The mere-exposure effect refers to the enhancement of attitude toward a stimulus as a result of repeated encounters with that stimulus. It has been found with a variety of stimuli (faces, ideographs, words, music, pictures, abstract patterns), using a variety of dependent measures (force-choice preference judgments, liking and pleasantness rating scales), in both positive and negative contexts (Saegert, Swap, & Zajonc, 1973), in laboratory (Moreland & Zajonc, 1976) and field settings (Schaffner, Wandersman, & Stang, 1981), and in nonhuman (Hill, 1978) as well as human animals (see Bornstein, 1989 for meta-analytic review). Furthermore, there is evidence within the realm of art that in addition to enhancing the enjoyment of a particular piece, mere exposure may also contribute to the maintenance of entire art canons (Cutting, 2003). Important for our proposal, mere exposure to a stimulus has been robustly shown to facilitate reprocessing of the stimulus, as indicated by faster identification and classification latencies for merely exposed as compared to novel items (see Haber & Hershenson, 1965; Jacoby & Dallas, 1981). In fact, several investigators have suggested, consistent with our proposal, that mere exposure enhances preference precisely because of this reprocessing benefit (see Bornstein & D'Agostino, 1994; Jacoby et al., 1989; Seamon, Brody, & Kauff, 1983; Whittlesea & Price, 2001). Unlike our proposal, however, these investigators see fluency simply as a cognitive cue to be interpreted by the perceiver in the context of an evaluative judgment (see Klinger & Greenwald, 1994). Contrary to this cold account, our hot account suggests that high fluency leads to liking because it elicits genuine, positive affect. Support for our proposal comes from several sources. At the behavioral level,

Monahan, Murphy, and Zajonc (2000) first subliminally exposed participants to either 25 different ideographs or to 5 different ideographs repeated 5 times each. Later, participants exposed repeatedly to the same 5 ideographs (high fluency condition) reported being in a better mood than participants exposed to 25 different ideographs (low fluency condition). At the psychophysiological level, Harmon-Jones and Allen (2001) found greater EMG activity in the zygomaticus major (indicative of positive affect) for merely exposed as compared with novel items. Taken together, these behavioral and psychophysiological results support our contention that the mere-exposure effect reflects hedonic marking of high processing fluency.

Structural Relation Preferences

The development of a preference for a stimulus does not necessarily depend upon a perceiver having previously processed that exact stimulus. Rather, this preference may develop merely from having previously processed structurally related stimuli. This was demonstrated by Gordon and Holyoak (1983) using a category-learning paradigm. Participants were first exposed to several letter strings conforming to a grammatical structure, and then provided liking ratings for novel grammatical and ungrammatical strings. The findings showed a structural relation preference: participants rated novel grammatical letter strings as more likeable than the ungrammatical ones. Sollberger and Reber (2004) subsequently confirmed and extended these findings using more meaningful tonal sequences: participants preferred both old and novel tonal sequences that were grammatical to novel tonal sequences that were ungrammatical. And just as mere exposure facilitates the extraction of information, the same appears to be true here as well. Specifically, in a study by Buckner (1994), after participants had been exposed to instances of an artificial grammar, they were asked to identify as quickly as possible novel grammatical and ungrammatical letter strings that were gradually revealed from beneath black patterned masks. Participants responded faster to grammatical letter strings than to ungrammatical ones, thus indicating that a prior learning experience with a category of items facilitates subsequent processing of novel items that bear some structural relationship to the previously learned category.

Prototypicality

The most structurally related member of a category is often referred to as the prototype. It represents an average or central tendency of all the members belonging to a category (Posner & Keele, 1968). The preference for prototypes is robust: people show it for living categories—human faces (Rhodes & Tremewan, 1996; Rhodes, Yoshikawa, Clark, Lee, McKay, & Akamatsu, 2001) as well as fish, dogs, and birds (Halberstadt & Rhodes, 2000, 2003)—and nonliving categories—color patches (Martindale & Moore, 1988), furniture (Whitfield & Slatter, 1979), and wristwatches and automobiles (Halberstadt & Rhodes, 2000, 2003). Given that prototypes are the most representative members of their categories, it is not surprising that they are also the most accurately and quickly classified members (Posner & Keele, 1968; Read, 1972). Recently, Winkielman, Halberstadt, Fazendeiro, and

Catty (2006) examined the connection between prototypicality, fluency, and attractiveness. Participants first learned a category of random dot patterns (Experiment 1) or common geometric patterns (Experiment 2) and then were presented with novel patterns that varied in level of prototypicality. Participants were required to classify the patterns into their respective categories as quickly as possible and to rate the attractiveness of each. A close relationship between the level of prototypicality, fluency, and attractiveness was observed: both fluency (as indexed by classification speed) and attractiveness increased as patterns became more prototypical, with the prototypes of each of the categories being the most fluently processed and rated the most attractive of all the patterns. Importantly, when fluency was statistically controlled, the relation between prototypicality and attractiveness dropped by half (though it remained significant). This suggests that processing facilitation is an important, though not the only, cause of the "beauty-in-averageness" effect.

Just as for the mere-exposure effect, however, these results could reflect a cold cognitive evaluation of the stimulus on the part of the participant ("The closer the item matches the prototype for the category, the higher the liking rating I will give it."). To examine if prototypes (more-fluently processed items) do in fact engender genuine, positive affective responses, Winkielman et al. (2006, Experiment 3) took facial EMG measures while participants viewed prepared prototypes (unseen prototypes for a category of dot patterns they had just been exposed to) and unprepared prototypes (unseen prototypes for a category of dot patterns they had not been exposed to). Consistent with our hedonic fluency proposal, viewing prepared prototypes elicited significantly greater zygomaticus activity and, therefore, presumably more aesthetic pleasure than viewing unprepared prototypes.

Priming-Based Preferences

It has long been known that processing fluency may be enhanced through the use of perceptual or conceptual priming procedures. Both types of procedures have been employed to assess the relationship between fluency and affect. In a perceptual priming study, Reber, Winkielman, and Schwarz (1998) presented participants with slightly degraded pictures of everyday objects (a desk, bird, plane) that were subliminally primed with either a matching contour or a mismatching contour. Some participants were required to identify the pictures as quickly as possible, while other participants were asked to judge how much they liked the pictures. Consistent with our fluency account, pictures primed by matching contours were recognized faster and liked more than pictures primed with mismatching contours. Winkielman and Cacioppo (2001, Study 1) subsequently replicated these results using EMG and in the process provided support for the hedonic marking of processing fluency: pictures primed by matching contours elicited greater zygomaticus activity than those primed by mismatching contours.

In a conceptual priming study, Winkielman and Fazendeiro (in preparation) used a cross-format semantic priming procedure to create three fluency conditions: (a) high fluency, where there was an exact perceptual and conceptual match between the prime and target (e.g., prime and target both consisted of either the word "dog" or a picture of a dog), (b) medium fluency, where the match between the prime and target was only conceptual (e.g., word "lock" priming a picture of a key or vice versa), and (c) low fluency, where there was a perceptual and conceptual mismatch between the prime and target (e.g., word "snow" priming a picture of a desk or vice versa). Regardless of whether participants saw the prime immediately before the target (study 1) or whether they saw the prime in a list during a previous phase (study 2), they rated targets most favorably under conditions of high processing fluency, next most favorably under conditions of medium processing fluency, and least favorably under conditions of low processing fluency.

To examine the relationship between fluency, affective experience, and judgment, Winkielman and Fazendeiro (in preparation) extended their conceptual priming paradigm with the use of a misattribution manipulation borrowed from the psychology of emotion. Specifically, they played new-age music in the background during the study and informed some participants that the music might influence how easily information comes to mind (their fluency experience) and others that it might influence feelings regarding the stimuli (their affective reactions). The results were highly informative. Telling participants that the music might influence how easily information comes to mind did not alter the effect of processing fluency on liking. However, suggesting to participants that the music might influence feelings toward the items eliminated the effect of processing fluency on liking: targets were judged as equally likeable across the three fluency conditions. This result suggests that participants were using their fluency-based affective reactions and not the fluency signal per se as the basis for the liking judgment, thus supporting our proposal that high fluency is hedonically marked.

Objective Features of Stimuli

Unlike psychologists, who tend to focus on how the learning history of the perceiver influences preferences, researchers in experimental aesthetics tend to focus on the role of object properties. Three such properties have been closely scrutinized: amount of information, symmetry, and contrast and clarity.

Amount of Information

The idea that the amount of information contained in a stimulus may be an important determinant of aesthetic appeal has long been of theoretical interest in the history of aesthetics (see Arnheim, 1974; Gombrich, 1984). Garner (1974) approached this idea empirically by assessing the relationship between amount of information and judgments of figural goodness. To do this, he operationalized the amount of information in terms of how many unique patterns could be produced by flipping or rotating a given pattern. The greater the number of unique patterns that could be produced, the higher the amount of information the pattern was assumed to contain. Using this operationalization of amount of information, he observed that the less information a pattern contained the higher its figural goodness was judged to be. And apparently this result is not confined to simple patterns. Nicki, Lee, and Moss (1981), for example, found that as ambiguity in cubist paintings decreased (the less information paintings contained) the more pleasant they were judged to be. Important for our proposal is that stimuli that possess less information have also been shown to be more fluently processed (as indexed by lower recognition latencies) than stimuli that possess relatively more information (Checkosky & Whitlock, 1973). This suggests that the appeal of items that are low in information may result from the higher fluency with which they are processed.

Symmetry

Given the findings in the previous section that amount of information is related to aesthetic appeal, it should not come as a surprise that there is a widespread preference for symmetry; all else being equal, symmetrical objects possess less information than their asymmetrical counterparts. According to our proposal, however, symmetry is appealing by virtue of its ability to facilitate information processing and not simply because objects possessing symmetry contain less overall information. Support for this assertion comes from studies by Palmer and his colleagues. Palmer (1991) presented the same symmetrical dot patterns (such that amount of information was held constant) in one of three orientations—vertically, diagonally, or horizontally—and required participants to rate the figural goodness of each of the patterns. He found that dot patterns presented in the vertically symmetrical orientation received the highest figural goodness ratings, followed by those presented in the horizontally symmetrical orientation, with those presented in the diagonally symmetrical orientation receiving the lowest figural goodness ratings. Most importantly, the figural goodness ratings paralleled earlier work by Palmer and Hemenway (1978) on ease of symmetry detection: symmetry in the dot patterns presented in vertically symmetrical orientations was detected the fastest, followed by the symmetry in the horizontally symmetrical orientations, with the symmetry of the dot patterns presented in diagonally symmetrical orientations being the most difficult to detect. Since each of the patterns in the three orientations contained the same amount of information, this result argues that symmetry makes any given stimulus more appealing because, beyond reducing amount of information, it (especially vertical symmetry) enhances processing fluency—facilitates the ability of the perceiver to detect redundant information and, as such, to more easily make sense of (identify or classify) the stimulus. Reber and Schwarz (2006) provided further support for this interpretation by showing that symmetry in abstract shapes not only makes those shapes more appealing but also makes them easier to identify than comparable shapes that are asymmetrical.

Contrast and Clarity

Contrast and clarity have repeatedly been identified as characteristics of aesthetically appealing objects (see Gombrich, 1984; Maritain, 1966; Solso, 1997). According to our proposal, this property confers aesthetic appeal because of its ability to facilitate extraction of information. There are in fact a number of studies demonstrating that as contrast and clarity increase, so does processing fluency. Checkosky and Whitlock (1973), for example, observed that recognition speed was faster for stimuli presented in higher rather than lower figure-ground contrast. Going on the assumption that increases in contrast facilitate processing fluency, Reber et al. (1998) presented circles that subtly varied in figure-ground contrast and asked participants to judge how pretty (or ugly) each was. As predicted by the processing fluency account, participants judged circles that were higher in figure-ground contrast (higher in fluency) to be prettier (or less ugly) than those presented in lower figure-ground contrast (lower in fluency). It is interesting to note that higher figure-ground contrast (and therefore higher fluency) was reliably associated with more favorable stimulus evaluations regardless of how the evaluative question was framed (whether the question focused on how pretty or how ugly the stimulus was). Previous work in the nonaffective domain showed that high processing fluency may lead to more extreme judgments. For example, Mandler, Nakamura, and Van Zandt (1987) found that high processing fluency increased judgments of both brightness and darkness, depending on the focus of the question. The fact that this was not the case in the Reber et al. (1998) study and, as far as we know, has never been the case for an affective judgment, with higher processing fluency always being associated with more favorable stimulus evaluations, argues in favor of an inherent connection between high processing fluency and positive affect.

Summary

In this section, we examined a number of preference effects that depend on the learning experiences of the perceiver as well as on the characteristics of objects. By demonstrating that these two factors may enhance fluency, we have provided a parsimonious explanation for a broad range of aesthetic-preference phenomena: for those originating from the cognitive and social sciences—mere exposure, structural relation preferences, prototypicality, and priming-based preferences—as well as for those most often associated with experimental aesthetics—amount of information, symmetry, and contrast and clarity. Additionally, by presenting both behavioral and psychophysiological evidence for the hedonic marking of high processing fluency, we have provided convergent support for our proposal that high fluency is one possible basis, and we think an important basis, for the felt pleasure of the aesthetic experience.

THE NEURAL BASIS OF HIGH PROCESSING FLUENCY AND AFFECT

There have been no investigations that have directly examined the neural basis of the connection between fluency and affect. However, a great deal of neuroscientific work has been done on the neural basis of priming (one variable we have identified as facilitating processing fluency) and the neural circuits involved in reinforcement and reward. We review this work here and highlight possible connections to processing fluency.

Neural Response Suppression as the Neural Correlate of High Processing Fluency

Most generally, priming refers to a change in the behavioral response to a target as a result of prior exposure to the identical or related item. Typically, the consequence of priming with identical or similar items is response facilitation (faster RT, more accurate classification), though it is possible to also produce response interference (Huber & O'Reilly, 2003). On the neural level, priming is supported by two mechanisms. Over short durations, a prime may briefly pre-activate the related representation, presumably lowering the threshold for the subsequent response. However, over the longer term, the consequence of priming is neural response suppression—a reduction in neural activity in those brain regions that were initially recruited to process the item (Wiggs & Martin, 1998). This reduction is seen both at the level of single cells in nonhuman primates (see Desimone, 1996) and across several cortical areas in humans (see Buckner, Peterson, Ojemann, & Miezin, 1995). Furthermore, it occurs in both the visual and auditory modalities (see Bergerbest, Ghahremani, & Gabrieli, 2004), and it is found with both perceptual (making judgments about repeated words or pictures) and conceptual (completing a word fragment for a previously seen word) priming procedures (see Buckner & Koutstaal, 1998 for review). Finally, it can also occur with structurally related items, including prototypes (Reber, Stark, & Squire, 1998). In short, neural-response suppression can be seen as the neural correlate of high processing fluency.

But why should facilitation in behavioral performance with an item correlate with reductions in neural activity? One speculation is that the suppression of neural responsiveness to primed items reflects a neural learning process in which neurons that initially responded to irrelevant features of the item (features not necessary for identification of the item) drop out of the response pool. This neural pruning has the effect of sharpening the representation of the item such that only those neurons that are optimally tuned for processing critical item features remain responsive. The end result is more efficient neural processing and, as such, facilitated behavioral performance—reductions in latencies to identify or classify the item (Maccotta & Buckner, 2004). We suspect that other variables that have been shown to facilitate processing fluency, such as symmetry and contrast and clarity, may enhance behavioral responding in a similar fashion by creating sharper and therefore less noisy neural representations. Though this conjecture has yet to be empirically tested, it is consistent with some recent neural modeling work (Winkielman & Nowak, 2005).

High Processing Fluency and the Neural Representation of Reward

According to our framework, high processing fluency serves as a cue that rapidly provides information about the rewarding properties of a stimulus. One neural region that has been implicated in assessing the reward value of a stimulus is the medial orbitofrontal cortex (OFC). Elliot, Dolan, and Frith (2000) pinpointed this structure as being particularly important for assessing behavioral outcomes when the perceiver is required to make a response to the stimulus on the basis of partial information (when close inspection of the stimulus is not feasible). If so, one might expect this structure to be sensitive to high processing fluency, using this signal as a cue to assess the reinforcing and rewarding properties of the stimulus under consideration. A number of neuroimaging studies, although not directly assessing fluency per se, provide some support for this speculation.

Macguire, Frith, and Morris (1999) had participants undergo PET while reading stories that varied in comprehensibility. They found the more subjectively comprehensible (and presumably the more fluent) the stories became, the greater the blood flow in the anterior region of the medial OFC. Frith (2000), also employing PET, reported a similar finding except with the use of a comprehensibility paradigm in which he required participants to provide word completions to constraining sentence stems. Participants showed greater anterior medial OFC activation (in almost the exact same location as the previous study) when they gave appropriate as opposed to inappropriate sentence-stem completions.

Elliot et al. (2000) reported an fMRI study they performed in order to identify the neural substrates of delayed matching compared with delayed nonmatching to sample. In such a task, participants are initially shown an item and then subsequently shown a pair of items whereby they have to identify either the item they saw or the one that they didn't see. Significantly more activity occurred in the ventromedial OFC in the matching condition (i.e., while reprocessing an old item) as compared with the nonmatching condition (i.e., while processing a novel item). Since the medial OFC exhibited significantly more activation when processing the merely exposed items than when processing the novel items and since mere exposure has been shown to enhance processing fluency, this study could be interpreted as suggesting that the medial OFC is sensitive to high processing fluency. This conclusion is consistent with results of an earlier PET study of the subliminal mere-exposure effect by Elliot and Dolan (1998). In their study, when participants made preference judgments, repeated stimuli activated the medial PFC, an area closely connected to the medial OFC and also known for its role in reward processing. Notably, these neuroimaging studies showing activation of neural circuits involved in reward to repeated stimuli fit nicely with the earlier reviewed Harmon-Jones and Allen (2001) EMG study showing greater zygomaticus activation to merely exposed items. Taken together, they highlight the multilevel hedonic consequences of mere exposure and, more generally perhaps, high processing fluency.

Finally, Volz and von Cramon (2006) performed an fMRI investigation of the neural underpinnings of insight. They briefly (for 400ms) presented fragmented line drawings of either possible (real) or impossible (nonsensical) objects and required participants to quickly respond (within 2s) based on a "gut feeling" as to whether they thought the objects were possible or impossible. They found medial OFC activation when participants judged the fragmented line drawings to be possible, and this activation was also shown to depend on how possible it actually was, based on the degree of fragmentation of the picture, to perceive a coherent gestalt. These results thus correlate progress toward achieving a coherent percept (without actually achieving that percept) with medial OFC activation, thus suggesting that the medial OFC is in fact sensitive to fluency of information processing.

Summary

In this section, we identified a neural correlate of high processing fluency: neural response suppression. We also reviewed studies that provide some preliminary support for the idea that the medial OFC is sensitive to high processing fluency, and therefore that the fluency signal may in fact be used by the medial OFC as a cue to rapidly assess the reinforcing and rewarding properties of a stimulus—that the stimulus should be approached, acquired, or consumed.

OVERALL SUMMARY AND CONCLUDING REMARKS

The concern of this chapter has been with understanding what we take to be the *sine qua non* of the aesthetic experience: aesthetic pleasure. We identified high processing fluency as being one possible route to aesthetic pleasure and, therefore, as being an important contributor to the aesthetic experience. We provided support for our proposal by presenting evidence from behavioral (preference judgments), psychophysiological (EMG reactions) and neuroscientific (activation of reward circuits) studies. Throughout, we showed how the concept of fluency provides us with a parsimonious explanation for a broad range of aesthetic phenomena. Readers interested in a further discussion of these issues, along with conditions that moderate the impact of fluency on affective experience, might wish to consult Reber et al. (2004).

We conclude by emphasizing the complexity of subjective experience, that there is clearly more to cognitive phenomenology than fluency and its attendant pleasure (Whittlesea, 2002), and that this is especially true for the aesthetic experience. Indeed, many of our aesthetic experiences compound several qualitatively different subjective states. While admiring a painting or even watching an action scene from a movie, for example, an observer may experience a combination of pleasantness, interest, tension, surprise, and awe, which may lead the observer, in retrospect, to describe the experience as thrilling. It is our hope that by achieving convergence across a variety of behavioral, psychophysiological, and neuroscientific measures, we will be able to better characterize the cognitive processes that underlie various subjective states, and that we will therefore be able to move toward achieving a fuller understanding of one of the most coveted of all human experiences, the aesthetic experience.

ACKNOWLEDGMENTS

We thank Norbert Schwarz, Rolf Reber, and Tedra Fazendeiro for many years of discussion about these ideas.

REFERENCES

Arnheim, R. (1974). *Art and visual perception. The new version*. Berkeley, CA: University of California Press.

Bergerbest, D., Ghahremani, D. G., & Gabrieli, J. D. E. (2004). Neural correlates of auditory repetition priming: Reduced fMRI activation in the auditory cortex. *Journal of Cognitive Neuroscience, 16,* 966-977.

Bornstein, R. F. (1989). Exposure and affect: Overview and meta-analysis of research 1968-1987. *Psychological Bulletin, 106,* 265-289.

Bornstein, R. F., & D'Agostino, P. R. (1994). The attribution and discounting of perceptual fluency: Preliminary tests of a perceptual fluency/attributional model of the mere exposure effect. *Social Cognition, 12,* 103-128.

Buckner, A. (1994). Indirect effects of synthetic grammar learning in an identification task. *Journal of Experimental Psychology: Learning, Memory, and Cognition, 20,* 550-566.

Buckner, R. L., & Koutstaal, W. (1998). Functional neuroimaging studies of encoding, priming, and explicit memory retrieval. *Proceedings of the National Academy of Sciences, 95,* 891-898.

Buckner, R. L., Peterson, S. E., Ojemann, J. G., & Miezin, F. M. (1995). Functional anatomical studies of explicit and implicit memory retrieval tasks. *Journal of Neuroscience, 15*(1), 12-29.

Cacioppo, J. T., Petty, R. E., Losch, M. E., & Kim, H. S. (1986). Electromyographic activity over facial muscle regions can differentiate the valence and intensity of affective reactions. *Journal of Personality and Social Psychology, 50,* 260-268.

Checkosky, S. F., & Whitlock, D. (1973). The effects of pattern goodness on recognition time in a memory search task. *Journal of Experimental Psychology, 100,* 341-348.

Cutting, J. E. (2003). Gustave Caillebotte, french impressionism, and mere exposure. *Psychonomic Bulletin & Review, 10,* 319-343.

Desimone, R. (1996). Neural mechanisms for visual memory and their role in attention. *Proceedings of the National Academy of Sciences, 93,* 13494-13499.

Elliott, R., & Dolan, R. (1998). Neural response during preference and memory judgments for subliminally presented stimuli: A functional neuroimaging study. *The Journal of Neuroscience, 18,* 4697-4704.

Elliot, R., Dolan, R. J., & Frith, C. D. (2000). Dissociable functions in the medial and lateral oribitofrontal cortex: Evidence from human neuroimaging studies. *Cerebral Cortex, 10,* 308-317.

Frith, C. D. (2000). The role of dorsolateral prefrontal cortex in the selection of action, as reveal by functional imaging. In S. Monsell & J. Driver (Eds), *Control of cognitive processes: Attention and performance XVIII* (pp. 549-565). Cambridge, MA: MIT Press.

Garner, W. R. (1974). *The processing of information structure*. Potomac, MD: Lawrence Erlbaum.

Gombrich, E. H. (1984). *A sense of order* (2nd ed.). London: Phaidon.

Gordon, P. C., & Holyoak, K. J. (1983). Implicit learning and generalization of the "mere exposure" effect. *Journal of Personality and Social Psychology, 45,* 492-500.

Haber, R. N., & Hershenson, M. (1965). The effects of repeated brief exposures on growth of a percept. *Journal of Experimental Psychology, 69,* 40-46.

Halberstadt, J. B., & Rhodes, G. (2000). The attractiveness of nonface averages: Implications for an evolutionary explanation of the attractiveness of average faces. *Psychological Science, 11,* 285-289.

Halberstadt, J. B., & Rhodes, G. (2003). It's not just average faces that are attractive: Computer manipulated averageness makes birds, fish and automobiles attractive. *Psychonomic Bulletin & Review, 11*(1), 149-156.

Harmon-Jones, E., & Allen, J. J. B. (2001). The role of affect in the mere exposure effect: Evidence from psychophysiological and individual differences approaches. *Personality and Social Psychology Bulletin*, *27*, 889-898.

Hill, W. F. (1978). Effects of mere exposure on preferences in nonhuman mammals. *Psychological Bulletin*, *85*, 1177-1198.

Huber, D. E., & O'Reilly, R. C. (2003). Persistence and accommodation in short-term priming and other perceptual paradigms: Temporal segregation through synaptic depression. *Cognitive Science*, *27*, 403-430.

Jacoby, L. L. (1983). Perceptual enhancement: Persistent effects of an experience. *Journal of Experimental Psychology: Learning, Memory, and Cognition*, *9(*1), 21-38.

Jacoby, L. L., & Dallas, M. (1981). On the relationship between autobiographical memory and perceptual learning. *Journal of Experimental Psychology: General*, *110*, 306-340.

Jacoby, L. L., Kelley, C. M., & Dywan, J. (1989). Memory attributions. In H. L. Roediger, & F. I. M. Craik (Eds.), *Varieties of memory and consciousness: Essays in honour of Endel Tulving* (pp. 391-422). Hillsdale, NJ: Erlbaum.

Klinger, M. R., & Greenwald A. G. (1994). Preferences need no inferences?: The cognitive basis of unconscious mere exposure effects. In P. M. Niedenthal & S. Kitayama (Eds.), *The heart's eye* (pp. 67-85). San Diego: Academic Press.

Lang, P. J., Greenwald, M. K., Bradley, M. M. & Hamm, A. O. (1993). Looking at pictures: Affective, facial, visceral, and behavioral reactions. *Psychophysiology*, *30*, 261-273.

Maccotta, L., & Buckner, R. L. (2004) Evidence for neural effects of repetition that directly correlate with behavioral priming. *Journal of Cognitive Neuroscience*, *9*, 1625-1632.

Macguire, E. A., Frith, C. D., & Morris, R. G. M. (1999). The functional neuroanatomy of comprehension and memory: The importance of prior knowledge. *Brain*, *122*, 1839-1850.

Mandler, G., Nakamura, Y., & Van Zandt, B. J. S. (1987). Nonspecific effects of exposure on stimuli that cannot be recognized. *Journal of Experimental Psychology: Learning, Memory, and Cognition*, *15*, 646-648.

Maritain, J. (1966). Beauty and imitation. In M. Rader (Ed.), *A modern book of esthetics* (3rd ed., pp. 27-34). New York: Holt, Rinehart and Winston.

Martindale, C., & Moore, K. (1988). Priming, prototypicality, and preference. *Journal of Experimental Psychology: Human Perception and Performance*, *14*, 661-670.

Monahan, J. L., Murphy, S. T., & Zajonc, R. B. (2000). Subliminal mere exposure: Specific, general, and diffuse effects. *Psychological Science*, *11*, 462-466.

Moreland, R. L., & Zajonc, R. B. (1976). A strong test of exposure effects. *Journal of Experimental Social Psychology, 12*(2), 170-179.

Nicki, R. M., Lee, P. L., & Moss, V. (1981). Ambiguity, cubist works of art, and preference. *Acta Psychologica*, *49*, 27-41.

Palmer, S. E. (1991). Goodness, Gestalt, groups, and Garner: Local symmetry subgroups as a theory of figural goodness. In G. R. Lockhead, & J. R. Pomerantz (Eds.), *The perception of structure* (pp. 23-39). Washington, DC: American Psychological Association.

Palmer, S. E., & Hemenway, K. (1978). Orientation and symmetry: Effects of multiple, near, and rotational symmetries. *Journal of Experimental Psychology: Human Perception and Performance*, *4*, 691-702.

Posner, M. I., & Keele, S. W. (1968). On the genesis of abstract ideas. *Journal of Experimental Psychology*, *77*, 353-363.

Read, H. (1972). *The meaning of art*. London: Faber & Faber.

Reber, P. J., Stark, C. E. L., & Squire, L. R. (1998). Cortical areas supporting category learning identified using functional MRI. *Proceedings of the National Academy of Science USA, 95,* 747-740.

Reber, R., & Schwarz, N. (2006). Perceptual fluency, preference, and evolution. *Polish Psychological Bulletin, 37*, 16-22.

Reber, R., Schwarz, N., & Winkielman, P. (2004). Processing fluency and aesthetic pleasure: Is beauty in the perceiver's processing experience? *Personality and Social Psychology Review, 8*, 364-382.

Reber, R., Winkielman, P., & Schwarz, N. (1998). Effects of perceptual fluency on affective judgments. *Psychological Science*, *9*, 45-48.

Rhodes, G., & Tremewan, T. (1996). Averageness, exaggeration, and facial attractiveness. *Psychological Science*, *7*, 105-110.

Rhodes, G., Yoshikawa, S., Clark, A., Lee, K., McKay, R., & Akamatsu, S. (2001). Attractiveness of facial averageness and symmetry in non-western cultures: In search of biologically based standards of beauty. *Perception*, *30*, 611-625.

Roediger, H. L. (1990). Implicit memory: Retention without remembering. *American Psychologist*, *45*(9), 1043-1056.

Saegert, S., Swap, W., & Zajonc, R. B. (1973). Exposure, context, and interpersonal attraction. *Journal of Personality and Social Psychology*, *25*, 234-242.

Schaffner, E. P., Wandersman, A., & Stang, D. (1981). Candidate name exposure and voting: Two field studies. *Basic and Applied Social Psychology, 2*(3), 195-203.

Schwarz, N. (2004). Meta-cognitive experiences in consumer judgment and decision making. *Journal of Consumer Psychology, 14*, 332-348.

Schwarz, N. (2006). On judgments of truth and beauty. *Daedalus, 135*, 136-138

Seamon, J. G., Brody, N., & Kauff, D. M. (1983). Affective discrimination of stimuli that are not recognized: Effects of shadowing, masking, and central laterality. *Journal of Experimental Psychology: Learning, Memory and Cognition*, *9*, 544-555.

Sollberger, B., & Reber, R. (2004). *Artificial grammar learning as a potential mechanism for the acquisition of music preference.* Unpublished manuscript.

Solso, R. L. (1997). *Cognition and the visual arts*. Cambridge, MA: MIT Press.

Tulving, E., & Schachter, D. L. (1990). Priming and human memory systems. *Science, 247*(4940), 301-306.

Volz, K. G., & von Cramon, D. Y. (2006). What neuroscience can tell us about intuitive processes in the context of discovery. *Journal of Cognitive Neuroscience, 18,* 2077-2087.

Whitfield, T. W. A., & Slatter, P. E. (1979). The effects of categorization and prototypicality on aesthetic choice in a furniture selection task. *British Journal of Psychology*, *70*, 65-75.

Whittlesea, B. W. A. (2002). On the construction of behavior and subjective experience: The production and evaluation of performance. In J. Bowers & C. Marsolek (Eds.), *Rethinking implicit memory* (pp. 239-260). Oxford, UK: Oxford University Press.

Whittlesea, B. W. A., Jacoby, L. L., & Girard, K. (1990). Illusions of immediate memory: Evidence of an attributional basis for feelings of familiarity and perceptual quality. *Journal of Memory and Language*, *29*, 716-732.

Whittlesea, B., & Price, J. (2001). Implicit/explicit memory versus analytic/nonanalytic processing: Rethinking the mere exposure effect. *Memory and Cognition, 29*, 234-246.

Wiggs, C. L., & Martin, A. (1998). Properties and mechanisms of perceptual priming. *Current Opinion in Neurobiology*, *8*, 227-233.

Winkielman, P., & Cacioppo, J. T. (2001). Mind at ease puts a smile on the face: Psychophysiological evidence that processing facilitation leads to positive affect. *Journal of Personality and Social Psychology*, *81*, 989-1000.

Winkielman, P., & Fazendeiro, T. (in preparation). *The role of conceptual fluency in preference and memory.*

Winkielman, P., Halberstadt, J., Fazendeiro, T., & Catty, S. (2006). Prototypes are attractive because they are easy on the mind. *Psychological Science, 17*, 799-806.

Winkielman, P., & Nowak, A. (2005). Dynamics of cognition-emotion interface: Coherence breeds familiarity and liking, and does it fast. *Behavioral and Brain Sciences, 28*, 222-223.

Winkielman, P., Schwarz, N., Fazendeiro, T., & Reber, R. (2003). The hedonic marking of processing fluency: Implications for evaluative judgment. In J. Musch & K. C. Klauer (Eds.), *The psychology of evaluation: Affective processes in cognition and emotion* (pp. 189-217). Mahwah, NJ: Lawrence Erlbaum.

Contributors

STEVEN BROWN is a cognitive neuroscientist working in the Department of Psychology, Neuroscience & Behaviour at McMaster University in Hamilton, Ontario. He received his Ph.D. in the department of Genetics at Columbia University in New York, and did postdoctoral research at the Pasteur Institute in Paris, the Karolinska Institute in Stockholm, the University of Texas Health Science Center in San Antonio, and Simon Fraser University in Vancouver. His research deals with the neural basis of human communication processes, with a focus on the arts. He is co-editor of two books: *The Origins of Music* (MIT Press) and *Music and Manipulation* (Berghahn Books).

MIQUEL CAPÓ (Mallorca, Spain, 1971) received his degree in philosophy and a Masters degree in human evolution and cognition, from the University of the Balearic Islands. He has carried out research concerning the cognitive, neural, and evolutionary bases of language, aesthetic preference, and morality, as well as philosophy of biology. He is currently Assistant Professor at the department of Philosophy of the University of the Balearic Islands.

CAMILO J. CELA-CONDE (Madrid, Spain, 1946) is Senior Professor of Anthropology at the University of the Balearic Islands (Palma de Mallorca, Spain). He is the Director of the Laboratory of Human Systematics (UIB). His latest book is *Human Evolution* (co-author Francisco J. Ayala), New York, Oxford University Press, 2007. He is Fellow of the American Association for the Advancement of Sciences (elected in 1999), Biology section. He is also a member of the Center of Academic Research and Training in Anthropogeny, Salk Institute, and the University of California, San Diego (elected in 2008).

ANJAN CHATTERJEE is Professor of Neurology and member of the Center for Cognitive Neuroscience at the University of Pennsylvania. After medical school at Penn, he completed a neurology residency at the University of Chicago, post-doctoral fellowship training in dementia at Case Western Reserve University and in cognitive neurology at the University of Florida. His clinical practice focuses on patients with cognitive disorders. His research focuses on spatial and temporal attention, the interface of space and language, neuroaesthetics, and neuroethics. In 2002, he was awarded the Norman Geschwind Prize in Behavioral and Cognitive Neurology by the American Academy of Neurology. He is an associate editor of the *Journal of Cognitive Neuroscience,* and on the editorial boards of *Empirical*

Studies of the Arts, Cognitive Neuropsychology, Neuropsychology, Cognitive and Behavioral Neurology, and *Behavioural Neurology*.

TROY CHENIER is currently pursuing his Ph.D. in social psychology at the University of California, San Diego. His research focuses on understanding cognitive phenomenology: How variations in the dynamics of information processing give rise to feelings (i.e., the feeling of familiarity), beliefs (i.e., about one's own assertiveness), and attitudes (i.e., liking). Of particular interest to him is the contribution that such cognitive mechanisms make to preference development and the aesthetic experience.

ELLEN DISSANAYAKE is an independent scholar and writer whose interdisciplinary work is concerned with the arts as evolved behaviors, inherent in human nature. Her books, *What Is Art For?, Homo Aestheticus: Where Art Comes From and Why*, and *Art and Intimacy: How the Arts Began*, are all published by the University of Washington Press; *Homo Aestheticus* has been translated into Chinese and Korean. She resides in Seattle where she is an Affiliate Professor in the School of Music at the University of Washington.

W. TECUMSEH FITCH is a biologist and cognitive scientist at the University of St Andrews. He received his B.A. in Biology and Medicine, and his Ph.D. in Cognitive and Linguistic Sciences, both at Brown University. His work focuses on the evolution of cognition and communication in a diverse group of species including humans; he is particularly interested in the biology and evolution of music, speech, and language.

TORBEN GRODAL is professor at the University of Copenhagen in Film and Media Studies. He is the author of *Moving Pictures. A New Theory of Film Genres, Feelings, and Cognition,* and *Embodied Visions: Evolution, Emotion, Culture, and Film*, both published by Oxford University Press, aside from books in Danish on cultural history and film and literary theory. He has published many articles that combine humanistic methods and brain science with special emphasis on the role of emotions in relation to subjects such as film theory and film analysis, aesthetic theory, and video game theory.

THOMAS JACOBSEN is associate professor of psychology (Oberassistent) at the Institute I of the University of Leipzig, Germany. His main research focus is on the experimental and cognitive neuroscience of pre-attentive cognitive processing of language and non-language sounds. He also works on the neurocognitive psychology of aesthetics.

GISÈLE MARTY (Geneva, Switzerland, 1951) is Senior Professor at the University of the Balearic Islands (Palma de Mallorca, Spain). Her research and teaching are focused on Psychology of Art and Psychology of memory. She has authored several books and numerous international journal papers. She is the main researcher of various research projects in Empirical Aesthetics that have approached this field using, among other methods, neuroimaging techniques. Her work has contributed to establishing a lasting research program in Psychology of Art in Spain.

DAVID S. MIALL is professor of English at the University of Alberta in Canada. Previous publications include, as editor, *Humanities and the Computer:*

New Directions (1990), *Romanticism: The CD-ROM* (1997), and a monograph, *Literary Reading: Empirical and Theoretical Studies* (2006). In addition he has authored over 90 chapters and journal articles. He specializes in literature of the British Romantic period, and the empirical study of literary reading—a field in which he has collaborated with Don Kuiken (Department of Psychology) since 1990. He teaches courses in Romantic literature, Gothic fiction, literary computing, and empirical and historical studies of literary reading.

ENRIC MUNAR (Mallorca, Spain, 1963) is Professor at the Department of Psychology (University of Balearic Islands). He obtained his psychologist degree in 1989 from the University Complutense (Madrid), and his doctorate in 2000 from the University of the Balearic Islands. Dr. Munar is a member of the *Human Evolution and Cognition* research group (www.evocog.com). His research interest is experimental cognitive psychology, in general, and human perception, in particular. He coordinated a handbook on the study of attention and perception, *Manual de Atención y Percepción* (1999). At this time, he is actively participating in several projects dealing with aesthetic preference, evolution of human cognition, and visual illusions.

MARCOS NADAL (Mallorca, Spain 1975) has a degree in Psychology, and a Ph.D. in Human Evolution and Cognition, from the University of the Balearic Islands. He has carried out research concerning the cognitive, neural and evolutionary underpinnings of language, aesthetic preference, and morality. He is currently Assistant Professor at the Department of Psychology of the University of the Balearic Islands.

ERIC NICOLAS is a musician and composer who lives and works in New York City. He received his B.A. in Literature and Society from Brown University. He composes, records, and performs in diverse popular styles including jazz, Brazilian and American pop, and rock. As a professional band leader and arranger he is very familiar with contemporary chart-writing conventions. For more information see www.ericnicolas.com.

MARI TERVANIEMI obtained her Ph.D. in Psychology in the University of Helsinki, Finland, in 1997. Since then, she has worked there as a researcher. In parallel, she has acted as a professor in the University of Jyväskylä, Finland, in 2000-2001 and as a Marie Curie fellow in Leipzig, Germany, 2001-2002. In 2004-2005 she worked as a senior lecturer at the University of Helsinki. In 2006-2009, she acts as a coordinator of an EU-funded research project Tuning the brain for music and in 2008-2010 as the vice-director of the Finnish Centre of Excellence for Interdisciplinary Music Research.

N. J. WADE received his B.Sc. in Psychology at the University of Edinburgh, and his Ph.D. in Psychology from Monash University in Australia. He was the recipient of a British Commonwealth Scholarship. He received a postdoctoral research fellowship from the Alexander von Humboldt Stiftung, at Max-Planck-Institute for Behavioural Physiology, Germany. He was Lecturer in psychology at the University of Dundee, Reader in Psychology at the University of Dundee, and is Professor of Visual Psychology at the University of Dundee from 1991. He is a fellow of the Royal Society of Edinburgh, and Honorary Professor at the University of Abertay

Dundee from 1997. His research is focused on the representation of space and motion in human vision, the history of research in visual science, and the relationship between visual science and visual art.

ANTJE VON GRAEVENITZ is an art historian, author, and editor specializing in avant-garde art of the 20th century. She is Professor Emeritus of Art History at the Kunsthistorisches Institut at the University of Cologne. She received her Ph.D. from the Ludwig-Maximilians-University of Munich in 1972 after studying art history, archeology, and ethnology, and she specializes in anthropological issues, such as rituals in art. Her work has focused on the art of the twenties and fifties, through to today including movements such as Surrealism, Kinetic Art, and performance art, and artists such as Duchamp, Giacometti, Brancusi, Beuys, and Nauman.

PIOTR WINKIELMAN is professor of psychology at the University of California, San Diego. Using methods drawn from social and cognitive psychology as well as the neurosciences, his research explores the interplay between cognition, emotion, embodiment, and consciousness. He is particularly interested in the implications of this work for social cognition—how cognitive and emotional processes interact to influence social judgment and decision making.

DAHLIA W. ZAIDEL began doing brain research in the field of hemispheric specialization by studying the commissurotomy ("split-brain") patients in Roger Sperry's lab at Caltech, emphasizing the functional lateralization of memory, problem solving, spatial perception, and motor control. Art became a fascinating empirical tool in her research to ferret out information about the cerebral hemispheres. Her interest in left-right asymmetries of brain or of face has continued to dominate her research as a Fulbright Scholar in Oxford and as faculty in the psychology department at UCLA where her focus now is on the intersection of neuroscience, beauty, face, art, and brain.

Index

For Product Safety Concerns and Information please contact our EU representative GPSR@taylorandfrancis.com Taylor & Francis Verlag GmbH, Kaufingerstraße 24, 80331 München, Germany

Batch number: 10726534

Printed by Printforce, the Netherlands